TRACKING TRUTH

Tracking Truth

Knowledge, Evidence, and Science

SHERRILYN ROUSH

CLARENDON PRESS · OXFORD

OXFORD
UNIVERSITY PRESS

Great Clarendon Street, Oxford OX2 6DP

Oxford University Press is a department of the University of Oxford.
It furthers the University's objective of excellence in research, scholarship,
and education by publishing worldwide in

Oxford New York

Auckland Cape Town Dar es Salaam Hong Kong Karachi
Kuala Lumpur Madrid Melbourne Mexico City Nairobi
New Delhi Shanghai Taipei Toronto

With offices in

Argentina Austria Brazil Chile Czech Republic France Greece
Guatemala Hungary Italy Japan Poland Portugal Singapore
South Korea Switzerland Thailand Turkey Ukraine Vietnam

Oxford is a registered trade mark of Oxford University Press
in the UK and in certain other countries

Published in the United States
by Oxford University Press Inc., New York

British Library Cataloguing in Publication Data

Data available

Library of Congress Cataloging in Publication Data

Data available

Typeset by SPI Publisher Services, Pondicherry, India

Printed in Great Britain
on acid-free paper by
Biddles Ltd.,
Kings Lynn, Norfolk

ISBN 0–19–927473–8   978–0–19–927473–4

1 3 5 7 9 10 8 6 4 2

In grateful memory of Robert Nozick
for his optimism

Preface

It is unfortunate and ironic that I cannot thank Robert Nozick for help in the preparation of this book. Unfortunate both because I could have benefited from his advice and talent for argument, and because the reason I didn't get it is that he was dead shortly before I had the brainstorm for this book, and quite a bit before his time. It is ironic that I never talked to Nozick about tracking because he was one of my dissertation advisors, and I believed in tracking even back then and before having the words for it. Maybe if I had not been such a slow student things would have been different. I can express gratitude for his example, and for his well-placed paternalism, which was the primary reason I managed to complete my Ph.D. before the bell rang.

I read Nozick's tracking account of knowledge and evidence near the end of graduate school (at the urging not of Nozick but of Hilary Putnam). Without any experience in analytic epistemology, I concluded that the view was plainly right, cited it where it seemed to boost the plausibility of certain points about evidence in philosophy of science, and put it aside. I don't remember being impressed with the response the tracking view provided to the skeptical problem; for me, the virtues of the view lay elsewhere. It was only a few years later that I discovered to my surprise that the epistemology community was impressed with the answer to skepticism, but had long since decided that the tracking view of knowledge was definitely not right. I am a decent enough probabilistic reasoner that I did not at that point indulge the delusion that I was right and everyone else was wrong. But I did keep notes about every complaint that preceded an announcement that the tracking view of knowledge was wrong, and continued to reflect on why I thought it was right. At a certain point I realized that a little imagination, and a little less deference to the original formulation of the view, would do the trick. I am sure that Nozick himself would have applauded my lack of deference, and even felt honored by it.

Fortunately or unfortunately, the result of a lot of notes, a little imagination, and a fair bit of obsession can be a hefty book. But I also had a lot of help in thinking through the material and revising the manuscript. Chief among the people I must thank is Branden Fitelson whose enthusiasm helped me through many a discouraging day, and the volume and quality of whose feedback was hard to reconcile with the fact that he has publications of his own. (I have considered the hypothesis that Branden Fitelson is actually two people flying under a single passport.) It was great good luck that he ended up being a reader of my manuscript and subsequent interlocutor. I am grateful as well to the other, anonymous, reader of my manuscript, for encouragement and helpful criticism from a different perspective. Though lucky for me, these choices were of course not accidental, and I thank my editor, Peter Momtchiloff, for wisdom in this and other matters, and Rebecca Bryant, Jackie Pritchard, and Rupert Cousens for making the production process smooth and enjoyable.

Writing this book was an exhilarating learning process. Brian Skyrms, Bas van Fraassen, Gil Harman, Pen Maddy, Eric Barnes, Jim Bogen, Fred Dretske, and Tamar

Szabó Gendler all read part(s) of the manuscript at some stage, and all taught me things through their comments. Elijah Millgram read the whole thing, some parts more than once, and his perceptions and dissatisfactions made the product more interesting than I had imagined it could be. Brian Skyrms deserves my special thanks for his encouragement, his approachability, and his patient answers to my questions, whether they were difficult or merely ignorant. Being his colleague for six months led me to think that paradise would involve, in addition to the flora of southern California, having an office down the hall from his.

I am indebted to several other people too for helpful discussions of the material, including John Norton, Jonathan Vogel, Kyle Stanford, Bill Demopoulos, Aaron James, Bill Bristow, Jason Grossman, Kai Wehmeier, James Pearson, Robert Howells, Alex Rosenberg, Dick Grandy, Richard Feldman, and Alan Chalmers. Vogel deserves a special spirit-of-philosophy prize for having serious discussions with me about a view he deeply disagrees with. I owe special thanks to Hartry Field for encouragement and for sharing his expertise with me and my theory on many occasions. Without his help the theory would be even more imperfect than it is.

First among the institutions I must thank is Rice University, and my department, especially for their generosity in giving me leave to take advantage of research opportunities elsewhere. I am grateful to the Center for Philosophy of Science at the University of Pittsburgh, and the Logic and Philosophy of Science department at the University of California, Irvine, for providing me with stimulating research environments and support during much of the writing of this book. The research for this book was also made possible by a teaching release fellowship from the Center for the Study of Cultures, and by many Jon and Paula Mosle Junior Faculty Research Awards over the years, at Rice University. Material in this book was presented to audiences at a Pacific APA session in 2003 where my commentator Robert Howells made me think, and at the Formal Epistemology Workshop in Berkeley in 2004 where James Justus did likewise. Some material was also presented at the Conference on Scientific Evidence at Johns Hopkins in 2003 and at various venues at the University of Pittsburgh and at UC, Irvine. The audience feedback in all the places I talked about this material, though not always positive, was always helpful to the project.

S. R.

Acknowledgement

Material from Chapter 5, 'Only probability,' first appeared in 'Discussion: Positive Relevance Defended,' *Philosophy of Science*, 71: 110–16. Copyright 2004 by the Philosophy of Science Association. All rights reserved. It is reprinted, with adaptations, by permission of the University of Chicago Press.

Contents

1. **Tracking: At Home on the Range** — 1

    Knowledge is power, and other intriguing banalities — 1
    Animals — 6
    Science — 10
    Testimony — 17
    Justification, knowledge, and the maintenance of true belief — 22
    Overview of chapters — 27
    Appendix 1.1. Knowledge without justification — 35

2. **Tracking with Closure** — 38

    1. Recursive tracking — 41
    2. Immediate implications — 51
    3. Tracking not too strong — 57
        Oscar and Dack — 57
        Not falsely believing — 59
        Disjunctions — 62
        Ice cubes, rookies, hit rock, and missed rock — 63
        Jesse James and method — 68
        Sensitivity training — 71
        Deities of questionable benevolence — 72

3. **Tracking: More and Better** — 75

    1. Tracking not too weak — 75
        Rules of application—the tracking conditions — 76
        Newspaper — 93
        Gumshoe and Tagalong — 96
        Judy and Trudy — 98
        Barns and fakery — 100
        Dumb luck and blind luck — 102
        Compulsive Mr Nogot — 107
        Conjunctions — 110
        Causal overdetermination — 112
    2. Knowledge of the future — 113

4. **Tracking over the Rivals** — 117

    Sensitivity and safety: higher-level knowledge — 118
    Sensitivity and safety: direction of fit — 121
    Sensitivity and safety: no trade-off — 123
    Why knowledge brings power — 126
    Relevant alternatives theories and 'lottery' propositions — 128

Knowledge of logical and other necessary truths 134
Appendix 4.1 Sensitivity and safety 148

5. **What is Evidence? Discrimination, Indication, and Leverage** 149

Knowledge and evidence 149
Desiderata for a concept of evidence 154
The discrimination condition on evidence 160
The indication condition on evidence 165
Only probability 178
Conclusion 183
Appendix 5.1 The Likelihood Ratio, high P(e), and high P(h/e) 187

6. **Real Anti-realism: The Evidential Approach** 189

Introduction 189
Lambs and sheep 194
Empty strutting? 197
Natural defenses 209
From EP to e·p·t: dream on 214
Conclusion 223

References 225
Index 231

How could history of science fail to be a source of phenomena to which theories about knowledge may legitimately be asked to apply?

Thomas S. Kuhn, *The Structure of Scientific Revolutions*

From this point of view all the sciences would only be unconscious applications of the calculus of probabilities. And if this calculus be condemned, then the whole of the sciences must also be condemned.

Henri Poincaré, *Science and Hypothesis*

1

Tracking: At Home on the Range

Knowledge is power, and other intriguing banalities

What do you do if you want to know whether and when your package has been delivered? You buy *tracking* from the US Postal Service (or UPS, or FedEx, or DHL). What do meteorologists do when they want to know where a storm system is and in what direction it is headed at what speed? They *track* it. In fact, in a handy *Hurricane Preparation Guide* available from Home Depot in regions bordering the Gulf of Mexico, you can 'track like the pros' by listening for the latest storm position and strength from the National Hurricane Center, and plotting the storm's progress on a 'Hurricane Tracking Map'. What do you do if you want an efficient way to learn about all and only the news that is important to you? You subscribe to the *Times News Tracker*, of course, and get all of the *New York Times* articles published on topics of your choice (and nothing else) delivered to your inbox when those articles appear. 'Never miss a thing . . .' Not all tracking is desirable, of course. There are some things we'd rather people didn't know. The same GPS device in your cell phone that allows your provider to locate you, and direct your call to the local police, when you dial 9-1-1—they call this 'tracking'—can also be used to track you when you haven't asked for it. The data miners that download themselves onto your computer, and gather information about where you go on the internet and how often, are commonly supplied by the vendor *Tracking Cookie*.

There is a picture of knowledge in which the dominant metaphor for describing what knowledge is involves the simple notion of following. We know things when we follow them. We understand something when we can truthfully answer 'yes' to the question 'Do you follow?' I take it that simple, spatio-temporal following, as when we follow a crawling insect with our eyes, or a hunter follows the footprints of prey with steps of his own, is the paradigm image of what it is for someone to track something. To track an insect crawling toward you is to know where that insect is, but to determine whether all knowledge is a matter of tracking, we must first say what tracking is in a general way.

Robert Nozick, who was the first to connect the word 'tracking' with knowledge (Nozick 1981), defined what it is for a belief to track the truth in terms of the fulfillment of subjunctive conditionals: a subject S's belief p tracks the truth if were p to be false S wouldn't believe it, and were p to be true S would believe it. (Cf. Dretske 1971, Armstrong 1973, Goldman 1976) A belief is knowledge if in addition to tracking the truth, it is also true as a matter of fact. As it happens, this formulation of what tracking is, and of how it should figure in an account of knowledge, runs into serious problems. However, critics have been too quick to reject the idea of tracking when they found the faults of this formulation. The purpose of this book is to give the respect due to the powerful intuitive appeal of this following, or tracking, idea of knowledge and ideas about evidence associated with it, and to trace some of their consequences. To do this I will define what I take to be the best possible version of the view, and give it the best defense I can. The new version of the tracking view replaces subjunctive conditionals with conditions on conditional probabilities, for example, but for most of the purposes of the present motivating chapter, Nozick's formulation will suffice.

One might wonder why we should have an account of what knowledge is, and why you, or anyone else, should read it.[1] An epistemologist does not regularly defend the activities that are central to his profession; he just does them. However, even within the community of epistemologists doubts have been raised as to whether the concept of knowledge is as important as it has been made out to be, compared to other concepts of epistemic interest, like *understanding* (Elgin 1996; Kvanvig 2003). For some philosophers it is the project of analysis of concepts that is suspicious, especially as carried out by epistemologists; how can it give us anything more than a rehashing of the practitioners' intuitions, culturally biased intuitions at that (Nichols et al. 2003)? And an outsider who tries to read in epistemology could be forgiven for thinking that the culture whose biases prevail is as small as the set of epistemologists themselves, for it can look to the uninitiated like an insider's parlor game. (Of course, NB, most academic discussions do.) The rules and even the point of the enterprise can seem elusive. Suppose we could get the concept right, though, and getting it right wasn't a mirage. Why would an account of what knowledge is be of any value to us?

Appreciation of the analysis of a concept requires a little bit of basic curiosity. Beyond that, the concept of knowledge can stand on its own, for an account of this concept can provide explanations of interesting things that we had no explanation of before. For example, the account of knowledge I will set forth in this book explains why we are at ease saying both that a scientist knows a kaon has decayed and that the dog knows there is someone at the door, despite the vast differences in intellectual resources and methods between the two subjects mentioned (and the fact, as I see it, that the claim about the dog is strictly false). The account also provides a deep explanation of the fact, obvious but not often discussed by epistemologists, that the better one's evidence for a hypothesis is, the better one's chances of knowing it.

There are other obvious things that one might like an explanation of. It is an assumption of the epistemological trade that knowledge is superior to mere true belief. Who can disagree, but why is it so? It is not enough to point out that mere true belief may be so accidentally, as when one throws a die to decide what time it is and happens to get the right answer. The word 'accidental' definitely sounds insulting, but why should I care whether my true belief is so accidentally; since I have the true belief—'the goods,' one might say—how can its accidentality yield any practical

---

[1] I must thank Elijah Millgram for pressing me to take this question seriously. I only discovered the tracking account of why knowledge is valuable and why knowledge brings power that is discussed below by trying to answer the question why an *account* of what knowledge is could be valuable.

worry? The traditional epistemologist will claim that the deeper requirement is that I be able to justify the belief, and the ability to justify will tend to remove that accidentality; it is because we need justification that we need knowledge rather than mere true belief. But this sounds like a requirement only an intellectual, or a lawyer, could love. Justification, in the traditional sense, does not necessarily remove accidentality, as we will see below, but even if it did we would have to contend with the fact that there are vast ranges of topics on which we have true, even knowing, beliefs that are very useful to us, and for which ordinary life almost never calls upon us to offer a justification. I know that vegetables are good for me, and though I might be inclined to proselytize on the matter to those I care about, I need not be able to justify this belief in order for the knowledge to be beneficial to me and, if those I care about are willing to trust me blindly, even to them.

It seems that since knowledge can be, and so often is, useful without our being called upon to exercise any ability to justify the beliefs that make it up, then unless either we define 'justification' as something more general than the ability to give reasons,[2] or explain why an ability that isn't used as such still has useful consequences, justification cannot be the whole story about why knowledge is more valuable than true belief. In fact, I think that even though justification is more general than the ability to offer reasons and arguments, it is not even part of the explanation of why knowledge is more valuable than mere true belief. The view of knowledge developed in this book yields an explanation of the value of knowledge, and of why accidentality matters, on quite other grounds, as I will explain more fully in the remainder of this chapter. To the extent that true belief is valuable in life, which on the practical side is admittedly not universal, knowledge is more valuable, and for the same ultimate reason.

An analysis of the concept of knowledge can give not only explanations but practical guidance, though this is less immediate and direct. Human beings are pretty good at acquiring knowledge, but what if we wanted to be more efficient at this? To achieve that it might be useful to know what it was about the things we do unreflectively to gain knowledge that is essential, and what inessential, to insuring that knowledge is the end product of the process; we might be able to stop wasting resources on the inessential bits. Of course, knowing what knowledge *is* is not the same thing as knowing what is essential to the process of acquiring it. However, it is hard to deny that the former could be helpful to achieving the latter. For example, any part of typical processes of acquiring knowledge whose only contribution was in yielding a part of the end product that was not required for knowledge, would not be

---

[2] I have in mind, for example, the view of justification offered by Alvin Goldman (1979, 2000), and more recently defended in Goldman (1999). This view would have to explain why knowledge is more valuable than true belief in terms of justification since, as on the traditional view, justification is still the essential way in which the two differ. Nothing I have yet said rules out such an explanation because on Goldman's view justification does not require the ability to produce an argument or reasons. On my own view of what justification is, which is not the topic of this book, justification could not be what makes knowledge more valuable than mere true belief because it follows from what it is that justification is not necessary for knowledge.

essential to a process we wanted to streamline for knowledge. An account of what knowledge is would help us identify these inessential parts.

Scientists probably have better instincts than any of us for how to extend our knowledge into new domains. But in new domains old habits may not work anymore, and may need to be modified or generalized. Which parts of the habits they have are more likely to be important to keep in the passage to a new domain, and which inessential to the new process? It is hard to believe that a reflective understanding of just what the goal is, or has been, when we seek knowledge can never be helpful to making such decisions. A similar point can be made about our goal in educating students; because of a sense that knowledge imparts greater capability to a student than does mere true belief (correct opinion) on the same matter, we aim to transmit knowledge. How could a finer-grained and more reflective understanding of what the end state of that goal is—knowledge in the student—and how it exceeds mere true opinion, not have some relevance to the question how better to achieve it?

One sometimes hears the saying 'Knowledge is power' in settings concerned with education or the politics of education, where we mean something like that a greater number of knowing beliefs allows a person to navigate the world better and, perhaps in other ways too, to have a better life. When this slogan was originally framed it meant something possibly related but more ambitious. Centuries ago when modern science was just beginning, Francis Bacon, its self-appointed prophet, used the memorable phrase *Knowledge is power* to sum up his vision of a future in which human beings had much more ability to control nature, avoiding or preventing its destructive tendencies, and harnessing its creative capacities.[3] Having lived his vision, we think we understand why his claim is true: having knowledge makes it possible to build gadgets, prescription drugs, weather predicting programs, rocket ships, hydrogen bombs, and other technology, and technology gives us power over nature (including other members of our own species). However, this is no explanation of why knowledge is power unless we also understand why knowledge makes it possible to build technology or, more generally, to *do* things. Unfortunately, no epistemologist I know of has asked this question: what is it about knowledge that makes it useful for building technology?

This may be because on the traditional view that knowledge is justified true belief, nothing does. A justified true belief has a connection with the way the world is in virtue of being true, but the requirements for justification of a belief traditionally have a subject's obligations end at the boundary of his accessible consciousness. This leads to the famous Gettier counterexamples which show that because justification and truth may coincide accidentally in a belief, the traditional view implies we can know things that our intuitions say we do not know. The problem is not that a belief may be justified and yet not true, which we all agree can happen and is not a case of knowledge due to the falsehood of the belief, but rather that one can have a justified true belief that isn't knowledge and the traditional view implies that it is knowledge. I will discuss these examples in their natural setting in Chapter 2, but my current concern is with a

[3] To avoid unintended identification of the two concepts, we could paraphrase the saying as 'Knowledge brings power.'

broader implication of this feature of the traditional view. Since, on this view, the obligations of justification end at the boundary of one's accessible consciousness, one may have a justified, true belief without having any capacity to *do* anything with that so-called knowledge. This, it seems to me, is the chief practical cost of the accidentality of mere coincidences between truth and justification in a belief, as well as of accidentality in mere coincidences between truth and belief.

One may have a justified true belief without being able to do anything with it because justification does not necessarily bring with it any ability to maintain a true belief about that matter through time and changing circumstances. One may lack the capacities mentioned, while having a justified true belief, because one may lack in one's accessible consciousness beliefs that are relevant to whether the claim would be true in different circumstances—and thereby lack the capacity to form the correct belief on the matter in different circumstances—while yet having justification for one's belief.[4] (Gettier's examples, discussed in Chapter 2, illustrate this nicely.) A fortiori, one may lack this capacity when one has a merely true belief. If one is not able to follow the truth on the matter into changed circumstances, then one cannot be assured of better than random success at doing things using this belief, because if one tries to *do* something with this purported knowledge, circumstances will be changed by that very fact. This is a problem because we all know that knowledge enables us to *do* things, including change the world to conform more nearly to our wishes.

Any 'anti-luck' epistemology, of which there are several, will do better than the traditional view of knowledge at ruling out accidentally true beliefs—and accidentally true *and* justified beliefs—from counting as knowledge. That does not imply, though, that these views perform equally well at explaining why knowledge makes technology possible. (Indeed they do not, as I will briefly explain in Chapter 4.) However, the tracking view, which is also an anti-luck epistemology, explains this feature of knowledge with grace and economy. In order to fulfill the first tracking conditional for a proposition p—if p weren't true you wouldn't believe it—it must be that if circumstances were different in such a way as to make p false, in any of the most plausible[5] ways this might happen, you would not believe p. If so, then when you have this knowledge-enabling property if the truth value of p *does* change in the future, in plausible ways, your belief *will* change to unbelief with it. Similarly, to fulfill the second tracking conditional—if p were true you would believe it—it must be that if circumstances were different from what they actually are, in plausible ways, but p were still true, then you would still believe p. Thus, as long as you have this

---

[4] In other words, on this view one may know that p without having ruled out probable alternate circumstances in which not-p, as long as one is not aware of whether or not those circumstances are probable or relevant.

[5] The clause 'in any of the most plausible ways this might happen' is not necessary in the subjunctive conditional formulation of the conditions, but I include it explicitly here to make clear to those unacquainted with the properties of this type of conditional that it does not require the consequent to be true in *all* possible ways of fulfilling the antecedent. I use the phrase 'most plausible' to be deliberately ambiguous between 'sufficiently probable', which will be the criterion for which possibilities matter in my own formulation, and 'closest', which is the usual criterion for subjunctive conditionals, a fine distinction that does not matter at the moment.

knowledge-enabling property if p *does* remain true while other things change in plausible ways, you will *continue* to believe p.

Notice what fulfillment of these conditions by a subject, for a p stating the behavior of an object, means about the capacity of the subject to project the behavior of that object in circumstances in which it was not seen to occur before, e.g., in a newly concocted machine, broadly construed. If those new circumstances bear no resemblance at all to any circumstances the subject has seen before, then it means nothing at all. But invention of tools is hit or miss in such situations as well. However, if the circumstances bear partial resemblances in certain ways to circumstances the subject has seen before—as machines often do since they are often concocted out of combinations of already understood parts—then they are likely to be partially comparable to circumstances I called 'plausible' above, that is, circumstances in which the subject who fulfills the tracking conditions will believe the right thing about how the object behaves. For this reason the subject who fulfills the tracking conditions will have informed and somewhat reliable hunches about how the object will behave in the novel circumstances. This will not give him foreknowledge of which machine ideas will work, but everyone knows that trial and error makes a contribution to the discovery of technology. What the role of tracking in knowledge does explain is the ability of someone with knowledge of parts to guess at better than random which new machine ideas using those parts will work. On the tracking view one does not gain knowledge without also gaining some capacity to act to shape what the world does. Knowledge is power *because* knowledge requires tracking.

Animals

The meerkat, a South African mammal of the mongoose family, made familiar by the character Timon in the movie *The Lion King*, is a highly cooperative species. Those who study these small animals say that human beings rival their cooperation only when we have a good day. It may be that they cooperate out of necessity; with limited defensive weapons, the meerkat—which is the size of a well-stuffed submarine sandwich—is prey for a number of larger animals. It lives in open areas, going into its hole-homes for sleeping, mating, and fleeing. Eating requires foraging and digging outside, though, and foraging in the brush of an open area is dangerous. Accordingly, the group forages together, with one of the meerkats standing guard on the highest ground in the vicinity. Such an arrangement is not uncommon among non-human animals. Nor is it unusual that the meerkat watchman has a signalling system to alert his fellows of danger. In some species the watchman even has distinct signals for different kinds of predator; an animal with more options than the meerkat—which can only retreat to a hole—has better chances of survival if it responds differently to snakes, tigers, and hawks, for example.

However, the meerkat watchman also has a continuous peeping song, uninterrupted as long as there is no reason to sound the alert. It is a signal that apparently indicates not only that it is safe but also that he is still watching. This kind of habit is intriguing because of the way that it adds a layer of security to the information the watchman conveys to his fellows. Cruel as it is, it appears that the probability that the watchman himself is overcome by a predator is high enough that his fellows need to be reassured continuously that this has not happened. That the watchman is not sounding the danger signal is apparently not enough to give insurance that there is no danger. He could be failing to sound the danger signal because he is dead (Clutton-Brock 2002).

The watchman's continuous song is a sign that he is watching, and therefore an indicator that if there were danger there would be a danger signal, whether a specialized cry or a sudden silence. If I am right about why the watchman has a habit of continuous peeping, then we could describe the function of the meerkat watchman system as contributing to fulfillment of the following subjunctive conditionals: if there were danger from predators, the foraging meerkat would be aware of it, or, if the area were not safe, the foraging meerkat would not continue foraging as if it were. The resemblance of these to Nozick's conditionals is clear. In this book I argue that fulfillment of conditions similar to these is what makes a true belief knowledge, and what makes some facts evidence for others. From the view that results it is easy to classify humble organisms like the meerkat as having a rudimentary version of what we call 'knowledge.' I regard this as a confirming consequence of the view, since it seems to me obvious that lower animals do have something like knowledge.

Our knowledge that there is a bee in my bonnet, and of other such commonplace p, makes up a small sample, not obviously representative, of the kinds of knowledge and near-knowledge there are in the world. It is uncontroversial, for example, that higher non-human animals have something similar to knowledge, something so similar that we are inclined to slip into speaking of them as knowing things, even if on reflection we do not think that is quite right. We can say that the dog knows there is someone at the door, or knows that the other dog is male or that his master needs help, that the cat knows there is a mouse (or at least an edible) behind the bookcase, and that the meerkat knows it is safe, without abusing our language terrifically.

Many older views in epistemology would have trouble explaining in what sense what lower animals have is similar to what we have in knowledge, primarily because of the tendency of these views, called 'internalist', to require for knowledge that a subject have, in addition to true belief, consciously accessible justification for her belief. We just saw that taking what follows from the subject's accessible consciousness as sufficient for justification in a view of knowledge made such a view too weak to explain why knowledge is power. But making conscious accessibility of reasons for belief necessary for knowledge is too strong to allow such a view to explain how there could be any similarity whatever between what other animals sometimes have and what humans have when we have knowledge. Even the highest non-human animals do not have conscious access, or partial access, to the grounds for their behavior, and one may slip into speaking of them as knowing things even if one does not think they have beliefs at all. It is hard to see how animals could have what we have to a lesser degree or partially on internalist views. Yet, as it seems to me, many of them obviously do. The animals that have glimmerings of awareness of something partially like mental contents that would justify their behavior are very few—chimpanzees perhaps—but the animals to which it is natural to ascribe something like knowledge are very many indeed.

Inability to explain what is similar about animals and ourselves with regard to knowledge is something I cannot help but regard as an abject failure on the part of internalist epistemology. Newer externalist views, which deny the need for conscious access to one's justification for belief in order to have knowledge, and locate what makes a belief knowledge instead in the relation that the belief bears to the way the world is, are obviously in a position to be more successful at identifying similarities between human knowledge and lower animals' near-knowledge.[6] The new tracking view of knowledge developed in this book is an externalist view of human knowledge, but it also offers a particular and unified way of understanding the senses in which human knowledge and animal near-knowledge are similar and different because one does not need to have beliefs in order to track the truth.

So, to make the view as uncontroversial as possible, suppose that non-human animals do not have beliefs. Anyway, any animals that we become convinced do have beliefs thereby become eligible for being counted as having full-blown knowledge like ours. Neither Nozick's original tracking view of knowledge nor my revision of it counts anything as knowledge that does not involve belief, but the idea of tracking has always been more general than that. We may define X TRACKS Y to mean that if Y were true then X would be true, and if Y were false then X would be false too. In this way, one fact may TRACK another, which is, as Nozick said and roughly as I will argue later, one of the things that happens when a fact is good evidence for a hypothesis. Though we suppose that animals do not have beliefs, they do have other media through which they TRACK the world, namely, awareness and responses. Higher animals have awareness of things that tend to be important to survival, such as the meerkat's awareness that it is or is not safe from predators, which is dependent on an awareness that there is or is not a peeping sound. And even the lowly paramecium has locomotive responses to its environment that are salient to its survival, moving toward sugar and away from obstacles. Watching a paramecium's behavior in a sugar gradient makes it quite intelligible, if also strictly incorrect, to say that this one-celled organism knows where the sugar is. And that is because if we watch it long enough we can see that it has a mechanism for insuring that for any direction around the paramecium if there were more sugar in it than in the place where the paramecium now is the organism would move toward it, and if there were not it would not.

Animals TRACK the world along some dimensions, and this TRACKING is responsible and gives a good reason, I claim, for our inclination to attribute near-knowledge to them. What does it mean for a meerkat's awareness to TRACK the truth? It means, for example, that if the meerkat were in danger then it would have a sense that it was in danger, and if it were not in danger then it would not have a sense that it was in danger. Y here is 'The meerkat is in danger' and X is 'The meerkat has a sense that it is in danger (fear)'; it is clear that when the watchman system is functioning correctly X TRACKS Y. Imagine an animal that does not TRACK the danger posed by large

---

[6] Other arguments for externalist views can be found in Ramsey (1960), Goldman (1967, 1976, 1979, 1986), Dretske (1971, 1981a), Armstrong (1973), Nozick (1981), Plantinga (1993), and Kornblith (2002). Goldman (1999) contains powerful arguments against internalism.

predators, or does so only sporadically. Perhaps it is a deaf meerkat which looks at the watchman from time to time while it is foraging to try to insure its safety, but cannot hear the danger signal or the absence of peeping. Then one of the two tracking conditionals is likely to fail. If this meerkat were in danger, it might not have a sense of fear, because it would have missed the danger signal and might well not have looked at the appropriate time to make up for that handicap. A sense of its general vulnerability might lead the animal to have a constant sense of fear, which would mean that it fulfilled the first tracking conditional: if it always had a sense of fear then it would also have a sense of fear when there was danger. However, this would ruin its fulfillment of the other tracking conditional because even if there were no danger it would have a sense of fear. And not only does this animal's awareness fail the tracking conditions, the thing that this failure makes it most natural to deny of the animal is something like that it has knowledge of whether it is in danger or not.

The epistemological internalist may grant the reasonableness of the thought that the dog knows there is someone at the door (even though I expect him to deny, as I do, its strict accuracy). What he is likely to object to is the idea that epistemology bears any responsibility to this thought about dogs. I might be told that the subject of epistemology is human knowledge, whatever other sorts of knowledge there might be in the world. However, it seems to me that traditionally epistemology took all knowledge as its subject matter, with our predecessors giving accounts, for example, of what knowing would be like if you were God or if you were an angel, to articulate more fully by contrast what it is like when you are human (e.g., Kant 1965: B71-2, B 138-9). Even if our focus is human knowledge, we cannot expect to get this subject matter right if it is an example of a larger phenomenon that we are ignoring. Human knowledge evolved out of more primitive behavior that other animals still possess. If our account of human knowledge cannot make sense of their behavior as a primitive version of our own, then it is inadequate.

An analogy will help to make my point. I have not met a non-human animal that I think has knowledge in the strict sense in which I will define that term, primarily because I do not think those animals have beliefs, and beliefs are required for knowledge.[7] I also do not think that non-human animals have language in the sense that we do, and that belief and language may have a relationship. Thus, I do not deny that a dramatic step occurred when knowledge evolved, as dramatic as the difference between ourselves and chimpanzees in the capacity for language. But admission that there is a large step between animals and ourselves works for my point and not against it. Consider what we expect of those who try to say what language is. Because we know that language evolved from more basic things, if primitive signaling systems were not recognizable as partial fulfillments of some of the conditions in an account of what

---

[7] Whether animals have beliefs is a controversial matter on which I am merely reporting my stand. As Kim Sterelny has convincingly argued (Sterelny 2003: ch. 3), the experiments that would tell us whether animals have decoupled representations (his term for what is distinctive about belief) have not been done. This is primarily because what they would be looking for, response *breadth*, is the opposite of what we have been looking for in experiments probing the extent of other animal capacities. Sterelny's articulation of what makes something a belief is especially useful because it can be described independently of whether or not an organism has language.

language is, we would (or should) take that account of language to be flawed. It seems true and illuminating, for example, that some animals use nouns, but that they lack a syntax which would enable them to distinguish, the way that sentences can, among the various relations the items those nouns refer to might stand in. Such comparisons should be and are possible in the study of language, and I am simply requiring the same breadth of accountability for study of the concept of knowledge. In fact, I am even more impressed with animals' near-knowledge than I am with their near-language, so it seems to me that the best account of knowledge may have explanations reaching even deeper into the animal kingdom than the correct account of language needs to. Tracking provides a particularly natural and easy account of similarities between other species and ourselves with respect to knowledge, and the account is consistent with, indeed ideal for, an evolutionary picture of the emergence of our special capabilities out of those of more primitive systems.[8] I do not see how internalism can succeed on either score without attributing to non-human animals much more consciousness and language than it is plausible to think they have.

Science

If we venture beyond the parochial domain of everyday human knowledge in the other direction, we find scientific knowledge. Epistemologists do not discuss scientific knowledge in any detail these days, having long since ceded the territory to philosophers of science. However, the generality of epistemology's charge to analyze the concept of knowledge brings with it an obligation to make claims that are true of this variety as well. Still, if we thought that epistemologists could learn something by consulting philosophers of science, we would be cut short by the fact that philosophers of science do not usually analyze the concept of knowledge, or even the concept of scientific knowledge. The reason for this, I think, is that philosophers of science implicitly assume that we would know what scientific knowledge was, or near enough, if only we knew what makes one statement evidence for another: a true belief is scientific knowledge, roughly, when one has good enough evidence for it. The question what evidence is takes pride of place over questions about knowledge in the part of philosophy of science devoted to epistemological issues, to the point of having an entire subfield, confirmation theory, devoted to its theoretical articulation. The reason for this, in turn, I think, is that the deliberate, conscious, and systematic pursuit and creation of evidence is one of the things that is distinctive about science and scientific knowledge. It is not that in ordinary life we do not possess evidence for our claims—we often do—but it usually comes to us inadvertently, without our making a special or systematic effort to acquire it, and it is often possessed unconsciously. When it is pursued deliberately and consciously by detectives, journalists, and lawyers, they too are engaging in something like science.

---

[8] Understanding knowledge as a matter of tracking makes it pretty obvious how it was possible for the aspect of knowledge that goes beyond true belief to evolve, because of the clear evolutionary advantages of what Sterelny calls 'robust tracking systems' over mere single-cue 'detection systems.' How belief, the medium of human beings' distinctive tracking capacities, evolved or could have evolved is a thornier matter, as his probing discussion displays (Sterelny 2003: ch. 3).

Whether or not these assumptions explain the behavior of philosophers of science, they are assumptions I will make. And whatever explains the disciplinary emphases of philosophy of science, the fact remains that if we want to take advantage of what these specialists have learned about scientific knowledge, we will only be able to do so by way of discussions of evidence. To keep the case of scientific knowledge in view, I present a new tracking view of evidence, in Chapter 5. One of the many charms of the tracking idea is the easy relationship that it yields between the view of evidence and the view of knowledge, which effortlessly explains our sense that better evidence makes it more likely that one knows on its basis. On Nozick's tracking view of evidence, e is strong evidence for h whenever if h were true then e would be true $(h \rightarrow e)$, and if h were false then e would be false $(-h \rightarrow -e)$. If you know e, you would believe h on its basis and wouldn't believe h if e weren't true, and e fulfills Nozick's condition on strong evidence, it is no surprise that you know h, either on the tracking view or in real life.[9]

Speaking autobiographically, it was the tracking view of evidence, and my sense of its striking fit with what scientists aim for in experiments, that led me to the conviction that tracking would also be the best account of knowledge. Consider why physicists think they know there is no ether drag, that is, no dependence of the speed of light on the motion of its source relative to the ether, the supposed medium of light transmission. Einstein apparently believed this on grounds of principle, without knowing the very latest relevant experiments when he published his special theory of relativity that assumed this in 1905. But Einstein also said that no one believes in a theory except its author, whereas everyone relies on an experiment except the physicist who conducted it.[10]

If asked why they believe there is no ether drag physicists will most often cite the Michelson–Morley experiment.[11] Arguably this response is shorthand for that particular experiment combined with the many repetitions of it by others through 1930, and the later execution of similar experiments using lasers, which put the result beyond dispute. What was brilliant about the experimental design was the way in which it linked any possible ether drag, that is, difference in the speed of light depending on the speed of its source, to changes in interference fringes that would be visible in a telescope. An interference fringe produced by two beams of light will change in response to as little as a fraction of a wavelength of change in the synchronization of its incoming sources. Michelson exploited this fact by setting up an apparatus in which interference fringes would be different if the speed of light was

---

[9] That this is so depends on the tracking relation possessing a transitivity property, since the fact that you track e and that e TRACKS h cannot otherwise yield any purchase on whether you track h. As I will explain in Chapter 5, although the tracking relation as I formulate it is not strictly transitive, it does have a weaker transitivity property that is sufficient for the purpose of explaining how knowledge gets transmitted over several tracking relations in the cases where that plausibly happens: errors magnify over chains of tracking relations at no more than an arithmetic rate.

[10] Remark attributed to Einstein in 1922. Source: Dr Herman F. Mark in an interview with A. Rabinovich in 'Questions of Relativity,' *Jerusalem Post*, 22 March 1979, 7, quoted in Galison (1987: 244).

[11] Michelson received the Nobel Prize in 1907 for the interferometer and techniques he used in this and earlier experiments measuring the speed of light.

different in different orientations of the apparatus to the earth's motion, as the hypothesis of ether drag said it was. Essentially, two beams of light from the same source would be made to travel out perpendicularly to each other over identical distances in long tubes at the end of which mirrors would bounce the beams back. If synchronized light beams traveled at different speeds in the two directions, then because they traveled the same distance they should be out of synch when they returned. Previous experiments looking for the ether drag had failed to find it. This apparatus took the investigation to a new level of sensitivity because changes in interference patterns represented a new level of magnification of the difference they were looking for.

Of course, it was not enough to make sure that if there was an ether drag then there would be a difference in the interference pattern. Other things could cause a difference in the pattern as well, such as a discrepancy in the lengths of the tubes, and this would throw off their measurements of the quantity of the drag. This particular problem could be addressed by adjusting the lengths of the tubes until an intensity peak was achieved in the interference between the two beams, and then rotating the apparatus to check for the ether drag effect by looking for a change. Ambient motion of the apparatus could also make a difference to the interference fringes, leading the experimenters to float the apparatus in a pool of mercury for stability. Much work was done to make sure that when they saw changes in the interference pattern those changes could be attributed to the ether drag alone, and could be measured. Measuring the ether drag, not proving its non-existence, was the purpose of Michelson and Morley.

It is clear that these scientists' aim in conducting the experiment was to set it up in such a way that anything that was not ether drag would not show up as a shift in the interference pattern, and anything that was ether drag would show up. The former was desired because they did not want the ether drag measurement to be falsely high, the latter because they did not want it to be falsely low. In so doing, they aimed to set up an apparatus that also happened to fulfill the conditions the tracking view says we would be most interested in if we wanted strong evidence for the presence or absence of an ether drag: if there were no ether drag then the interference fringes would show no appreciable shift, and if there were an ether drag then it would show significant shift. To their surprise and dismay, Michelson and Morley's hope to measure the ether drag was disappointed, since they detected no more than one fortieth of the theoretically expected shift in the interference pattern. And it is clear that it is to the extent that we regard their experiment as fulfilling the conditionals I have listed that we regard it as successful in giving strong reason to think there is no ether drag. It is said that James Clerk Maxwell inadvertently goaded Michelson into measuring the ether drag by remarking that the effect was too small for any experiment to find. Michelson would not have met the challenge if the reason he did not find the drag was because the experimental set-up was not good enough to show it.

Not everyone thought or thinks these two individuals showed the result that there is no ether drag conclusively. Some say it was not shown until the later laser experiments. Others stress alternative theories of the ether that were offered to explain the null (no effect) result. My aim is not to take a stand in this debate about whether their experiment succeeded in securing the conclusion we now believe is true. My point is rather about what counts as success, and the doubts that have been cast on this experiment illustrate further the central role of tracking in this. One of the early doubters was Michelson himself, who considered the possibility that they were failing to see drag not because it was not there, but because the apparatus was too close to the earth, where the ether might cling to the earth and follow its motion. Consequently he tried the apparatus at a variety of altitudes, where an experiment he still regarded as unsuccessful might give him the result he believed it should. Attempts like this to explain the null result while maintaining that light does have different speeds depending on its motion relative to an ether further illustrate that tracking captures what we regard as essential to the experiment's success in showing that there is no ether drag. The possibility that altitude made a difference to the experiment cast doubt on the significance of the result because it cast doubt on the following tracking conditional: if there were an ether drag then the interference fringes would have changed significantly. Other objections, whether experimental or theoretical, can be understood quite naturally according to the same scheme.

The Michelson–Morley experiment is one where the result was unexpected and null. Consider the equally vaunted Rutherford scattering experiment, where the result was an unexpected effect. According to his own recollection Ernest Rutherford suggested that Hans Geiger train Ernest Marsden by having him check whether alpha particles (helium nuclei) shot through thin films of heavy metal would ever be deflected through angles larger than 90 degrees. Rutherford had been shooting alpha particles at things, and even at films of heavy metal, for some time, and he was pretty confident of the outcome of this exercise: back-deflection was not possible. Geiger and Marsden would shoot a stream of positively charged alpha particles at a gold film no more than 400 atoms thick, and detect where the alphas landed at a screen on the other side. The physics of scattering was well enough understood that the pattern on the screen could be used to infer something of the structure of the film the particles had passed through. On the basis of J. J. Thomson's 'plum-pudding' picture of the structure of the atom, Rutherford expected the alpha particles to more or less go through the foil in a straight line. Since according to Thomson's model the atom was a uniformly distributed pudding of positive charge, with individual electrons randomly distributed like plums throughout, the hefty alpha particle, which was fully 8,000 times more massive than an electron and moving at a high velocity, would knock out of the way any of the tiny units it might hit, and the repulsion of the positive charge in the atom was too spread out to exert a strong deflecting force. The chance of getting back-deflection was very tiny, and this could be calculated.

Rutherford later called it 'quite the most incredible event that ever happened to me in my life,' when Geiger reported that they had been able to get several alpha particles deflected back. 'It was almost as incredible as if you had fired a 15-inch shell at a piece of tissue paper and it came back and hit you' (Pais 1986; 189). Rutherford and the scientific community eventually concluded that this experiment had shown that the plum-pudding model of the atom was wrong, and that most of the mass of the atom (and all of the positive charge) was instead concentrated in a small central nucleus. They did so, I submit, on the basis of conviction that certain tracking conditionals were fulfilled. One of them was that if the plum-pudding model of the atom were correct then backward deflections of the alpha particles would not be a common occurrence, producible at will. Their confidence in this was of course based on a myriad of assumptions both experimental and theoretical, for example that the alpha beam was hitting the gold foil and not the metal tube that was holding it up, that the thin gold foil did not contain impurities such as chunks of concrete, that positive charge distributed over the entire atom provided too weak a force for such deflection, and that alpha particles were 8,000 times as massive as electrons. But the force of their conviction that what Geiger and Marsden saw eliminated Thomson's model came from the fact that these well-grounded assumptions lent support to the tracking conditional.

In their conclusion that the experiment supported an alternative model in which the atom had a small core of concentrated mass, belief in tracking conditionals had to have an equally crucial role. To be confident of this conclusion they had to be confident that if the nuclear model were correct then large-angle scattering could be expected (h → e). This was relatively easy on basic theoretical grounds since the charge of the atom minus its electrons was more than enough to deflect an alpha particle if that charge was concentrated densely. Equally importantly, they needed to be confident that if the nuclear model were not correct this large-angle scattering would not happen. (−h → −e) Obviously, Rutherford's arguments that the plum-pudding model would not yield this effect were a start on this. But he went further. Rutherford made explicit arguments to the effect that a concentrated nucleus was the only way such deflections could possibly occur (Rutherford 1911: 687). These arguments were of course fallible. They were based on the assumption that the force of electromagnetism dominated the effect, and the fact that in this force a scattering angle of greater than 90 degrees was impossible unless the target was more charged than the projectile. We now know that there were forces that Rutherford and his contemporaries did not know about, the strong and weak nuclear forces. But luckily those unknown forces did not make a difference to the fulfillment of the tracking conditional that needed to be true for this experiment to provide good evidence for the nuclear model. And Rutherford's effort, if not his achievement, was to rule out all possible alternatives, not only the alternatives that had been imagined.

A final example from biology will be helpful; in contrast to the physics examples I have cited, this is a case where scientists confirmed the view they expected to be true. When James Watson and Francis Crick published their result on the structure of the DNA molecule they also suggested a mechanism through which it replicated itself (Watson and Crick 1953). Matthew Meselson and Franklin Stahl at the California Institute of Technology soon confirmed their suggestion (Meselson and Stahl 1958). The way in which they did this, what they took to be important to doing this, highlights the centrality of tracking to the production of evidence.

Merely producing data that Watson and Crick's proposal would have predicted was not enough to confirm the suggestion, nor would any scientist have dreamed that it was. Meselson and Stahl needed to produce evidence that would rule out alternative ways replication might take place in order to zero in on what was actually happening. They investigated three possible ways the double-stranded molecule could reproduce itself, which they took to be exhaustive. A molecule would somehow have to use its own structure and the soup of nucleic-acid building blocks it was floating in to bring the result of more than one DNA molecule where there had been only one before. Watson and Crick had proposed that replication was a doubling, a production of two daughter molecules where there had been one parent before. Meselson and Stahl confirmed that it was a doubling in their first experimental result, and this narrowed the possible mechanisms down to three.

The molecular structure they already knew, combined with a little applied Euclidean geometry and an assumption of conservation of matter, implied that there were only three ways a doubling of this molecule could happen in the conditions imagined. In the 'conservative' scenario one of the two resulting molecules would be the parent while the other consisted entirely of building blocks assembled out of the soup. In the 'semi-conservative' scenario suggested by Watson and Crick each of the daughter molecules would contain a strand from the parent and a strand made up entirely of new building blocks. In the 'random dispersive' model neither daughter molecule would contain an original strand from the parent; each strand of each daughter molecule would be a cut and pasted combination of pieces of the original strands and pieces picked up from the soup. It is hard to argue with the claim that these were the only possibilities given what they knew; it is the claim that all, some, or none of an original strand appears in a daughter molecule, and all, some, or none exhaust the possibilities. The genius of the investigation, perhaps, was to have pitched the question at a level of description where this exhaustiveness could be achieved in a simple way.

These three possibilities would be distinct in the first generation of replication, and the experimenters could figure out which was happening if they could figure out how to discriminate them. They did this by means of heavy and light isotopes of nitrogen, an element that they confirmed would be incorporated uniformly as replication proceeded. DNA molecules denser or rarer by the kinds of amounts the isotopes would make them differ by could be separated with an ultracentrifuge, a fact Meselson and Stahl confirmed independently. The *E. coli* source of DNA was grown for many generations in heavy nitrogen, then switched to light nitrogen and checked for its density profile every generation after the switch. If replication was conservative, then after the first generation there should be two peaks of density, one corresponding to the heavy parent molecules and the other to their entirely new daughters. Instead what they observed was only one band, of a density intermediate between that expected for molecules with only heavy nitrogen and that expected for molecules with only light nitrogen. This ruled out the conservative model, but did not distinguish between the remaining semi-conservative and random dispersive models, since these models both predicted molecules with old and new parts, and thus with a mixture of the two types of nitrogen.

Knowing the structure of the DNA molecule helped them once again, because this told them that though the overall density of the first-generation daughter molecules would be the same whether they were produced semi-conservatively or by random dispersion, the individual strands of these DNA molecules would have different density profiles. If they could get the individual strands on the centrifuge, then if the daughters were produced semi-conservatively there would be two density peaks, one for the heavy parent strands and one for the lighter new strands. On the other hand, if they were produced by random dispersion then since both strands of each molecule would be cut and paste products there would be only one peak, because all of the individual strands would have similar intermediate densities.

They were able to get the individual strands on the ultracentrifuge because they learned that when enough heat is applied to *E. coli* DNA to break the hydrogen bonds (called 'denaturing'), the DNA molecule is chopped at the rungs of the ladder, leaving individual strands. (This was confirmed by the fact that the molecular weight of the product of heating *E. coli* DNA was roughly halved, whereas, for example, with salmon DNA the molecular weight is unchanged.) When they heat-denatured the first-generation products and compared their centrifuge bands to samples known to be heavy and light, they found that indeed there were two peaks this time, corresponding exactly to the positions for DNA with heavy and light nitrogen. This, they concluded, ruled out the random dispersive model.

I have suppressed an enormous amount of detail in the description of this series of experiments. I have not mentioned the role of cesium chloride, or EDTA, or ultraviolet absorption photography, or described how they knew exactly when one generation of replication had been accomplished or how long the ultracentrifuge should run. However, there is a good reason why the level of description I have just given is the textbook version of the story, which is that this is the level one needs to understand in order to have a first grasp of why what they found showed that, in *E. coli* at least, DNA replication is semi-conservative. This description contains what all of Meselson and Stahl's fine work was aiming for: the securing of certain tracking conditionals. These are, namely, if replication were semi-conservative then for first-generation, double-stranded DNA there would be a single peak at a precise (intermediate) density and first-generation single-stranded DNA would show two peaks at precise locations, and if replication were not semi-conservative then the double-stranded first-generation product would show two peaks at precise locations (conservative), or the single-stranded first-generation product would show one peak at a precise location (random dispersive).

These conditionals even explain to us why the details matter. For example, why does it matter how long the centrifuge runs? Here is one reason: if the centrifuge did not have enough time to bring the materials to equilibrium it might not separate materials that could be separated. That is, one might get one band (peak) where one should have gotten two. This kind of mistake would ruin the first part of the second tracking conditional that says that if replication were conservative one would get two peaks. If one has not centrifuged to equilibrium, then even if replication were conservative one might not get two peaks. It is because the scientists satisfied themselves of the truth of the tracking conditionals noted that when they actually got a single intermediate peak from the double-stranded DNA and two peaks for the single-stranded DNA they were confident that this meant replication, at least in *E. coli*, was semi-conservative. In addition to the fact that how DNA replicates is of wide-ranging significance for their field, it is the fact that these scientists established such firm tracking connections that makes us regard this as a classic experiment.

Testimony

One might have expected that an idea that worked so well on animal near-knowledge would dumb down the notion of human knowledge, but instead the tracking idea seems very natural at the highly conscious and deliberate 'higher' end of knowledge, too, where we find experimental scientists. This impressive range leads me to expect that the idea can account for the everyday human knowledge that stands somewhere in between. One species of everyday knowledge, the kind we acquire by believing what others attest to, has received a good deal of attention in recent years in epistemology (Coady 1992; Fricker 1987, 1995; Adler 1994; Audi 1997). Philosophers of science have taken an interest in the topic too, since the dependence of scientific knowledge on trust in the beliefs of other scientists plays a key role in the growth of knowledge, a realization we owe to John Hardwig and others (Hardwig 1985, 1991; Shapin 1994; Lipton 1998; Kusch and Lipton 2002). This book will not give an extensive tracking-based discussion of testimony, but I wish to describe in this introduction why the tracking idea is as at home with knowledge by testimony as with the other kinds of examples we have seen. I will use Nozick's conditions for this, though a precise account would require my revised analysis of knowledge, found in Chapters 2, 3, and 4. Thus, suppose that S's true belief p is knowledge just in case (1) if p were not true S would not believe it, and (2) if p were true then S would believe it, and that false beliefs are not knowledge under any circumstances.

In many, perhaps most, cases in which we count a subject S as knowing p on the basis of the testimony of another, W, that p, W knows p. One might think that the testifier's knowing p is required for knowledge that p by his testimony, on the basis of the thought that no one can give what he doesn't have. However, this consequence of the 'transmission' picture of knowledge by testimony is not true in general, as Jennifer Lackey has shown (Lackey 1999). Nozick's tracking conditions perform very well in this area because they both support the transmission picture where it is appealing and correct, and correctly identify exceptions to it.

On Nozick's tracking view of what it is for W to know p there are two ways for W to fail, assuming that W believes p and attests to p. One way is for p to be false, the other is for at least one of the tracking conditionals to be false for W and p. Let us suppose, for the sake of simplicity, that S actually believes W and nothing would change about S's believing W unless something about W or the circumstances changed. If p is false, then of course S cannot know p by W's testimony, since no one can know a statement that is false, by any means.

What if W's belief that p fails to track p although p is true? This can happen in two ways. One is if were p to be false W might well still believe it. This could be so if W were gullible, incompetent, or had the right kind of conflict of interest, e.g., a parent who believes that his or her child is not guilty of a crime. In most of the cases I can think of where W might well believe p though p was false, S would be mistaken (if possibly justified) in believing p on the basis of W's testimony that p. The tracking view implies the same, for notice that if S believes p on the basis of W's testimony that p but W might well believe p even if p was false, then S's belief that p fails to track the truth too. If p were false, then S might well believe p, since she gets her information from W who might have. Thus, on the tracking view S fails to know p. Of course, an exception to this will occur if S has a definite way of sensing when W's flaw is at work, and hence when not to trust him, though W has no similar sense. In this case the problem with W will not affect S's knowledge on the tracking view, because S tracks the truth though W does not. But counting S as knowing in such a case is as it should be. This is so despite the fact that it is a case where the usual transmission picture of testimony fails, since W has given what he does not have.

The other way for W's belief to fail to track the truth is if were p to be true W might not believe it. That is, even though W actually believes p his belief is not modally stable in that circumstances could fairly easily change his belief though p remained true. Imagine, for example, that W is impressionable, easily influenced by lawyers or donors, easily cowed by authority, or just not very sure of what he saw. In such a case S's belief that p would fail to track the truth in the same way that W's did: if p were true S might well not believe it because her source might well not have believed it. (I assume for simplicity that W's attestation is S's only potential source of reasons to believe p.) Of course, once again, if S is responsive to when W's faults are at work though W himself is not, then S may get knowledge from W despite those faults, both on the tracking view and in real life.

Other ways for W to fail to know p and thereby for S to fail to know p by believing W's testimony, on the tracking account, arise if W does not believe p though he attests to it. If W does not believe p and p is not true, then S, a subject who comes to believe p through W's testimony, does not know p because of p's falsehood, as already noted. What if W does not believe p but p is true? This means that though he doesn't believe p, W is testifying to it. If he does this unconvincingly, which is one of the possibilities, then S will not believe him if she has some discriminating ability. In this case S will not come to know p by W's testimony because she doesn't come to believe p by means of W's testimony. If S does come to believe p by W's testimony then, on the assumption it was unconvincing, she must have some disposition to be fooled by W either because she is distracted by W's charm or because she lacks minimal lie-detection mechanisms. Intuitively, this is enough to disqualify her from having knowledge in normal circumstances. It is enough on the tracking account too, provided that there is no regularity insuring that W's attestations are always in line with the truth, which is unlikely due to W's commitment to attest to what he does not believe. (Cases violating this proviso will be discussed presently.)

What if W does this testifying so convincingly as to pass all of S's sound lie-detection mechanisms? In that case, S will come to believe p through W's testimony, but she gets knowledge thereby, on the (Nozick) tracking view, if and only if this belief tracks the truth of p. We can suppose that S not only actually believes W but also S's belief that p tracks W's attestations about p, since if it doesn't she isn't fully trusting him on this topic; she has not put her belief fully in dependence on his testimony. The tracking view also says she hasn't come to know in case she isn't trusting W, since lack of tracking there ruins the only possible tracking relation to the truth that S has any access to.

If S tracks W's attestations about p, then whether her belief that p tracks the truth depends on whether W's attestations track the truth,[12] and that is not determined merely by whether W's attestation is actually true. As in the previous case, we need to consider in addition something about W's dispositions. Of course, a W who actually believes a falsehood and attests to the opposite is not likely to be very reliable about any of the important steps, so his attestation probably does not track the truth. In this normal kind of case, if S's lie-detection mechanisms are fooled by W's testimony, as we are supposing, then she does not get knowledge, on the tracking view, because her belief's tracking of the truth fails somewhere along the line of the relation between W's attestation and the truth. This conforms to our intuitions, since getting fooled by a very skilled liar who is incompetent about whether p is true is not a way of coming to know p, even if one's resulting belief in p happens to be true.

The case of mismatch between what W attests to and what W believes looks different if it is not due to lying but rather, for example, to duty diligently performed. In Lackey's (1999) example, a teacher who does not believe evolutionary theory teaches it to her students in an effective and reliable way because she has been instructed to do so and she obeys orders. The students get knowledge thereby, if they are paying attention and assuming evolutionary theory is true, and we think so despite the fact that we cannot count the teacher as knowing since she does not believe, that is, despite the fact that the teacher transmits what she does not have. The tracking view is in line with our intuitions in this example because our intuitions counting the teacher as transmitting knowledge depend on an assumption that she has been diligent in preparing her testimony in such a way that it effectively conveys what a skilled and believing advocate of the theory would convey. Though her belief does not track the truth, her testimony does, and this is why she can transmit what she does not have. If we did not think her testimony tracked the truth, we would not think the students got knowledge from their experience with her either.

It is also possible to imagine a case where W's attestations about p are in a very dependable relation to the truth though W's intention is not duty: suppose his attestations are always true when p is true and false when p is false, while his beliefs about p are always false when p is true and true when p is not. Perhaps W is perfectly counter-competent but also always does what he thinks is lying.[13] Such a W, who, because his beliefs are false does not possess knowledge of p, can give S knowledge of p on the tracking view as long as his testimony is unfailingly convincing and S is disposed to respond appropriately to that. This consequence is admittedly somewhat strange, if, as we are supposing, far from being aware of W's perfect countercompetence and unfailing intention to lie, S is not even unconsciously picking up on them. However, this strange consequence is not the burden of the tracking view alone. On the basis of what has been described we can say not only that S tracks the truth that p, but also that S has formed her belief through a reliable process, and also that S's belief is justified. It is even

---

[12] Note that this claim depends on the weak transitivity property of tracking discussed above.

[13] I owe thanks to Stefan Brandt for transforming the example I had into this more extreme and thereby more illustrative case.

indefeasibly justified since though S's justification is defeated by W's intention to lie, that defeater is itself defeated by W's perfect countercompetence. Since S's belief is also true she counts as having got knowledge from W on all of these views.

The externalist will have less trouble accepting this consequence, but also, it seems to me, more resources for handling it. The problem, if there is one, is in the facts external to S's possible awareness; only a further externalist condition can pick up on this.[14] The best the internalist can do, it seems to me, is to classify this example with extreme skeptical scenarios and declare it in need of special treatment. However that may be, the last few paragraphs have shown that the tracking account agrees with the rule of thumb that S usually cannot come to know p via the testimony of a witness who does not know p, with important exceptions well accommodated as noted.

There are other ways for S's trust in a witness W's attestation that p to fail to give her knowledge, than that W did not know p. S might have been a bad judge of whether W should have been believed, e.g., S is a silly person, who believes W because W is wearing a red tie. Suppose W does know p, and S believes W's testimony that p for this silly reason. Then S does not know p, and the second tracking conditional tells us why: if p were true but W had put on a different tie that morning, something that it seems could have happened easily, then S would not believe W's testimony, and so would not believe p. If one believes for the wrong reasons the tracking account has a tendency to ferret that out. Suppose, on the other hand, that S is a good judge of whether to believe witnesses like W. This seems to mean, at least, that S would not believe W if W were incompetent or a liar, and would believe W if he weren't these things. If so, then S knows p on the basis of W's testimony when she actually believes p and p is true, because S wouldn't believe p if p weren't true, and would believe it if it were.[15] (If p weren't true, then W wouldn't believe it, or if he did S wouldn't have believed W, etc.) This is the paradigm case of successful transmission of knowledge by testimony. By attending to the four major nodes on a flow chart of what can happen in a case of testimony, namely, whether p is true or false, whether W knows p or doesn't, whether W attests to p or doesn't, and whether S trusts W or doesn't, we have seen that the tracking conditionals illuminate the reasons for the answers we standardly give as to whether S knows p on the basis of W's testimony.

When we look into the eyes of a witness and try to decide whether to believe what he says, we are trying to track the truth. However, the decision whether to believe what another asserts is not always preceded by deliberation, and believing is not always preceded by a decision. In fact, many have recently argued that this kind of case involving decision and deliberation is the exception rather than the rule (e.g., Coady 1992). We believe a great many of the things that other people say, and we think that a great many of those beliefs are knowledge, despite the fact that the beliefs arose in us

---

[14] In fact, I think there is an externalist condition that will show S's failing here, for notice that S does not track the fact that her belief in p tracks the truth. We could make tracking that you track a condition for justification, and declare, as I discuss below, that justified knowledge requires more than mere knowledge. In this case there would be something that our S lacks though she has knowledge; she lacks justification.

[15] Use is made of a transitivity property here and elsewhere in what follows. I will not continue to identify the cases.

with very little, if any, thought. The tracking view has no trouble delivering the conclusion that such beliefs are knowledge despite our lack of deliberation or decision, because what makes a belief knowledge on this account is not our awareness that tracking relations hold, but the mere fact that they do hold. Thus, when I unconsciously assess the facial movements of a speaker and distrust him because of the smirk he wears, I needn't be aware that this is the reason I distrust him. It will be enough if that smirk in fact tracks his lying, and I track the smirk.

Our mechanisms for detecting lies are not perfect but most people's are rather substantial, even though we are often unaware of how exactly these mechanisms work. The mere fact that they do track whether a person is lying, though, means that the tracking view can count us as knowing things that we have learned through unreflective belief in the testimony of others when it is appropriate to do so. Thus, for example, the tracking view will have no problem counting us as knowing (true) things that we believe on the testimony of respected scientists, or that they believe on the testimony of each other, and we will not have to regard gullibility as a virtue in order to have it do so. There are hundreds of cues that we and scientists pick up on that help to determine whether we believe what a scientist says, and many of these cues support tracking relations between our beliefs based on them and the truth. For example, we are more likely to believe a result reported in the journal *Nature* than to believe a claim published in a vanity-press book by an author whose Ph.D. credential is explicitly listed after his or her name. And one is right to so behave since the highly selective refereeing process *Nature* engages in, and that the vanity press does not, makes it more likely that *Nature* will publish not only claims that are in fact true, but also claims that track the truth by fulfilling the conditions listed above. Moreover, possessing the appropriate deference will be enough to know the truths we believe on the basis of scientists' testimony; we do not also have to know why that deference is appropriate.

The fact that a tracking view can allow us to attribute knowledge in this situation exhibits an advantage of externalism over internalism about knowledge, at least as viewed by an externalist. It is widely agreed, even by those who disagree about the epistemology of testimony, that we believe a great deal of testimony without consciously evaluating the competence or sincerity of the speaker, and we think that in many cases we get knowledge doing so. We seem to have two choices of what to say about this. Either, in those cases, we actually do not evaluate the competence or sincerity of the speaker, or we do so evaluate but unconsciously. If we want to continue believing that such testimony gives us knowledge then if we take the first option we must adopt some kind of principle that says we have a presumptive right to believe testimony just as such, without evidence, as long as we have no evidence that says we should not (Fricker 1995). Allowing this principle seems unavoidable for children, who need to trust in order to get started learning, but it seems out of place for a mature adult. Given everything we know about human beings' capacity for lying and incompetence, this option, which appears to elevate gullibility to a virtue, and regard it as a transmitter of knowledge, is at the very least uncomfortable.

The other option, in which we do evaluate speakers, but do so unconsciously, which I appealed to in explaining how the tracking view delivers the verdict that commonplace testimony can give us knowledge, seems a truer description of things.

(Adler 1994; Fricker 1995; Faulkner 2002).[16] However, it does not sit as easily with internalism as it does with externalism about knowledge, because of the premium internalism places on the accessibility of one's reasons for belief. One can well imagine cases where a subject has unconsciously evaluated the speaker according to criteria we regard as quite good, and this determined that he believed the speaker, but the subject is unable to dredge up the reasons for which he trusted the testimony.[17] When asked, he may be able to come up with nothing more to say than that it was obvious he should. An externalist can count this case nevertheless as one of knowledge. It seems that an internalist cannot. This is not a decisive blow, since the internalist may be fully prepared to deny knowledge by testimony to such a subject. However, the more such cases there are as a matter of fact, the more the internalist position looks like denying the knowledge the doctrine of unconscious evaluation was set out in order to admit.

Justification, knowledge, and the maintenance of true belief

Though it is clear from my comments that I think the internalist about knowledge should at the very least reconsider, and though the defense of a particular externalist view against challenges that have dogged all forms of externalism, as I attempt in this book, gives support to externalism in general, it is not the main concern of this book to convince a committed internalist to become an externalist. There is even room for combining the view I develop here about knowledge with an internalist view of justification, although I make no promises that the seams will be easy to sew. It is possible to have such a combination view if one grants that justification is not necessary for knowledge, for then one is not forced to identify the tracking conditions as themselves an explication of justification, and is free to define justification as one wishes. Thus an internalist may be able to retrieve everything she wants in the domain of justification that I have denied in the domain of knowledge, though at what will seem to her a cost of denying the necessary connection the philosophical tradition has claimed between the two concepts.

The tracking conditions, whether Nozick's or mine, are not offered as an analysis of the concept of justification, though one could imagine construing them so since, on Nozick's view, they fully answer the question what the missing ingredient to know-ledge is beyond true belief, where traditionally one found the concept of justification. The internalist could not tolerate the tracking conditions as an account of justification because they make no demand of conscious access to reasons—it is enough to track, those conditions say, you do not also have to be able to be *aware* that you track. I do

---

[16] Such unconscious evaluation is compatible with a filter conception of trusting, where we withhold trust only when cues call the trustworthiness of the speaker into question, and otherwise trust. However, it rules out the idea that we have a primitive right to credulity, because one is expected to evaluate whether or not a defeating cue is present before one has the right to trust. (Cf. Fricker 1995: 397–9.)

[17] An earlier case might provide an example of the other combination, where we mistrust for good reasons we cannot dredge up: how many of us can explain why there is good reason to mistrust books whose authors' Ph.D.'s are explicitly listed on the cover? It does not follow ineluctably from the fact that one's evaluation of a speaker has been unconscious that one *could* not reconstruct the process. But it seems to me there will be many such cases.

not take the tracking conditions as explicating justification because they are not the right externalist account, though I think that an externalist account of justification defined in the terms of tracking can be given. An ideal account of this sort would allow for, and even explain, the fact that some justification is consciously accessible, but not require like the internalist that all justification is so. I will not develop an account of justification as I see it in this book—though I do have a suggestion that will pop up from time to time—but it will be helpful if I make a few more confessions here about how I see the relation of justification to knowledge. This, I hope, will head off the impression that there is no way the view of knowledge developed in this book, which makes no mention of justification, could be plausible given the larger assumptions often made about the relation between these two concepts.

I do not regard justification as necessary for knowledge. The plausibility of this option was first suggested to me by a type of counterexample proposed to Alvin Goldman's externalist account of justification (Goldman 1979, 2000). Consider the simple clairvoyant, a case due originally to Laurence BonJour (1980, 1985: 34–57). This is a subject, S, who believes a truth p in accordance with whatever criterion the externalist wants to set. For our purposes it will be that he tracks p: if p weren't true, then S wouldn't believe it, and if p were true he would. The clairvoyant is not aware, and never will be, of the process through which his valuable power brings him the right answers, and let us suppose that he is not capable of performing a track-record argument on himself, an argument in which he reflects on his past successes and performs an induction. This lack of all of the normal steps that might accompany acquisition of knowledge by means of reasons, and the fact that his belief nevertheless tracks the truth, is what makes him a clairvoyant. The internalist feels, and I agree, that it is quite strange to attribute justification to such a person's true belief that p. From this it follows that justification is not likely to be simply the tracking of truth. However, I think that more follows, because I also have a strong intuition that the clairvoyant knows. In fact, what is spooky about an imagined clairvoyant, I think, is precisely that he has knowledge without justification.

The claim that there can be knowledge without justification leaves a glaring question in its wake: why is it that knowledge is so often found *with* justification, or the ability to justify, often enough, at least, for millennia of philosophers to have regarded the latter as a necessary condition for knowledge?[18] Of course, how often knowledge is judged to be found with justification depends on what one takes to be required for justification; the more consciousness is required for justification, the smaller will be the set of beliefs that have it. Thus, a full answer to this question must be postponed to a future project explicating justification. Generally speaking, though, part of the revolution that externalism represents is the acknowledgement that less conscious deliberative ability with respect to a subject matter is needed for knowledge of that subject matter than philosophers, with an obvious bias toward the skills most developed in themselves, once assumed. Since it is natural at least to associate the ability to deliberate consciously with the ability to give a justification of one's beliefs, it

---

[18] Though I would like to have thought of this question myself, I must thank Bill Bristow for pointing out this yawning gap in my story.

may be that the cases where knowledge and justification do coincide are a smaller fraction of the whole than we once thought, leaving me with less to explain. (For an example of knowledge without justification that is more realistic than the clairvoyant, see Appendix 1.1.)

If I had to try to explain, at this early stage of development of my views about justification, why justification is ever present when knowledge is, I would have to guess that the ability to seek and concoct justifications is one of our species' many tools for trying to track the truth, that is, for trying to gain knowledge; justification is thus a means to the end of knowledge, but not the only means. Even when justification is not a conscious setting forth of an argument, it is a more elaborate affair, I think, than tracking the truth simply. Yet following, or tracking, the truth must be its ultimate epistemic goal. It is not the tool used in every case of truth-tracking for the same reason that consciousness is not involved in many of our behaviors: the cost, in resources and mistakes, of using a more elaborate tool outweighs the benefit in some situations. The views one takes of what knowledge and justification are (when the two concepts are taken not to coincide in the domain of true belief) ought to imply that justified knowledge has more to it than mere knowledge. However, there are likely many situations in which the more that consciously accessible justification gives has no value, in much the same way that in normal circumstances understanding digestion confers no benefit on the eater as eater.

Equally obviously, a doctor's understanding of the digestive system can confer great benefit on an eater as eater if this understanding is used to advise an ailing patient on what foods to exclude to improve digestion. Similarly, there are situations in which the ability to produce explicit justifying arguments, and receive and judge the same from others, enables an agent to do better at tracking truths than he would without this ability. A subject without the ability to justify or to judge the justifications others offer, who lives in a community where others do have the ability to traffic in justifications— for example, in a community of human beings—will have access to the tracking of fewer truths than those others will. Such a subject will be able to expand his base of beliefs that track truth by perception and by blindly trusting the professions of familiar trustworthy individuals. But the set of markers by which he can judge whether to believe the profession of an unfamiliar individual or source will be much more limited than the set that the other subjects can use. For example, in addition to watching for shifty eyes in the speaker, which the subjects without justifications can respond to, the others will be able to judge whether an argument is deductively valid and whether its premises cohere with beliefs they already have. They will be able to add beliefs that track the truth on the basis of the justificatory arguments offered by others in situations where one who cannot argue or judge others' arguments cannot. The non-justifying subject might be able to carry out investigations of his own in order to acquire a truth-tracking belief on the topic in question, but the subject who traffics in justification can save resources by piggy-backing on the investigations of others. I conjecture that we do not need to look further than the goal of having more truth-tracking beliefs and fewer non-truth-tracking beliefs for a lower cost to the individual, to find the ultimate epistemic purpose of the activity of justifying beliefs.

To say that the ultimate epistemic purpose of practices of justifying belief is the cheaper tracking of a greater number of truths, and cheaper avoidance of non-truth-tracking beliefs, is not to deny that justifications have many intermediate goals along the way.[19] For example, justification that takes the form of an ability to produce an explicit valid argument from shared premises is in many circumstances the most efficient way to *transmit* beliefs that track truth from one subject to another. If it is true that my car handles better than most cars on the highway, and I track this truth, you may come to track the same truth by hearing me profess this and trusting what I say (as long as the professing, hearing, and trusting preserves the tracking relation to the truth of the matter), or you may track that truth by driving the car yourself (if I let you). However, in the first case you are at the mercy not only of my character but also of my competence at judging a car's handling as it compares to that of other car types, and in the second case you expend resources in the form of time spent driving and of the social cost involved in asking permission to drive it—*What*, I might say, *you don't believe me?* And in the second case you cannot track the truth unless you also have a repertoire of comparison experiences to take with you driving.

If I have the ability to frame, and you have the ability to judge, a deductive argument, then you can come to know the truth about my car's handling more easily than all of this by believing my claim that the car is a BMW, assuming that you have background knowledge on which to judge my claim about what this implies. Though I might (and would) be lying about my car's being a BMW, I am less likely to be mistaken about the make of the car I own than I am to be mistaken about how the handling of the car compares to that of other makes. The ability to traffic in justification makes the transmission of this knowledge about my car from me to you cheaper and easier.[20] It seems plausible, too, that the more efficient we are at tracking truths the more resources we will have at our disposal for attempting to raise the complexity of the truths that we track.

The ability to produce and judge justifications for belief can also have benefits for a lone individual. One cannot have the ability to produce or explicitly to judge justifications of beliefs without having the ability to reason deductively and inductively. If a person does have these abilities then she is capable of expanding and contracting her set of beliefs in a fashion that is responsive to whether they are true, and in ways that one who cannot so reason will not be able to do. Some deductive consequences and inductive generalizations of a given claim are obvious, and one would not need to reason explicitly in order to acquire the belief in such a consequence of a belief one already possesses. But many interesting deductive consequences

[19] Obviously, the practices also have non-epistemic goals, such as the establishment of authority and thereby power for the person who justifies (although this only works in special types of community), and the persuasion of others to act in a particular way.

[20] One might think that circumstances in which knowledge of how my car handles would be useful to you at all, e.g., if you were considering buying it, would automatically be circumstances in which you might as well do a test drive, so that justification does not make the transmission of knowledge cheaper in this case. But this isn't so. We could be about to go on a road trip together and under time pressure to decide whether to take my car or yours.

and inductive generalizations of claims are not obvious. One who reasons consciously will, while one who does not so reason will not, or not reliably, be able to seek and find such consequences of knowing beliefs she already has and add them to her stock of knowing beliefs. In the case of inductions these additions will not expand the truths among one's beliefs infallibly—falsehoods can also creep in—but if the reasoning is sound then the net results will be better than random.

Ability to reason deductively in complex cases, and to reflect on a multiplicity of beliefs all at once, neither of which is required for the tracking of some truths, can also help the subject rid herself of false beliefs. For when she looks at a set of her beliefs in tandem she may notice that they are inconsistent, conclude that one of them must be false, and proceed to reason about which beliefs are likeliest to be the rotten apples. There is also a use of deductive and inductive skills that can directly improve one's tracking in a given situation. A reflective organism can produce an image or representation of the process through which she is trying to form a belief, and apply deduction and induction to that representation in order to doublecheck that the process will give her a belief that tracks; if she finds that it doesn't, she can take steps to improve the situation. Of course, the representation has to be sufficiently accurate for this to be helpful to tracking, but often the challenge isn't making an accurate representation of the process but correctly interpreting what its outcomes mean, and the flowchart is too complicated for the subject to assess unconsciously. We will see examples in Chapter 3 that illustrate the power this reflective capacity has to help the subject to track at her first level of belief, by looking at subjects who did not use it but should have ('Dumb luck and blind luck'). Thus abilities that we associate with justification provide a layer of checks that false beliefs have not crept in, which may give more power to track truths and avoid falsehoods than do the mechanisms through which beliefs tracked or did not track the truth when they were acquired, and these advantages accrue to the individual all on her own.

I have described several reasons why we should expect the ability to justify beliefs to be present with knowledge in many cases, and in doing so there was no need to assume that this ability is what makes a true belief knowledge or that it is what makes knowledge more valuable than true belief. The latter is still an open question. If the purpose of practices of justifying beliefs is improved tracking of truths, what is the purpose, and value, of knowledge? Surely the ultimate goal of knowledge is true belief. Why is it, then, that true belief that p is not sufficient for knowledge that p? Related to the question why knowledge is more than true belief is the question why knowledge is more valuable than mere true belief. Given that what I think distinguishes knowledge from mere true belief is tracking, this becomes the question why true belief that in addition *tracks* the truth is more valuable than mere true belief.

We have seen above a practical advantage of a true belief that tracks the truth over a mere true belief: tracking truth gives one a greater capacity to do things with the true belief. But it does not follow from this that the value of true, tracking beliefs is exhausted by their practical import. I am not personally a fan of the language of intrinsic value, but if true beliefs do have intrinsic value, then true, tracking beliefs will have, I submit, greater intrinsic value. This is because of the more general fact from which we derived the practical advantage of true, tracking belief over mere true belief:

one who has a true, tracking belief will have a capacity to maintain true belief on that matter and avoid false belief on that matter over time and changing circumstances that the owner of a merely true belief will not possess. From the practical point of view this property yielded an ability to *do*. If true belief in p is intrinsically valuable, then a true belief in p is valuable whether or not it gives one any ability to carry out activities on its basis. If a true belief is intrinsically valuable at time t then it has got to be more intrinsically valuable to have a true or at least to avoid a false belief concerning the matter of p at many future times. (Unlike practical value, intrinsic value presumably does not expire, so we can sum over times.) If true belief is intrinsically valuable then true, tracking belief is more so.

Perhaps one does not think that the purpose and value of knowledge is a capacity to maintain true and avoid false beliefs over time and changes in circumstances. If so, then one will need to supply a different answer to this question, and I cannot see what it would be. If this is the purpose and value of knowledge then it is of special interest that it looks as if tracking is not just one way to achieve it, but the only way. That is, not only is it the case that if one tracks the truth that p one has some capacity to maintain true belief and avoid false belief in p over time and change in circumstances, but also, it seems, that any mechanism that allows one to maintain a true and avoid a false belief in the matter of p over time and change in circumstances is a mechanism through which one tracks the truth. It is not that there will be no other ways of describing what that mechanism is—there will—but whatever else the mechanism does and however else it can be described, it seems that the mechanism must support tracking of the truth if it is to give one the capacity named. And so, it is the tracking that the mechanism supports that *makes* it a mechanism that yields the special qualities of the thing we call 'knowledge.' Why should we care about knowledge? Because, or to the extent that, we want to maintain true beliefs over time. Why should we think that knowledge is a matter of tracking? Because tracking explains why knowledge has this valuable feature.

Overview of chapters

Some of the arguments I have made in this chapter are programmatic. Their details would have to be worked out to make them stand up to scrutiny. Their purpose has been to make plausible that it matters what knowledge is, that tracking explains widely different types of knowledge, and that there are interesting and attractive implications to taking knowledge to be a matter of tracking. These implications cannot get going, though, unless there is a solid and thorough account of what the tracking view of knowledge is that they can be based on. Giving such an account is the first objective of what follows in this book.

In the years since its introduction Nozick's account of knowledge has met with many problems and dissatisfactions: a raft of counterexamples that have not been overturned, a property (lack of closure under known implication) that most people who have thought about knowledge find unacceptable, complaints that the subjunctive conditionals through which he formulated the account are not themselves well understood, and, as a consequence of the former, suspicions that entirely too much of how the view determines what counts as knowledge happens, as it were, 'offstage,' without explicit rules. Taking these problems together and assuming, as it seems, that they are independent of each other, it is not too surprising that most epistemologists have written off the view as a non-starter.

This long list of troubles would appear less damning if the problems involved could be seen as all depending on just two misfortunes of formulation, and this indeed is what we will see. Some in the long list of counterexamples are alternative illustrations of the same problem, and some distinct problems have the same root cause. The total number of root causes is two, both fixable. Lack of closure under known implication in Nozick's view of knowledge is felt by many to be unpalatable all on its own, and a dozen counterexamples showing that his view of knowledge is too strong appear to be so many added reasons to dismiss the view. However, first, the fact that the original tracking view lacked closure was a historical accident, the consequence of a decision that with equal right could have been made otherwise, and easily can be made otherwise by us. It was not, as it is often presumed to be, a deep feature essential to any tracking view of knowledge. I impose the closure property on knowledge—roughly, if you know p and you know that p implies q, then you know q—by defining knowledge recursively, with known implication as the mechanism of recursion. Second, as I show in Chapter 2, if we add closure then all of the counterexamples tending to show that tracking is too strong are overturned. Thus, remarkably, a baker's dozen of seemingly hopeless problems turn out really to be one fixable problem. In addition, the view can be simplified, since once closure is added there is no need for the relativization to method of belief formation that Nozick added to address certain difficulties, difficulties that, once again, no one expected had anything to do with lack of closure.

The critics were right, and for some of the right reasons, that formulating the tracking view in terms of subjunctive conditionals cannot be adequate. What they missed is that formulating the view in terms of conditional probability not only moots the theoretical worries—general and specific—about using subjunctives in analysis, but also allows one to turn back all of the counterexamples showing that the original tracking view was too weak in its requirements for knowledge. Chapter 3 is devoted to showing all of these things. Those counterexamples were not independent problems, but difficulties highly dependent on the idea that one evaluates a subjunctive conditional by asking whether the consequent is true in a single closest possible world or the first few closest. It is obvious that a tracking view would want to take more than one or a few scenarios different from the actual scenario into account when it asks what the subject would believe were things different than they are in some respects—Nozick said as much. It is not as obvious how to formulate this within existing theories of counterfactuals. I think that an interpretation of counterfactuals could be given, by someone more talented and patient than I, which would suit the needs of the tracking view on this point. However, such an interpretation might not be a plausible account of the counterfactuals of ordinary language, and I see no reason to do all of this when I can take a theory off the shelf—the theory of probability—that is already highly determinate and developed, both qualitatively and quantitatively, with regard to this and many other matters. For example, the conditional probability claims with which

I replace Nozick's subjunctive conditionals automatically require evaluation of the subject's belief-forming behavior in many scenarios different from the actual one, as I will explain in Chapter 3.

The impression that too much of how the tracking view determines which particular cases count as knowledge takes place 'offstage' came from the use of subjunctive conditionals. But the problem is not merely that subjunctive conditionals are not well understood. That fact helped to hide a deeper problem that appears to challenge all forms of externalism about knowledge in one way or another. This is the generality problem, the problem of fixing the level of generality of the description of the facts that are going to determine whether a given case is one of knowledge (Conee and Feldman 1998). The generality problem was first noticed by Goldman (1979, 2000) in his development of process reliabilism—a true belief is knowledge when and only when it was formed by a reliable process—but its lesson appears to apply to any account of knowledge that uses facts about the world to determine whether a given belief is knowledge, that is, to any form of externalism.

Facts about the world can be described at any level of specificity or generality, and those descriptions do not in general all have the same implications. In particular, they do not generally have the same implications about whether a belief, or a true belief, is usually formed by a process. A single process may be reliable or unreliable at forming true beliefs about a matter depending on the level of generality at which that process is described. Thus, the process reliabilist will have to count a true belief formed by that process as knowledge or not knowledge depending on the level of generality at which the process is described. Which level of generality is the appropriate one? The internalist does not have this worry about descriptions of facts because her concern is not the causal (or natural) process through which the belief was formed. The appropriate level, or range of levels, of generality for propositions—in her case believed propositions—that will confer knowledge is automatically fixed by the proposition that is a candidate for knowledge, and the rational order. If another belief deductively implies or inductively confirms the candidate proposition, then the former is automatically, by that very fact, of the right level of generality to *justify* the candidate proposition; and if it does not, then it automatically is not. And justification, for an internalist, is the key to knowledge.

Thus, to compete with internalism any form of externalism must face the problem of generality explicitly: how does one fix the level of generality of the description of facts about the world that make something a case of knowledge? This can be accomplished by intuition in particular cases, but that gives us no account of what the cases have in common and hence of what it is about them that makes them cases of knowledge. Consequently, it leaves us without an account of what knowledge is. The challenge, then, is to give a rule for determining the appropriate level of generality of description in all cases. This seems like a daunting challenge, even a devastating objection, as it stands, but when we formulate an account of knowledge in terms of probability, as I will, this looks instead like a work-a-day problem faced by all probabilistic modeling of phenomena in the world. The problem may not be solvable in a given case, but the mere fact that the question exists is not a fault, since it always exists in probabilistic modeling.

A probability is defined only relative to a model—here, a set of propositions delineating the set of possible events, and a probability function that assigns a number to each member of this set. It is, then, always a problem to identify what determines the set of possible events and the probability function for each case. If rules cannot be found so as to give the expected probabilities in known cases, this does not imply that there can be no probabilistic models of the thing being studied, but rather suggests that either one is not dealing with a single phenomenon or one has the wrong general idea of how it works. The fact that one needs to specify how levels of generality of description will be determined in order to have a theory that gives determinate answers in particular cases is not by itself an objection. In Chapter 3 I give the general rules that make it possible to apply conditional probability to particular cases to determine whether tracking, and hence knowledge, is present. One of the chief advantages, then, of conditional probability over subjunctive conditionals in the formulation of the requirements for tracking is the ability to deal explicitly with a major problem facing not only the tracking view but all forms of externalism. Of course, the solution to be given here works only for the tracking view, since the problem arises on this view in its own peculiar way.

Chapters 1 through 3 of this book are devoted to showing that a tracking view of knowledge is possible and viable. In Chapter 4 I argue that it is preferable to other externalist views on offer. Over other externalisms one of the advantages, apart from an explicit solution to the generality problem, is in how tracking deals with reflective, or higher-level, knowledge. As I show, the tracking view blocks a manifestly circular and unacceptable way of gaining knowledge, that two other externalisms—process reliabilism and the 'safety' view—have no resources to block. How an externalist view deals with reflective knowledge is a crucial test of its viability. Externalism was designed with the idea in mind to do justice to those cases of knowledge in which subjects do not reflect; it would not therefore be surprising if externalist views performed poorly in cases where subjects do reflect, as we find with two non-tracking externalisms. This is not good enough, though, because, of course, internalism performs extremely well with reflective knowledge, and there is no denying that we have a lot of this type of knowledge.

Succeeding where other externalisms fail in accounting for reflective knowledge is sufficient to explain why tracking is superior to those views. However, a particular externalist view built around a counterfactual property called 'safety'—your belief is *safe* if it couldn't easily be false—has gotten a good deal of attention lately, so even though that view fails the reflective knowledge test it deserves to be further compared to the similar-sounding tracking view so that we may appreciate the fact that the superiority of a tracking view is overwhelming. In this vein I argue, in Chapter 4, that taking safety as defining knowledge gets the direction of fit wrong in how our beliefs should relate to the truth, which leads to a class of counterexamples, and that the tracking view gets the direction of fit right. It is not that safety is a bad property, but it is not what makes a true belief knowledge. In acknowledging that safety is a good property, I find another reason to prefer tracking as the defining quality of knowledge. Neither safety nor tracking implies the other, as is well known. However, in Chapter 4 I argue that there is an asymmetry between safety and tracking in that though a true belief's safety does nothing to insure us that it tracks the truth, a true belief that tracks the truth is more likely than not to be safe. Only true beliefs matter here, since false beliefs are disqualified from being knowledge by dint of their falseness. Thus, there is a sense in which tracking brings along safety for free, but safety does not bring along tracking. This should give pause to an advocate of a safety view who concedes that there is anything positive about tracking. The direction of fit and the relative weakness of the safety property compared to tracking also explain why tracking provides a better explanation of the power property that knowledge has. I briefly discuss the inferiority of process reliabilism, as well, in explaining the power property.

One of the well-known successes of the original tracking view was its ability to explain our intuitions about lottery propositions. The namesake of this class of propositions is the claim that my single lottery ticket will not win (in a fair and very large lottery). Despite the fact that the probability that my ticket will win is vanishingly small, and I know this, we have some hesitation against declaring that I *know* it won't win, and the hesitation remains no matter how high the probability against my winning. Tracking explains this hesitation because I do not track that my lottery ticket will not win, even if this is true: if it *were* going to win, nothing about that would change my tendency to believe that it will not. Most accounts of knowledge have trouble with this type of case, but in Chapter 4 I single out relevant alternatives theories, especially a recent such theory due to David Lewis (1996), since this is the remaining type of rival to the tracking view that has not been shown inferior on other grounds. I rely on the work of others to explain what is inadequate about a relevant alternatives theory in this area, and explain how the addition of closure in the new tracking view sews up a small hole that remained in lottery cases for the old tracking view.

Knowledge of logical and other necessary truths was a problem for the old tracking view, since, as we will see, one of its conditions could not easily be defined for these cases and the other condition is too weak to work alone; substituting conditional probability for subjunctive conditionals does not change this situation for the better. However, we should not suppose that other externalist views and relevant alternatives theories do better in this area. As I explain in Chapter 4, they actually do worse. The solution to the problem of giving an externalist account of knowledge of logical truth, in my view, is to require the subject's responsiveness to, though not knowledge of, the fact that the proposition which is a logical truth is implied by every proposition. I define a view which incorporates this idea, and which with appropriate supplements yields accounts of non-logical necessary truths if desired. The account of knowledge of necessary truth that I offer could, I think, be appended to any externalist view of knowledge of contingent truth without contradiction. However, its natural home is with a tracking view, since although the account does not involve tracking it does share with tracking a more general feature that makes tracking the best account of knowledge of contingent truth: both accounts require the subject's beliefs to be responsive to the way things are.

The attraction of a tracking view of what evidence is comes from the fact that the two conditions—in Nozick's most extreme formulation, if the hypothesis were true then the evidence would be true, and if the hypothesis weren't true then the evidence wouldn't be true—embody the ideas that evidence *indicates* the truth of the hypothesis, and that evidence *discriminates* between the truth and falsity of a hypothesis. I argue in Chapter 5 that the best way to modernize, i.e., probabilize, these ideas is to formulate conditions on likelihoods, looking for a high probability that the evidence statement is true given that the hypothesis is true (high P(e/h)), and a low probability that the evidence statement is true given that the hypothesis is false (low P(e/−h)).[21] Once we are to this point in formulating what the tracking view takes to be important in evidence, confirmation theory tells us that to prefer the tracking view in this domain is to prefer the Likelihood Ratio measure of confirmation—the ratio of the first probability named above to the second—since this is the only viable measure we know of that uses both of those probabilities and only those probabilities.

I take the question about evidence further to ask not only about degree of support, that is, what it is for evidence to give us more reason to believe a hypothesis than we had without it, but also what it is for evidence to give us a good reason to believe a hypothesis full stop. I take it that intuitively this means that the evidence makes the hypothesis have a sufficiently high posterior probability. Since a high Likelihood Ratio puts no constraint on the posterior probability of a hypothesis, a further condition must be added to high Likelihood Ratio if we are to give an analysis of the notion of evidence that gives a good reason to believe. I present such a condition, namely a lower bound on the probability of the evidence, and show mathematically that this together with a high Likelihood Ratio produces a lower bound on the posterior probability of the hypothesis. I begin the process of interpreting what the term 'P(e)' must mean if we are to make sense of this result. Finally, in Chapter 5, I defend the project of understanding evidence purely in terms of probability against some recent objections to this approach, and prove that the tracking relation has a transitivity property sufficiently strong to allow us to understand why having better evidence makes it more likely that you know.

The probabilistic study of evidence has yielded a great deal of understanding in the many decades since, for example, Hans Reichenbach and Rudolf Carnap brought the tools of probability to the problems of induction and confirmation. Philosophical discussions of whether we should be epistemological realists or anti-realists about scientific theories—i.e., whether we do or do not have good reason to believe our best theories are true—depend crucially, as it is not difficult to show, on claims about evidence. In particular, they depend on claims about whether observational evidence can confirm or disconfirm theories that contain names or descriptions of unobservable entities. Yet the philosophical discussion of realism and anti-realism has not evolved to include a check with confirmation theory as to which claims about evidence are viable. If I convince you of nothing else in Chapter 6, I hope to convince you that confirmation theory yields non-trivial conclusions about epistemological realism and anti-realism.

---

[21] The innovation here is to call the probabilistic formulation an improvement, for Nozick also named these likelihoods as part of a way to think about his tracking view of evidence. He seems to have regarded them as inferior to the subjunctive conditionals, though, and he also put the likelihoods together in a way that resulted in a measure of confirmation that is not viable, as we will see in Chapter 5.

For example, as I argue, the anti-realist view of Bas van Fraassen—Constructive Empiricism—depends crucially on a claim I call 'Equal Punishment': no observational evidence can disconfirm a theory more than it disconfirms the set of things the theory says about observables. As it turns out, whether this claim is true depends on which measure of confirmation is chosen. On the Likelihood Ratio measure, which you would choose if you were a friend of tracking, the Equal Punishment (EP) claim is provably false. There is only one plausible measure out of the ones that are popular today on which EP is true, the so-called ratio measure. However, even this apparent way of defending a Constructive Empiricist view turns out to fail for the following reason. Because of the way probability works, and because of the terms that have to be evaluated in any of the measures considered in order to render a judgment of whether one claim confirms another, even the ratio measure cannot avoid the fact that claims about unobservables have to be evaluated even in order to render judgments about whether observed data confirm claims about *observables*. To conform to any probabilistic confirmation theory of a sort we currently understand, one will have to be either much more of a skeptic or much more of a realist than the Constructive Empiricist wants to be.

Constructive Empiricism is not the only position that runs into trouble when we think carefully about what is required for evidence. The folly of the realist is typically to ignore what is known as the problem of the catch-all, the problem that we usually cannot evaluate for a high-level theory the term $P(e/-h)$. That this term exists explicitly in the Likelihood Ratio (LR) measure makes this measure of confirmation a good choice for the realist, because it is this term that is responsible for the fact that EP is false on the LR measure, giving the realist a way and a rationale for rejecting Constructive Empiricism. However, the typical realist overreaches, since though it may be that we can have evidence for and against high-level theories, and will have some day, nevertheless because of the problem of the catch-all, the realist has no grounds for asserting that we do have such evidence *today* for any high-level theory claim. On the other hand, against the Constructive Empiricist, we do successfully evaluate this term, and hence evidence claims, for hypotheses that go slightly beyond the realm of observables. Thus whether or not we successfully evaluate the catch-all, and not per se observable vs. unobservable, is the distinction epistemologically most salient to the debate between realism and anti-realism. In Chapter 6 I begin a discussion that tries to understand why the catch-all term becomes so much harder to evaluate as the hypothesis in question comes to look more like an abstract theory and less like a mere claim of correlation among observables.

Any anti-realist who was more modest than the Constructive Empiricist, and stuck to claims about the inadequacy of our *actual* evidence for high-level theories, has been right all along because of the difficulty we have evaluating the catch-all term for theories, and because, as I argue, the catch-all term must be evaluated in order to support an evidence claim. It is this somber note that makes the position I defend in the final chapter a variety of anti-realism. However, alongside the famous pessimistic induction over the history of science that points out that all of our past theories have been false and asks why we should think our current theories are any different, we should put a new positive induction. This would come from the fact that over the course of centuries we have improved our ability to evaluate the catch-all term very impressively. We can do it now for cases we could not have done it for 100 years ago. We have learned methods for doing it without explicitly conceiving of all of the alternative possibilities to the hypothesis. Because of this progress, we lack grounds for putting a limit ahead of time on how elaborate a theory we will ever be able to confirm. Thus, the realist was always right to reject the idea that we could be confident about such limits. The positive induction even suggests reason for hope.

This book spills a great deal of ink in an effort to develop viable tracking accounts of knowledge and evidence, and to draw out their implications for what we have a right to say about scientific knowledge, and I expect that a lot more could be developed. However, even if these accounts are not ultimately convincing to every reader I hope that two general points will stand. First, that epistemologists can gain valuable perspective on the relative merits of their theories of knowledge by paying closer attention to what is a plausible account of scientific knowledge. Second, that discussions of realism and anti-realism about scientific theories cannot afford to ignore the confirmation theory done by formal epistemologists.

APPENDIX 1.1

Knowledge without justification

For an example of knowledge without justification, consider a person who read a *New York Times* science page account of the evidence that broccoli has special health benefits and subsequently forgot the evidence and the source she got it from but retains the belief in this benefit a year later. Goldman thinks that this belief is justified, points out that a great many beliefs all of us depend on are like this, and faults the internalist for the skeptical consequences of counting the belief as unjustified (Goldman 1999: 280). If knowledge is justified true belief, then denying that a belief is justified is, indeed, denying that it is knowledge. However, it seems to me equally plausible, if not more so, on the facts of the case, that the broccoli-believer's belief is not justified, but that all the same the situation might be such that we should not deny her knowledge. A tracking view of knowledge that does not take justification as necessary for knowledge can deliver this verdict.

Whether she knows p, that broccoli has special health benefits, supposing that it does, will depend, on the tracking view, on whether she wouldn't believe that broccoli has special benefits if it does not, and would believe it if it does. Thus, she may know p from having read that one *New York Times* article in at least two ways. First, she may know if (1) that article presented results that were close to definitive—that is, as long as if p were false the results would have been different and if p were true they would have been the same—and (2) the newspaper would not have presented them as definitive if they were not, and would have presented them if definitive despite pressure not to from, say, the beef lobby, and (3) she would have believed p if reported and not believed p if not reported. Second, our subject may know if though the results she read about were not definitive, if p were false then scientists would have discovered it, newspapers would have reported it, and she would have read about it and ceased to believe p in the interim, and otherwise—that is, if p were true—she would have stuck to her belief.[1] In Goldman's original example she does not, as a matter of fact, encounter supporting or undermining evidence in the interim between acquiring her belief and possessing it without its evidence—in order to set her up to have no evidence at all when we are asking about her—but that is consistent with truth or falsity of the subjunctive conditionals just listed. If our subject and the scientific and journalistic community she depends on have the right behaviors and habits, she may track the truth about broccoli without currently having evidence on the matter.

However, though the subject may still track the truth after all this time, the claim that her current belief is justified is rather puzzling. It is at least in need of further justification. The reason Goldman gives for thinking her belief is still justified is that her past acquisition of this belief was epistemically proper, but while it is true that it was proper on anyone's account, it is unclear why this is supposed to be sufficient for the belief being justified now, a year later. What she has done in the meantime is presumed not to matter to whether she is justified now, except that she must not have encountered any further confirming or disconfirming evidence.

---

[1] Note that the possibility of knowledge on the tracking view here depends on the weak transitivity property discussed in footnotes in Chapter 1 and proven, for the new tracking view, in Chapter 5. Otherwise tracking a source that tracks the truth would not necessarily be a way of tracking that truth oneself.

Goldman points out that the reason a certain kind of internalist does not count this as a case of justification is because for this internalist only current mental states are justifiers and, thus, the subject's past acquisition of a justification is external and irrelevant to whether she is justified now. The suggestion is that the only way one could object to the idea that this subject's belief is now justified is if one were such an internalist. However, it is clearly logically possible to object to the idea that the belief is now justified on purely externalist grounds: one might think that encountering, as a matter of fact, neither confirming nor disconfirming evidence concerning broccoli's health benefits in the intervening year is not sufficient to *maintain* justified belief over time. This way of caring about the history of the belief since the initial justification is not merely a logical possibility either. It is natural to think that behavior with certain justification-preserving properties is required to maintain a justified belief over time.

What if our subject encountered no further evidence on the matter because she stopped reading and watching all news sources, perhaps due to obsessive work on an art project, and it just so happened that this topic never came up in conversations with her friends? Meanwhile, though, two studies were reported suggesting that broccoli ingestion causes cancer in laboratory rats, and these reports got a lot of media attention for obvious reasons. (Such evidence is possible even if the original belief about broccoli is true.) It seems wrong to say that our broccoli-believer is still justified; it seems like rewarding her for epistemic negligence, since if she had behaved a little better, she would be more informed, and we would not be counting her as justified anymore if she retained that belief.[2] One may think that her later belief is not justified not because she lacks consciousness of her original reasons, or any reasons, but rather because she has behaved poorly in maintaining her justified belief in the meantime.[3] It seems to me plausible that her belief is not justified merely in virtue of the facts Goldman lists, and that the preferable way to avoid skeptical consequences is to accept this and deny that knowledge requires justification.[4]

One might object that I have shown how the belief about the broccoli could now be unjustified within the parameters Goldman set for the example, and also how the belief about broccoli could be knowledge within the parameters he set, but I have not shown how this could be an example of both properties at once. Isn't anything the subject does in the meantime since acquiring the belief that helps her belief fulfill the tracking conditions going to mean automatically that she maintains her belief in a way that preserves justification, at least by

---

[2] This point exploits the phenomenon discussed as evidence one does not possess by Gilbert Harman (1973, 1980) and others.

[3] It may be that the source of Goldman's intuition in this case is the view of justified belief as belief formed by a reliable process that he offered elsewhere (1979, 2000). On a crude understanding, this view would support the intuition because forming by a reliable process—a process that generally produces truths—a belief about a matter whose truth value doesn't change and then putting that belief on the shelf, is a reliable process. The existence, unknown to you, of further undermining evidence would not affect the fact that the original process exceeded a certain threshold of reliability. Though this view of justification supports his intuition, it does not serve the argument Goldman (1999) is making, since that was supposed to be an argument against internalism from neutral ground. The example seems to me instead to cast doubt on the view of justified belief as belief formed by a reliable process. The more nuanced final formulation of process reliabilism, found in (10) of Goldman's (1979, 2000), says that formation of the belief by a reliable process is not sufficient for justification; there must also not be any other process of belief formation available to the subject which would give her a different belief. However, the way that Goldman seems to intend 'available' does not change the assessment of this example, and if it did we would be back to the question what supports the supposed intuition that the broccoli-believer is justified.

[4] For good reasons to think that justification is not the mark of knowledge, see also David Lewis (1996).

an externalist's lights? Not necessarily, because stronger and weaker externalist conditions can be placed on the history of the belief. For my part, I would make the condition that must be fulfilled for justification stronger than tracking alone. An example of a property that is stronger than tracking alone is tracking that one's belief tracks. Our subject could track the truth about broccoli's health benefits a year after acquiring her belief merely by reading the *New York Times* science section every Tuesday religiously, as long as the newspaper and the scientific community in fact behave in a way that maintains the truth of the tracking conditions about her belief. However she would not by that fact alone track the fact that her belief about broccoli tracks. She would trust that her belief tracks the truth, but not *track* that it tracks. The distinction has to do with whether she is sensitive to the truth about the quality of the newspaper and the scientific community. If she is merely trusting that they track the truth, she may be right to do so, and gain knowledge thereby about broccoli, but she may not by those facts alone be justified in her belief about broccoli.

2

Tracking with Closure

The tracking view of knowledge is strongly associated in the minds of epistemologists with a certain ingenious reply to skepticism that it made possible, in which we can know that there are tables in front of us without having to know that we are not brains in vats, a consequence that I will say more about below. However, while this defanging of the skeptic was elegant, we should be careful not to be dazzled into thinking that this was the most attractive part of the tracking view of knowledge. It is significant that I have been able to sing the praises of tracking for an entire chapter already without mentioning this consequence about skepticism. My revision of the tracking view of knowledge goes a step further still from the idea that a certain response to skepticism is what is most essential and attractive about a tracking view; the famous result about skepticism does not survive the revision.

Epistemologists have largely abandoned hope for tracking views of knowledge due to the accumulated defects of the original version of the idea (Nozick 1981). Keith DeRose's more recent contextualist version of tracking (DeRose 1995, 1996) inherits at least one glaring fault from the original view (see 'Not falsely believing', below) and is thereby also suspect. It may be that those attempting to use tracking primarily as a way of delivering a split decision about skepticism have come to the end of the line. I do not know. However, there is much territory unexplored in which we use the tracking ideas to understand knowledge, and tolerate other kinds of reply to skepticism than Nozick gave us. This chapter introduces the basics of the attractive view of knowledge that I find in this territory. It is a simplified variant of the old tracking view that sidesteps all of the familiar fault lines. In this chapter I will argue that the new view survives all of the objections that say tracking is too strong. (I ask the reader's indulgence in case the litany of examples becomes tedious—the rhetorical situation demands that I be comprehensive.) In Chapter 3 I will discuss further subtleties of the view and argue that it survives the objections saying that tracking is too weak. (Indulgence again, dear reader.) In Chapter 4 I will argue that the new tracking view is superior to other approaches to knowledge, including process reliabilism, safety, and relevant alternatives views.

What is so attractive about tracking as the key notion in a view of knowledge? Consider a case of coerced confession. Corrupt law enforcement officers, motivated by their dislike for Joe Blow on the one hand and their need to present a certain murder as solved on the other, proceed to kill two birds with one stone. They bring Blow into the precinct and threaten his forearms with lit cigarette ends until he breaks down and signs a document that says he did the deed and makes a tape recording to the same effect. Suppose that these officers are so corrupt and thoughtless that they do not realize they have engaged in coercion, and so come themselves fully to believe the document and recording that are the outcome of their adventure: they believe that Blow committed the murder. There are obvious moral and legal problems with these actions, but focus instead on the epistemological side, the clear intuition that the officers do not know that Blow committed the murder, even if he did. Why is it so clear that they do not know? Nozick's first tracking condition hits the nail on the head. This condition requires of the subject who knows p that if p weren't true then the subject wouldn't believe p. In this case it requires that if Blow hadn't committed the murder the officers wouldn't believe that he had. And of course it is precisely because, or to the extent that, we think this isn't true that we think they do not have knowledge. It is because, or to the extent that their coercive procedure would have made the officers believe Blow was guilty *even if he was not* that we think they do not know that Blow committed the murder even if he did. What explains their lack of knowledge is that their belief fails the first tracking condition.

Nozick's second tracking condition is equally intuitive and powerful. Suppose that the president of the United States believes that Bob Woodward is a good journalist, and suppose that Woodward is a good journalist. The president's belief is true, but we all know that knowledge requires more than that, so we need more information. Suppose, then, that the president believes Woodward is a good journalist because of nothing except the fact that Woodward published a flattering book about him. I take it as obvious that this president does not know that Woodward is a good journalist, even if, as we are supposing, he is.

The tracking view has a good explanation of why we take such a president to lack knowledge. The second tracking condition says that the belief of a subject who knows p must be such that if p were true but other things slightly different, then the subject would believe p. One fails this requirement if the conditional is false, that is, if there are close possible scenarios in which p is true but the subject might not believe p. One way to fulfill the antecedent of this conditional for our case is through a scenario in which Woodward is a good journalist and he publishes an *unflattering* book about the president in question, a conjunction of things that can be seen as a close possibility. (A good journalist publishes what he finds without bias, so his being a good journalist does not alone make it more or less likely that his writings will be flattering to the president.) In this scenario the president in question might not believe that Woodward is a good journalist because of what we assumed about why he believes that Woodward is a good journalist in actual fact: the flattery that made him believe Woodward a good journalist is not present in this new case, so he might not believe, indeed, probably *would not* believe, that Woodward is a good journalist in the new scenario. The president fails the second tracking condition and that is why he doesn't know that Woodward is a good journalist: he is tracking whether Woodward flatters him, not whether Woodward is a good journalist.

The tracking conditions are intuitive and powerful. As we will see shortly, they handle Gettier-type counterexamples to the traditional view of knowledge readily. In these examples the problem is that the link between a subject's belief and the truth of that belief is accidental, a matter of mere luck. To take these examples seriously is to presume that there should not be too much luck in the relation between the fact that a belief is held and the fact that the belief is true, if the belief in question is to be knowledge. The tracking view responds to this demand extremely directly, almost as if it takes this feature to be the most important aspect of knowledge. Instead of detours through talk about whether the subject would be able to make an argument, as in a justificationist view, or even talk of the properties of the process through which a belief was formed, as in process reliabilism, the tracking view makes a straightforward demand for a certain kind of strong correlation between the fact that a proposition is true and the fact that the proposition is believed.

The nature of this correlation will occupy us below, but there are a number of general things to notice about the approach. Unlike, for example, the causal view of knowledge, the tracking view is indifferent to the type of process that connects a fact and the holding of a belief about that fact. As long as the proper correlational relation holds between the endpoints the process may be anything or, indeed, nothing at all. If magic does not bring knowledge, for example, on a tracking view this will be a contingent fact due to the inability of magic to underwrite the correlational properties. However, while the tracking approach is indifferent to certain things, it is highly particular about others. The kind of correlation that is required between a belief and the truth of that belief is not only stronger than mere positive correlation, in which that a belief and the truth of that belief occur together is more probable than that they occur independently. It is also directional, whereas positive correlation is symmetric between the two correlates. In a tracking view we ask what would happen to the subject's belief were the world to be so and so. The state of things is always the antecedent, the subject's belief the consequent. The state of things is, if you like, the independent variable, the subject's belief the dependent variable, and we take the question of whether someone knows to be a matter of whether her belief depends in the right way on the state of the world on the topic the belief is about. The tracking view thus takes knowledge to be fundamentally a matter of responsiveness to the way the world is, however that responsiveness may be achieved.

Attractive as it is, the tracking view has fallen into disfavor of late, not only because of examples where the anti-luck strategy seems imperfect, and other proposed counterexamples to the original view that never got rebuttals, but also on grounds of principle. The implication of that view that knowledge is not closed under known implication—a feature embraced as a virtue by both Fred Dretske (1970) and Robert Nozick—is widely regarded among epistemologists as intolerably counterintuitive. Ernest Sosa (1999*a*) has argued that an alternative counterfactual view, based not on sensitivity as with tracking but on the slightly different counterfactual notion of safety, not only lacks the problems attributed to the notion of sensitivity, but also calls into doubt the significance of our intuitions in favor of the latter, because it shows how easily we can confuse the two. Timothy Williamson (2000) has used marginal cases to make a fresh attack on the idea that sensitivity should have a role in the analysis of knowledge. Lurking in the background are the doubts of some philosophers (Williams 1991; Fogelin 1994) about the wisdom of using subjunctive conditionals in the analysis of knowledge when we do not seem to understand them any better than we do the analysand. There are also the doubts of others (McGinn 1984) that counterfactuals could give the last analysis even if we did understand them, because they have 'dependent' truth values for which it is supposed that there must be some further explanation. Moreover, to date no one has defined a uniform similarity relation that resists counterexamples in a sensitivity-based counterfactual account of knowledge. The current chapter deals with the marginal-cases argument and most of the worries about counterfactuals, leaving the remainder for the next chapter, and I postpone discussion of the rivalry between sensitivity and safety to Chapter 4.

As we will see in more detail and more concretely in what follows, the new view I advocate is a fallibilist and non-contextual tracking view in which knowledge is closed under known implication, and the view deals handily with all of these concerns. The most dramatic difference between the new view and that of Nozick is imposition of the closure property whose absence has been considered a defect. This makes the tracking requirements sufficient but not necessary for a true belief to be knowledge, thus weakening the requirements for knowledge, and moots a host of well-known complaints, including some not taken to be related to lack of closure. The two remaining modifications of the original view represent salutary simplifications: (1) the view is not relativized to the method through which one comes to believe, since once the closure property is added this is unnecessary, and (2) well-defined conditional probabilities replace the dodgy subjunctive conditionals of the usual formulations.

1. RECURSIVE TRACKING

Roughly speaking, knowledge is closed if when you know something, and you know that something else follows deductively from it, then you know the some-thing else.[1] It is a logical truth that deduction preserves truth; the issue here is whether deduction also preserves knowledge, which we know requires more than truth. We believe that knowledge has the closure property if we believe that known implication preserves not only truth but also knowledge. The tracking view of knowledge is strongly associated with rejection of this closure property for know-ledge because this is a feature of the only non-contextual tracking views that have been investigated. Assuming the standard semantics of counterfactuals, non-closure is implied by Nozick's tracking view since on his view tracking is a necessary condition of knowledge, and deduction does not preserve tracking. (An example below illustrates this latter fact.)

Both Nozick and Dretske embraced non-closure in knowledge, and this property is especially useful for giving a clever response to skepticism. However, these two authors are in the minority: most have found rejection of closure for knowledge too hard to swallow intuitively, even for a nice answer to skepticism. I am with the majority on this issue since I do not find any of the purported counterexamples to closure plausible

---

[1] Some people would add the qualification 'provided that your belief in the second is *based* on your belief in the first' but we will see that my formulation of knowledge of implication allows us to dispense with explicit expression of this idea.

independently of anxiety about the consequences of this issue for skepticism (Vogel 1990; Feldman 1995). Closure is good, and tracking is good, and though no actual theory has yet put the two features together, that does not imply that it is logically impossible to do so. The possibility of a tracking view with closure, and without contextualism either about knowledge or about counterfactuals, deserves to be explored systematically.[2] In this section I introduce such a view, and in the rest of the chapter I explore its consequences and defend it from charges that the tracking conditions are too strong to figure in a plausible account of knowledge.

To first approximation, the new tracking view involves a simple and natural modification of Nozick's (1981) view, a revision that makes the analysis of knowledge recursive. Suppose p is a proposition. First analyze the base case: if

(1) p is true,
(2) S believes that p,
(3) if* p were not true then* S would not believe that p, and
(4) if* p were true then* S would believe that p (and would not believe that not-p),

then I will say that S 'Nozick-knows' that p, and otherwise not. (Nozick would have said that her belief 'tracks' p, but I will reserve the term 'tracking' for my final formulation.)

Condition (3) is Nozick's *variation* condition and (4) is his *adherence* condition. Condition (3) requires that in nearby possible scenarios in which the truth value of p is different from the actual value, S's belief varies with that truth value. Condition (4) says that in nearby possible scenarios in which p is true but other circumstances are different from the actual, S still believes p. Circumstances are varied in the evaluation of the so-called adherence condition, but the truth value of p is not, and under these conditions we expect the subject to stick with what she believes in the actual world. I follow Nozick in understanding the 'if-then' of these conditions in such a way that (4) does not follow from the truth of p and S's belief in p, because (4) concerns possible scenarios and more than one must be evaluated even when the antecedent is true in the actual world. This intended 'if-then' does not seem to me to be the subjunctive conditional of ordinary language, as I have flagged by the asterisks. Saying what we want to say in this respect will require a further modification of the view, to be introduced below. It is primarily this feature that makes what I am now explaining only an approximation of my considered view.

The new tracking view differs from the old view, in the first place, because on the new view Nozick-knowing is not the only way to know. From what we Nozick-know we can get by known implication to other beliefs that are also knowledge. Thus, to

---

[2] Wright (1983) and Williams (1991: 336–46) have pointed out that Nozick's tracking view does not strictly imply that knowledge is not closed. Nozick's view implies this only in combination with the assumption that counterfactuals are not contextually determined. DeRose (1995, 1996) develops a tracking-type view in which knowledge is context-dependent but closed within contexts. The present account is not contextualist in either sense, or in the more general sense; the features of knowledge I am concerned to identify do not vary in kind with context, though thresholds may vary by degree.

analyze the concept of knowledge I combine the notion of Nozick-knowing with a recursion clause: For subject S and proposition p, S *knows* that p if and only if:

S Nozick-knows that p,

or

p is true, S believes p, and there is a q not equivalent to p such that q implies p, S knows that q implies p, and S knows that q.[3]

According to this analysis, anything that you derive from something you Nozick-know by n steps of deduction, for some finite n, is also something you know. This is because doing an explicit, valid derivation of p from q means that you know that q implies p, at least in the moment. However, in keeping with my avowed externalism, I do not take this to be the only way to know that q implies p. One may know this without doing any explicit or conscious reasoning, as when we know that if r then s and r together imply s without thinking about it and, indeed, without being capable even in principle of giving a non-circular justification for this belief. (Recall what the tortoise said to Achilles (Carroll 1895).)

I have two options for how to make clear what it is for S to know that q implies p in the recursion clause above. I can leave the analysis as it stands, in which case (on pain of circularity) knowing that q implies p will require Nozick-knowing it, that is, tracking the fact that q implies p. Alternatively, I can supply a special account of the notion of knowing that q implies p. If I leave the analysis without special provisions for knowledge of logical and other necessary truths, of which knowledge that q implies p is one type of case, then we will have the awkward consequence that Nozick's variation condition, in which we ask what would happen when the proposition in question is negated, will be very difficult to evaluate: who of us knows what happens in a logically impossible world, such as the one where a q that logically implies p is true but p is false? Indeed, in my final formulation of the new account of knowledge in terms of conditional probability, the variation condition will be strictly undefined for logically necessary truths. The adherence condition alone gives a decent first approximation of an account of knowledge of necessary truth, but I do not think it is adequate, and I have a better view to offer.

I will give that account of knowledge of necessary truth in Chapter 4, but for now let me give a first approximation of the special case of knowing that q implies p, in order to complete the first approximation of the recursive tracking view of knowledge. This particular case is special in another way, since my general account of knowledge of necessary truth, which avoids the awkwardness of the variation condition as applied to these cases, will be built out of insights about knowledge of logical implication. S *knows that* q *implies* p, on the first approximation of my view, just in case

---

[3] Note that this analysis is not circular because the final clause 'S knows that q' can be replaced with 'S Nozick-knows that q or for some n there exist r_1 through r_n none of which is equivalent to q such that S Nozick-knows r_1 and S knows that r_1 implies r_2 and S knows that r_2 implies r_3 and ... S knows that r_{n-1} implies r_n and S knows that r_n implies q.' The notion of Nozick-knowing makes no use of the concept of knowledge and the notion of knowing that one claim implies another is defined independently below. Knowledge of implication is defined for the multiple-premise case in the final formulation of my view of knowledge below, but here I use the single-premise case for simplicity of initial presentation.

(1′) it is true that q implies p,
(2′) S believes that q implies p,
(3′) if* S did not believe p then* S would not believe q,
(4′) if* S did believe q then* S would believe p, and
(5′) if (2′) is fulfilled because of inference(s) S made from q to p, then every step of inference in this chain is one where S knows that the premise implies the conclusion.

(3′) is motivated by the fact that if you do not believe p and you know that q implies p then you ought not to believe q. Similarly, if you believe q and you know that q implies p then you ought to believe p.

Notice that conditions (3′) and (4′) are disanalogous to conditions (3) and (4) above in that the order of the antecedent and consequent propositions is not the same in (4′) as it is in (3′), whereas they are kept the same, but for negation, in (3) and (4). This is because I am not trying to capture the notion that S's belief in p tracks her belief in q, but instead the notion that the behavior of S's beliefs shows proper responsiveness to the relation between q and p. The relation between a q and a p for which q implies p is not necessarily such that when q is false p is also false—to think so would be to commit the fallacy of affirming the antecedent—but rather such that if p is false then q is false. Fulfilling condition (4′) will mean that S's belief behavior is responsive to this fact. The other way in which conditions (3′) and (4′) are disanalogous to (3) and (4) is that the latter are co-variation conditions between beliefs and the matters of fact those beliefs are about whereas the former are co-variation conditions between beliefs and other beliefs. This is because the fact that q implies p says nothing about whether q or p is true. Therefore, our conditions for knowing the implication should not require the subject's beliefs to be sensitive to the facts of whether q or p is actually true. The clause (5′) is the best way I can see using only behavioral criteria to insure that there are no mistakes in any inference of more than one step that might be the basis for the subject's belief in the implication. This clause will not lead to regresses because every chain of inferences is discrete, meaning that eventually we will arrive at inferences whose implications the subject must know according to (1′) through (4′) if she is to know the implication in question between the endpoints of her chain of inferences. This completes specification of the first approximation of the recursive tracking view of knowledge.

One might think that in order to avoid counterexamples I would need to add to the recursion clause which allows the subject to expand her knowledge by means of knowledge of implications, a clause that requires that her belief in p actually be based on her knowledge of the fact that p follows deductively from q. Perhaps she knows q and that p follows from q, goes the worry, but these facts are not what *makes* her believe p. Perhaps instead she believes p because she believes untrustworthy testimony to that effect. Remarkably, such a clause is not necessary, because of the way I have specified what knowledge that q implies p amounts to. If S believes p because of something other than her knowing belief that q, then there is a close possible world in which she believes q and yet does not believe p, namely, the world in which the untrustworthy testimony was not available to her. This follows from the assumption of the counterexample that it was the untrustworthy testimony that *made* her believe p, which implies that she wouldn't believe p if not for that testimony. This is because we cannot imagine the testimony as responsible for her belief without giving it some status as a necessary condition for that belief.[4] But if there is this possibility in which S believes q but fails to believe p, and this possibility is close, then she fails to know that q implies p, on my view, because she fails condition (4′). A subject can know p by knowing q and that q implies p according to this view only if these latter two facts are the things responsible for her belief that p, but to state that explicitly would be pleonastic.

There are many reasons, as I have discussed above and in the previous chapter, to be dissatisfied with the use of subjunctive conditionals of ordinary language in this formulation. They inhibit us from determinate, explicit, quantitative analysis, and they do not even seem to behave the way I want a tracking condition to behave, considering more than one or a few alternative scenarios to the actual one.[5] The conditional probabilities that I will substitute for these conditionals have a further advantage that will be attractive to those of a Humean persuasion: whereas it is controversial whether counterfactuals can be interpreted purely in terms of correlations among things in the actual world, it is uncontroversial that probability can be interpreted so. Not every interpretation of probability is so, but one kind of frequency interpretation would have a statement of probability be a prediction of outcomes of future actual trials, and the most popular subjective interpretation has a statement of probability be a report of some (rational) subject's actual degree of belief.

Use of conditional probabilities will represent a step toward clarification, determinate commitments, and Humean options. Thus, my official recursive tracking view of knowledge has a revised set of conditions in the base case, whose resemblance to the Nozick conditions should be obvious. S *knows* p *by tracking* p if and only if:

    I. p is true,
    II. S believes that p,
    III. $P(-b(p)/-p) > t$, and
    IV. $P(b(p)/p) > t$, and $P(b(-p)/p) < 1-t$,[6]

---

[4] One may worry that this claim is not true in cases of overdetermination. In that case not everything that brings about the belief is a necessary condition for it since the absence of either cause would not change the effect. In these cases consider both causes of the belief and what the subject would believe if both were absent. She would not believe because the disjunction of all of the causes that make up an overdetermination is necessary for the effect. One might worry that denying all of those overdetermining causes would not put us in the closest possible world, but this worry is dealt with in the final formulation in terms of conditional probabilities, where all somewhat probable alternate scenarios matter to the evaluation, not just a few close ones.

[5] For an example of others' dissatisfactions with subjunctive conditionals, consider Robert Fogelin's claim that ambiguity makes subjunctive conditionals useless for the analysis of knowledge (Fogelin 1994: 73). Whether that is true or not, the conditional probability is not ambiguous. So, for example, for $P(p/q)$ for $q = x$ and p — Bizet and Verdi were compatriots to be high, x must often be true not only in the scenarios where Bizet was Italian, but also in the scenarios where Verdi was French, since these are equally probable ways in which their being compatriots could have been achieved as far as the statement has specified.

[6] We do not want to count someone's belief in p as tracking p if she would believe −p in addition to p when p is true. We could achieve the same as the second clause of IV does by requiring that any

where '$-b(p)$' says that S does not believe that p, neither p nor the claim that S believes p is assumed as background in any of the probability judgments in III and IV, and P is governed by the Kolmogorov axioms.[7] It is natural to say that S's (true) belief that p *tracks* p if and only if that belief fulfills conditions III and IV. I will give the full exposition of the rules of application for conditions III and IV in the next chapter, where they are especially salient to the conceptual issues about knowledge. We should understand t and $1-t$ as high and low thresholds respectively, so that conditions III and IV require certain probabilities to be high and low respectively. The default value I will use until further notice is $t = 0.95$, and thus $1-t = 0.05$.[8]

'$P(-b(p)/-p)$ is high' gives the answer 'No' to the question: Is it likely that S believes p given that p is false? '$P(b(p)/p)$ is high' gives the answer 'Yes' to the question: Is it likely that S believes p given that p is true? The fact that these probabilities are not required to be 1 but only sufficiently high is what makes the view of knowledge fallibilist, since it means that you may be counted as having knowledge even if there exist possible scenarios in which you believe the wrong thing; it's just that those scenarios must be improbable. In other words, it is possible, though improbable, for a false belief in p to satisfy both tracking conditions. In many cases these constraints formulated in terms of conditional probabilities give the same results about whether S knows as the subjunctive conditionals did, and the change makes no difference to cases or issues in the preliminary discussion of the new view in this chapter.[9] I will explain

subject whose beliefs are in question is rational by the lights of the probability axioms, but that is a much stronger assumption that few if any actual people fulfill. The point-consistency that the criterion for belief introduces below is not, I think, sufficient to make the second clause of IV unnecessary since the belief criterion is applied under undisturbed conditions and the second clause of IV is not so restricted.

[7] It would be functionally equivalent to say instead that the statements that p and that S believes p are not assigned probability 1 by the function P. The point is that we do not want to allow these things to be assumed, or assigned probability 1, because then the relevance of other facts to them will not be visible. More specifications of this sort will be given in the next chapter with the rules of application for conditions III and IV. The probability function P may be interpreted objectively or subjectively, but if we choose the latter then when the subject applies the conditions to herself the conditions may be undefined or trivialized. Condition III will be undefined if the subject's degree of belief in p, that is $P_S(p)$, equals 1, and condition IV will be trivialized if the subject's degree of belief in p equals 1. One may worry about Moorean paradoxes too ('p but I don't believe p'), but where these arise the subject will be taken to fail to have knowledge for failing condition IV, which is as it should be. For example, if $P_S(p) = 0.99$, while $P_S(b(p)/p) = 0.2$, it is natural to understand this as a situation where the subject asserts (or believes) p but also asserts (or believes) that she does not believe p. She is no doubt confused, but what matters for our purposes is that $P_S(b(p)/p) = 0.2$ insures that she does not have knowledge of p, via condition IV.

[8] The parameter t makes a weak contextualism readily available, in which whether the subject knows depends on what the threshold t is for that context. One could go further by using different parameters for conditions III and IV, and allowing that a context may have different requirements concerning false positives and false negatives in the determination of whether a subject knows. Of course, the context-independent fact remains that parameters like t have to be high, because as t goes closer to 0.5 the relationships expressed by III and IV between the belief and the truth reduce to no better than random. In this book I am concerned with this context-independent aspect.

[9] In the preliminary discussion, the expression 'S knows p by tracking p' will be used for cases which fulfill both the new and the old (Nozick-knowing) requirements. I will frequently abbreviate this phrase to 'S tracks p' for economy. I will frequently verify that the new probabilistic requirements give the same answers as the old subjunctive requirements in the examples treated in this chapter. The remainder are left to the reader.

the precise advantages of the change in the next chapter where it does make a difference.

Finally, the full recursive tracking view of knowledge adds a recursion clause to the base case. Thus, S *knows* that p if and only if

S knows p by tracking p

or

p is true, S believes p, and there are $q_1, \ldots, q_n$ none of which is equivalent to p, such that $q_1, \ldots, q_n$ together imply p, S knows that $q_1, \ldots, q_n$ imply p, and S knows $q_1, \ldots, q_n$[10]

where S *knows that* $q_1, \ldots, q_n$ *imply* p if and only if

(a) it is true that $q_1, \ldots, q_n$ imply p,
(b) S believes that $q_1, \ldots, q_n$ imply p,[11]
(c) $P((-b(q_1) \vee \ldots \vee -b(q_n))/-b(p)) > s$,
(d) $P(b(p)/b(q_1).\ldots.b(q_n)) > s$, and
(e) if (b) is fulfilled because of inferences S made from $q_1, \ldots, q_n$ to p, then every step of inference in this chain is one where S knows that the premises imply the conclusion.

The threshold s may be the same as t above or different. I will take s to equal t = 0.95 in this book. I have generalized to multiple-premise implication so that the account works for every case of known implication. This is the final recursive tracking view of knowledge, modulo the rules of application to be specified more closely in the next chapter and in Chapter 4, and discussion of knowledge of necessary truths that are not implications in Chapter 4.

It is important to keep in mind as I contract the phrase 'recursive tracking view of knowledge' to 'recursive tracking' for brevity, that the word 'recursive' does not modify the word 'tracking' but the word 'view'. That is, addition of the recursion clause does nothing at all to alter what it is to track the truth, and thus nothing to alter the size of the set of propositions that we track; in particular, it does not expand the set of truths that we are counted as tracking, though it does expand the set of truths we are counted as knowing. The set of propositions we track is altered, mostly in the direction of contraction as we will see in the next chapter, by the shift from subjunctive conditionals to conditional probabilities. What the recursion clause alters is not what it takes to track the truth, but what it takes to know the truth; with the recursion clause you need not track p in order to know p, although you must track some $q_1, \ldots, q_n$ that imply p.

[10] If one is concerned that use of the word 'knows' in this clause makes the account circular, see n. 3 above.
[11] It sometimes seems to me that this clause is too strong, since it seems that a subject may know that q implies p, at any rate in a way sufficient for securing knowledge of p from knowledge of q, without being sure of what the word 'implies' means. Thus, in a further refinement of the view it might be good to weaken this clause so that one is not required to believe the proposition 'q implies p' in order to know that q implies p. Instead of requiring the subject to have appropriate betting dispositions toward the statement that q implies p one could require her to have a strong disposition to bet on p rather than −p when told she should assume that q is true.

It is natural to wonder what I take to be required for a subject to believe a proposition. Though I do not have a full-blown account of what it is to have a belief, the social scientist's behavioral criterion for determining whether a person has a belief will suffice for my purposes here. In my version, then, a subject S has a belief that p if and only if

> in a situation controlled for disturbing factors in which S distributed betting money over p and −p, with equal payoff per amount bet for p and −p, S would bet at least 19 times more on p than on −p.[12]

The seemingly magic number 19 results from the fact that if we take degrees of belief to be constrained by the axioms of probability then to believe p to degree 0.95 requires believing −p to degree 0.05, and 95/5 = 19/1.[13] This does not mean that I am assuming the subject conforms fully to the rationality constraints embodied in the probability axioms, but does mean I assume the subject is what we might call 'point-consistent'; though she may have betting behavior and a belief set that is incoherent when taken as a whole, she does not believe both p and −p when the two are presented to her simultaneously and explicitly in this form.[14] These reflections give us a rough idea of what it takes, on my view, for us to judge that a subject fulfills the belief clauses in this view of knowledge. The betting criterion has the virtue of measuring commitment to the proposition in question, which a criterion based merely on testifying behavior would not do. It also has the virtue of not requiring a person to have a thought that p in order to possess a belief that p, which is as I think it should be. A person need not have such a thought in order to possess a belief, on this view, as long as she would respond appropriately in betting behavior when presented with the statement.

It is easy to verify that on the recursive tracking view knowledge is closed under known implication.[15] The fact that the analysis uses known implication explicitly as its mechanism for recursion automatically means that whatever is known to be implied by known things is also a known thing. It is also easy to verify that the view handles Gettier-type examples. First consider one of Gettier's own examples (Gettier

---

[12] The account is thus limited to the rather idealized case of full belief, and ignores issues surrounding partial belief and what kind of partial knowledge might be associated with it. However, the criterion for full belief is lenient in that one counts as having the belief even if one's degree of belief is only 0.95.

[13] Note that it is coincidence that the threshold 0.95 shows up here for belief and earlier in the conditions for tracking; these are different thresholds. I chose 0.95 for both thresholds because I wanted a high percentage. 0.95 is, for example, somewhere between the cutoffs for A and A+ in student grades.

[14] I understand the view not as implying that it is impossible for a person to believe an outright contradiction, but rather as only applying to cases where the person does not so believe. Thus, I am idealizing away the possible cases where the subject believes both p and −p at the step of whether to count such a case as believing p at all. I sometimes think it is impossible for a person to believe an outright contradiction, but there is also a significant intuition in favor of a view that can count a subject who so believes as wrong. By idealizing these cases away I am refraining from taking a stand on this issue.

[15] I make this claim for the final formulation of the view. The recursion clause of the first approximation is too restrictive to give us all known implication, of course, because it is limited to the case of single-premise implication.

1963). Smith believes on strong evidence that Jones will get the job that both he and Jones have applied for, and that Jones has ten coins in his pocket. (Perhaps the president of the company has told Smith that Jones will get the job, and Jones has counted his coins in front of Smith.) Smith infers validly from this conjunction that the man who will get the job has ten coins in his pocket. In actual fact, Smith is going to get the job despite his evidence to the contrary, and Smith also happens to have ten coins in his pocket, though he has no idea of this. Thus Smith's belief that the man who will get the job has ten coins in his pocket is true and justified, though as with all Gettier-type cases what makes the belief true is only accidentally related to what makes the belief justified. What makes Smith's belief true is facts about Smith, whereas what makes Smith's belief justified is evidence he has about Jones.

As is familiar, the traditional view of knowledge as justified true belief founders on such cases since it must count them as cases of knowledge when they are patently not. The original tracking view nailed the problem here without fuss: Smith does not know that the man who will get the job has ten coins in his pocket because if it were not the case that the man who will get the job (Smith) had ten coins in his pocket, Smith might still believe he did, since Smith has not counted the coins in his own pocket, but only those in Jones's. The new tracking view agrees that Smith does not know that the man who will get the job has ten coins in his pocket because, in the first place, Smith does not track the fact: the probability that he believes the job-winner has ten coins in his pocket supposing that the man does not is quite low, since Smith has misidentified the job-winner as someone who he believes *does* have ten coins in his pocket. Secondly, he cannot know that the job-winner has ten coins in his pocket via the recursion clause because that only allows us to know things by known implication from known things, hence from *true* beliefs.[16] However, the belief from which Smith infers that the job-winner has ten coins in his pocket, namely, that Jones will get the job and Jones has ten coins in his pocket, is false.

There are also Gettier-type cases that do not involve inference from a false premise. We can make our current case into one of these by supposing that Smith does not infer his belief that the one who gets the job has ten coins in his pocket from the false belief that Jones is the one who gets the job and Jones has ten coins in his pocket. Instead he forms the belief that the one who will get the job has ten coins in his pocket directly from his true evidential beliefs—that the president of the company told him Jones will get the job and that Jones counted the coins in his pocket before Smith's very eyes—without drawing any intermediate conclusion. The verdict of recursive tracking is the same, of course, for his belief that the one who will get the job has ten coins in his pocket no more tracks the truth of this belief than it did above. The vast majority of all non-inferential Gettier-type cases will be the same; they will not count as knowledge because of failure of the tracking conditions. There are exceptions, discussed in Chapter 3, which involve what I call 'dumb luck' or 'blind luck' and which the new

---

[16] That is, the recursive tracking view abides by Gilbert Harman's Principle P (Harman 1973; Clark 1963) for *deductive* inference. The view implies that non-deductive inference yields knowledge if and only if its conclusion tracks the truth, and this latter condition does not imply that all of such inferences' intermediate premises and conclusions are true. Thus Principle P is not generally true on the recursive tracking view.

tracking view classifies as knowledge. But this view also explains why we typically don't get knowledge in these ways, citing more than the mere fact that extreme good luck of the sort involved is rare. There are also fancy Gettier cases, where one has the subject inferring, via misleading evidence, from a truth without getting knowledge, e.g., Compulsive Mr Nogot. These require further discussion that I postpone until the next chapter.

Having a concrete example in mind provides an opportunity to clarify the use of probability in the tracking conditions of my formulation, and to head off possible objections that are wide of the mark. Note that condition III requires of, say, subject Smith that the probability be high that he not believe the job-winner has ten coins in his pocket supposing that the job-winner does not have ten coins in his pocket. A high value for this probability does not require *Smith* to assign a probability to the matter. Thus, it is no objection to point out that an ordinary Smith does not assign probabilities to such matters. The subject need have no beliefs at all about his beliefs in order to have knowledge, which is as it should be in an externalist view.

Even though Smith is off the hook, we might think that the one who uses conditions III and IV to determine whether Smith has knowledge will have to assign probabilities to certain statements.[17] However, though this may be true, it is not necessarily so, for it depends on the interpretation of probability employed. If a subjective interpretation of probability is used with these conditions, then a probability is identified with a degree of belief. Thus to say that condition III or IV is fulfilled is not to say that the one using the conditions is *assigning* probabilities to Smith's beliefs in various circumstances, but simply that he or she possesses degrees of belief concerning Smith's beliefs in various circumstances. If an objective interpretation of probability is employed for these conditions, then the conditions say that certain probabilistic matters of fact obtain, and one who evaluates the conditions is indeed estimating the objective probabilities that obtain. It is in the spirit of an externalist view of knowledge that views whether a subject has knowledge as a matter of fact and not merely of ascription, that conditions III and IV be interpreted using objective probability.[18] However, even so, in actual fact, in our incomplete state of knowledge even with respect to whether subjects actually have knowledge, one uses subjective probabilities if necessary to evaluate these conditions, and replaces them with the preferable objective probability estimates where and when those become available.

If we are proceeding rationally, then our subjective probabilities will correspond to our best estimates of objective probabilities (assuming we believe the latter exist). Thus, in evaluating the tracking conditions in particular cases, as we will need to do

---

[17] As explained above in n. 7, one who applies these conditions to herself may find that they are trivial.

[18] One may use this tracking view of knowledge not as an explication of a matter of fact concerning whether a person does or does not have knowledge, but instead only as a way of articulating the conditions under which we ascribe or ought to ascribe knowledge. That is, a tracking-type externalist may be an ascriptionist. In that case, the subjective interpretation of probability is most suitable because the conditions then say that it is appropriate for the judger to ascribe knowledge to S when the judger's degrees of belief about S's beliefs in various circumstances are so and so. In that case the conditions' fulfillment does not imply that the judger's beliefs correspond to a matter of fact about whether the subject knows.

below, we can use our subjective probabilities as our best estimate of the probabilities that determine whether the tracking conditions are fulfilled. Subjective probabilities are degrees of belief, so when in doubt about whether a tracking condition is fulfilled we should use the betting criterion on ourselves with respect to the relevant propositions, to determine whether our beliefs exceed the thresholds. What are the relevant propositions?

The tracking conditions III and IV are conditions on conditional probabilities of the form $P(C/A)$. 'C/A' is not a proposition of ordinary language; there are good reasons for thinking it is not equivalent to the conditional 'if A then C' (Adams 1965, 1966; Lewis 1976). However, $P(C/A)$ is equivalent to other more useful formulations, and it is one of these that I propose as the court of last appeal in judging whether the tracking conditions are fulfilled in a given case. $P(C/A)$ is close to 1 if and only if $P(A.C)$ is much greater than $P(A.-C)$, that is, if the probability of A and C is much greater than the probability of A and $-C$. In particular $P(C/A) \geq 0.95$ if and only if $P(A.C)$ is at least 19 times greater than $P(A.-C)$. Translating this into degrees of belief, we judge tracking condition III to be fulfilled when we are willing to bet at least 19 times more on $(-p.-b(p))$ than we are on $(-p.b(p))$, assuming the payoff per amount bet is the same for the two. That is, we would bet much more on a certain kind of match between the subject's belief and the truth than on a certain kind of mismatch between the two. It is useful to translate the constraint into a comparison of conjunctions in this way, because human beings are known to have systematic tendencies to error in comparing conjunctions with their individual conjuncts. To the complaint that we are not usually able to assign precise numbers corresponding to probabilities, even when the latter are understood as degrees of belief, I say that the view of knowledge here loses little force if all we are able to do is to make ordinal comparisons and qualitative judgments of high and low. Specifying thresholds is an idealization that is convenient for theorizing and exposition.

2. IMMEDIATE IMPLICATIONS

The recursive tracking analysis obviously takes inspiration from the Nozick account, but the key difference between them makes an important difference to the structure of knowledge, and a dramatic difference to how one may respond to skepticism. Whereas the original tracking view made it a condition on every individual belief that to be knowledge the tracking conditions must hold for it, in the recursive view we distinguish two broad cases: those beliefs that are knowledge because they track the truth, and those that are knowledge because they are known to follow deductively from other beliefs that track the truth. The addition of closure thus imparts a structure to knowledge in which some knowledge is primary, because these beliefs 'keep track of' what they are beliefs about, and other knowledge is derivative, gained via known implication from beliefs that are already knowledge. The account thus has in common with an account that makes a place for 'basic knowledge' that a certain set of beliefs within the subject's knowledge is distinguished as being more closely related to its ground than are other beliefs that count as knowledge.

However, this analogy would be highly misleading if taken any further, since it would mischaracterize the primary knowledge of the recursive tracking account. The beliefs we have that track the truth can be, and often are, very far from basic or immediately known. We know complex empirical generalizations such as occur among scientists' beliefs about the physical world when those beliefs track the truth. But when they do track the truth it is because of complex and controlled experiments, not, say, because of immediate intuitions. Physicists know that there is no ether drag to second order because of the Michelson–Morley and similar experiments, which (we believe we know) would show the drag if it existed. Among the scientist's knowing beliefs such beliefs are distinguished as being tightly responsive to their subject matter, as we can see by the fact that they track the truth, but these beliefs are not basic or immediate in any obvious sense; for one thing, their formation requires a great deal of deliberate work. They are not direct in some senses either: the experimental apparatus that stands between the belief and the thing believed is a complicated medium. However, I call them 'primary', and they are special, because they fulfill the tracking conditions, which are the conditions through which any content must first pass before it becomes available as empirical knowledge.

There will be no empirical statement that we know by the recursion clause of the tracking view that was not first contained, as deductively implied content, in some statements that we knew by tracking. Thus the tracking conditions are the limiting step for empirical knowledge. We can see this in another way, for it is clear that on this view all inductive routes to knowledge must be such that through them we satisfy the tracking conditions. This is because the only other way to have knowledge is by known implication (from knowing beliefs), and inductive support does not meet the standard of implication.[19] The core of our empirical knowledge is our primary knowledge, the beliefs that fulfill the tracking conditions and that thereby have a tightly responsive tether to the particular truths they are about. This primary knowledge is of a higher grade than the derivative knowledge in another way, for it is only these beliefs that necessarily have the power property associated with knowledge that I discussed in the previous chapter. This is because the power property is due to tracking, and tracking is not necessarily preserved by deduction. Even so, derivative knowledge is not so very poor; every belief that is derivative knowledge will be an implication of some beliefs that *do* have the power property.

The recursive tracking analysis has the criteria for knowledge follow how our beliefs are actually acquired more closely than the original analysis did. Much of our knowledge is direct or inductive, as with our particular perceptual beliefs and generalizations properly acquired from them—both of which arguably fulfill the tracking conditions.[20] However, some of our knowledge is derivative; we literally

---

[19] Put another way, any induction that did meet the standard of implication we would count as implication and cease to call 'induction'. The claim I am making here does not deny that implication counts as the limiting case of induction.

[20] Generalizations we know will track the truth because part of what I think it means to do induction properly is that you induce from a representative sample. The more representative the sample, the less likely it is that on its basis you would believe the generalization if it were false. This is built in to what the recursive tracking view requires for knowledge of contingent generalizations that

derive it from other knowledge or know it by knowing that it is implied by other knowledge. Moreover, some of those derivative beliefs should clearly count as knowledge even though they do not track the truth. Thus, independently of the concern that knowledge be closed, the structure that the recursive analysis imparts to knowledge should seem very natural.

For example, Sherlock Holmes can know that the intruder was not a stranger because if he were the dog would have barked, Holmes would know the dog had barked—because it would have awakened the stable boys, which they would have told him—and Holmes would not believe it was not a stranger (Conan Doyle 1986). In this case Holmes's belief tracks the truth. He can also know that it is improbable that the corpse he left in the room where the murder occurred is levitating, even though since Holmes is now standing on the sidewalk outside he would not believe it was probable that it was levitating even if it were probable (say, because the perverted murderer filled the corpse with helium and discreetly sealed it). This is because (Holmes knows that) that it is not probable that the corpse upstairs is levitating follows from the fact that corpses do not generally levitate, a general fact that Holmes knows because if corpses did generally levitate then he would have heard about it, investigated it, and believed it. Some beliefs that are knowledge are related to what makes them knowledge attentively, and others are related derivatively, in particular by known implication from things that are related attentively. The recursive tracking analysis of knowledge incorporates this. This Sherlock Holmes case also illustrates the fact that deduction does not preserve tracking, since Holmes tracks the generalization that corpses do not generally levitate but does not track the instance that follows from it, that the corpse he left upstairs probably is not levitating. This case is one of a type into which several counterexamples put forward against Nozick's view fall, and which the new view handles readily, as I will discuss below.

The most obvious effect of the imposition of closure on the tracking view and, perhaps, the reason why the possibility has not been systematically investigated until now, is that it ruins Nozick's attractive response to skepticism, which is his view's distinguishing mark and claim to fame. It so happens that on Nozick's view not only does knowledge fail to be closed, but it fails to be closed in just the right way for me to be able to know that there is a table in front of me and yet not know that I am not a brain in a vat, a brain, with no table in front of it, suspended in a fluid and attached to electrodes that make me have all of the same sensations and perceptions that I am now having and usually have. I know that there is a table in front of me (supposing there is) because my belief that there is a table tracks the fact that there is. In the close possible scenarios where there is no table I do not believe there is because my eyes are working and I see that there is no table, or if my eyes are not working I have indications of this. However, even if it is true that I am not a brain in a vat I do not track that fact because if it were false—that is, if I *were* a brain in a vat—I would still believe it—that is, I would believe that I was not a brain in a vat—because of the precise way in which brains in vats are reality-challenged: all of their impressions are normal, like they

were not deduced from others, and is consistent with the view of evidence and of its relation to knowledge developed in Chapter 5.

would be if they were not envatted. All of this is so despite the fact that, on the usual assumptions about the brains-in-a-vat scenario, it follows deductively from there being a table in front of me that I am not a brain in a vat.[21] Deduction does not preserve tracking.

What is attractive about this feature of Nozick's view is that with it we can concede something to the skeptic—that we do not know we are not brains in vats—without that concession propagating back to cast doubt on our ordinary knowledge. We can thereby explain with some dignity why the skeptic is capable of taking such strong hold of our thoughts—namely, because he is right about something—and yet with equal dignity cast his doubts aside insofar as they touch the things we normally think we know.

Patently, imposing closure on the tracking view means that if I know there is a table in front of me, then I know whatever I know is implied by that. In particular, if I know there is a table in front of me then I know, on the usual assumptions, that I am not a brain in a vat. And if I do not know that I am not a brain in a vat, then I do not know that there is a table in front of me, by contraposition. If we think I do not know that I am not a brain in a vat, then we are forced to a skeptical view of my entire situation. If we are more persuaded that I know that there is a table in front of me, we are forced to follow G. E. Moore in averring that I know a lot more besides (Moore 1962: 144–8). Adding closure to tracking destroys the attractive middle way.

Many people seem to think that what a view of knowledge must explain about skepticism is why we seem to ourselves to know many things in ordinary life, and then after skeptical reflection seem not to know them. Dretske and Nozick found ways to say both that we know ordinary things, and that we do not know that skeptical hypotheses are false. A contextualist will say that the explanation of the apparent disappearance of our knowledge under questioning is that the knowledge actually disappears in the transition to the skeptical context. But I am not convinced that what the skeptic destroys is our knowledge (unless he destroys our belief), and I think that the phenomenon that most needs explanation from a view of knowledge is more basic than what either of these avenues have us suppose. What most need explaining are the brute fact, and the frustration, of how miserably incapable we are of refuting the skeptic, the consequent seeming futility of the exercise, and our continued confidence that there are sometimes tables in front of us.

It is familiar that if we were brains in vats we would have no indication of that. Therefore, nothing we could cite as evidence would be different (from the inside) from what a brain in a vat could cite. It is obvious that this affects our ability to give justifications for our beliefs. It is not obvious that this affects our knowledge. An inability to justify our beliefs is part of the frustration of the skeptical hypothesis, but

---

[21] It is interesting that the possibility that I am dreaming does not work quite the same way. It is not implied by my dreaming that there is a table in front of me that there is not a table in front of me, and it would be unnatural to impose it. However, I do know that I know that there is a table in front of me if there is, on either tracking view, and this does imply that I am not dreaming, since even though dreaming that p is not incompatible with p, dreaming that p is incompatible with knowing p. Thus, what I discuss in the text for the brains-in-a vat scenario happens for the dreaming scenario at the next higher level of knowledge.

there seems to be a general severance of our efforts from our knowledge in this case. What we discover on skeptical reflection is not precisely that we don't have knowledge, but rather that nothing we could do, no exertion we could make, would make any difference to whether we know that the skeptical hypothesis is false, and that if it isn't false, then most of our knowledge is implicated. We learn that we are helpless to improve our situation, because it is always in the nature of the skeptical hypothesis that all of our tools are wanting.

For example, on the brains-in-a-vat scenario where we are all envatted, all of our perceptions would be the same whether we were envatted or not, and no scientist could turn up any tell-tale sign of our envattment, since he or she is envatted too. Importantly, this disconcerting helplessness does not imply that we don't know, or that we know some things, but not all of their implications, or even that we know sometimes (when no one is questioning us) and not others (when the skeptic is around). Instead, it could mean that whether we know is, at a fundamental level, though not at every level, out of our hands. Either we know, or we do not know, that we are not brains in vats, and whichever way it is it is so regardless of context, and of the skeptic's questions, in my view. What we learn on skeptical reflection is how difficult it is to find conclusive reasons for believing that we know, even if our ordinary beliefs *are* knowledge.

The recursive tracking view does not settle the skeptical question—a fortiori it does not refute the skeptic—but it classifies and explains our experience of skepticism well. According to this view of knowledge I may know that there is a table in front of me, in which case I also know that I am not a brain in a vat (by known implication), or I may not know that there is a table in front of me, because I do not know that I am not a brain in a vat.[22] Recursive tracking does not determine which of these positions one must adopt, but does tell us what my knowing that I am not a brain in a vat depends on, and thus why my situation is frustrating. Notice that under the typical assumption that I have formed a belief that there is a table in front of me on the basis of visual impressions, and then concluded therefrom that I'm not a brain in a vat, the recursive tracking view implies that I know that I'm not a brain in a vat if and only if I'm not a brain in a vat (or any other kind of deceived and deceiving thing) in fact. Roughly, I know that p if and only if p is true, for this kind of p. In the circumstances assumed, there is virtually nothing except the truth or falsity of this p that determines whether I know it, and this corresponds to the fact that there is nothing I can use as leverage to improve my situation with respect to it. This explains our experience of helplessness in the face of the skeptical proposition.

---

[22] One might worry that according to recursive tracking we can get knowledge that the skeptical hypothesis is false on the cheap: the tracking conditions on 'There is a table in front of me' do not require me to be failsafe against the possibility that the skeptical hypothesis is true, since only 'close' possibilities matter and the skeptical scenario is not close. However, notice that I can't know the skeptical hypothesis is false if it is not false, and its being true would undermine the truth of the claim 'There is a table in front of me' and hence undermine the status of the latter as knowledge. The skeptical hypothesis has to *be* false in order for me to know that there is a table in front of me, though the latter does not require me to *track* its falsity.

This is in contrast to the proposition that there is a table in front of me. Tracking this proposition does not require anything in particular of my dispositions in the scenario where I am a brain in a vat, since that is a faraway scenario and the tracking conditions applied to the table statement thus ignore it. The ways in which I could fail to track that there is a table in front of me are mundane; for example, I could have my eyes closed or my eyesight could fail. However, if I had my eyes closed I could open them, and if my eyesight failed I could use my hands to decide whether there was a table in front of me, or I could ask my trustworthy neighbor. With non-skeptical statements, whether we know is responsive to our effort. We can improve our tracking of them through exerting ourselves. With the skeptical statements it is not so, for once we do the normal thing nothing further we do will make any difference to whether or not we know that the skeptical hypothesis is false. The recursive tracking view thus provides a useful classification of hypotheses into skeptical and non-skeptical: skeptical hypotheses are statements whose falsity we might know but *could not* track no matter how great our effort. Non-skeptical hypotheses we may in fact fail to track or to know but nothing about them implies a priori that our efforts to track or to know them are in vain. This classification also explains the empirical scientist's lack of interest in philosophical skepticism. The business of empirical science is an effort to know; where effort is in vain because irrelevant to whether we know, there is no reason for the scientist to waste her time.

Moore's performances may seem glib. *Here is one hand and here is another. It follows deductively that external things exist* (Moore 1962: 144–8). However, the recursive tracking view that gives him wide berth can also identify what is haunting about skeptical hypotheses: we know, or we do not know, but we are probably not going to articulate good reasons to believe one way or the other for these well-constructed statements. In light of this, Moore's 'arguments' could be understood as psychological efforts to persuade us to embrace again our naïve beliefs, rather than as (failed) attempts to provide conclusive reasons to think we know what we ordinarily think we know. I am inclined to think that the lesson is that though we may, and ordinarily think we do, have knowledge that we are not brains in vats, we lack, and will always lack, the ability to offer justification for such claims. This would mean there can be knowledge without justification, a view that I hold on other grounds, as explained in Chapter 1.

Whether or not one likes the Moorean option, it is significant that it is available in a tracking view, since most have assumed that it is not. We often hear that putting a condition like (3) above on knowledge 'commits one to the disjunction of non-closure and rampant skepticism' (Williamson 2000: 151). True if (3) is taken as a necessary condition for knowledge, but there are other formulations. Recursive tracking, which is a disjunctive account, achieves a delicate balance by making (3)'s descendant III a necessary condition on the base case—the kind of knowledge from which all of our other knowledge derives—but not a necessary condition on all knowledge. Thus it incorporates the importance of 'sensitivity', a word that has come to be associated with tracking, without importing its skeptical consequences. DeRose's tracking view achieves this latter goal too, but at the price of accepting a thorough-going contextualism, a price that I am not willing to pay (DeRose 1995, 1996). Moreover, on

DeRose's way of achieving this, no (endorsable) Moorean option is preserved since that would require a cross-context closure that he denies.

I regard the consequence recursive tracking has about skepticism as illuminating, but even if my opponent grants that it is adequate—perhaps because a view of what makes a true belief knowledge is not necessarily obligated to refute the skeptic or to settle the skeptical question—he will wonder why I should bother to have a Nozick-type view when my modification destroys the most attractive feature of such a view. The answer, to repeat myself, is that though I recognize the appeal of the middle way with skepticism, I do not regard the fine-grained consequence about skepticism as the most attractive, or plausible, aspect of Nozick's view. What is most compelling about the idea of tracking is the light it sheds on knowledge of various sorts. A view of knowledge had better not have plainly false consequences about skepticism, but the question what to say about skeptical hypotheses should not, I think, drive one's view of what knowledge is. As I have said in Chapter 1, my own attraction to tracking came from the obvious fit of conditions (3) and (4) with what scientists explicitly aim for in constructing experiments, and from the ability of tracking conditions to explain why what many animals have strikes us as so similar to knowledge. Tracking's fit with both the most deliberate and conscious cases of knowledge and the most instinctive and unconscious cases of proto-knowledge is an impressive range that leads me to expect that, in some form, it is also the right account of the everyday human knowledge that stands between the two.

3. TRACKING NOT TOO STRONG

Before discussing positive advantages of the recursive tracking view over its externalist rivals, we need to dispense with known counterexamples to tracking, to assure ourselves that the new view is worth investigating. These examples fall into two classes, those tending to show that tracking is too strong to be the missing ingredient in knowledge beyond true belief, and those tending to show that it is too weak. I discuss the latter in the next chapter. Here we focus on those suggesting that tracking is too strong.

Oscar and Dack

Recursiveness saves the tracking view from Alvin Goldman's well-known counter-example to Nozick—Oscar, who sees a dachshund in front of him, and knows there is a dog before him, although he does not Nozick-know it (Goldman 1983: 84–5). Oscar sees Dack the dachshund and believes there is a dog before him, which, indeed, there is. The trouble is that according to the example if there were not a dog before him there would be a hyena, which Oscar would misclassify as a dog. Tracking conditions (3) and III are violated, so Oscar does not Nozick-know or track that there is a dog in front of him. Yet, surely, Oscar knows.

The reason we think Oscar knows derives from the fact that he can know that a dachshund is a dog without knowing precisely the outer boundaries of the concept *dog*, therefore without being able to tell that a hyena is not a dog. When tracking condition (3) or III expects Oscar to be able to differentiate a hyena from a dog, it is as if one is supposing that the way that Oscar knows there is a dog in front of him is by seeing in Dack the complete essence of dogness, checking each and every necessary and sufficient condition for dogness. That is the only way it would make sense to expect him to know the full contours of the concept, rather than only to be able to identify paradigm cases.

But that is not how Oscar knows there is a dog in front of him. He knows this because he knows there is a [dachshund] in front of him, he knows that a [dachshund] is a dog, and he knows that it follows from these two facts that there is a dog in front of him. Note that Oscar need not know the word 'dachshund' or have a well-developed concept of it for this to be so, as I have indicated by the brackets around this word in reporting why he knows. Thus in order to know what I say he knows implies there is a dog in front of him he needn't be able to distinguish a dachshund from an exotic Chinese breed of dog that looks very similar. He probably could not do that, but he also does not need to because I do not claim that he knows there is a dachshund in front of him, only that he knows there is a [dachshund] in front of him.

This bracketed word is a placeholder for what Oscar sees of the properties of the mammal in front of him. Oscar knows that there is a four-legged, floppy-eared, friendly animal with short fur, short legs, disproportionately long body, wagging tail, etc., etc.[23] The beliefs that the specimen in front of him is so and so, and the claim that such an organism counts as a dog, are beliefs of Oscar's that presumably track the truth. If this animal in front of him were not four-legged, floppy-eared, friendly, etc., then he would not believe it was. In the new terms, surely we are very confident that Oscar does not believe all of these things when at least one of them is false. Something would be wrong with Oscar's perceptual or mental capacities that would also prevent him from knowing that what was in front of him was a dog if he could not tell whether these features were present. If the animal in front of Oscar were a hyena, then it would not be friendly and would not be wagging its tail, but whereas these facts might leave Oscar unsure of whether it was a dog or even believing that it was, they would not leave him unsure of whether those particular traits were exhibited; he would not believe they were.

In addition, if an animal with all the traits he believes the animal in front of him has did not count as a dog, then surely Oscar would not believe it did since the same skills and attention that gave him this much of the actual concept *dog* would have tipped him off if things had been different with the concept.[24] In the new terms, we can be confident that assuming these traits are not sufficient for doghood Oscar does not believe they are because we assume he is a mature enough and competent speaker of

---

[23] As I have alluded to, these features are indifferent between those of a dachshund and those of a similar-looking but distinct breed, thus conceding Williamson's point that knowledge is compatible with some insensitivity (Williamson 2000: 159). Oscar's beliefs about the features of the dog will likely involve vague predicates.

[24] I assume that the concept in question is the ordinary concept *dog* and not one based on, for example, DNA classifications, since the former is all that our Oscar would be able to know applies to the animal he sees in front of him.

the language who learned it in the usual way. The adherence conditions are likewise satisfied both for Oscar's beliefs about the traits and for his belief that they are sufficient for doghood. That these beliefs track the truth is enough to make Oscar's belief that he knows is implied by these, namely, that there is a dog in front of him, knowledge by the recursive tracking account.

Goldman's example brings out the fact that we can know that a thing is or is not an instance of a concept without tracking these facts. Tracking that a thing is or is not an instance would require hefty acquaintance with all of the necessary and sufficient conditions for application of the concept, but we can know that a thing is or is not a case of a type without all of that as long as it falls within the set of clear cases or the set of clear non-cases of that type. That is, we can know that a thing is or is not an instance of a concept if we know that it exhibits traits that we know are jointly sufficient for application of the concept or jointly sufficient for withholding application of the concept, even if we wouldn't know what to say about borderline cases. For an example of this in the negative direction, replace the dachshund in Goldman's example with a human being and suppose that, for whatever reason, Oscar forms the belief that the thing in front of him is not a dog. Suppose too, though, that if it were a dog it would be a kind that was so odd Oscar would believe it was not a dog. Though this prevents him from tracking that the human being is not a dog it does not prevent him from knowing it. He knows this because he knows by sight, and tracks, that the animal in front of him is bipedal with fingers and toes, fingernails and toenails, and he knows, that is, he tracks, that these traits are sufficient to rule out doghood.

Recursive tracking is able to honor this phenomenon in our knowledge of when a thing is an instance of a type because we have obvious ability to track whether specific traits are present and also to track whether those traits are jointly sufficient for application or withholding of the concept. These two kinds of beliefs together imply statements of the form 'x is (or is not) a Y' and it is easy for us to know that. Thus, recursive tracking can explain these kinds of cases where the original tracking view could not.

Not falsely believing

It is a regular complaint about tracking that survives DeRose's contextualization of the view, that it fails in cases of S believing that she does not falsely believe p, for p some statement she knows, e.g., 'I have hands' (Vogel 1987: 203, 2000: 609; Sosa 1999*a*: 145). S's belief that she does not falsely believe p is not something she Nozick-knows (or tracks) because her belief fails condition (3) (and condition III): if S did falsely believe she had hands, she might, and probably would, believe that her belief was not false. This is because in the stated situation S *does* believe falsely that she has hands, so whatever it was that made her belief false was not something she was picking up on, and so not something that would prompt her to change her reflective belief that her belief was not false either. However, our intuitions say that when S knows that she has hands—a belief that normally does track the truth—she surely also has knowledge that she does not falsely believe she has hands, as long as she has a belief about this matter, as we are assuming she does.

It is characteristic of an externalist view to distinguish sharply between the conditions for first-order knowledge and those for reflective or higher-level knowledge about that knowledge, and I think that tracking and other externalist views are right to do so. One does not *automatically* have reflective knowledge in virtue of having the knowledge that reflective knowledge is about. That said, it does seem that the original tracking view has made the distinction wrongly in the case cited when the proposition involved in reflection is 'I do not falsely believe that p.' However, the case cited and all those usually cited in counterexamples of this form are taken from among our most basic and trusted beliefs; one would have to be a skeptic to suppose that these beliefs of ours are not knowledge. The intuition that if one has knowledge that p then one has knowledge that one does not falsely believe p is not so obvious, I think, when the case is of a different sort.

Consider a person's belief p that there is no motion of the earth relative to the ether. Supposing that this belief is knowledge does not seem to bring automatically in its wake the consequence that the person knows she does not falsely believe p. This may be because we are aware that a person may fail to have this reflective belief out of due respect for the fallibility of science. 'I may believe p falsely' does not sit well with 'I do not falsely believe p' so if she has the first belief she probably will not fully have the second. But the situation in question above is one where the subject does have the reflective belief, so suppose that she does. Still, though it does seem possible that her reflective belief is knowledge we seem to need to know more than that she knows p in order to see her as knowing that she does not falsely believe p, even when she believes the latter. And it seems we may need to put more effort into it than in the case of 'I have hands.' Putting this example alongside the original examples, I conclude that it ought to follow from a view of knowledge that there are ways of acquiring the reflective knowledge in question but that it is not automatic, and less effort may be needed for this in the case of easily known statements like 'I have hands' than is required for more elaborate beliefs whose status as knowledge itself required much more deliberate effort (on the part of someone, not necessarily the subject).

On the recursive tracking view there are (at least) two ways that a subject may know that she does not falsely believe p when she knows p, and though neither follows automatically from her knowledge that p and her belief that her belief p is not false, both seem to be exemplified in the usual situation for the belief 'I have hands.' For the first way, note that my knowing that I have hands implies that I do not falsely believe I have hands, and I know that. (That I know implies that I do not falsely believe, and I know that.) Moreover, I do know that I know that I have hands, because my belief that I know that I have hands tracks the truth. If it were not the case that I know that I have hands then either it would be false that I have hands or I would not believe that I had hands or I would not be tracking that I have hands. In the first case I would not believe that I knew I had hands because I would not have hands and I would be able to see that, and in the second case I wouldn't believe I *knew* I had hands because I wouldn't believe I had hands. Some versions of the last possibility where I fail to track that I have hands are disqualified because they represent faraway, skeptical scenarios. The mundane ways in which I might fail to be tracking that I have hands would be failures I would be aware of—paralysis combined with blindness, for example—and that awareness would lead me to refrain from believing I knew that I had hands. Knowing that you know is not implied by knowing on the recursive tracking view any more than on the original tracking view, but in the kinds of basic cases where knowing that one does not falsely believe seems to come along with knowing, knowing that you know comes along too by a contingent rather than necessary connection.[25]

It is clear that knowing that one does not falsely believe that there is no motion of the earth through the ether in the same general way will require more than it did for my belief that I have hands. The person who knows this p may easily fail to know that she knows. She may have read and believed a report in the *New York Times* science section to this effect and though that report tracked the truth the question of whether it did or not is not something she has a belief about. Even if she does have such a belief that belief may not be knowledge because *it* does not track and she does not know that it follows from something she knows. After all, tracking whether the *Times* is tracking the truth about a matter like this would require following in some way both their methods of reporting and whether the science itself is tracking the truth. The subject will by no means obviously be doing these things just because she knows that there is no motion of the earth through the ether. Nor need there be anything she knows from which it follows that the *Times* is tracking the truth. This consequence of the recursive tracking view that while it is certainly possible to acquire reflective knowledge that one does not falsely believe this p it is not obvious that one has it just because one knows p, and it may not even be easy to have it, corresponds to one of our intuitions about this case of more recherché knowledge.

The other way in which recursive tracking allows one to know that she does not falsely believe p when she knows p also requires more than simply that she knows p, but it is equally easy to fulfill in the two types of cases we have considered. This is via knowledge of an instance of the equivalence schema for truth, e.g., that p is true if and only if p. [26] Knowledge of an instance of the equivalence schema is not trivial on the recursive tracking view, but it does not require the reflective thought that 'p is true if and only if p' that it may be only philosophers possess, and then only sometimes. This is, in the first place, because belief that p is true if and only if p does not require the thought that p is true if and only if p, on my view, but only the fact that one's bets would be appropriate when presented with this statement and its negation. Secondly, though the equivalence in question may not be exactly logical in nature one will count

---

[25] I will discuss some cases where knowing something does not mean you know that you do not falsely believe it, in Chapter 4. These are also cases where you fail to have the higher-level knowledge that you know that you know, confirming the association I have made here.

[26] I owe thanks to Brian Skyrms for pointing out this solution to me, and to Hartry Field for help in thinking it through. Note that the main disagreement among theories of truth is not as to whether the equivalence schema is right (in non-paradoxical cases) but whether it exhausts what there is to say about what truth is. There are theories of truth that might not accept the equivalence schema, e.g. a coherence view, but those views probably would not sit well with a tracking approach to knowledge anyway. There are also instances of the schema that might not be true, for example, where p is the sentence 'This sentence is false,' but I doubt that we have clear intuitions that people know such statements or that such statements are not false either. If one thinks there are p that fail to have truth values then one will be willing to assert −true(p) and not willing to assert −p, violating the equivalence schema, but presumably one would not in that case assert p either, and we would not count such a person as knowing p or −p because she would not have the corresponding beliefs.

as knowing it on my view if one fulfills the conditions for knowing that p is true implies p and that p implies p is true given above, because those conditions are the ones I will use for knowledge of any implication where 'p implies q' is a necessary truth. Thus, a subject will know the equivalence schema instantiated for p if her betting on that instance of the schema would be right and her beliefs are such that

$$P(-b(p \text{ is true})/-b(p)) \geq 0.95$$
$$P(b(p)/b(p \text{ is true})) \geq 0.95$$
$$P(-b(p)/-b(p \text{ is true})) \geq 0.95$$
$$P(b(p \text{ is true})/b(p)) \geq 0.95$$

One's belief that p and one's belief that p is true must be tightly correlated in order for one to know the equivalence schema instantiated for p. However, if they are not so correlated then I see no reason to grant without further assumptions that a subject knows she does not falsely believe p when she knows p. If she does know the equivalence schema for this instance then knowledge that she does not falsely believe p is easy, no matter what p may be, as long as she believes p. This is because p implies that p is true (which she knows), and that p is true implies that her belief that p is not false, since true implies not false (which she presumably also knows).

Our intuitions about not falsely believing a proposition one knows are mixed, I think. When one considers a wide range of examples one realizes that it might be easy to have this knowledge or it might be hard, and this seems in part to depend on the example. Recursive tracking agrees and adds that it depends on the way in which one comes to the belief that one does not falsely believe. If it is via the equivalence schema then it is easy, and equally easy for any p. If it is via knowledge that one knows then while this is easy for some p, e.g. 'I have hands,' it could be quite difficult for others.

Disjunctions

Jonathan Vogel has pointed out that the original tracking view has a peculiar consequence when it comes to knowledge of disjunctions. While a disjunction is never logically stronger, and is usually logically weaker, than each of its disjuncts, it seems more difficult to know a disjunction than to know one of the disjuncts on the original tracking view. This is because the variation condition requires us to consider scenarios in which the negation of the proposition in question is true, and the negation of a disjunction is a conjunction of negations. The latter is not only logically stronger than the negation of one of the disjuncts alone, but is also more different from the actual world than is the negation of either of the disjuncts, since it denies two features of the actual world whereas the negation of a single disjunct denies only one. That makes these scenarios farther away (on the subjunctive formulation) and less probable (on the conditional probability formulation). The original tracking view would require the subject to be disposed to do the right thing in those scenarios in order to know the disjunction though she did not have this requirement for coming to know one of the disjuncts. Thus, it seems, the original tracking view makes it harder to know a disjunction than to know a logically stronger disjunct.

I am not convinced that the feature cited implies in general that it is more difficult for the subject to know a disjunction than to know one of its disjuncts. After all, although she must be able to do the right thing in a farther away or less probable scenario, her content-to-cue-ratio is not reduced over what it is with a proposition that is not a disjunction, namely 1; this scenario has two components but it also has two possible sets of cues for her to make use of, coming from the falsity of each of the disjuncts, just as the falsity of one non-disjunctive proposition yields one set of cues. I am also not convinced that it is easier in general to know a disjunction than to know one of the disjuncts just because the latter is logically stronger. I think that when we think so our intuitions are dominated by a kind of case that does not settle the general question, namely a case where we do know one of the disjuncts.

Knowing one of the disjuncts does not necessarily get us anywhere in knowing the disjunction on a tracking view without closure. This is because $P(-b(p)/-p)$, for example, may be high while $P(-b(p \vee q)/ (-p.-q))$ is low. However, with recursive tracking it is easy to know a disjunction $p \vee q$ once you know one of the disjuncts, say p. You know the disjunction in that case as long as you satisfy requirements (*a*) through (*e*) above for knowing that p implies $p \vee q$, which is fairly easy to do. Thus recursive tracking accommodates the fact that disjunctions are easier to know than disjuncts to the extent that I think it is clear we need to.

Ice cubes, rookies, hit rock, and missed rock

Oscar knows things that are not as specific as the things he tracks: he knows that there is a dog before him and doesn't track that but does track that the animal has a long list of specific characteristics and the fact that these are jointly sufficient for doghood. He has knowledge of the doghood of what is in front of him because what he tracks implies the less specific fact, and he knows that. There are many forms in which we might find a situation where although a person does not track what we think she knows, there are deductively stronger propositions that she does track and from which she knows the other claim follows. In the case of not falsely believing it was the deductively stronger claim that she knows that she has hands or p augmented by an instance of the equivalence schema. A particularly simple form of this relationship is where the proposition tracked is a generalization, and the proposition known but not tracked is an implied instance, as in the Sherlock Holmes case above. The literature has provided us with many examples of this broad type, of which I will discuss several here.

Vogel (1987) presented two examples of this sort. In the first, it is August and I take a drink with ice cubes in it outside to the garden, but before too long I leave my drink outside and go back inside the house to cool off because it is 95 degrees out there. Several hours later, not having gone or looked outside again, I surely can be said to know that those ice cubes have melted, writes Vogel. The trouble is that the crucial subjunctive conditional that should have been true if I was to Nozick-know this—

If the ice cubes hadn't melted, I wouldn't believe, by the method I actually used to form my belief, that they had.

—comes out false. If the ice cubes had not melted, then I 'would have been sitting inside thinking that they had, on the basis of all [my] past experience with ice, heat, and the like' (Vogel 1987: 206).[27]

In a second counterexample due to Vogel the problem is similar. Two policemen, one a rookie the other a veteran, confront a mugger at some distance. The veteran knows that the rookie is trying to disarm the mugger by shooting a bullet down the barrel of the mugger's gun (which we assume is next to impossible at a distance). The veteran sees the rookie fire his gun but does not see (or hear) the result. The veteran thinks to himself that the rookie missed, and it would seem to be fair to say that he knows that the rookie missed, if he did. But again the subjunctive conditional that would need to be true for the veteran to Nozick-know that the rookie missed, namely,

> If the rookie had not missed then the veteran would not have believed (by the method he actually used to form his belief) that the rookie had missed.

is surely false. Whatever would have happened in the world that allowed the rookie to succeed would not also have affected the veteran's well-founded expectation that the rookie failed.

Peter Klein's hit rock and missed rock cases, though superficially different, present a similar challenge (Klein 1987). In hit rock my gas tank is empty, and I believe it is empty on the basis of the gauge reading 'empty.' But unbeknownst to me just moments before I read the gauge a rock kicked up by one of the tires disconnected the wire that connected the gauge to the gas tank. As a consequence, the gauge would have read 'empty' even if there were gas in the tank. In this case Nozick's account fares well because I clearly do not know that my gas tank is empty, and conformably tracking condition (3) fails. Tracking condition III also fails because we cannot be confident in this case that given that the tank is not empty I do not believe that the tank is not empty, since I follow the gauge which is going to be wrong. In missed rock everything is the same except that the rock just misses the connecting wire, leaving the gauge set up to report the state of the gas tank reliably. The gas tank is empty, and I know it.

Nevertheless, in the missed rock case there is a close possible world in which the gas tank is not empty but I still believe it is empty. This is the world where the weight of the gas in the tank changes the way the car is riding so that the rock, which has the same trajectory as it has in the actual world, this time hits the connecting wire and ruins the reliable reporting of the gauge. Thus I know that my tank is empty, but tracking condition (3) is not fulfilled since if the tank had been full I might have believed it was empty since the rock might have hit the wire.[28] Nozickean tracking does not match our intuition. Nor does condition III since, put in probabilistic terms, there was a significant chance that the rock hit the wire even though it actually did not, and this means there was a significant chance I believed the wrong thing even though

---

[27] That the condition fails is independent of whether one relativizes to method of belief formation, and also independent of whether one uses subjunctive conditionals or the conditional probabilities that I prefer.

[28] The tank has to be full for this to be plausible. Charitably, I ignore the fact that being full is not a *close* way of being not empty.

I actually did not. The basic point is the same as with Vogel's examples: there are individual events or processes the subject is not tracking which we would nevertheless grant the subject knows something about. Here it is the connecting wires and events with rocks under the car as one is driving it.

Nozick flirted with backtracking compounds as a way of eliminating these problems. A backtracking compound that would take care of the first case would say that if the ice cubes had not melted then my previous experience would have been different in ways that would have led me not to expect the ice cubes to melt. Not only is this particular statement hard to evaluate (and when one gets a handle it seems false), but backtracking compounds in general are dubious because the backward conditionals they involve, with consequent temporally prior to antecedent, are not generally determinate (Lewis 1979).

However, no such extreme measure is needed if we revise the tracking view to make it recursive. I know that the ice cubes have probably melted, if they have, because, or to the extent that, I know that ice cubes left in high temperatures generally melt, and I know that it follows that these particular ice cubes most probably have. Similarly, the veteran knows that the rookie has probably missed in his attempt to stop the mugger, if the rookie has missed, because the veteran knows that shooting in the hopes of matching one particular trajectory generally fails, and he knows that it follows from this that it is extremely unlikely for the rookie in particular to be able to achieve this. I know that my gas tank is probably empty in the missed rock case in virtue of the fact that I know the indicator is a generally reliable instrument, and I know that it follows from this and what the indicator says that the gas tank is most probably empty. Intuition says that knowledge that exceptional events have probably not occurred can be had indirectly through knowledge of the generalizations to which those events would be exceptions. The recursive tracking view agrees.[29] The subjects in these cases know these generalizations because they track them. For example, we can surely be confident that assuming that ice does not generally melt when left outside in high temperatures, that is, given that there are regularly exceptions, I also do not believe that ice generally melts in those conditions.

---

[29] Nozick allowed that sometimes knowledge can be had through inference from known things. However, he made a condition for knowledge of p that is the result of an inference of p from known q that if p were false then the subject S would not believe that q (or S would not infer p from q) (Nozick 1981: 231). This is too strong to deal with the cases here, since it would require that if the ice cubes had not melted then I would not believe that ice cubes regularly melt in 95 degrees (or at least would not have inferred from that claim that these particular ice cubes would melt), and that if the rookie had not missed then the veteran would not believe that it is very unlikely that anyone can shoot a bullet down the barrel of a gun at a distance (or at least would not have inferred from that claim that the rookie would miss). These conditionals are not compelling since in both cases the exceptional occurrence is possible in the actual world but that does not change our beliefs about the generalizations or our inclination to infer from them.

This recursive tracking recipe also handles an interesting case presented by Ernest Sosa, in which I drop trash down a chute at my high-rise, and presumably know that it has reached the bottom (supposing it has) (Sosa 1999*a*: 145–6). If it had not reached the bottom through some fluke, then I would have no indication of that, so I do not track the fact that it has reached the bottom. However, I do track the generalization that trash thrown down the chute generally gets to the bottom. (I would have heard if it regularly failed.) It follows from this, and the fact that I have thrown the trash, that it has probably reached the bottom, etc.

One may have noticed that the recursion clause gets us only to knowledge that the ice cubes have *very probably* melted, that the rookie's shot *most probably* failed, and that the tank is *probably* empty. That is as far as the recursion clause can take us because the generalizations I know from which the instances follow deductively are not strict. Their truth is consistent with the existence of exceptional cases, in the first case because the laws of thermodynamics are statistical in nature, in the second because it is not physically impossible to shoot down the barrel of a gun, and in the third because gas gauges do fail from time to time. Also, the statistical regularity in question may not fail in our case but simply be inapplicable; because the subject isn't following the ice cubes, she has no evidence that the neighbor didn't come by and put them in her freezer for safe keeping. Whatever is happening here matters, too, since it is clear that there will be many such cases; non-strict generalizations and ceteris paribus clauses are commonplace both in ordinary and scientific knowledge. Some epistemologists think that attributing to the subject in the house the knowledge merely that the ice cubes' melting is highly probable, or to the veteran the knowledge merely that the rookie very probably failed, is not enough. In these cases they say, if the belief is true then the subject should be counted as knowing it, not merely as knowing that it is probably so.

In ordinary contexts that may seem right. It seems fussy to deny that the veteran knows no more than that his partner very probably failed. However, it would be wrong to generalize this aversion to fussiness. Notice that if we attributed knowledge that the ice cubes melted, and not merely that they probably melted, to the person in the house, then by closure our subject would, if he or she were sufficiently reflective, thereby have knowledge that this instance was not one of those exceptional cases. This is because this follows deductively from the generalization and the instance, both of which our subject knows. But that this was not an exceptional case is precisely what our subject does not know because of failure to track the instance. In a scientific context this would matter, and scientists would not attribute knowledge of more than high probability that the untracked instance behaved as expected.

On balance I think it best to leave the tracking view as it is, able only to yield the verdict that these subjects know that the ice cubes very probably melted, the rookie very probably failed, and the gas tank is very probably empty. Since they are out of touch with the particular instances in question I do not think these subjects do know more than claims of high probability. In conversation I have found that feelings about whether this is right are highly correlated with one's self-identification as a philosopher of science or an analytic philosopher, with the latter tending to be quite convinced that the verdict that the subject knows 'very probably —' is not good enough. People would assert these things, full stop, not merely that they are very probably so, say they. I am not sure what the majority of people would choose if given the choice between saying they know that the ice cubes have melted and they know that they have *very probably* melted, though I would bet on their favoring the latter. But in any case, people say a lot of things. In particular, we allow ourselves to say a lot of things that, on reflection, we must conclude are not strictly correct but are shortcuts we employ for linguistic economy. I think this is one of those cases. If we did only know *very probably* p, it would be natural for linguistic convention to allow us to assert more than we knew, namely, p, and it would be natural for us to believe more than we knew, namely, p. [30]

One might take issue with my description of the subjects in these examples as knowing what they know via the recursion clause and knowledge of a statistical generalization. One might think instead that they know what they know via instance-to-instance induction that does not go through belief in a generalization. This description will not fit the veteran's evaluation of the rookie's performance with the gun, since it is implausible to suppose that the veteran has seen many attempts of this sort in the heat of action. However, it is a plausible way to describe the other cases. Is the reason the new tracking view can attribute to the subjects no more than knowledge that the instance in question is very probably as they think it is that the new tracking view does not approve of instance-to-instance induction? Fortunately for the new view this is not the case. As the next chapter shows in the section on knowledge of the future, instance-to-instance induction to knowledge of propositions that are not qualified by probability is possible according to the tracking conditions. Still, the current cases do not qualify. As the reader can verify, on the new tracking account if the subject in the house is doing instance-to-instance induction, then she does not know that the ice cubes have melted, although, just as with imagining her going through the generalization, she does know that they *very probably* have melted.

The deciding factor here is not which type of inductive inference the subject makes, but rather that the propositions in question are like the proposition that I will not win the lottery. Knowledge I have about there being a large number of eligible tickets and that the drawing is fair give me knowledge that my ticket will very probably not win, but it is generally agreed that I do not know that my ticket will not win. Either tracking view has a neat explanation of this fact since if my ticket were going to win I might, and probably would, still believe that it was not, because I am isolated from any indication that it will win even if it will. It is similar with the ice cubes not melting and the other cases here. The subject is isolated from any indication of things not going in the expected way, and so does not know that they definitely have not, only that they very probably have not. It is because the tracking view deals so handily with lottery propositions, as we will see in Chapter 4, that it has the consequences it does here.

Vogel is right that 'Nozick's tracking condition is inconsistent with our knowing that unobserved exceptions to natural law don't occur' (Vogel 1987: 209). However, most of the 'natural laws' in question are not exceptionless, we can track the statistical laws, and, on the recursive tracking view we can know that it follows from them that an exception is very improbable even in a case we are not in fact tracking. Indeed, we can even track that the exceptional thing is very probably not happening. Thus, my simple modification of Nozick's view addresses Vogel's and Klein's worries, and does

---

[30] There is another change to the view that might be necessary and that might yield the consequence the analytic philosopher wants here, which is the addition of a recursion clause for inductive reasoning. Before making that addition, though, I would have to see examples more convincing than these of good induction that does not preserve tracking but does preserve knowledge, examples where the resulting putative knowledge did not give us the consequence that the subject knows an exceptional case did not occur when she obviously doesn't know this.

so while retaining the point of the tracking view, that what makes knowledge knowledge is that it is present when and only when beliefs are responsive to the truth.

Jesse James and method

The adherence condition, (4), which says that if p were true and other things slightly different then S would still believe p, can also seem too strong. It certainly is too strong in Nozick's account, but its descendant IV is just right once we add the recursion clause. The situations that make the condition seem excessive are often cases where the circumstances that put the subject in a position to know are accidental. Because they could easily have not happened, the scenarios in which they did not happen are close, which leads to the conclusion that the subject would not have formed the belief she did in a close world in which the belief is true. Fortunately for the new tracking view, in such situations there nevertheless will typically be many things that the subject does Nozick-know and know according to condition IV, which can easily be known to imply other things we think she knows.

Consider the case in which Betsy happens to be standing in a good spot for witnessing a man with a gun rushing out of a bank just as his mask slips off (Nozick 1981: 193; Shope 1984: 35–6; Forbes 1984: 47–8). She recognizes the face as that of Jesse James, so she knows that Jesse James is the bank robber. Betsy's knowledge is so good that she will probably be put in a witness protection program, but her belief does not track the truth, and she does not Nozick-know that James is the robber, because in the close world where James is the robber but his mask does not fall off, Betsy does not form the belief that James is the robber, violating condition (4). In the final formulation of the recursive tracking view, of course, close possible worlds is not the language with which to speak about what the tracking conditions are checking, but that makes no difference to the sort of example now in question. The subject violates condition IV too because assuming that Jesse James is the bank robber allows for a significant probability that his mask does not fall, a situation in which Betsy does not have an opportunity to form her belief.

The answer to this challenge has by now a familiar ring. Note that Betsy has many knowing and tracking beliefs regarding the incident she witnessed, and all we need to do is find one or more from which it follows that James is the robber or is very probably the robber. This is easy. Let p = 'There was a man with a gun in his hand whose face looked like that of Jesse James from the "WANTED" posters running out of the bank in front of me at such-and-such a time.' Betsy surely has such a belief, and it tracks the truth. If there wasn't a man of this description running out of the bank then she wouldn't believe there was. And if there was such a man then changing the fact that his mask fell is not among our options in evaluating the adherence condition (however we do it) since affirming the proposition means affirming its presuppositions, in particular, in this case, that his face was visible.[31] We are permitted to change things such as whether the robber bumped into anyone as he was running out as also whether

---

[31] Note that we would be in deep waters if the condition that currently needed our help were the variation condition, because then the question would be about what is involved in negating a

an onlooker fell to the ground with a heart attack at the sight of the famed criminal, but such things would not affect the formation of Betsy's belief if, as we must suppose, she looked at the robber's face. It is part of our assumption in the example that Betsy is a good eyewitness so if the robber's face did not look like that of Jesse James from the 'WANTED' posters then she would not believe it did. From Betsy's belief that p she is entitled to deduce that the robber is very probably Jesse James, and even if she does not explicitly so reason she knows that this is implied.

Arguably, this is how Betsy actually came to her belief in a realistic example of this sort, though there is no reason to suppose that she was conscious of the steps at the time. She might well have become conscious of them, parsed in just this way, though, when she was cross-examined on the witness stand by a defense attorney. Some may be bothered once again by the fact that the most we can get out of the tracking view is that she knows the robber was *very probably* Jesse James. But an objection here seems to me even less plausible than it was in the previous cases since eyewitness testimony is notoriously unreliable. Moreover, clinical experiments show that some properties people tend to take to be highly correlated with trustworthiness of testimony—stress in the witnessed situation, confidence of the witness while testifying—are not (Loftus 1996).

Nozick's response to the Jesse James sort of example was tightening of the individuation of the method through which the subject came to her belief. Individuating the method finely enough makes the accidental event that made belief formation possible part of the method, and hence something that in his view is fixed over all variation in worlds or scenarios that occurs while checking the two tracking conditions. If we called Betsy's method 'looking at the face of the man' rather than 'looking with her eyes', then we would not need to check any possibility in which the face of the man was not visible. The trouble is that there are other types of case where it would be useful to individuate the method coarsely. Individuation of method should be principled and uniform across examples lest this become an elastic waistband with which the view is made to fit every example. However, saying up front for all cases how the method is to be described strikes me as a task that is as hopeless as it would be necessary for giving a proper analysis in which method was mentioned. The problem is analogous to the generality problem for reliabilism: one must, and yet it seems to me cannot, say up front in that reliabilist analysis of knowledge at what level of generality the process forming the belief is to be described (Conee and Feldman 1998).

There is another problem with relativizing to method. If the view of knowledge is relativized, then the method is fixed in the variation of worlds that we do to check the tracking conditions. This means that the tracking conditions won't be checking whether the method actually used was chosen accidentally, and this will make cases

---

proposition that has a presupposition: is denying the presupposition a way of denying the proposition, or is it a way of making the proposition lack truth value? Fortunately we can steer clear of heavy commitments in the philosophy of language since the problem we are now considering would not arise for the variation condition. This is because it is the problem that since in the actual world the method used was available accidentally the subject might not form the belief in an alternate scenario where she should, but fulfilling the variation condition requires that the subject *not* form the belief in a type of alternate scenario.

count as knowledge that would not count intuitively. Imagine a person who forms beliefs about what the weather will be like by consulting a thing he's found on the web that displays numbers roughly in the range of realistic temperatures but that have no other claims associated with them. Suppose, though this may be hard to do psychologically, that the person views this as a good way of figuring out what the weather will be like with no reason for viewing it so. He just fixed on it, and continues in this way. Suppose further that it so happens that this is a successful way of forming beliefs about the weather because if the temperature were not going to be the number this thing displays then it would not display that number, and if it were it would.[32] If we relativize to actual method then this person knows what the temperature will be because he actually uses a good method, but surely he does not know. If we do not relativize to method we can register appropriate disapproval of the fact that this is a guy who might have believed anything because we can ask about his dispositions to choose methods.

Fortunately, as far as I can see there is no reason to relativize the tracking view of knowledge to method at all once the recursion clause is added. Closure removes the need for reference to method in one of the standard cases where it was thought necessary, the Jesse James case. There is another well-worn example, the one that apparently prompted Nozick to appeal to method in the first place, that is susceptible to a similar treatment: the grandmother. An elderly woman sees her grandson in front of her and believes that he is ambulatory because she sees him walk up to her. If he were not ambulatory, though, the rest of the family would have shielded her from awareness of that, so her belief fails condition (3). Nevertheless, surely the grandmother knows he is ambulatory when he walks right in front of her and she sees him do this. If we relativize to method then we say that the grandmother knows on the basis of the method she actually used, of seeing her grandchild in front of her, though she would not know if she had actually used the method of relying on the reports of relatives, because of their propensity to shield her from bad news. Conformably, the tracking conditions are fulfilled in the first case and not in the second. The grandmother knows because she is actually in the first case.

So far so good. However, relativization to method gives rise to baroque problems when more than one method is actually employed, leading Nozick to a less than complete effort to define an extra notion of 'outweighing' among methods. Fortunately, then, on the new view talk of method is not necessary to address the grandmother case, since the recursion clause saves the day. As is by now familiar, there are plenty of things grandma tracks from which it obviously follows that her grandson is ambulatory or probably ambulatory. Here is one: 'My grandson is walking towards me.' If it were not the case that her grandson was walking towards her she would surely not believe he was. If it were someone else walking toward her then in order to think she would believe it was her grandson we would have to suppose she could not recognize her grandson, but that would ruin the intuition this example was supposed to provoke, that this is a grandma who knows her grandson is ambulatory by seeing

---

[32] I have colonized this example from Robert Howells, who used it against me in his commentary on my APA paper on the recursive tracking view.

him walk. On the other hand, if it was her grandson but he were not walking toward her then he would be doing something else and she would not see him walking towards her. (Supposing grandma senile or blind once again goes against the assumption of the example that she knows her grandson is ambulatory.) From this belief of grandma's that her grandson is walking towards her, it follows that her grandson can walk, since what is actual is possible. Thus, it follows that he is ambulatory, and grandma knows this. After the grandson sits down, of course, it does not follow necessarily from what grandma sees then that he is ambulatory, but it follows from the fact that he was just walking and that nothing visibly harmed him in the meantime that he very probably is still ambulatory.

Notice that the recursive way of handling this example also gives the right answer about the possibility where her source of belief is her relatives. The more basic, tracking beliefs she would get from that process—e.g., 'Jane says he is ambulatory'—do not imply that he can walk, or even that he probably can walk, without a further premise to the effect that Jane probably wouldn't lie to her. If that premise isn't true then the grandmother does not have knowledge of her grandson's health according to the recursive tracking view, which is just as it should be.

My hope and expectation is that relativization of knowledge to the method through which a belief was actually acquired can be fully excised from the tracking view. I will discuss in Chapter 3 further details of how this is achieved, in particular how exactly the rules of application of the tracking conditions determine what is fixed and what varies when we evaluate what the subject does in scenarios different from the actual.

Sensitivity training

Williamson (2000: 147–63) has directly attacked the idea that sensitivity should be a necessary condition for knowledge. Though condition (3) is not a necessary condition for knowledge on my account, its descendant III is necessary in the base case, and Williamson's argument concerning possible marginal cases thus appears to threaten.

Williamson asks us to consider a man with a tendency to underestimate distance when the case is a close call. Thus, when he sees a distance of twenty-one meters he judges it to be less than twenty meters, though he would not judge twenty-three meters to be less than twenty meters. We are next to imagine him presented with a distance which is about one meter. He judges this distance to be less than twenty meters. He is not only right, but also in possession of knowledge, and this is so, Williamson believes, even if we add to the setup the condition that if the distance were not less than twenty meters, it would be a distance subject to our man's habitual underestimation, say twenty and one half meters. Twenty and one half meters is not close to the actual distance of one meter, but in this case, as with Oscar and Dack above, we are rigging the possible scenarios in such a way as to give our man a hard time. That if the distance were not under twenty meters then our subject might believe it was (because it would be twenty and one half meters) is irrelevant, it seems, to whether he has knowledge when the distance is actually only one meter. This, it seems, means that the variation condition is irrelevant to whether our man has knowledge.

However, the irrelevance of the tracking condition comes only from a presuppos-ition we made, namely, that our man knows this case is not a close call. If we suppose that he does not know whether it is a close call, then his incompetence at close calls ceases to seem irrelevant. If it were a close call, then he could easily believe a falsehood about it. For the tracking condition to be irrelevant intuitively, our man must know that this case is not a close call. How is that achieved? Williamson insists that this man may know that the distance is less than twenty meters without having any other belief about the matter than that it is less than twenty meters. That is, he need not have formed the belief that it is less than two meters, or about one meter, or rather small. This leaves it mysterious how the man knows that this case is not a close call.

It would be implausible to assert that the man knows that the distance is less than twenty meters if when prompted he would deny all assertions of the following sort: it is less than two meters, it is less than three meters, etc., it is about one meter, it is rather small. It is implausible that he even believes the one meter distance is less than twenty meters if when given money to bet his bets would not cluster around a few of the statements 'It is less than n meters' for $n = 1/2–30$, in increments of $1/2$, if he is given equal payoffs per amount bet for each n. But if he would be willing to bet at least 95 per cent of the money we give him on the three options $1/2$, 1, and $1\ 1/2$, then according to my criterion for belief he has a belief that the distance is very roughly one meter.[33]

This belief presumably tracks the truth, since if the distance were not very roughly one meter it would have to have a value substantially far away, say four meters. If the distance were four meters would our man believe it was roughly one meter? No, because this is not a close call, so not subject to his tendency to underestimate in close call situations. That the distance is very roughly one meter implies that the distance is less than twenty meters, and our subject knows that if he knows anything. An analogous argument can be made in case the man's tendency to underestimate grows with the absolute size of the distance. The keys to the solution, of course, are the fact that I use a notion of belief that does not require the subject to entertain the thought that p in order to believe that p and, both in consequence and independently, the implausibility of the idea that the subject who knows the distance is less than twenty meters when it is about one meter has no belief at all about roughly what the distance is.

Deities of questionable benevolence

It seems that on the view of Descartes a subject has to be able to rule out the possibility that an evil demon is deceiving her with fake impressions in order to know that there is

---

[33] Of course, what I really need in order for the man to fulfill my criterion for the belief in question strictly is not that he bets at least 95% of the money on the three options, $1/2$, 1, $1\frac{1}{2}$, but that he bets at least 95% of the money on one option presented as a disjunction of the three. Because of sensitivity to framing a typical human being may differ in these two bets, betting more when the same region of possibility space is presented as split into three options than when it is coalesced into one. I assume in this case, then, that our man is rational enough not to be affected by framing. It would probably also be possible to redescribe the experiment to get the desired result without an assumption quite this strong.

a table in front of her. To review what we have seen earlier in discussing skepticism, this does not follow on Nozick's view, since tracking the table does not require being good against the possibility of anything as recherché as an evil demon. Thus, as long as your sense organs are working properly and there is in fact a table in front of you, your belief that there is a table there is knowledge. The same is true on the new tracking view. Of course, on Nozick's view none of this implies that you know you are not being fed false impressions by an evil demon. On my view it does, as long as you know that your not being so deceived is implied by the facts that there is a table in front of you and that you have an impression of a table, which implication we may assume you know on anyone's account.

In an effort to show the flaws in Nozick's view of knowledge Colin McGinn (1984: 531–2) has us imagine, instead of possible evil demons, actual deities—whom he calls 'benevolent'—whose effect is merely counterfactual. For example, suppose that there are material objects all around, but there is also a deity who watches over our sense impressions. In the event of a cataclysm that destroyed all material objects (but, presumably, left our belief-forming processes intact), this deity would step in to supply impressions of material objects. Thereby, we have the falsity of the subjunctive conditional 'If there were not material objects around me, then I would not believe there are,' and failure of the variation condition, which is a necessary condition for knowledge on Nozick's view. However, surely, says McGinn, even in a world where such a deity was standing by I would know that there are material objects around me when there are, because I would see them in the usual way, my belief in them would not be accidental, and with the deity we can make the probability of the cataclysm in question as low as we like while maintaining the falsity of the variation condition for p = 'There are material objects around.'

Such an actual deity has the same deleterious effect on the variation tracking condition for p = 'There are material objects around' as a possible evil demon does, and I agree with McGinn that though we do not track p that does not disqualify us from knowing p in these cases. But my view, unlike Nozick's, has the resources for delivering this verdict since my view has the recursion clause. The plan of the actual deity described in the example only kicks in when all material objects are destroyed. All material objects being destroyed is not a close (or probable) way for there to fail to be a table in front of me, and not a close or probable way for there to fail to be a chair under me. Thus, assuming that everything is in fact normal, I track the fact that there is a table in front of me and I track the fact that there is a chair under me, without being good against that faraway possibility. Since I track that there is a table in front of me and I track that there is a chair under me, I know that there is a table in front of me and I know that there is a chair under me. I also know that these claims imply that there are material objects around. Thus, I know that there are material objects around, assuming there are, even though I do not track the fact. Where Nozick's view had a counterintuitive consequence mine does not, for reasons that are by now familiar.

What if the impression-sustaining intentions of the deity in question are restricted to this table in front of me? We might think that this affects whether I track the table by implying that I fail to fulfill the variation condition for 'There is a table in front of me.' However this does not follow, for the table going out of existence—which is the condition for the deity's plan to kick in—is not a close or probable way for there to fail to be a table in front of me. And if we change the deity's intentions so that he would supply me with continuous impressions of the table in front of me even if I moved the table with my hands or left the table to get a drink, then the intuition that I know there is a table in front of me disappears, it seems to me. There isn't a way I can see that demons or deities can get the better of the new tracking view.

In sum, the new tracking view handles readily all of the challenges that say that tracking is too strong. In several cases this is unexpected, since though the lack of closure in the original tracking view had been viewed with disapproval, it had not been seen as the operative problem in the putative counterexamples.

3

Tracking: More and Better

1. TRACKING NOT TOO WEAK

The recursion I have added to the original tracking view imparts leniency to the view, expanding the set of cases we can count as knowledge compared to the original tracking view. Thus, it can be of no assistance in charges that tracking is too weak to rule out cases we do not want to count as knowledge. However, as I will show in this chapter, purported counterexamples of this variety disappear when we employ conditional probabilities instead of subjunctive conditionals in defining the tracking conditions. This move allows us to incorporate Nozick's idea that more than one or a few alternate scenarios must be evaluated in judging whether a belief is knowledge, and allows for a uniform way of determining which possibilities must be considered that avoids the charges of adhocness that could be leveled against use of similarity relations over possible worlds that are defined on an as-needed basis. It allows us to sidestep gnarly questions about what subjunctive conditionals or counterfactuals are and how to evaluate them, since we will not use either device.

As we will see below, the examples that have been presented to show that tracking is too weak can be addressed by expanding the 'circle' of alternate scenarios considered in the tracking requirements to include more of the most probable alternatives. Critics have sometimes ignored Nozick's stipulation that more than one scenario be evaluated, and they were helped along by the fact that the subjunctive conditional of ordinary language that he used does not, I think, really work as Nozick wanted his view to work. Thus, we are left with a somewhat technical question of how to formulate the intended view. The best way to do this is the formulation in terms of conditional probabilities I stated in the previous chapter. In order for a belief p to track the truth p it must be that:

III. $P(-b(p)/-p)$ is high, and
IV. $P(b(p)/p)$ is high, and $P(b(-p)/p)$ is low.

These conditions are not well defined, of course, until a probability function is specified. In the cases we saw in the previous chapter the choice of probability function—which is, among other things, the choice of which statements to fix as they are in the actual world and which to allow to take other values—was natural and easy to agree on. In order for the view of knowledge to be well-defined, though, there must be a general rule for choosing the probability function in a given case.

This becomes especially apparent in the cases that have been used to argue that tracking is too weak, because I have said that the key to overturning them is to expand the 'circle' of alternate scenarios that the subject's belief patterns must be good against, and choices about the probability function will determine which scenarios go into that expanded circle. Since which cases get counted as knowledge depends sensitively on which scenarios are in that expanded circle, it is natural for my opponent to demand that there be general principles for determining the probability function, and thereby the circle.

If I succeed in giving a set of rules for determining the probability functions to use in evaluating conditions III and IV, then, in particular, I will have solved the generality problem for the tracking view. This, recall, is the problem, encountered in some form by any externalist view, I think, of saying in general and in a principled way the level of generality or specificity at which facts about the world are to be described when they enter into judgments of whether the subject's belief has the right relation to the facts to be counted as knowledge. For the tracking view this problem takes the form of the question: at what level of generality are facts about the actual circumstances in which a subject forms her belief to be fixed when we vary scenarios? If I can give general rules for choosing the right probability functions for evaluating the conditions, then this problem will automatically be solved. To see how conditions III and IV work in detail, and that they work in examples that have been thought to be challenges, we need to consider how conditional probability works in general, and set the rules I refer to for the application of conditions III and IV.

Rules of application—the tracking conditions

Consider how condition III works. The condition:

$P(-b(p)/-p)$ is high,

is equivalent to the following:

$P(-b(p).-p)/P(-p)$ is high.[1]

This says that the probability of two things, S's not believing p and p's not being true, is only slightly less than the probability of the second, p's not being true, alone. It is as if the occurrence of the second 'brings along' the first. To speak metaphorically, one might say that the second 'makes' the first likely. This explains why the simpler, purely correlational, probability statement is a good ersatz for the idea that p's being false should 'make' the subject unlikely to believe p if the subject is to be counted as having (base-case) knowledge.

Next consider which alternatives to p's being true are under consideration in evaluating $P(-b(p).-p)/P(-p)$. The answer is that all of the $-p$ alternatives not assigned probability 0 by the probability function—on the personalist interpretation

---

[1] This is true on the Kolmogorov axiomatization of probability, but not on the axiomatization of probability in terms of Popper functions, which takes conditional probability as a primitive. The 'brings along' story I tell here would not be available if we used Popper functions, but I think that a similarly serviceable story could be told using the constraints that account provides on probabilistic independence, though the story would be longer.

all alternatives consistent with background knowledge—are considered, but only the reasonably probable make much difference to this ratio. To see both of these points consider that

$$P(-p) = P(A_1) + P(A_2) + \ldots + P(A_n),$$

where $-p$ is equivalent to $A_1 \lor A_2 \lor \ldots \lor A_n$, for A_1 through A_n mutually exclusive and jointly exhaustive ways in which $-p$ could be true. Those A_i that have low probability relative to $-p$, i.e., for which $P(A_i/-p)$ is very low, contribute only a small share to $P(-p)$, and thereby make very little difference to the ratio $P(-b(p).-p)/P(-p)$.[2] If in one of those scenarios S believes p (falsely) then that will put a drag on the ratio, but only by a tiny amount. More intuitively, if all of the alternative, that is, $-p$, scenarios in which the subject believes p have very low probability, they will not make a crucial difference to our ratio, which is as it should be. In other words, the alternative scenarios that matter to the criteria we are using for knowledge are the probable ones. Note that in this framework it would make no sense to expect in general that there is some one most probable $-p$ scenario the subject's disposition to react to which alone determines whether she has knowledge, the analog of what people tend to expect when they use subjunctive conditionals to formulate and criticize the tracking conditions. The evaluation would look that way in my formulation only in a very special case where there was one $-p$ scenario that had a probability (on $-p$) that was 0.95 or greater; we do not encounter this in the examples that generally get discussed.

The adherence condition, IV, that

$P(b(p)/p)$ is high, and $P(b(-p)/p)$ is low,

similarly considers all the ways the given statement, here p, could be true that are not themselves assigned probability 0 by P (on the personalist interpretation those that are consistent with background knowledge). $P(b(p)/p)$ will be high if p's occurrence 'brings along' the occurrence of $b(p)$, that is, if p's being true 'makes' it likely that S believes p. $P(b(-p)/p)$ will be low if p's occurrence 'makes' it unlikely that S believes $-p$. As with III, only what happens to the subject's belief in the ways for p to be true that have significant probability will affect the ratio much.

Obviously, whether a conditional probability involving a pair of propositions is high or low depends on the probability function. What is the probability function that we use for these evaluations? There is not a single function used to evaluate all cases because the questions we want conditions III and IV to answer are different for every p and situation in which a subject comes to believe p. So the question is rather what the rule is for identifying the right functions to use for evaluating III and IV for a given case. I will give these rules over the course of the next pages, developing the reasons for them gradually. Notice, first, that some things need not have a special rule

---

[2] Note that here I am not citing the false HITI assumption, that one can approximate $P(A/B)$ by ignoring improbable alternatives to A, an assumption so called after the idea that Highly Improbable Theories are Irrelevant. I am instead citing the true claim that one can approximate $P(B/A)$ by ignoring improbable ways of realizing A. For proof of the latter, and proof that HITI is false, see Fitelson and Thomason (forthcoming).

fixing them, since they are fixed for free. We need not make any special rule to assign probability 1 to anything implied by the −p or p that are the antecedents in the conditional probabilities of III and IV, since such statements will get probability 1 automatically in that situation due to the fact that the p or −p effectively gets probability 1 for the occasion. (Note that I am using the word 'antecedent' to refer to what occupies the p position in P(q/p) in a conditional probability, in order to avoid confusingly overusing the word 'condition' in what follows.)

For example, in evaluating the adherence tracking condition taking p to be the claim that dinosaurs existed, we will not have to consider possible scenarios in which there never were material objects, since those are scenarios inconsistent with the existence of dinosaurs in the past. Another general point relevant to the probability function is that, as I said earlier (Chapter 2), the fact that S believes p is not to be fixed as it actually is. b(p) should not to be assigned probability 1, whether or not that is the probability it actually has, because that would make the probability of b(p) given X equal to 1 for any X with a non-zero probability, rendering the tracking conditions useless, since condition III would never be fulfilled and condition IV would always be fulfilled. I will not take b(p), −b(p), b(−p) or −b(−p) to be fixed at 1, or any other particular value either, since we are interested in how the probabilities of these matters respond to changes in other matters.

However, there are other general questions about what matters are to be fixed, in the probability functions we use to evaluate III and IV, to be just as they are in the actual world. Suppose that we fix very little to be as it actually is, and therefore that much is allowed to vary. If we suppose, for example, that nothing except general facts about things and the way they work is fixed then a great deal will be allowed to vary in both conditions III and IV. That would have at least one kind of disastrous consequence. For example, subjects would not fulfill condition IV when the p or −p in question did not heavily constrain events after a certain point in time, and some node in the causal chain after that time through which the subject was brought to the present went the way it did with only low probability. In this case p's being true would not 'make' it probable that S believed p, though it is clear from the following example that the implication of this is inappropriate for a view of knowledge. Suppose p = Dinosaur Bob was a vegetarian, and S, a paleontologist investigating Bob, believes p because she has gathered good evidence for p. From the point of view of a world where there was a male vegetarian dinosaur at the appropriate time and other things are constrained to be as they have been since only insofar as p's truth and the way things generally work constrain that, S cannot be said to be likely to form any belief at all about Bob. She might have been a carpenter or taxicab driver or any number of other things instead of a paleontologist. In fact, S might not even have existed at all, or might have existed but died in that car crash she narrowly escaped ten years ago, all of which says that condition IV is not fulfilled. However, this does not affect our willingness to attribute knowledge to her now.

More needs to be fixed to be as it actually is than general facts about how the world works, but saying how to make the right choices means running into a functional equivalent of the generality problem that plagues process reliabilism. For example, we could force S to have formed some belief or other on the matter of p by assuming facts about the method she actually used to come to believe p in our evaluation of whether she knows, but this would force us to specify in general at what level a method is to be described. As I said in the last chapter, I avoid relativization to method and I regard this as fortunate because I think this generality problem would be unsolvable. There is an easy way to get around the particular problem that S must have some belief or other about p, which is to stipulate that the probability functions used to evaluate IV assign probability 1 to the claim that either S believes p or S believes −p. Other obvious things need fixing too, so along with this disjunctive claim about S's beliefs for condition IV we will also take for both conditions III and IV her identity, facts about her general tendencies, and her general placement in the situation in which she has actually formed and actually has a belief. I will make these rules more determinate presently.

The disjunction—S believes p or S believes −p—has a restrictive function, having us ignore the scenarios in which S didn't come to a belief at all about the matter of p. If S believes p or S believes −p, and S is an epistemologically responsible person, then S will have used the best method she could for finding out whether p is true, and will have trusted its results. She will not always know in such circumstances, since she will not always thereby track the truth. For example, a person to whom no good method is available will have a probability of 50 per cent of coming to believe p and 50 per cent of coming to believe −p. But if so then the adherence condition is not fulfilled, and she does not know, in conformity with our intuition in such a case.

The rules I have given for fixing certain things in evaluation of conditions III and IV do not yet quite solve the generality problem. For a tracking view this problem becomes most apparent in the question how much is fixed about the actual situation in which the subject came to believe, and her placement in it, and at what level of detail. I said that we would fix her general placement in her situation because if we did not fix something here, then there could be an overwhelming number of scenarios considered in which our subject was not even present and so would have a 50–50 chance of forming either belief on the assumption that she formed one or the other belief. The swamping effect of all those scenarios would mean that on that mode of application there are many propositions that we think people know but which no subject could ever know.

But how general is 'general'? I said that we would fix the subject's general situation and her placement in it when she came to believe p, but what does this entail?[3] This cannot simply be left to judgment, since the answers we get as to whether a subject knows will depend sensitively on how much we hold fixed about the actual situation when we consider what the subject would believe were that situation to vary. If we have not given a rule for determining what to hold fixed, then we will not have illuminated what it is to know. And the rule 'fix only general matters' is not determinate enough to give us answers in many disputable cases.

I propose a solution to this generality problem, for the new tracking view, in the form of a determinate pair of rules. I will first motivate these rules intuitively, then precisely state their official versions. Afterward, we will see how they work in important examples. The general idea behind the tracking view is that (leaving the

---

[3] I am grateful to Aaron James for pressing me as to why going only so far as saying we fix the situation generally was solving the generality problem more effectively than process reliabilism had.

recursion clause to one side) a subject who knows p should be responsive in her p-belief behavior to changes that p's being false rather than true would make to the world (condition III), and to the difference that p's truth makes to the world, but unresponsive or rigid in her p-belief behavior in the face of changes to the world that are not relevant to p (condition IV).

To make this concrete I am going to say that the set of scenarios we want conditions III and IV to test the subject's responsiveness to is the set of scenarios that can be generated by varying the matters that are more 'influenced' by the truth value of p than the truth value of p is 'influenced' by them. In particular, for condition III they are the things whose truth value is more sensitive to p's being false than p's being false is sensitive to their truth values. This leads to the following criterion: for all q not equal to p, −p, b(p), −b(p), b(−p), or −b(−p), and not of the form r.s or ∀xFx, if

$$|P(q/-p) - P(q/p)| \le |P(-p/q) - P(-p/-q)| \text{ and}$$
$$|P(-q/-p) - P(-q/p)| \le |P(-p/q) - P(-p/-q)| \qquad *$$

then hold P(q) fixed at its actual value. Otherwise do not hold P(q) fixed at its actual value. Criterion * says that p's being false rather than true makes less or the same difference to q's being true, and to q's being false, than the difference that q's being true or false makes to p's being false. (Making the same difference includes the case where p and q make no difference to each other, i.e., when they are probabilistically independent or irrelevant.) q that fulfill this criterion ought to be fixed as they actually are because −p does not differentially affect them; −p is more affected by their being true or false than either they or their negations are by it versus p. We get what we need, that is, variation of those matters that are differentially affected by −p, by allowing all q that do not fulfill criterion * to vary. For those q we can inspect the subject's disposition to respond in her p-belief to the variety of possible values for P(q) that −p and the fixed probabilities of the q's that fulfill the criterion allow.

Another way to state what we are doing here is that we are determining which statements or their negations −p is more relevant to than they are relevant to −p, and those matters we are going to leave open for variation, while we fix everything else (except p, −p, b(p), −b(p), b(−p), and −b(−p)). Then we will require of the subject who fulfills the variation condition that she is appropriately responsive to these things −p is differentially relevant to, strongly tending not to believe p when these things that indicate p's falsehood occur. In order to have knowledge of p by tracking p, after all, the subject must be sufficiently able to pick up on the difference that the falsehood of p would make to the world. With criterion * we are simply being explicit about what 'the difference that the falsehood of p would make to the world' means.[4]

---

[4] There is more than one way to measure the 'difference' that the truth or falsity of a statement makes to the world. For example, we could measure the difference that B makes to A by the ratio P(A/B)/P(A). But if we did that, then we would not be able to pick up on any asymmetry of degree of relevance or 'influence', as we have done with the terms I use involving negations, for by Bayes's Theorem P(A/B)/P(A) = P(B/A)/P(B). Likelihood Ratios use the terms with negations that I have used here, but they are too sensitive to the direction of 'influence' and I needed to measure simply its magnitude. This left me comparing absolute values of differences of likelihoods on propositions and their negations.

For the adherence condition we do a related but different thing, for here we want to allow variation in those matters that the truth value of p makes no difference to, and allow variation in those things that the truth of p makes more of a difference to than they make to p, and make sure the subject does not respond to irrelevant changes as if they were relevant to p and is able sufficiently to pick up on the difference that the truth of p makes through the possible noise. This leads to criterion **: for all q not equal to b(p), −b(p), b(−p), or −b(−p), and not of the form r.s or ∀xFx, if

$$|P(q/p) - P(q/-p)| < |P(p/q) - P(p/-q)| \text{ and }$$
$$|P(-q/p) - P(-q/-p)| < |P(p/q) - P(p/-q)| \qquad **$$

then hold P(q) fixed to its actual value.[5] Otherwise do not hold P(q) fixed to its actual value. The matters that are probabilistically irrelevant to p will have both left-hand side and right-hand side of both of these inequalities equal to 0. They will not fulfill criterion **, and they will be allowed to vary. (This is an idealization, of course; I will count roughly irrelevant as irrelevant, both for ** and for *.)

We allow matters irrelevant to p to vary in order that in the next step we can check that S's belief in p does not vary with them. Matters that p is more relevant to than they are to it will also be allowed to vary; this is so that when the adherence condition is applied we make sure that there was sufficient disposition for the truth of p to produce S's belief in p, and S didn't just get lucky in the actual case. Of course, when we check P(b(p)/p) those matters will only be able to vary as much as the truth of p allows them to, which is just as it should be. The facts in the actual world that 'brought about' the truth of p will be fixed, as they should be, since they will be more probabilistically relevant to p than p is to them or their negations. A few more fixing rules will be specified below, but criteria * and ** are central to the account. As I will explain more explicitly below, criteria * and ** are to be judged from the point of view of the actual world.

It is helpful to illustrate these criteria with an example. Consider Goldman's case (colonized from Dretske) with the child, the parent, and the thermometer. A mother takes her child's temperature with a thermometer, which says that the child's temperature is normal. Suppose that it is true that the child's temperature is normal, and that the thermometer is also working normally. If this were all there was to the case, then we would say the mother knows her child's temperature is normal. However, suppose that there were hundreds of thermometers in the medicine chest, all but one of which was defective, and the particular way in which that majority was defective is that they all read 98.6 regardless of the circumstances. The mother happened to choose the only functional thermometer out of hundreds when she went to the chest to get the thermometer she was going to use. With this new information our sense that the mother knows her child's temperature is normal tends to recede (Goldman 1986: 45).

---

[5] We do not need a clause excepting p and −p from this criterion since neither fulfills it; p does not fulfill the first clause because for p the two sides are equal, and −p does not fulfill the first clause because for −p the right side is undefined.

Suppose p is the claim that the child's temperature is normal. On Nozick's view the actual method of belief formation is held fixed, so which thermometer the mother actually used in forming the belief in p is held fixed. This is bad, of course, because it ruins any grounds we would have for saying that if the child's temperature were not normal his mother might well still believe it was, and thereby that she does not have knowledge. She would not still believe it was normal if it was not, because the thermometer she actually used is not defective, and it would tell her that the temperature was abnormal if it was. Fixing the actual method of belief formation made Nozick's view unable to reach back to those possibilities that surround the mother's choice of thermometer, yielding a counterintuitive conclusion in this case.

As I have explained, actual method of belief formation is not fixed in my tracking view. As shown in the previous chapter, in the cases that prompted Nozick to relativize to method my view turns out the right answer with no special treatments. I do not have any problems generated by a rule that says to fix the actual method, because I have no such rule. But there is still the question of how my view does handle the thermometer case, and criterion * allows us to answer. Intuitively, we expect the mother to fail the variation condition, if the mother fails at all to have knowledge on the tracking view. In order for the mother to fail tracking condition III,

$$P(-b(p)/-p) > 0.95$$

there must be a sufficiently probable scenario consistent with −p in which the mother believes p, and which is among the possibilities generated by the things that criterion * allows to vary from the way they are in the actual world. The following statement,

q = The mother gets this thermometer out of the medicine chest.

fails to satisfy criterion * for p = The child's temperature is normal, and understanding 'this thermometer' as referring to the one she actually used. For this reason q is a statement whose truth value will be allowed to vary. Varying this q will then expose the flaw in the mother's belief.

To see that this q does not satisfy the criterion (and hence should not be fixed) note first that even though in the actual world it is highly likely that the mother goes to the medicine chest, still the mother is more likely to go to the medicine chest if the child's temperature is abnormal than if it is normal, since if the temperature is abnormal the child is more likely to feel sick and exhibit other symptoms that prompt the taking of a temperature. If she does go to the medicine chest then of course she has the same chances of pulling out this thermometer among the many thermometers whether the child's temperature is abnormal or not. However, whether the child's temperature is abnormal influences significantly whether she goes to the chest at all, which going is a necessary condition for getting this thermometer. This means that the left-hand side of the first inequality in * is significant.

The right-hand side of that inequality is not significantly greater than 0. This is because the probability of her going to the chest is high in the actual world, and is not affected by whether she gets this thermometer (q) or not (−q), since in the actual world there are several hundred ways of going to the chest even if she does not get this thermometer. Her getting or not getting this thermometer can only make a difference to the very low probability in the actual world that the child's temperature is abnormal by making a difference to whether the mother goes to the chest, but it has no means to do that since she goes to the chest with the same probability whether she does or does not get this thermometer.

Since q does not satisfy criterion* it is one of the things that will not be fixed when we evaluate whether the mother withholds belief in p when p is false. That there are hundreds of defective thermometers in her chest will be fixed since it is roughly probabilistically irrelevant to whether the child's temperature is elevated on this occasion and the temperature on this occasion is roughly irrelevant to it, making both terms of the first inequality * roughly equal to 0, and both terms of the second inequality * roughly equal to 0, meaning that this meets criterion * for being fixed. In order to see whether the mother fails condition III, we ask what she believes when the child's temperature is not normal. We can assume that in this case the mother is likely to go to the medicine chest to get a thermometer because the child is likely to feel ill or hot, since if she isn't so inclined then she will believe the child's temperature is normal and we are done. Which thermometer the mother gets is not fixed so she is likely to get a defective one, by sheer force of numbers. She takes the temperature and believes what the thermometer says, as was her disposition in the actual world, so since the defective thermometer says 98.6 she believes the child's temperature is normal, even though it is not. Thus, she fails condition III, and does not have knowledge, as our intuitions suggest.

One would be right to wonder what probability function we are to use in determining for a given q whether it satisfies criterion * for a particular p. I wrote 'P' for both the criteria * and **, and condition III, but these are not the same probability function. (In fact, as we will see, the judgments that correspond to conditions III and IV are not even judgments that a certain probability function takes a certain value on a certain argument, but rather judgments as to whether a quantification over a certain set of probability functions is true.) The function to be used for evaluating both * and ** is the probability function that is maximally specific, up to what our language allows, in the possibilities that are expressed by the propositions that make up its arguments, and that takes the values that those arguments have in the actual world, with a proviso that I will come to. I call this function P_u, the ur-probability function, because it serves as the first step in defining the set of functions we will deal with in evaluating conditions III and IV.

The domain of the function P_u is the set of statements of our language, where two sentences are counted as the same statement if they have the same meaning, and its range is the probabilities those statements have in the actual world, but under the stipulation that no propositions get the extreme probability values 1 and 0 except logical truths and falsehoods respectively. This is so as to avoid destruction of the relevance relations we are looking to discern with criteria * and **. We can see the significance of staying away from the extreme probabilities for contingent propositions with an example. Suppose p, the ice cream is frozen, is true in the actual world and q is the claim that the ice cream is taken out of the freezer where it now actually sits. If we assign p probability 1 due to its truth then the conditional probability $P(p/q)$ will also be 1. But that would obscure the fact that taking the ice cream out of the freezer makes a difference to whether it is frozen.

This stipulation of no extreme probabilities for contingent propositions requires us to take further precautions. Assigning the same probability to every true proposition would also ruin probabilistic relations we want to preserve. For example, often a conjunction is less probable than one of its conjuncts. Thus, we should imagine ourselves assigning, say, the probability 0.999 to all atomic propositions, and 0.001 to all negations of atomic propositions, with other probabilities determined in a way that depends on these. My calling a function a probability function means that I assume it fulfills the (Kolmogorov) axioms for probability, which imposes a good deal of helpful coherence in this and subsequent steps of application of conditions III and IV. Although I have not fully defined the function P_u I think we have good instincts about it. We use these instincts about P_u to determine for each q whether criteria * and ** are fulfilled, with the p given by the case of belief we are evaluating as to whether it is knowledge.

When in scrutinizing theories of knowledge we consider a hypothetical scenario to judge whether it should count as a case of knowledge, we are of course not describing the actual world, but we are describing a way that we imagine the actual world could be and it is on that assumption that our intuitions are generated. Thus, the appropriate procedure for hypothetical scenarios, like the examples considered below, is to imagine P_u modified in the way the imagined case requires, and go on from there.

When we know which q satisfy criterion * and which q satisfy criterion **, we know a lot about which things are to be fixed and which allowed to vary when we apply conditions III and IV respectively. We combine these criteria with the rules that for the adherence condition it is fixed that the subject believes p or the subject believes $-p$, and for both conditions that the laws of nature and other regularities are fixed, the subject's existence, identity, dispositions, and state of duress are fixed, and the subject's location in space and time when she formed the belief and (if different) when she has the belief in question are fixed. These latter rules trump criteria * and ** and are always respected. I will explain the additional fixings presently, but the question that presses now is exactly how the fixing and varying I have referred to that determines whether conditions III and IV are fulfilled, is expressed and executed.

Because we need to know what a variety of different scenarios would make our subject do with regard to belief in p, we really need to ask what values a variety of probability functions give to the argument b(p) when p or $-p$ is assumed. That is, we need to ask after the truth value of a quantification that states something about all of a set of probability functions P_i that meet the condition that for the q that we decide should be fixed as they are in the actual world, $P_i(q) = P_u(q)$. In other words we set a requirement on all those probability functions that give the same probability as the function describing the actual world does to the matters our rules tell us to fix. We get the universe of probability functions that we are going to quantify over by taking all probability functions that have the same domain as P_u. That is, we generate the set of probability functions at issue by taking the same possibilities as those described by the statements in P_u's domain, and assigning all possible values (probabilities) to those arguments. Each difference in value represents a different probability function.

The variety of values we assign to generate these functions are continuum-many between 0 and 1. Like P_u these functions all assign probability 1 to (the same) logical truths, probability 0 to logical falsehoods, and assign extreme probabilities in no other situations, except, for condition IV only, that the disjunction 'S believes p or S believes $-p$' can be assigned probability 1.

We will take condition III to be fulfilled, then, for a subject S who actually believes p, when the following quantified statement is true:

For all Pi such that

(1) $P_i(s) = P_u(s)$ for s any statement regarding the subject's existence, identity, dispositions, location in space and time when she formed the belief and, if different, when she has the belief, s the statement that the subject is under extreme duress, and s any statement that is a law of nature or other regularity, and

(2) for all q that are atomic sentences or disjunctions of atomic sentences and negations of atomic sentences, or are existential quantifications, and are not equivalent to p, $-p$, b(p), $-b(p)$, b($-p$), or $-b(-p)$, and such that if
$$| P_u(q/-p) - P_u(q/p)| \leq | P_u(-p/q) - P_u(-p/-q)| \text{ and}$$
$$| P_u(-q/-p) - P_u(-q/p) | \leq |P_u(-p/q) - P_u(-p/-q)|$$
$$\text{then } P_i(q) = P_u(q),$$
$$P_i(-b(p)/-p) > 0.95$$

We will take condition IV to be fulfilled when the following quantified statement is true:

For all P_i such that

(1) $P_i('S \text{ believes } p \text{ or } S \text{ believes not-p'}) = 1$

(2) $P_i(s) = P_u(s)$ for s any statement regarding the subject's existence, identity, dispositions, and location in space and time when she formed the belief and, if different, when she has the belief, s the statement that the subject is under extreme duress, and s any statement that is a law of nature or other regularity (including logical truths), and

(3) for all q that are atomic sentences or disjunctions of atomic sentences and negations of atomic sentences, or existential quantifications, and are not equivalent to b(p), $-b(p)$, b($-p$), or $-b(-p)$, and such that if

$$| P_u(q/p) - P_u(q/-p)| < |P_u(p/q) - P_u(p/-q)| \text{ and}$$
$$|P_u(-q/p) - P_u(-q/-p)| < |P_u(p/q) - P_u(p/-q)|$$
$$\text{then } P_i(q) = P_u(q),$$
$$P_i(b(p)/p) > 0.95 \text{ and } P_i(b(-p)/p) < 0.05$$

These quantified statements are a more rigorous fleshing out of the procedure for evaluating conditions III and IV that we have imagined intuitively, with a few additions I will explain.

I have restricted application of criteria * and ** (clauses 2 and 3, respectively) to q that are atomic sentences or disjunctions of atomic sentences and negations of atomic sentences because the criteria are not well defined for conjunctions, hence also for universal quantifications; they can give different answers as to whether to fix one of these types of statements depending on whether we apply the criteria to the statement or to its component statements. We will follow the verdict of the component statements, so that a conjunction or universal quantification may be fixed, but only if the appropriate atomic conjuncts are fixed (or the statement is a quantification and it has been fixed by the rule about laws of nature and other regularities). Note that atomicity of the statements does not imply that their predicates are monadic; for example, atomic statements may involve the dyadic predicate of equality, as I expect instances of laws of nature would.

One may worry that though it is determinate for a defined language which statements are atomic it may not be for our natural language. For example, we treat the statement 'Mary is pregnant' as atomic for many purposes though presumably it can be broken down to a conjunction of component statements, so which is it? I don't know how to answer that question, but I don't think I need to because we can go with the way we treat the statement in the context in question. If we treat a statement as atomic then that is probably atomic enough for application of our criteria because my surmise is that we treat a statement so only when the component conjunct statements tend to stand and fall together. If so, then the conjunction can be treated as atomic because it will not present the problem I restricted the criteria to atomic statements (and their disjunctions, etc.) in order to avoid. One may notice that I have admitted that judgments about probability go towards determining which statements are atomic, and that which statements are atomic has a role in determining probabilities that concern us here. I think this circle is unavoidable, and may be related to our inability to offer a non-circular justification for projecting the predicate *green* but not projecting the predicate *grue*; notice that one could say 'x is green' is atomic, and 'x is grue' is not, and we do not project the latter because we regard it as improbable that that property will continue to be exhibited. In any case, though I think there is a circle in this neighborhood it is not my problem, since I am not here giving an analysis of *probability* or *atomicity*, but of *knowledge*.

For condition III, we fix the subject's existence, identity, dispositions, and location in space and time when she formed the belief, and also when she has the belief we are judging as to whether it is knowledge in case that is different, whether the subject is under extreme duress, laws of nature and other regularities, and all those matters that are not within the area of differential 'influence' of $-p$ as judged by the standards of the actual world (except, where applicable, the subject's belief behavior regarding p and $-p$). Holding all of that fixed, which puts us in most but not all respects in the actual world, we ask whether the subject is likely to refrain from believing p assuming that p is false. This takes the form of asking whether she is so likely according to every probability function that is consistent with the fixings.

I fix the probability that the subject is under extreme duress at its actual value in order to allow duress to be relevant (if it should be) to whether we count her as knowing if she is actually under duress, and to throw away alternate scenarios in which she is under extreme duress when she is not so situated in the actual world. What a subject would believe if she were under duress doesn't matter to whether she knows when she is nowhere near that state, so we do not want to consider probability functions that assign high probabilities to that state. We might think that since belief is not really voluntary duress also couldn't cause one to change a belief. However, though it may be true that one wouldn't change one's belief voluntarily in such a circumstance, that doesn't imply that one's belief would not be changed. (Consider the scene from Orwell's *1984* in which the interrogator is not satisfied to get the prisoner to report the wrong number of fingers in front of his face, but through torture, supposedly, actually gets the prisoner to *see* the wrong number of fingers.) Even if it is a regularity that duress cannot cause change of belief, which would then get fixed by the rule about regularities, this other rule fixing the actual probability of duress will cause no harm.

We must stipulate that the laws of nature and other regularities are fixed if we want them to be fixed because though the regularities will often be probabilistically independent of p they are not considered by * as regularities but only via their instances. We do want the laws of nature fixed at their actual probabilities since scenarios in which they are different are not usually relevant to the question whether S knows that p. Where those scenarios are relevant to the question whether S knows, our conditions will be able to pick up on that because no empirical statement, including the laws, is given a completely inert extreme probability. We want logical truths to be fixed at their actual probability, 1, because what a subject is disposed to believe in a contra-logical world is never relevant to whether she actually knows. This is stipulated in IV's criterion ** but needn't be in III; criterion * imposes it automatically because a logical truth is probabilistically irrelevant to every p.

In the rule for condition IV we assume that the subject has formed some belief or other and fix the subject's existence, identity, dispositions, and location in space and time when she formed the belief and, if different, when she has the belief in question, whether she is under extreme duress, and all of the laws of nature and other regularities. We also fix all of those matters that p is within the area of differential 'influence' of as judged by the standards of the actual world, i.e., the things that are more relevant to p than p is to them. With condition IV we want to vary things irrelevant to p, and check to see that the subject does not mistakenly jump on them as indications of p's falsehood and stop believing p. However, criterion ** alone would have us vary everything irrelevant to p, and that would rock the world more than would be suitable. This is because there could be laws of nature that are not particularly relevant to p, so criterion ** would not fix them, but varying them would upset the world quite a bit, in ways that we are not concerned about when we ask whether S knows that p. Thus we need to fix the laws of nature. Once again, since they are not given extreme probabilities they will be malleable where they should be, for example, as I think, when knowledge of laws of nature is in question.

After fixing these things, we then ask whether allowing the remaining matters to vary it is likely that S believes p assuming that p is true. I conjecture that we don't need to fix any more than these things in order to get as much as is appropriate to be fixed about the actual situation. This is because the antecedent of the conditional probability in condition IV is p, meaning that anything presupposed by p will automatically get fixed at probability 1 for the occasion, and because ** allows us to fix anything that 'brought about' p in the actual world. However, obviously, if these rules did not fix enough more fixing could be imposed.

A few words are in order about what the 'fixing' I have prescribed entails. As can be seen from the quantified condition, the fixing of, say, q, is a fixing not of the truth value of q but of the probability that all of the P_i (that we ask condition III or IV of) assign to q at the same value as P_u assigned to q. This puts limits on what any of the P_i can assign to some other statements. For example, those statements logically implied by the statement in question must be given probabilities greater than or equal to that of the statement in question by all the P_i in question. However, it does not imply that the probability of q cannot be affected by variation in the probabilities of other statements in our final evaluation of, say, $P_i(-b(p)/-p)$ for a given i. This is because $P_i(q) = P_u(q)$ does not imply that $P_i(q/t) = P_u(q)$ for any t. The possible t in question are of two sorts: either they have themselves been fixed or they have not. If t has been fixed then although $P_i(q/t)$ may not equal $P_u(q)$, still $P_i(q/t)$ will equal $P_u(q/t)$. That is, the probability of q given t will be the same according to P_i as it is in the actual world. If t was not fixed then (for condition III) that was because p vs. −p mattered more to it or to its negation than it mattered to −p. Therefore, although the varying t takes many different absolute probabilities in the various P_i, the probability t takes conditional on p or −p is significantly affected by p or −p in all the P_i. Thus, when we evaluate $P_i(-b(p)/-p)$ for each P_i, though the probability of t may affect the probability of q it will do so only after having its own probability significantly influenced by the supposition of the antecedent −p.

Thus, the extent to which a fixed q can have its probability changed from $P_u(q)$ in evaluation of the variation or adherence condition is limited, and the alterations that are allowed are restricted by the antecedent p or −p of that final conditional probability $P(-b(p)/-p)$, $P(b(p)/p)$, or $P(b(-p)/p)$ in the respective condition. Fixing q imposes inertia in favor of the actual probability of q in another way, of course, since even if things that are allowed to vary affect the probability of q, where that probability starts out for every P_i is the probability given by the actual world. Fixing q as opposed to letting it vary provides a strong ballast in favor of the actual probability of q since when the rules allow q to vary, each P_i takes a different value for $P_i(q)$, but when q is fixed, every P_i takes the same value for $P_i(q)$. This means, in particular, that even if q describes a circumstance in which the subject has a 0.999 probability of believing the wrong thing or not believing the right thing, as long as $P_u(q)$ was less than or equal to 0.05 (and the antecedent p or −p of the condition doesn't make it greater than 0.05) that scenario will not cause us to count the subject as violating condition III or IV. Notice also that if the antecedent p or −p does make the probability of that scenario in which the subject will make a mistake greater than 0.05 then, intuitively, we ought not to count the subject as knowing.[6] Overall, even though it is probabilistic, what I am calling 'fixing' is worthy of the word.

---

[6] An illustration of this parenthetical effect would be if the supposition that there was not a table in front of me made the chances greater than 5% that I am a brain in a vat. Although there being no table in front of me raises the probability that I am a brain in a vat from what it was supposing there is a table in front of me (zero), surely it does not make that probability greater than 5%. However, if there being no table in front of me did raise the probability that I am a brain in a vat to greater than 5% then the fact that I can't tell that I'm a brain in a vat when I am would make us withhold the knowledge label. Thus the condition works just as it should.

One may wonder how this set of rules deals with skeptical hypotheses, both as alternate possibilities that might or might not interfere with our ability to know ordinary statements and as hypotheses in their own right which we may or may not know to be false. If we are asking whether I know an ordinary p, such as that there is a table in front of me, and we are wondering how the precise tracking conditions deal with this, then we are assuming that p is true and that I believe p in the usual way, and the question is whether skeptical possibilities interfere with my tracking it. To figure out how the precise tracking conditions handle this we have to ask whether the q that says I am a brain in a vat (in a world with no tables) gets its probability fixed or is allowed to have it vary when the conditions III and IV are applied.

To answer this for condition III, we ask whether q satisfies * for this p. It can easily be verified that it does. There is a symmetry between the difference that there being a table in front of me or not makes to whether I am a brain in a vat or not and the difference that my being a brain in a vat or not makes to whether there is a table in front of me or not (since on the usual brains-in-a-vat hypothesis that I am using there are no tables in the world, and if there are any tables then that hypothesis is false). But criterion * asks a slightly asymmetrical question focused on the significance of −p. Thus, on the right-hand sides of both inequalities in * we have the difference that q versus −q makes to −p without any mention of p. In this way the criterion is able to pick up on our intuitive sense that the truth or falsity of the skeptical hypothesis is more potent than is the claim that there is no table in front of me.

The other crucial ingredient in seeing that q = 'I am a brain in a vat' satisfies * for p = 'There is a table in front of me,' is that in the actual world the probability of q is exceedingly low and the probability of p is, in the case in question, exceedingly high. Keeping this in mind we note the following. That there is not a table in front of me would not make it much more probable that I was a brain in a vat than it was with the table, although the latter probability is zero. Whether there is or there is not a table in front of me the probability that I am a brain in a vat is exceedingly small, making $|P(q/-p) - P(q/p)|$ very tiny. However, whereas in the actual world the probability that there is no table in front of me is very low, and my not being a brain in a vat does nothing to change this, so $P(-p/-q)$ is very tiny, my being a brain in a vat would bring the probability that there is no table in front of me up to 1, meaning $P(-p/q) = 1$. (q logically implies p, given how I have defined q, so this is allowed an extreme probability.) The difference between nearly 0 and nearly 1 is significant indeed, so $|P(q/-p) - P(q/p)| < |P(-p/q) - P(-p/-q)|$ because the left-hand side is nearly 0 and the right-hand side is nearly 1. A similar argument holds for the second inequality in *.

Thus, when we ask whether the variation condition is fulfilled by a subject who believes truly that there is a table in front of her, the skeptical hypothesis that she is a brain in a vat is fixed at its actual exceedingly low probability. This means that all the P_i of which we ask whether $P_i(-b(p)/-p) > 0.95$ have assigned this q an exceedingly low probability, much lower than 0.05. Thus, the fact that she is likely to believe p assuming p false and q true does not bring this conditional probability below 0.95. This is just the way we expect the variation tracking condition to work intuitively.

Criterion ** asks another asymmetrical question, this time focused on the significance of p rather than the significance of −p. But the evaluations are very similar in that just as for *, the right-hand sides of both inequalities are nearly 1 while the left-hand sides are nearly 0, meaning that for evaluation of condition IV, the adherence condition, the skeptical hypothesis gets fixed at the very tiny probability it has in the actual world. This does not actually matter to whether the adherence condition gives the answer it should, since that condition only docks the subject if she fails to believe p in an alternate scenario where she shouldn't give up the belief, and the skeptical hypothesis is concocted in such a way that none of the sensations the subject uses to form any of her beliefs about things like tables are changed, giving her zero encouragement to give up belief in p. Nevertheless it is reassuring that ** yields the expected verdict on whether to fix or vary the probability of the skeptical hypothesis since this supports the idea that we have correctly identified the general criterion. To summarize so far, we have the expected conclusion that I do track the fact that there is a table in front of me, despite the existence of the possibility that I am a brain in a vat.

What happens if p, the statement we are judging my knowledge of, is itself the falsity of the skeptical hypothesis? That is, p = I am not a brain in a vat. Suppose that p is true, so it is assigned an extremely high (non-unitary) probability by P_u. Suppose also that there is a table in front of me—perhaps I thump it as I declare my non-envatment. Call this claim q, and q will also be assigned a high (non-unitary) probability by P_u. We wonder whether when we evaluate conditions III and IV for this p statements like q will be fixed at their usual probabilities or be allowed to vary. In this case criteria * and ** once again yield the verdicts that we should expect, since they say that −p, that I am a brain in a vat, is more potent than q vs. −q, whether or not there is a table in front of me. As can be verified, all of the inequalities in * and ** have left-hand sides greater than right-hand sides, meaning that q, there being a table in front of me, is not fixed at its actual high probability when we evaluate conditions III and IV. Whether there is a table in front of me will be susceptible to variation in light of changes in assumptions about whether I am a brain in a vat.

This is as it should be, but there being a table in front of me or not would be subject to variation in evaluation of condition III even if it had passed criterion *. This is because −p, that I am a brain in a vat, is the antecedent in the conditional probability we check, $P(-b(p)/-p)$, and even if $P(q)$ is fixed at its actual value, that actual value will not be 1 since only logical matters are assigned extreme probabilities by P_u. Thus, when in evaluating $P(-b(p)/-p)$ we ask whether the subject believes p, we are asking it on the assumption of −p, that I am a brain in a vat, which implies −q, that there is no table in front of me, and that is allowed to affect our assumptions about −q because −q has not been taken out of play by being given an extreme probability.

This is also as it should be, but as important as what is varied is what is not varied, because of course the problem with the skeptical hypothesis, and the reason that one does not track its falsehood, is that one will not notice the differences in the world that its truth would make. Through evaluation of conditions III and IV my sensations of a table in front of me must be held as they are in the actual world in order for the expected answers, violation and fulfillment respectively, to drop out. How is this insured? For the variation condition this is easy because the antecedent of the conditional probability we eventually check for all P_i, $P(-b(p)/-p)$, is the skeptical hypothesis that I am a brain in a vat, and the skeptical hypothesis implies that all my sensations are as they normally are.

We do not get the same reassurance from the antecedent of the conditional probability, $P(b(p)/p)$, of the adherence condition, for that antecedent says only that I am not a brain in a vat. As far as that antecedent will fix it for us, I could be a frisbee or a slice of pizza. But the other rules for the adherence condition fix the claim that my sense organs exist and behave normally at an earlier stage. These claims fail criterion **, as they should since whether or not I am a brain in a vat is potently relevant to them. However, the claim that I have sense organs of the normal sort gets fixed because of another clause. Roughly how my sense organs usually work, and thus roughly what they would normally deliver to me in a given situation, should be fixed since it is a regularity that they work roughly as they do. Thus I pass the adherence condition for the claim p that I am not a brain in a vat, because nothing that changes when we evaluate $P(b(p)/p)$ changes anything relevant to whether I will believe I am not envatted. In addition to following in general the tracking intuitions about what we should be checking when we decide whether someone has knowledge, the scheme I have described delivers the conclusions we would expect about whether I track the negation of the skeptical hypothesis. On the new tracking view, as on the old tracking view, I do not track this claim. On the new view I do know it, but this is because I know it is implied by claims that I (presumably) do track, e.g., that there is a table in front of me.

I count the scheme given by the rigorous quantifications above as a full solution to the generality problem for the tracking view (assuming that it gives plausible answers in examples, not all of which I have checked, of course), because these rules put the new tracking view on a par with internalism on the question what is the level of generality of the statements that must be considered in determining whether the subject is to be counted as knowing. Recall that the internalist has no generality problem because the level of generality of the true beliefs of the subject that are relevant to the question whether she has justification for her belief in p is fixed by p and the rational order. Only those beliefs of the right level of generality to be rationally related to p, either deductively or inductively, can be part of a justification of p. We find all such relevant beliefs (or other sorts of justifiers) the subject has and ask whether they do justify p. It is similar for the new tracking view now that we have the criteria * and **: the level of generality of description of the facts that determine whether the subject knows that p is determined by p and the natural order, since the natural order determines of every q whether it satisfies criteria * and ** for p, because it determines all probabilistic relevance relations.

The statement p itself has a particular level of generality; whether any other given statement is (differentially) probabilistically relevant to p or $-p$ (or p or $-p$ to it) is in part determined by whether the other statement is of the right level of generality to be so. Then, whether q satisfies * and ** determines (modulo the special clauses, which introduce no generality problem) whether q is to be assumed when we ask how the subject behaves in scenarios that are not the actual scenario. Recall that which aspects of the actual situation were to be fixed, and how specifically described, in evaluating the subject's potential behavior, was the place where a generality problem showed up for the tracking view. Our rules, aided especially by the criteria * and **, answer this question completely generally. Like the internalist, we take our bearings for determining what level of generality of description is relevant to judging whether S knows that p from the level of generality of the statement p itself. Where we part company is in the next step in which the internalist judges relevance by the rational order, and we appeal to probabilistic relevance relations in the natural order.

This analysis does not use subjunctive conditionals, but since the conditional probabilities it does use work so much like subjunctive conditionals were intended to it is worth worrying whether objections that have been made against using the latter in analysis have indeed been mooted or addressed. Michael Williams's (1991) objection that we do not sufficiently understand subjunctive conditionals for appeal to them to be helpful hardly applies to conditional probability. While there are many interpretations, and even a few distinct axiomatizations of probability, there is little fundamental unclarity about how each of these axiomatizations behaves or about what it takes to evaluate a probability, in principle, once an interpretation, axiomatization, and probability function have been specified. Since I have given an explicit rule for choosing the probability function and chosen the Kolmogorov axiomatization, the probability values relevant to whether knowledge is present are well defined, even if in fact we cannot evaluate them in particular cases. Subjunctive conditionals are not so well defined in every case, as Robert Fogelin (1994) has noted, but this need not concern us.

Since no uniform similarity relation has been able to give the right answers for all cases in a tracking view formulated in terms of subjunctive conditionals, one wonders what in the new account does the work of the similarity relation. The work of the similarity relation was to determine which possible worlds different from the actual one the subject's belief behavior would be evaluated in by determining which possible worlds were close to the actual one. Close worlds are those similar to the actual one. Which scenarios the subject's belief behavior is evaluated in is determined differently on the new view. Much of the work for this is done by the fixing rules, and especially criteria * and **. The question how specific are the statements that get considered for fixing by these rules is answered by the domain of the ur-probability function P_u, which is the set of maximally specific statements of the language. The function P_u is also, of course, crucial in determining which statements satisfy criteria * and **.

As noted in the previous chapter, Colin McGinn (1984: 535) has expressed doubt that counterfactuals can give a full analysis of any concept. These propositions have 'dependent' truth values, he claims, meaning that there are always some categorical statements that make them true. Thus, he thinks, to offer up counterfactual propositions is not to do a complete analysis of a concept, because there is a deeper level at which one states the categorical propositions that ground the counterfactuals. Does conditional probability have or avoid a similar problem? Conditional probability may face a similar challenge, since any conditional probability can be rewritten as the ratio of the unconditional probabilities of a conjunction and of a conjunct, thus:

$$P(A/B) = P(A.B)/P(B)$$

However, while it may apply, I do not think the challenge holds water for either conditional probability or counterfactuals, and I suspect that to commit ourselves to its conclusion would be to disallow the analysis of any concept as a relation.

Suppose we wanted to analyze the concept of two objects being 'nearby' each other in a grid. This word means that their positions are very close as measured by the grid. Now, whether the two objects are nearby each other does depend on the absolute positions each stands at. But the concept of being nearby does not depend on what those positions are. Instead it depends on the magnitude of the difference between the coordinates of the one object and the coordinates of the other. Thus, to analyze the concept 'nearby' for this grid, we would state an equation for that difference and specify a cutoff (possibly vague) greater than which the difference does not allow the objects to count as nearby. There would be no further level of analysis at which we mentioned the absolute positions of these objects; to the extent those are needed, they are referred to in the equation that measures the difference between their positions. The concept 'nearby' is fully analyzed when we specify how to measure the spatial distance between two objects and a cutoff.

There are concepts of things that are relations, so the idea behind McGinn's objection cannot stand in its full generality. A tracking theorist thinks that knowledge is a special relation between a subject's belief and the way the world is, so will not be impressed with the objection from the getgo. But there is more to say. We have discussed enough examples to see that there is a vast range of types of categorical or unconditional facts that support or thwart fulfillment of the tracking conditions. While the view is quite stringent about what counts as knowledge, it is also exceedingly general, even more general than a view that focuses on causal relations. Facts about causes are parts of many chains of facts that support fulfillment of the tracking conditions, as with perception of objects, but those conditions do not have to be fulfilled by causal chains. The disposition a subject has to trust a witness's testimony can be well defined enough for the tracking conditions regardless of whether we think that trusting someone can be cashed out in a purely causal story, for example. The reason the tracking analysis stops where it does with relations between the subject's belief and the truth is that there is nothing general (and non-trivial) to be said about what all of the facts that support tracking relations have in common. It is in virtue of these special relations, and not primarily of the categorical or unconditional facts that support them, that a subject can be said to have knowledge, just as it is in virtue of the small difference between two positions, and not primarily of the positions themselves, that two objects can be said to be nearby each other.

Newspaper

There are a number of purported counterexamples to the original tracking view of knowledge which we can now see lose their sting on the new tracking view. Indeed, the new tracking view does not merely survive them, but handles them impressively. In a case due to Gilbert Harman, S believes the true report in a generally reliable newspaper that p: 'The dictator has been killed.' That paper carried the report only because of an enterprising journalist at the scene who saw the assassination, and whose report has been published verbatim. Due to machinations of the dead dictator's associates, televised news reports throughout the country have denied the assassination, falsely, but S does not see or hear about those reports. Everyone except S and the political conspirators who arranged the false reports has reacted by disbelieving p or suspending belief. S, who remained unaware of the false reports, continues to believe p (Harman 1973: 142–54; Nozick 1981: 177). Most people think that S does not know p. Yet it appears that Nozick's tracking conditions are fulfilled.

Nozick's treatment of this example was not satisfactory since in it he broke his own rule of holding the method fixed. He said that the key was that if S had seen those other reports she would have formed a false belief too or suspended belief, violating the adherence condition, but seeing the report she did was surely part of her method. At least, it was if we describe her method at the level of specificity that some other examples seem to require (Shope 1984: 37). As we know, my view does not have a rule fixing the method, so as long as none of my other rules fixes the method we can take advantage of the reply Nozick wanted to make. Indeed, even if we force the method to be fixed my view is going to give the correct verdict about whether the subject knows. A plausible way of forcing the method to be fixed would be to add to the example itself the idea that the subject is a recluse who never watches television, never listens to radio, and reads only the newspaper she actually read this time. Her reclusive disposition means that she will not be hearing people talking about other reports, her propensity to read only this newspaper will mean that she does not read other reports, and her aversion to television and radio will mean that she neither sees nor hears other reports. Still, it seems to me that her reading the true report does not give her knowledge that the dictator was killed.

The reason we do not think S knows in this example, whether she is dispositionally stuck on this one newspaper and nothing else or not, is that her connection to the truth is chancy. Her connection to the truth is chancy in the original case because she might have heard talk of those other reports, and not believed the dictator was killed, and because her own newspaper might have reported otherwise than it did, in which case she would not have believed the dictator was killed. Her connection to the truth is chancy in the case where she is a recluse because her own newspaper might too easily have issued a false report that the dictator was not killed. The basic source of excessive chanciness here is the fact that in a situation where a dictator was killed *any* news source, even a generally reliable one, has at least a 5 per cent chance of issuing a false denial that he was, withdrawing its assertion that he was, or reporting that it is unclear whether he was. The new tracking conditions expose this, using conditional probability in which many alternate scenarios are considered and criteria that tell us what is fixed and what varies when we evaluate the conditions. Condition III will behave similarly to (3) in Nozick's account and will not disqualify S from knowing that the dictator has been killed, but condition IV behaves better than (4) did.

In evaluating condition IV, we want to know what the subject is likely to believe given that the dictator was killed but things that are irrelevant to that, and things that are responsive to that, are allowed to vary, while lots of things about the subject's dispositions and so on are held the same. The fact that laws of nature and other regularities are held the same means in particular that the general reliability of all of the actual newspapers that are generally reliable is fixed at a high probability. How many newspapers there are is not fixed because whether the dictator was killed is irrelevant to it, but it is a rough regularity that communities big enough to have leaders referred to as 'dictators' have more than one newspaper. Also, it is a regularity that certain newspapers are delivered every day, so their availability is not left to chance.

Which paper she read (if more than one exists) is not going to be fixed unless she is supposed to have a disposition to read a particular paper, because without that disposition which newspaper she read is probabilistically irrelevant to whether the dictator was killed. Likewise, whether she talked to anyone about this matter will not be fixed unless she has a disposition to be reclusive (or the opposite), since it is roughly probabilistically irrelevant to whether the dictator was killed. We should suppose for the sake of argument that she does have a disposition to read some paper or other, since if she does not then it is too easy to have her fail the adherence condition. Also, for the same reason, our subject should be supposed to have a disposition to believe generally reliable newspapers that she reads and to be able to tell which these are.

There are other important matters that definitely are not fixed. Give the enterprising reporter of S's preferred newspaper a name, Fred, and adopt a name for the location where the assassination took place, Plaza Square, and say the assassination actually occurred at 2 p.m. sharp. If q = Fred was at Plaza Square at 2 p.m., then q does not fulfill criterion ** because it is roughly independent of whether the dictator was killed. That the newspaper in question had a reporter at the square at all might be fixed at its actual probability, if for example the rate at which this paper sends a reporter to events involving the dictator is a regularity. However, that it was the enterprising reporter Fred who was sent to cover the dictator-event is surely not a regularity. Not just because this doesn't sound plausible but if it were so, then our intuition that a person who reads the newspaper Fred works for doesn't know the dictator was killed tends to recede.

However, we can even allow Fred's presence and witnessing of the assassination to be fixed, and we will still get the verdict that the subject does not know. This is because what cannot be fixed is that Fred got back to his newspaper to deliver that eyewitness report of the event that he saw. The reason it cannot be fixed is that whether or not the dictator was killed matters a whole lot more to the probability that he gets his report back to his newspaper than whether he gets his report back to the newspaper matters to the probability that the dictator was killed. Thus this q fails criterion **. In evaluating condition IV we have that it is not fixed that this reporter gets back with his report, and it is fixed that our consumer subject on the other end is highly likely to believe what her newspaper says, and that if this reporter does not get back then the newspaper will in all probability do what a newspaper always does in such situations, namely, check the wires, and therefore it will print either a denial of the killing of the dictator or a statement of the unclarity on this matter. Given all this, in order to determine whether condition IV is fulfilled for the subject's belief that the dictator has been killed we ask whether the things that do get fixed allow for a scenario in which there is a probability greater than 5 per cent that Fred does not make it back with his report (before the printing of the edition of his paper that the subject reads).

This depends, of course, on what happens at the scene where the dictator is killed. Is it fixed that the conspirators immediately take steps to suppress information that he has been killed? This is not fixed, because the probability that the individuals in question do this is more affected by whether the dictator has been killed or not than the probability that the dictator has been killed depends on whether they do this or not. That is, this claim fails criterion **. This claim is not fixed, but some more general claims are because they are regularities. For example, there is a significant probability of information suppression after the assassination of a dictator as the assassins, or the dictator's henchmen, try to consolidate new power, or cling to old power. In a political power vacuum at the top the stakes are high and control of information is of obvious utility to anyone looking to fill the vacuum or to deny that it has opened.

Thus the antecedent p, the dictator was killed, of our conditional probability $P(b(p)/p)$ is going to have some tendency in all of the P_i to interfere with the flow of information. All we need in order to show that condition IV is violated is to show that there is a 5 per cent chance in one of the P_i that the information that p does not get through to S, and it seems to me we have that easily, for any paper she might care to read, and even if she has a disposition to read one in particular. It is even more likely that she doesn't believe p when p is true if she isn't a recluse and sometimes watches television or listens to radio, because then she has some probability of hearing about the other reports or the confusion (that have fairly high probabilities in at least one P_i). Remember, that she talks to anyone in particular, etc. is not fixed at its actual extremely low probability if she is not a recluse because these things are roughly probabilistically irrelevant to whether the dictator was killed. Even though S's belief that the dictator was killed is true, it is too tenuous to be knowledge, and tracking condition IV, using conditional probability and precise criteria of fixing and varying, tells us why.

Gumshoe and Tagalong

Another example benefits from the expansion of the set of alternative scenarios we check, this time in the variation condition rather than the adherence condition. This is Raymond Martin's Gumshoe and Tagalong, a pair of horses S is betting on at the race track (Martin 1983). S bets on Gumshoe to win in the first race and Tagalong to win in the second, in such a way that if she is right about either one or both she wins ten dollars. S doesn't watch the race and forms a belief about who won in a peculiar way: after the races she goes to the automatic teller, which can't give information about who won, and if she receives ten dollars then she believes p, that Gumshoe won in the first, and otherwise she believes that Gumshoe didn't win. It so happens that Gumshoe wins the first and Tagalong comes in last in the second, so S forms the belief that Gumshoe won, and this belief is true, but surely, one wants to say, it isn't knowledge. However, says Martin, Nozick's variation condition is fulfilled: if Gumshoe had not won the first then S would not believe that he had. This is true because the possible world closest to the actual world where Gumshoe doesn't win is one where only Gumshoe's winning has been changed. In that world, Tagalong comes in last just as he does in the actual world, the automatic teller does not give S ten dollars, and assuming S uses the method she actually uses S does not believe that Gumshoe won.

All this is true, but getting this example to work as Martin has is highly dependent on the practice of considering only one closest alternative scenario in which the believed proposition is false. Things are different if we look at all the reasonably probable alternate scenarios. These include Tagalong winning his race and Gumshoe not winning his, in which case if S uses her actual method then when the teller gives S ten dollars S acquires the false belief that Gumshoe won. It is obvious, I think, that it is precisely because S's belief isn't good against that scenario, in which Gumshoe doesn't win and Tagalong does, that we don't think S knows about Gumshoe even though her belief is true. Taking this alternative scenario into account is essentially why the new tracking view gives the right answer here. However, we need to proceed carefully since, as we know, the new view does not per se hold fixed which method the subject uses to form her belief, and that she uses the same method was assumed in the inference we just made about what the subject would believe in the scenario where Gumshoe loses but Tagalong wins. Also, we need to verify that the scenario I have said matters is among those that are probable enough to make an appropriate difference to fulfillment of the variation condition when we vary what the rules allow us to vary.

As it turns out, several things about the method through which S actually forms her belief in this case get fixed by the rules, not because they make up the method she actually uses but rather because they are probabilistically independent of p, the claim that Gumshoe won in the first, in the actual world, and therefore also independent of $-p$, the claim that Gumshoe didn't win.[7] One such q is that she places a bet that means she will win ten dollars if either Gumshoe wins in the first or Tagalong wins in the second or both. Another is that the teller gives no information about which horses won which races but only gives winnings, if any. Still another is that if she wins ten dollars then S believes that Gumshoe won in the first. S may have no strong disposition toward this mistake but only have made it in the actual case, but the facts that she did make it in the actual case, and that this claim is probabilistically independent of whether Gumshoe wins in the first in the actual world, mean that it gets fixed with probability 0.999 (or some such) in all the P_i we consider for the variation condition.

It remains to verify that the scenario in which Tagalong wins and Gumshoe loses is sufficiently probable to affect the verdict of condition III. The antecedent, $-p$, of condition III, $P(-b(p)/-p)$, has Gumshoe losing his race, so the question is whether q, Tagalong's loss in his race in the actual world, gets fixed or is allowed to vary. One might think that it would be fixed, because the outcomes of the two separate horse races are surely probabilistically independent. However, those two events are prob-

---

[7] These things are probabilistically independent of p even when we take into account, as we must, the fact that P_u assigns a very high probability to the claim that S won a particular bet involving Gumshoe. Interestingly, one can see my formulation of the tracking view as a generalization of Nozick's on the point of whether the method gets fixed, for on my view the method often will get fixed for the variation condition because many aspects of the method and the fact that it was used often will be probabilistically independent of p, and therefore of $-p$. Fixing the method was just an incorrectly specific description of why that should occur in many cases.

abilistically independent only if considered in isolation, and there is no isolation in the way the probability function P_u determines whether the outcome of Tagalong's race is independent of the outcome of Gumshoe's race. In the actual world S made and won a certain bet, Gumshoe won, and Tagalong lost. Thus all of these statements have probability roughly 0.999 according to P_u. These assignments contribute to the relevance relations that determine whether Tagalong's loss in the actual world fulfills criterion *.

As it turns out, Tagalong's loss, q, does not fulfill criterion *, as we can see from its failure in the second inequality. The probability that Tagalong won, −q, given that Gumshoe lost, −p, is roughly 0.999 because S won the bet so one of her horses won, while the probability that Tagalong won given that Gumshoe won is the same as it is in the actual world, nearly 0, because Gumshoe's winning combined with the bet that was won does nothing to improve the chances of a Tagalong win. Thus, the left-hand side of the second inequality in * is nearly 1. Since Gumshoe won in the actual world, $P_u(-p)$ is nearly 0, and whether Tagalong wins or not does nothing to affect that, even taking the won bet into account. Assuming Tagalong wins, the won bet does nothing to restrict Gumshoe from winning too, and a Tagalong loss forces a Gumshoe win, but that does not affect the probability that Gumshoe won since that was high on its own. Thus, the right-hand side of the second inequality in * is nearly 0. With left-hand side nearly 1 and right-hand side nearly 0 in the second inequality in *, q, Tagalong's loss, fails the criterion and is allowed to vary.

From here it is easy to verify that S does not know that Gumshoe won the first, because she fails condition III. For many of the P_i for which we ask after the value of $P_i(-b(p)/-p)$, Tagalong has a chance significantly greater than 5 per cent of winning his race assuming Gumshoe loses his. Thus, since for all of those P_i the chances of S believing Gumshoe won assuming that she won her bet is about 0.999, there are P_i for which $P_i(-b(p)/-p)$ is less than 0.95. S fails the variation condition in this case, just as we would expect. The status of this case as a counterexample to tracking was an artifact of the use of subjunctive conditionals to express the tracking view, which forced one to consider only the closest alternative scenarios instead of taking all but the least probable alternate scenarios into account as happens with conditional probability.

Judy and Trudy

Alvin Goldman (1986: 46) pointed out that the subjunctive conditional tracking view is more permissive than a view that requires the subject's belief to be good against relevant alternatives, and too permissive in general, and illustrated this with the case of the twins Judy and Trudy. The new tracking view corrects the permissiveness of the old tracking view in this case, just as it has in others, by requiring us to consider a greater number of possible scenarios.

In this case the subject Sam sees Judy from across the street and correctly concludes that it is Judy. But Judy has a twin and, says Goldman, '[a]s long as there is a serious possibility that the person across the street might have been Trudy rather than Judy (even if Sam does not realize this), we would deny that Sam knows.' The Nozickean tracking view does not deliver this verdict since if it weren't Judy across the street then it would be Judy's colleague who lost the coin toss Judy actually lost and had to fetch lunch in her place, or it would be no one, or it would be a stranger who got there at the time in question while Judy got there ten minutes later. In none of these cases would Sam believe it was Judy, so Sam fulfills the variation tracking condition on Nozick's account.

It is essential to maintaining the intuition that Sam does not know it is Judy that we suppose that the possibility that it was Trudy rather than Judy is what Goldman called 'serious'. If I found out that my friend had a twin who lived on a different continent, I would not come to doubt that I know that my friend is standing in front of me. Moreover, the seriousness that matters, it seems to me, should be cashed out in terms of probability; it is because it is so improbable that my friend's twin should pop up when he lives on another continent, that I continue in confidence that I know it is my friend in front of me. Thus, the situation that challenges the tracking view must be one in which we assume there is a significant probability that Trudy be the person across the street at the time and in the spot where Sam looks. Otherwise, our intuition that he does not know it is Judy collapses.

Now, whereas for a tracking view using subjunctive conditionals the possibility that it was Trudy has to be close or closest among the alternate possibilities in order for the subject to be required to be good against the possibility, on my view using conditional probability it need not be probable or the most probable among the possibilities in order to have the effect it should. This scenario need only have a slightly greater than 5 per cent probability in order to have the potential to affect the verdict of the variation condition since, we may assume, Sam cannot distinguish the twins visually from across the street so if Trudy is across the street instead of Judy that definitely will not stop him from believing it is Judy. The other ingredient to this scenario having the right effect is that the claim that Trudy is not across the street must not be fixed at its actual value of roughly 0.999, because then the possibility that it is Trudy if it is not Judy would not be able to get high enough in any P_i to matter when we inspect $P_i(-b(p)/-p)$.

The claim q that Trudy is not across the street is not fixed at its actual probability because this q violates criterion *. If we look at the left-hand side of the first inequality we see that it is nearly 1 since though the probability that Trudy is not there given that Judy is takes its actual value, roughly 0.999, the probability that Trudy is not there given that Judy is not is very low, because if Judy is not across the street there has to be something to account for the fact that Sam has Judy-like sensations, as P_u says it is very probable he does. On the right-hand side notice that the probability that Judy is not there given that Trudy is not there, $P_u(-p/q)$, is 0.001, because we judge by the actual scenario and in that scenario Judy is across the street. $P_u(-p/-q)$ is roughly 0.001 too, since if Trudy is across the street this will give Sam Trudy sensations he did not have in the actual world, but that need not take anything away from the claim that Judy is across the street or the Judy sensations Sam has in the actual world.

Now we can see that on the new tracking view this case does not fulfill the variation condition. All we need is that there be at least one P_i for which the probability that Trudy is across the street given that Judy is not has a probability greater than 0.05, for then $P_i(-b(p)/-p)$ will be 0.95 or less for that i. There is such a P_i, since Trudy's being across the street is not fixed at the minuscule probability that it has in P_u due to being false in the actual world, so the P_i take on all otherwise allowable values for the arguments q and $-$q. Thus, on the recursive tracking view Sam does not know Judy is across the street due to failure of the variation condition. Like so many others, this counterexample to a tracking view was an artifact of the formulation of that view in terms of subjunctive conditionals.

Barns and fakery

In influential examples presented by Saul Kripke, S is driving through the countryside in a place where there are both normal barns and barn façades put up by a clever stage builder (Lehrer 2000: 221). These façades are very well made and no one looking from the highway would be able to tell that any of them were not barns. S looks at what is in fact a barn and forms a belief that it is a barn, but surely, we would say, this is not knowledge. So far, the original tracking view looks good: even if what S was looking at while driving a given stretch of road was a barn, her belief that it was a barn does not seem like knowledge since there are all those fake barns around and she cannot tell the difference between fake ones and real ones. Conformably, Nozick's first tracking conditional is not fulfilled: if that were not a barn she might well still believe it was because the closest possible world in which it is not a barn looks to be one where it is a façade which she cannot distinguish from a barn. Condition III behaves analogously.

However, with Kripke's barns there are further details. In the color red there are both barns and barn façades in this region, but in blue there are only real barns, the prankster not having actually made any blue barn façades. S comes upon a blue barn, and believes from what she sees that there is a blue barn in front of her. Once again, says Kripke, her true belief is not knowledge, because S cannot tell a barn from a barn façade and there are barn façades around. However, as it seems, Nozick's tracking conditions check out: if that were not a blue barn S would not believe it was a blue barn, and if it were she would. The first checks out because there are not any blue barn façades, so the close worlds in which it is not a blue barn do not include any where the barn in question is a blue barn façade and thus do not include any S would mistake for a blue barn. They include worlds where it is a red barn or perhaps a red barn façade or nothing at all, but other possibilities are not close because of the prankster's decision not to make any blue façades in this region. Kripke apparently allows evaluation of the subjunctive conditional at more than one closest world, but scenarios with blue façades still do not make it in. In a further twist, Kripke points out that Nozick would have S knowing that there is a blue barn in front of her while at the same time still not knowing that there is a barn in front of her, since the fact remains that if it were not a barn, it could well be a barn façade, in which case she would believe it was a barn.

Things look different when we use condition III. The issue is just the same as in the Gumshoe and Tagalong case and the case of Judy and Trudy, and the rules for applying the new tracking conditions expressed as conditional probabilities eliminate the problem in the same way. The problem here, as there, is that the subjunctive conditional does not force us to consider sufficiently many alternate scenarios to the actual one, the scenario in which she would definitely believe the wrong thing is not considered, and thus the Nozickean tracking condition is fulfilled. The same does not happen with conditional probability and the rules of application developed here.

A lot of things about the actual situation described get fixed according to my rules. For example, that there are blue barns in the region (not counting this one) is fixed at probability roughly 0.999, because what relevance it and the claim that there is a blue barn in front of S have to each other is roughly equal in magnitude in the actual world, making the left-hand side and the right-hand side roughly equal for both inequalities in *. The same is true for the existence of red barns in the region. If q is the claim that there is a barn-façade-making prankster around, then the evaluation becomes slightly more complex. Since P_u assigns probability roughly 0.999 to the claim that there are red and blue barns around, the claim that there is a barn-façade-making prankster around is as likely if there is a blue barn in front of S or not from the point of view of what such a prankster may need for his trickery: the presence of the other barns is sufficient attraction if he needs it. However, in the actual world S has vivid sensations of a blue barn in front of her, so P_u assigns that claim probability roughly 0.999. This means that when we ask how likely it is that there is a prankster of the specified sort given that there is or is not a barn in front of her, and whether there is not a barn given that there is or is not a prankster, we must assume that her sensations are likely blue-barn-ish. This appears to make whether there is a blue barn in front of S and whether there is a barn-façade-making prankster in the vicinity probabilistically relevant to each other.

Whether there is a blue barn there, p, and whether there is a barn-façade-making prankster in the vicinity, q, are probabilistically relevant to each other because the subject has blue barn sensations. However, criterion * is concerned with the magnitude of the relevance in certain directions and is judged using the probability function of the actual world, P_u, which assigns probability roughly 0.999 to the claims that there is a blue barn there and that there is a barn-façade-making prankster around. Thus, consider the left-hand side of the first inequality in criterion *: though assuming that the subject has blue barn sensations, there not being a blue barn in front of her makes it likely that there is a barn-façade-making prankster about, the probability that such a prankster is about is already about 0.999 and cannot be made much higher since there are other logically possible explanations of the mismatch between her sensations and reality. Therefore, the left-hand side of the first inequality is nearly zero. The right-hand side is similar. $P_u(-p/q)$ will take its actual value of roughly 0.001, since the antecedent q is just as in the actual world—a prankster about—and so does not change p from its actual probability, roughly 0.999, which leaves $P_u(-p/q)$ at about 0.001. The term $P_u(-p/-q)$ is not significantly different from this, since though assuming the subject has blue barn sensations and that there is not a prankster around makes it likely that there is a blue barn, it is already extremely likely that there is a blue barn there, so $P_u(-p/-q)$ could be less than 0.001 but not by much. The left-hand side and right-hand side of the first inequality are roughly the same. The second inequality is also fulfilled, which can be seen by similar considerations. So it is going to be fixed that there is a barn-façade-making prankster about.

However, it will not be fixed that he made or did not make any blue barn façades, so the criterion dictates. $P_u(q)$, for q the proposition that he did not make any blue barn façades, is roughly 0.999, because he actually didn't. But while $P_u(q/p)$ takes roughly the very high actual probability of q because the antecedent p is true in the actual world, $P_u(q/-p)$ is significantly different from $P_u(q)$. Since the subject has blue barn sensations, assuming that there is not a blue barn in front of her makes it pretty likely that the prankster made a blue barn façade and put it in the spot in front of her, though that is not what he actually did. This makes the left-hand side of the first inequality middling to high. The right-hand side is not zero but it is lower than the left-hand side. This is because the probability that there is no blue barn in front of the subject is not a great deal different from 0.001 whether the prankster made a blue barn façade in this area or not. The existence of at least one blue barn façade in the area makes the non-existence of a blue barn in front of the subject marginally more likely than it would be if the blue façade didn't exist since it provides a competing explanation for her blue barn sensations. But this difference is not as great as the difference that the existence or not of a blue barn makes to whether there is a blue façade, assuming the subject has blue barn sensations. Thus, it is not fixed (for condition III) that the prankster made no blue barn façades, since this proposition fails criterion *.

With these things in mind, we can see that S fails to know that there is a blue barn in front of her by failing condition III. Since it is not fixed that the barn-façade-making prankster made no blue façades, the P_i of which we ask whether the variation condition is fulfilled take the whole range of possible values for the probability that he made at least one blue barn façade, that are consistent with the probabilities of other claims that are fixed. Thus, for at least one P_i for which we ask after the value of $P_i(-b(p)/-p)$ there is a greater than 5 per cent chance given that there is no blue barn where the subject is looking that the prankster made a blue barn façade on that spot. Since for all the probability functions under consideration the chances of S believing that it is a blue barn given that it is a cleverly made blue barn façade are about 0.999, there are P_i for which $P_i(-b(p)/-p)$ is below 0.95, and S does not know it is a blue barn before her. And, of course, the other problem Kripke highlighted, in which on Nozick's view she might know it was a blue barn without knowing it was a barn, does not arise for us since the closure under known implication that recursive tracking has means that if (contrary to the described case) she did know it was a blue barn, it would be very easy also to know it was a barn because that implication is obvious.

Dumb luck and blind luck

As standardly described, the Kripke barns are no problem for the recursive tracking view. However, one could rig the blue barn example further to have the effect Kripke intended. In the terms of my view this would require a change in the story that would fix the claim that the prankster did not make any blue façades.[8] This could be achieved

---

[8] This amounts to considering a challenge Jonathan Schaffer has put to me this way: what if it were a *deep nomological fact* that there were no blue façades around?

by supposing that the actual prankster has a deep aversion to using blue in any fakery he performs. (Perhaps he thinks the color is sacred or something of this sort.) This deep aversion fixes the claim that there are no blue façades around, as can be verified using criterion *, because P_u gives the probability roughly 0.999 to the claim that the prankster has a deep aversion to faking with blue. It then follows that there are no P_i among the ones whose values of $P_i(-b(p)/-p)$ we consider for condition III for which a scenario with no blue barn in the relevant spot but a blue barn façade instead gets a probability greater than 0.05, since for all the P_i the probability is roughly 0.999 that the prankster did not make any blue fakes. This forces us to say that the subject fulfills condition III—in scenarios with no blue barn she also does not believe there is a blue barn—and thus that she knows there is a blue barn in front of her.

Before commenting on whether we should be impressed with this case, I would like to describe other examples of the same phenomenon some of which are more realistic. The best case, I think, arises when we imagine the Gumshoe and Tagalong case with a twist the subject is not aware of and has no thoughts about. We imagine that the jockey who is riding Tagalong has been paid to throw the race, that is, to make sure the horse he is riding loses. Those who have paid or coerced him to do this will profit handsomely since they've done this rigging for all of the horses in that race except one, and bet accordingly. In these circumstances what our subject S does to form her belief about whether Gumshoe won is good against any scenario with a non-negligible probability. She bet that one or both of Gumshoe and Tagalong would win their races, and if she wins her bet then she believes that Gumshoe won. But this will always get her the right belief because it does not just so happen that Tagalong loses; Tagalong will lose no matter what. If this is our story then the recursive tracking view must count the subject as knowing that Gumshoe won even though she used the strange method, because Tagalong's losing gets fixed at its actual extremely high probability.[9]

This case is more interesting than the blue barn case or even the souped-up blue barn case not only because it is more realistic, but also because it shows an advantage of justificationist views that the barn cases do not show. The subject looking at the blue barn who, recall, is unaware of any façades round about, not only knows that it is a blue barn by the Nozickean tracking view. She is also justified in believing that it is a blue barn by an internalist standard, and it is a blue barn. These things make the case one of knowledge by traditional internalist lights. We can soup up the blue barn case so that there could not easily be blue fakes around, and this will make my tracking view count the case as one of knowledge. But this souped-up version will also present a problem for one who strengthens an internalist justification criterion for knowledge with an indefeasibility clause, one who says that in order to be knowledge a belief must be not just justified but justified in such a way that there are no facts that would defeat the justification were the subject to become aware of them. It is well known that such a clause must be made weaker than what I just reported so as not to count misleading or

---

[9] This is because whether or not the jockey throws the race makes a great deal of difference to whether Gumshoe won, assuming, as P_u reflects, that S bet on Gumshoe or Tagalong and won, whereas whether Gumshoe won or not makes little difference to whether or not the jockey threw the race even assuming S bet as she did and won. This means that criterion * is fulfilled for q that the jockey throws the race.

defeated counter-evidence that the subject does not possess as a destroyer of knowledge (Harman 1973).

What this means for the case at hand is that while the fact that there is a barn-
façade-making prankster about is a defeater of the subject's justification for believing
there is a blue barn in front of her, in the souped-up version this defeater is defeated by
the fact that the prankster would never make a blue fake. The existence of the barn-
façade-maker is evidence the subject does not possess against her belief that it is a blue
barn in front of her, but it is misleading evidence of the sort that an indefeasibility
view must rule out of account in general. Because of this such a view must count the
subject in the souped-up barn example as knowing there is a blue barn in front of her,
just as my view does. Thus, the blue barn cases present no comparative disadvantage
for my view over an internalist justificationist view. A case I discussed in Chapter 1 is
similar, where the subject believes a convincing and perfectly countercompetent
testifier who unfailingly tries to lie. Many aspects of the process through which the
subject comes to believe the testifier are defeaters of justification for so believing,
though they are not things she is aware of. However, those things are themselves
defeated by other perfectly compensating aspects of the situation, so they cannot
count against the indefeasibility of the subject's justification.

The case of Gumshoe and Tagalong looks potentially more threatening, since while
my view cannot disqualify the souped-up version of this case from being knowledge,
the (internalist) justificationist about knowledge can say that our subject lacks
knowledge because she lacks justification. That you won a bet that either Gumshoe
or Tagalong would win is obviously not a justification for believing that Gumshoe
won by anyone's standard. This could become a justification if rigging of the Tagalong
race was cited in addition, but that fact is not available to the subject to be part of her
reason for believing what she does.

Another case from Goldman (1986: 46) is similar, where the subject walks by a
smiling man on the street and because of the smile comes to believe correctly that the
man just won the lottery. We may suppose that this man is a peculiar person who
would never smile unless he won the lottery, so if the man had not won the lottery he
would not be smiling and our subject wouldn't believe the man had won the lottery.
Thus our subject fulfills the original tracking variation condition. The perfect relationship between the man's smiling and his lottery winning is fixed on my tracking
view, because it is a regularity.[10] And, to cut to the chase, this means that the subject
fulfills the new condition III as well. Our subject counts as knowing the man won the
lottery on the new tracking view as well as on the old. However, it is easy to see
intuitively that the subject has no justification for her belief that the man won the
lottery; no fact she is responsive to makes his smile a sufficient reason to believe he
won the lottery. So, the traditional internalist justificationist can declare our subject
unknowing because unjustified. These cases are more threatening than the souped-up

---

[10] This would have been fixed anyway by criterion *, since probabilistically it matters more to his
not winning the lottery (assuming, as in the actual world, that he smiled) than does his winning the
lottery or not matter to his having this peculiar disposition (on the same assumption).

barn case because they represent a serious difference between the traditional view and recursive tracking in which it looks as if the former has the advantage.

However, this apparent advantage is largely neutralized, I think, once we appreciate the bigger picture of things the recursive tracking view has to say about such cases. It is true that our intuitions feel something out of place in saying that the subjects in these cases know, but that sense that something is wrong is sufficiently vague that it is accommodated by the many things the recursive tracking view also says are wrong with these cases. For example, one could never rationally adopt smile inspection as a forward-looking strategy or plan for gaining knowledge of which people won the lottery because it would not regularly succeed due to the fact that real people do not restrict their smiles to such circumstances. But the recursive tracking view says nothing to suggest that this would be a good plan for gaining knowledge. It only says that if you are lucky enough to run into a man who never smiles except after he has won the lottery, and you are dumb enough to take his smile to mean he won the lottery even though you don't know about his smile behavior, then you do in fact know he won the lottery.

'Dumb enough' is a crucial part of this description, for the recursive tracking view can describe a problem at the reflective level in these cases of dumb luck, and if the subject reflected she would see it too, and probably be cured of her first-level belief and thereby lose her knowledge. The problem is this: though in these cases the subject's belief tracks the truth, the subject does not track that she tracks. That is, she does not have a belief that she tracks that tracks the fact that she tracks. In the terms of our cases, though the subject's belief tracks the fact that Gumshoe won due to the happy coincidence of her mistake and a rigged race, she does not track the fact that her belief tracks the truth. Indeed, if she reflected at all on the information available to her she likely would conclude that her first-level belief does not track the truth. Likewise, though it so happens that the second subject's belief that the man won the lottery tracks the fact that he did because of a strange property of the man's disposition to smile, this subject does not track the fact that her belief tracks that truth. In fact, if she reflected on the information available to her she would think that it does *not* track that truth.

It is essential to these cases of dumb luck that the subject does not reflect, and that the second-order tracking level is not just missing, but if it were there, as it easily could be because the subject has the information for it, it would be out of synch with the first level because the subject would believe she *did not* track. In cases of knowledge that we consider normal the second level is not so badly out of synch with the first level. For example, in a simple successful case of perceptual knowledge the subject not only tracks the flower pot in front of her but also to some extent tracks the fact that she tracks: if her perceptual organs were not working normally then in the normal ways that could happen she would have some indication of that and not trust them; and if they were working she would trust them. Externalist views famously have the property of its not being automatic if one knows that one also knows that one knows, and both tracking views conform to this; one need not so much as have a belief about whether one tracks in order to track the truth. However, one can track while not tracking that one tracks without the two levels being out of synch. The second level may just not exist since the subject does not have enough information for it. In the dumb luck cases the subject has enough information to see that her first-level belief does not track but does not use this information, and this is why we disapprove of counting her as knowing.

Tracking at the second level, which is accessible to the subject herself only by reflection though can be operative without reflection, performs a valuable service to tracking at the first level (knowledge) when it is present since it acts as a doublecheck. Belief that does not have this second-level tracking can still be knowledge, but we expect people to use judgments about second-level tracking when they have the information for it because this is a doublecheck, and we are organisms capable of second-level tracking and inclined habitually to do it to some extent without even thinking about it. Second-level tracking is a doublecheck to the extent that we are inclined to harken to negative verdicts at the second level by giving up the relevant belief at the first level. This is why it strikes us as strange to call the dumb luck cases knowledge: we are not likely to get knowledge this way because in these cases our habitual second-level tracking mechanisms would have a good chance of putting a stop to the initial belief. We are responsive to the fact that the ways the subjects in these cases form their beliefs are not generally ways to form beliefs that track the truth. We track that beliefs formed in these ways do not generally track, and we expect any knower to recognize the same.

I associate a subject's tracking that her belief tracks the truth with that belief's being justified—see Appendix 1.1—and though I have not developed the suggestion in this book one of its consequences is of interest here. If a belief's being justified is a matter of its bearer tracking that the belief tracks the truth, then we can agree with the internalist that the dumb luck cases involve beliefs that are not justified. Where we disagree in our verdicts then, is only as to whether the lack of justification automatically disqualifies a belief from being knowledge. I say, as I have above, that there can be knowledge without justification, and must also admit that these are examples of it. The contingent fact that we have mechanisms that tend to prevent us gaining knowledge in this way is enough to account for our intuitive misgivings about counting these as cases of knowledge.

The new tracking view has less that is damning to say about the earlier cases of lucky knowledge that seemed initially less threatening, but what it does have to say is to my mind enough. These were the souped-up barn case and the case of the convincing but perfectly countercompetent and 'lying' testifier, cases in which the traditional internalist could not declare the belief unjustified and so, like a tracking view, could not declare a lack of knowledge. In these cases the subject tracks the truth but does not track that she tracks, roughly because she is not responsive to what is really happening in the process through which she comes to her belief. For example, one way the subject who believes the testifier could fail to track is if the testifier's countercompetence was sufficiently imperfect, meaning that he had a significant number of true beliefs and thus could easily testify to a falsehood. There is no reason to think that his having true beliefs (leading to false testimony) would diminish his convincingness, though, which is the only thing about the process of her belief formation to which the subject is responsive.

However, in these cases the subject also does not have enough information to see that she does not track that her belief tracks the truth, even by reflection; things are abnormal in ways she is not aware of. This means that we cannot say, as we did of the recent dumb luck cases, that if she had just reflected that would have put a stop to her initial belief. That would imply that the case we entertain is radically unlike cases most familiar to us, which is sufficient to explain our surprise at the verdict that it is knowledge. We cannot say this, and we might say that the reason is these cases of lucky knowledge are not so much dumb as blind.

Nevertheless, there are two negative things the new tracking account can say about this knowledge by blind luck. First, just as with the dumb luck cases, my suggestion about what justification is means that these beliefs are not justified because the subject does not track that she tracks, even though she does track. This is interesting because it is a place where this imagined externalist account of justification imposes a higher standard than the traditional internalist view of justification does; these subjects do not have access to enough information to see that they ought not hold to their beliefs, but my externalist criterion for justification does not excuse them where an internalist standard would.

The second negative thing about these cases is that whereas the processes through which the subjects form their beliefs in the dumb luck cases could not be endorsed as a sound policy or plan for gaining knowledge because they would generally fail, the processes through which the subjects in the blind luck cases gain their beliefs could not even be a (non-trivial) policy or plan for gaining knowledge. This is because to recognize that one is in one of these situations which will, as it happens, lead by blind luck to a knowing belief is ipso facto not to be in such a situation because one is not blind. And to recognize that one is in a situation that *might* lead to a knowing belief by blind luck, is simply to recognize a situation that one is always in, a complicated world about which one doesn't know everything.

Compulsive Mr Nogot

Compulsions and aversions are powerful tools by which the epistemologist can try to imagine cases that satisfy externalist criteria for knowledge requiring regularities in the relations between facts and beliefs about those facts but which we feel strange calling knowledge. Of course, the result is usually cases that we feel strange about in general. But the exercise has the valuable point of highlighting issues about dumb luck that I have just addressed. The case I will now discuss, involving a Mr Nogot with a compulsion to get people to believe true propositions through fake evidence, stands separate from the dumb luck cases because I do not think it succeeds in tricking the tracking conditions into counting the beliefs he induces as knowledge. It stands separate from the other cases above because the issue with this example is not that subjunctive conditional tracking conditions fail to deliver the right verdict where conditional probability tracking conditions succeed—I think both formulations succeed—but rather that commentators on this case have failed to appreciate the full implications of the compulsion they are imagining. We might say the lesson here is: be careful what you wish for.

Mr Nogot and Mr Havit are in S's office. Mr Havit owns a Ford while Mr Nogot does not. But what Nogot does have is a special compulsion: to trick people into believing true things by giving them fake evidence. Nogot knows that Havit owns a Ford, and Nogot goes through a sham presentation of things like a fake title that are evidence that he, Nogot, owns a Ford. In this way he gets S to believe that p, 'Someone in the office owns a Ford,' by inferring it from the true existential generalization: 'Someone in the office has presented evidence that he owns a Ford.'[11] If p were not true then S would not believe it, we are told, because Nogot would not have gone through the charade. (He has no other reason to trick S.) And if p were true, then S would believe it, we are told, because it is no simple matter to change Nogot's compulsion. Thus it looks like S's belief that p is knowledge on Nozick's tracking account (Shope 1984: 38–9). Yet, surely, it is not knowledge.

It goes without saying that Nogot is a strange person, but Nogot is strange in more ways than have been noticed, and these are pertinent to whether his behavior counts against tracking. For notice that although the goal of his compulsion is to get people to believe true things, he has to make them believe a lot of false things along the way to that goal. For example, S will likely believe that Nogot owns a Ford, even if she does not make an inference from this belief, since it is implausible that S believes only statements involving the indeterminate 'someone' as she goes about her inferences. This is especially so using my criterion of belief that p which does not require a thought that p but only appropriate commitment. (See Chapter 2.) S will also believe that she has seen the title to Nogot's Ford, and S will believe that Nogot has been reliable in the past, which he cannot have been if he has had this unchangeable compulsion leaving so many false beliefs in its wake. S believes lots of false things by Nogot's influence, along with that one true proposition: 'Someone in the office owns a Ford.'

The reason why all of these false beliefs matter is related to what makes us intuitively think that S does not know. We think S does not know because her belief that p, though true, is dependent on the behavior of tricky Mr Nogot. There is something too chancy about getting a true belief from an experience with Nogot, though it is hard to say why because his compulsion is set up so carefully. It is suggested by the example that what Nogot did to S could not vary, because his compulsion is not easily changed. However, this is a mistaken impression, since without changing his compulsion we can imagine him doing a variety of things with the materials he has on hand. For example, he could have taken it as a goal to get S to believe the true proposition that no one in the office is on his way to the Ford mechanic, by inferring it from the false proposition that no one in the office owns a Ford (and the suggestion that no one would go to the Ford mechanic unless he did). Nothing about the compulsion to make people believe true propositions on the basis of fake evidence dictates which propositions will be singled out for true belief, and which will be all those false propositions the victim needs to believe in order to infer

---

[11] The unrealistic inference the example has S making here is set up this way in order to produce a Gettier example that gets around the solution to Gettier problems via Harman's Principle P, which allows one to gain knowledge by reasoning only if all intermediate conclusions are true. The implications of new tracking for principle P were discussed in Chapter 2.

the true ones. The fact that Nogot has to induce false beliefs in his victim in order to induce one true belief makes whether any given belief he induces in you is true a chancy matter.

To see why these facts about his compulsion matter to whether the subject tracks the truth consider the key things that are fixed and vary in our evaluation of tracking condition IV for this case. It is fixed that Nogot will trick someone into believing a true proposition by fake evidence because this compulsion of his is a regularity. It is fixed that S is in the office in question because that is what the rule demands. It is also fixed that this is a habitual place for Nogot to be because that is a regularity. (If it isn't, then it is implausible that S believes him because he is then a stranger who pops in to mount a gratuitous display of argumentation to the effect that someone owns a certain type of car, which is suspicious.) With all of these things fixed, it is fixed at a fairly high probability that S falls victim to Nogot. (If she doesn't then she fails the adherence condition anyway since she otherwise has nothing to go on—if she did the Nogot case would not work as it is supposed to—so assuming she formed a belief, which the adherence condition does assume, she has excellent chances of forming the wrong one.)

Crucially, what is not fixed is which proposition Nogot decides to play his trick with. 'Someone in the office owns a Ford' was chosen for misleading in the actual case, but criterion ** does not allow us to fix that. (Nor does *.) To see this note that the left-hand side of the first inequality is significant, since whether or not it is true that someone in the office owns a Ford makes a big difference to whether this proposition is chosen for misleading. This is because the compulsion demands that those propositions chosen for misleading be true. However, the right-hand side of that inequality is not significant since the probability is high in the actual world that someone in the office owns a Ford regardless of whether this proposition was chosen for trickery.

With this in mind it is clear that our subject does not fulfill the adherence condition for p. For there is an i for which $P_i(b(p)/p)$ is not greater than 0.95, because there is a probability function that assigns a high probability to the claim that Nogot chooses a different true proposition to play tricks with. It cannot be, after all, that he does not know any other (true) propositions since if he didn't he wouldn't be very functional at all, and still less skillful at elaborate displays of misleading evidence. That function will then also assign a significant probability to our subject's not believing that someone in the office owns a Ford, because she is fixed as forming a belief on the matter but now with no input at all, so she could as easily believe that no one in the office owns a Ford (and let us assume she is point-consistent).

There is probably an i for which $P_i(b(-p)/p)$ is greater than 0.05 for a different reason, because there is a P_i which assigns a significant probability to the claim that Nogot chooses for his trickery the claim that no one is on his way to the Ford mechanic. The probability is high for all P_i, given that he so chose, that he will present false evidence that no one in the office owns a Ford, since that is a perfect candidate false proposition to play a supporting role in getting the subject to believe that no one in the office is on his way to the Ford mechanic. Both of the foregoing sets of assignments are allowed because Nogot's compulsion, but not which proposition he uses it on, was fixed in the evaluation. Fixed though it is, that compulsion does not determine, or even probabilify, which true proposition it will be acted out on, and hence which false propositions get believed.

It is hard to show that the variation condition fails without helping oneself to invented facts that are not given, or given as known by Nogot, in the original scenario. But though in the example we are given little for Nogot to work with, real life would probably present Nogot with quite a lot to work with, and therefore quite a lot of different possibilities for which true beliefs, and hence which false beliefs, he was going to induce in S. The fact that he chose the ones he did is entirely too chancy, and this corresponds to the fact that it could have been otherwise in a probable alternate scenario. Some versions of this example stipulate that Mr Nogot actually has no other easy trick to play on S which accords with his compulsion, but this is not a matter that is open to stipulation. Anyone who was smart enough to do the trick Nogot actually did will be capable of imagining the alternative trick I described, and anyone with Nogot's capacities walks into that office knowing a lot of propositions to make tricks with.

A question remains about the possibility that Nogot's compulsion is confined to a single proposition, p. He goes around trying to make people believe that one true proposition on the basis of fake evidence, but with other propositions he behaves normally. In this case the recursive tracking view says that S knows p if she becomes a victim of Nogot's compulsion with respect to p, since everything is the same as it was above, but there is no probable scenario under which Nogot would have varied by making S not believe p or believe −p. But this is a case of blind luck of the sort discussed in the previous section and, though counting it as knowledge, the new tracking view has some disapproving things to say about it.

Conjunctions

Worries have been raised for Nozick's view about cheap knowledge of conjunctions. If I know p and do not know q, then, intuitively, I do not know p.q. But what if were that conjunction to be false it would be p that went false? Then, using Nozick's account, because I do know p and therefore track p I wouldn't believe p if p were false, and so I wouldn't believe the conjunction if it were false either. It follows then that as long as I believe the conjunction of p and q I know that conjunction even though, as we assumed, I do not know q. And isn't this problem exacerbated on a recursive account, since I can deduce q from p.q, and thereby be counted as knowing q when I did nothing to achieve this status?[12]

The first thing to say about this challenge is that the problem once again trades on the fact that the subjunctive conditional does not force us to consider as many alternate scenarios as conditional probability does. In particular, in order to rig this example with subjunctive conditionals it is enough to say that p's being false is the possibility first in line if the conjunction of p and q is false. This is far from enough with conditional probability where in order for scenarios in which q is false to be out

---

[12] I am grateful to an anonymous reader of the manuscript for alerting me to this problem.

of consideration when we judge whether the subject tracks the conjunction p.q it must be that $P(-q/-(p.q))$ is less than 0.05. The only easy ways I can see for this to happen are if either p is a necessary falsehood or q is a necessary truth. If p were a necessary falsehood that would ruin the example, since it is supposed to be that the subject knows p.q and falsehoods cannot be known. So it must be that q is a necessary truth, or at least it is true in some very sturdy sort of way.

It must be that p is actually true, because otherwise the tracking view would not count the subject as knowing the conjunction of p and q as we are supposing it does. Going further, in order for the subject to know the conjunction in the way that the example trades on she must track the conjunction, which includes fulfillment of the adherence condition. Therefore, $P(b(p.q)/(p.q))$ must be high. Since p is actually true, this implies that $P(b(q)/q)$ is high too, and thus (presuming her consistency) that the subject fulfills the adherence condition for q. The assumption is that the subject does not know q, and this can be so only by her not tracking q because she has to believe q and it has to be true in order for her to know the conjunction of p and q, on the tracking view or any other. However, we just saw that the subject must fulfill the adherence condition for q in order to know the conjunction p.q, so it must be the variation condition that the subject does not fulfill when we say, in line with a tracking view, that she does not know q.

In the initial challenge it looked like a subject could be counted by a tracking view as having knowledge of an arbitrary q just by conjoining that q with a p she knew whose falsehood was closer to the actual world than the falsehood of q was. However, not only does the subject have to fulfill the adherence condition for q in order for this gambit to work, but also on the new tracking view the q in question needs to be close to being a necessary truth. If q is close to being a necessary truth and the subject's only failing is that in a circumstance where q is false there is a greater than 5 per cent chance that she believes q, there will be almost no circumstance in which she has the wrong belief behavior towards q because there is hardly a circumstance in which q is false. In fact, she has no greater chance of having the wrong belief about q than she would have if she did fulfill the variation condition. This is altogether less impressive than the imagined problem with which we began.

There is a little dumb luck in any such example, but it has the same saving quality as we saw with the smiling lottery winner case and the case where Tagalong's race was thrown: reflection should have prevented her from having this belief in q. In this case, of course, first-level tracking of q is not quite happening. But the reason we can be sure that the subject does not track whether her belief in q tracks the truth is that if she did reflect on the only information we are supposing she has she would also conclude that she does not track q, and, if she was rational, that she ought not to believe q. We know that q is close to being a necessary truth, and therefore that failing the variation condition won't get her into any more trouble than if she fulfilled it. But there is no information we are supposing she has which could tell her that. Therefore, if she reflected on what she had she would likely not believe q. Since we are supposing she does believe q her second-level tracking mechanisms are not working. These facts account for our discomfort in counting her as knowing. Dumb luck is dumb, and our normal mechanisms for knowing insure that we do not usually know this way because we do not normally hold onto such beliefs due to our responsiveness to the improbability in general that such a strategy would bring knowledge, an improbability that the tracking view of knowledge can explain.

Causal overdetermination

Nozick touted his view of knowledge over the causal view that he was generalizing, on the basis of his view's superiority in dealing with difficult cases of causal overdetermination. In these cases more than one set of causes is actually efficacious in bringing it about that the subject believes p but one of the sets of causes is a good way of coming to know while the other is not and the subject would be moved by the bad set of causes, and not by the good set, if, contrary to fact, p were false. The classic case of this, first discussed by D. M. Armstrong (1973: 209), is the father who truly believes that his son is innocent of a crime of which he has been accused and believes this both on the basis of faith in his son and on the basis of the outcome of a well-conducted trial, but would have followed his faith had the trial's outcome been different. Since in the actual world the trial was a cause of the man's belief, and since a well-conducted trial is causally connected in the right sort of way to the fact of the defendant's innocence, the causal view of knowledge must count the father as knowing. But our intuitions tell us he does not know. A counterfactual (sensitivity) view has an obvious advantage here— if the son had not been innocent the father would still have believed that he was—but the way that Nozick actually got his view to give the right verdict depended on the relativization of his view to method. Since I have discarded the relativization to method, have I also ruined the verdicts in such cases?

Far from ruining the verdicts in these cases, not relativizing to method makes them easier to get. Getting the right verdicts should have been easy, but relativizing to method put a stumbling block in the way since the relativization said that all methods actually used must be fixed in the evaluation of the conditions. This meant that the good method got fixed too, even though the subject wouldn't have trusted it if it gave the answer he didn't want to hear. This forced Nozick to add an additional criterion to the analysis that determined whether the subject had knowledge by performing the evaluation on the method that *outweighed* (or at least was not outweighed by) the other methods actually used. A full explication was not given of what counts as outweighing but, ironically, the idea has a counterfactual flavor since intuitively, roughly, a method outweighs another if the subject would use it even in non-actual situations where he would not use the other.

When we discard the relativization to method, we can also discard the extra notion of outweighing because the tracking conditions using conditional probability pick up on that outweighing phenomenon without any special help, as long as we do not thwart them from considering which method the subject relies on in non-actual situations by stipulating that the methods are fixed at whatever they actually are. What condition III does with the case of the father is a good model. Notice that if q = 'The father believes concerning his son's innocence what the outcome of the trial tells him,' criterion * does not fix q. When p = 'the son is innocent,' q is not probabilistically independent of −p because if the son is not innocent the trial is likely to have a guilty verdict, in which case q will be false, whereas q is true when p is true. Indeed, whether the son is innocent or not matters a lot more to the probability that the father trusts the outcome of the trial than does whether the father has a disposition to trust the trial or not matter to the probability that the son is not innocent. Thus, q fails criterion * and does not get fixed in the evaluation of condition III. q' = 'The father follows his faith in his son' does get fixed because it is probabilistically independent of whether or not his son is innocent, by stipulation in the example.

Now the verdict is clear, since there is at least one i for which $P_i(b(p).-p) > 0.5$, meaning that there is at least one i for which $P_i(-b(p)/-p)$ is not greater than 0.95. To find such an i choose any of the probability functions that assign a high probability to the trial giving a verdict that matches the truth. Thus, the father fails to know because he fails condition III. This is just as we expect the evaluation to go intuitively. Nozick had reasons for relativizing to method, since not doing so made his view too strong in certain classes of examples. However, we have dealt with those examples in a different way, through the deductive closure imposed by the recursion clause. (See 'Jesse James and method' in Chapter 2.) It is a good thing too, since not relativizing to method simplifies the evaluation of cases of multiple methods, streamlining the analysis to appeal to as few independent concepts as possible.

2. KNOWLEDGE OF THE FUTURE

In Chapter 2 I explained how closure under known implication allows us to avoid appealing to backtracking counterfactuals to explain how we can know, for example, that the ice cubes left outside in the heat but not since inspected have probably melted. We know lots of generalizations, I said, because we track them, and we know that their instances follow deductively. Therefore, we know the instances. In particular, ice cubes left in heat for hours generally melt, and those I left outside are an instance of this. However, Nozick needed backtracking counterfactuals for other kinds of examples too, and might I not know that those particular ice cubes have melted from other instances, without going through the generalization?

Both kinds of worries can be addressed now that we have gone more carefully into the rules of application for the variation condition and adherence condition expressed in terms of conditional probability. Our knowledge of the future will provide a nice illustration because of the obvious usefulness in this case of backtracking counterfactuals. In order to know that the sun will rise tomorrow (on the original tracking view) we must fulfill the variation condition that says if it were not going to rise tomorrow we wouldn't believe it was. But in order for that to be true we would have to be able to expect some indication *now* of the sun's impending change of course for tomorrow. And in order to be able to expect that, a backtracking counterfactual would have to be true: if the sun were not going to rise tomorrow, then there would be some indication of this today (or before today). Unlike the backtracking counterfactual about the ice cubes, this claim seems to be true, so the original tracking view can explain our knowledge that the sun will rise tomorrow.

The new tracking view, of course, has available the mechanism of knowing an instance by knowing that it follows from a generalization we know. In this case, the generalization is that (in the current era) the sun rises roughly every twenty-four hours by the clock, and we track this. But surely, one might say, we can also know that the sun will rise tomorrow by doing enumerative induction from the instances we have seen or had other evidence of to the next instance, bypassing the generalization. So the question arises whether the new tracking view has something like the backtracking counterfactual to support an explanation of knowledge so acquired.

The tracking conditions expressed in terms of conditional probability can support this explanation, because where appropriate conditional probability allows for something like backtracking. This is not because there is a special provision for cases in which the consequent of the conditional probability statement precedes the antecedent in time. Rather, it is because probabilistic relevance makes no special provision for a temporal ordering at all. A is positively probabilistically relevant to B just in case A's being true makes B more likely than it would otherwise be, regardless of whether A is supposed to precede B or vice versa. And B may be probable or improbable given A regardless of the temporal ordering of the two. For example, it is very probable given that our subject in the Gumshoe and Tagalong case collected ten dollars from the cashier that either Gumshoe won or Tagalong won or both although that collection occurred after the races and also had no role in bringing about the races' outcomes. Although probability can be used to illuminate the asymmetries of causation and of time because the latter orderings leave traces in probabilistic relations, probability is more general and is not limited by these orderings.

If the ice cubes left outside for hours in the summer did not melt, that could have been due to a variety of quite mundane events. The nosy neighbor lady might have seen the poor abandoned ice cubes, scooped them up, and put them in her own freezer for safe keeping. The rabble-rousing teenage neighbor boy might have taken them to add to the collection of ice that was cooling his illegal keg of beer; packed with all the other ice, these cubes would take much longer to melt. And so on. This is essentially why when sitting inside the house we don't track that the ice cubes melted: there are ways they could have failed to melt that have a probability greater than 5 per cent assuming they did not melt, which would have given us no indication of their not melting as we sat indoors.

If the sun didn't rise tomorrow, by contrast, there would not be a mundane explanation for this. Something big would have happened. The only way we can suppose that the sun could fail to rise tomorrow without our having some indication today is by supposing that the big thing that made the sun not rise could fairly easily happen suddenly, without any precursors. Big things can happen suddenly and without precursors (we know of) in nature; earthquakes are an example. But all of the likely ways that the sun could fail to come up on our horizon through natural causes would have precursors we could see indications of. For example, the sun becoming a red giant will be a somewhat gradual process visible from the earth as the sun's color changes and the orbits of the planets decay. The supernova transformation is quick, but our sun is not heavy enough to become a supernova. One might protest that when one attributes to oneself knowledge that the sun will rise tomorrow it is not because one thinks of the fact that the sun will not supernova, for one did not even know that the sun will not supernova until one read it here. Be that as it may, one is in touch with the stability facts I am referring to, because one is in touch through long experience with the fact that the local heavens are stable and the changes that do occur tend to happen either daily or seasonally, or gradually and by decay. Appreciation of that stability plays a role in our willingness to attribute knowledge to ourselves in this case.

There are two ways I can think of for the sun failing to rise tomorrow to be so without precursors we would respond to, and both are non-natural. One is a man-made explosion of a magnitude to knock the earth out of its orbit. There would be precursors of this in the plans of the executors, of course, but these are not precursors we would have access to. The other way for the sun to fail to rise without precursors is an act of God not in the insurance sense but in the literal sense, an intervention that broke natural law and instantaneously changed the orbits of the earth and sun. Neither of these possibilities has a probability of greater than 5 per cent assuming the sun does fail to rise tomorrow, it seems to me. For the first this is because of the magnitude of explosion required to change the earth's orbit significantly. The second seems implausible even for theists since it looks capricious.

However, the exception proves the rule, for if you did think that either of these had a probability of greater than 5 per cent given that the sun doesn't rise tomorrow, then it seems to me you ought to lose the intuition that you now know the sun will rise tomorrow. If the way it would happen were it to happen has a significant probability to be something with no warning whatsoever, then why should you think that you now know it is not going to happen tomorrow morning? If a security expert had reason to worry that all of the nuclear weapons on earth could be detonated in a single spot, then I think he would also lose his confidence that he knows the sun will rise tomorrow. And in some religious traditions—varieties of Islam and Quakerism come to mind—practitioners show their humble acceptance that the future is in God's hands in every way by adding to declarations about the future the phrase 'if God wills it'. This it seems to me is also a broadcast saying that they do not claim to *know* the future.

It is overwhelmingly likely, it seems to me, assuming that the sun does not rise tomorrow, that there are precursors of this. The sun not rising brings about, and hence requires, changes not only in that regularity but in many others. It is because of our sense of this, and because other big changes in the heavens haven't come, that we think we know that the sun will rise tomorrow. When we evaluate condition III for this case all of the regularities about the heavens are fixed like other regularities. But, remember, what this means is that they have probability roughly 0.999 according to all of the P_i that are under consideration in evaluating $P_i(-b(p)/-p)$. It does not mean that their probabilities conditional on $-p$ are 0.999, because 0.999 is not an inert, extreme probability but is malleable if the right sort of antecedent comes along. The sun not rising tomorrow is the right kind of antecedent for changing the probabilities of many regularities about the heavens today because the sun not rising tomorrow pretty much requires such changes if it is to happen naturally. Thus conditional probability, with the rules of application I have described, behaves in such a way as to allow backtracking when it should, as in cases of knowledge of the future.

The new tracking view performs impressively in a vast range of cases of empirical knowledge, and has an answer for all of the cases that were supposed to have presented trouble for a tracking view. In our detailed development of the account of knowledge on offer it remains to see how the new tracking view should understand knowledge of logical and other necessary truths, which I discuss at the end of the next chapter. It occurs there as a natural part of a discussion of the advantages of tracking over other views.

4

Tracking over the Rivals

The recursive tracking view is not only attractive in its own right, but also demonstrably superior to process reliabilism, neighborhood reliabilist ('safety') views, and relevant alternatives views. In my estimation, the generality problem that faces the process reliabilist approach to knowledge is deep and unsolvable. I have shown above, in Chapter 3, how the recursive tracking view solves its analogous problem, and this represents one way in which the new tracking view is superior to process reliabilism. Other disadvantages of process reliabilism will show up below in discussion of reflective knowledge and of explanations of the power property. The first main topic I will treat in this chapter is the rivalry between the two counterfactual approaches to knowledge, those using the notion of sensitivity (tracking views) and those using the property of safety to distinguish knowledge from mere true belief. The second major topic of this chapter is the advantage of recursive tracking over relevant alternatives views, which is especially visible in the former's more successful treatment of lottery propositions. Finally I will present a novel account of knowledge of logical and other necessary truths, building from the account of knowledge of implication given in Chapter 2 (whose rules of application will be detailed here). Logical and other necessary truths present a problem for externalist views, and for tracking views in light of (either version of) the variation condition, but there is a very attractive solution for the new tracking view.

For a belief to fulfill a sensitivity criterion, in the terms these matters are commonly discussed in, it must be that if it were not true the subject would not believe it. A belief is safe when it could not easily be false, that is, the belief is not false in a neighborhood of possible worlds around the actual world. There are three important areas where sensitivity (or its probabilistic counterpart) succeeds and safety (or its probabilistic counterpart) fails as the extra ingredient required for knowledge. The first is that safety views have while the new sensitivity view lacks a problem accounting for reflective, or higher-level, knowledge (Vogel 2000). Process reliabilism succumbs to this same problem. Secondly, as I will argue here, safety gets the direction of fit wrong in its picture of knowledge as a relation between a subject and the world. Finally, the fact that neither safety nor sensitivity implies the other property leads to the impression that we must choose between the two. However, there is no trade-off of the sort imagined. As I will show, in the domain of true belief sensitivity is strictly stronger than safety, and if we choose sensitivity we more or less get safety for free. The same is not true in reverse; the safety property does not bring sensitivity with it in the domain of true belief. Thus, as long as it causes no other problems, as I have endeavored to show in this book so far that the new use of a new sensitivity property does not, we should prefer sensitivity to safety in our account of knowledge.

Sensitivity and safety: higher-level knowledge

Many epistemologists attracted to a counterfactual view of knowledge have in recent times flown to the notion of safety over that of sensitivity; whereas a sensitive belief wouldn't be believed if it weren't true, a safe belief wouldn't easily be false if it were believed. Safety has been attractive because it allows the Moorean response to skepticism, and does not have the not-falsely-believing and other problems associated with tracking (Sosa 1999*a*). I have shown in Chapter 2 that these areas do not present any problem for recursive tracking, that is, to a recursive use of a suitable sensitivity property, but this amounts to arguing safety theorists to a draw. Why should one jump ship?

There are good answers to this question. First, I take seriously the difficulties Vogel has presented for all kinds of reliabilism in accounting for reflective knowledge (Vogel 2000). Avoiding attributing to us too little or too much of this kind of knowledge seems to me a challenge any externalist view must squarely face. However, the argument Vogel presents against a sensitivity criterion will not get any traction against recursive tracking, because the kind of case he presents can be handled in the same way as the problem of not falsely believing treated in Chapter 2. His second argument, which is aimed against process reliabilism and what he calls 'neighborhood reliabilism' and others call 'safety', is trenchant, but no example of the sort he presents can be constructed in the recursive tracking view.

Imagine that you have a friend Omar who is a straightforward, trustworthy, and competent fellow, and one day you notice a shine at his feet that suggests that he has new shoes. You ask Omar: Are those new shoes? Omar replies: Why, yes, they are. Obviously, you now know that Omar has new shoes. And you know more besides. You know, for example, that your belief that Omar has new shoes is not false. Presumably, you know that your belief that Omar has new shoes is true. However, if we take sensitivity as a necessary condition for knowledge then we cannot render these obvious verdicts. For notice that if your belief that your belief that Omar has new shoes is not false *were* false, then you would probably believe that it is true. This is because an alternative scenario in which everything is as it actually is except that your belief that Omar has new shoes is false is a scenario in which you believe that Omar has new shoes. Believing both q and that your belief that q is false is paradoxical and difficult to imagine psychologically. The upshot is that even though you track the fact that Omar has new shoes you do not track the fact that you do not believe this falsely. The original tracking view has you knowing p while denying you the reflective knowledge that your belief that p is not false. It also denies you knowledge that your belief that p is true, since the same argument can be run for 'true' as we just did for 'not false.'

The problem here, as we saw in Chapter 2, stems from the lack of closure in the original tracking view of knowledge. For notice the peculiar fact that though the original tracking view denies you knowledge that your belief that Omar has new shoes is true, it grants you knowledge of the deductively stronger claim that you know that you know that Omar has new shoes.[1] This claim is deductively stronger because knowing implies believing truly, though not vice versa. Thus, because you know that you know that Omar has new shoes, and you have knowledge of trivial implications, you also know that you do not believe this falsely. You know that you know that Omar has new shoes because you track the fact. (You also Nozick-know it.) On the new formulation: with the reasonably probable ways for you not to know that Omar has new shoes, you are likely aware of that, and do not believe that you know that Omar has new shoes. Alternatively, you may know that your belief that Omar has new shoes is not false because you track the equivalence schema for the statement 'Omar has new shoes'—'Omar has new shoes' is true if and only if Omar has new shoes—and the equivalence schema plus the statement itself imply that your belief is not false, which you know. The tracking criteria do not deny us all reflective knowledge, and the obvious remedy for the problem that they deny us some is the closure that recursive tracking incorporates. Thus, recursive tracking does not have Vogel's first problem with reflective knowledge.

Where Vogel's first argument showed that the original tracking view was too strong because it excluded us from higher-level knowledge that we have, his second argument indicts the other types of externalist view for being too weak because they count us as having higher-level knowledge that we do not have. The worry is that these views have nothing to say that would be grounds for disqualifying a patently circular bootstrapping argument from giving knowledge. Consider Vogel's example, in which S is driving a car. We suppose that though S believes what her gas gauge says, and though her gas gauge is in fact reliable, S neither knows nor has any reason to believe that her gas gauge is reliable. She has never given a thought to it, and has never received any assurance of it. Now suppose that S engages in the following peculiar steps of reasoning. She looks at the gauge, forms a belief that the gauge says 'F', where F means that the tank is full, on that basis forms a belief that F, and conjoins these two beliefs. So, S believes that 'F and the gauge says "F",' and it becomes obvious to her that this implies that the gauge was accurate this time. She does this whole sequence repeatedly, and by induction over these many instances concludes that the gas gauge is reliable (Vogel 2000: 612–14).

It is obvious that S's belief so formed that the gas gauge is reliable is not knowledge, because she has no source for the belief that the gauge is reliable, or the beliefs that it was accurate on given occasions, except the gauge itself. She has parlayed beliefs based upon nothing except what the gauge says into a belief that the gauge is reliable, and this has to be illegitimate by anyone's intuitive standards. However, process reliabilist and safety views cannot render this verdict. Reliability of the process through which the belief was formed is the extra ingredient that a true belief needs to qualify as knowledge on the process reliabilist account. Because S's perception that the gauge says 'F' goes by a reliable process, and her gauge is in fact reliable, the true beliefs she

---

[1] Vogel expected the opposite when he wrote: 'Thus, it [tracking] also seems to exclude your knowing that any of your beliefs is reliable, or that any of your beliefs is knowledge. That is going far too far, in my book' (Vogel 2000: 611).

forms that the gauge says 'F' and that F are knowledge on that reliabilist account. Conjunction of two reliable beliefs does not in general yield a reliable belief, because each conjunct may be just barely above the reliability threshold. However, we may assume that each conjunct is well above that threshold in our case, from which it follows that the conjunction of her two knowing beliefs is also knowledge. Valid deduction is a (conditionally) reliable process if ever there was one, so S's true belief that the gauge was accurate this time is also knowledge. And we cannot object to her doing induction over these instances to come to her belief that the gauge is reliable, since if we did we would have to disqualify as unreliable a good portion of the inferences we typically use to get knowledge. There is no getting around the conclusion that S knows her gauge is reliable on the process reliabilist account of knowledge.[2]

A similarly devastating conclusion follows on the safety view, according to which what is needed for knowledge in addition to true belief is that the belief be one which could not easily be false. On Vogel's helpful characterization of safety, a safe belief is one that turns out to be true when it is held in a neighborhood of worlds not too far away from the actual world. S's belief that the gauge says 'F' is one which would be true in all nearby worlds, and the fact that her gauge is reliable means that her belief in F could not easily be false, so these two beliefs are knowledge. Conjunction of these two safe beliefs will also be safe, and so also be knowledge. S's true belief that the gauge was accurate this time is also knowledge since it is true in any of the worlds in which the conjunction is true. And once again we cannot object that S's inductive conclusion that the gauge is reliable is not safe enough for knowledge without disqualifying many more other examples than we otherwise would; the problem with that inference is not that the belief it yields is not safe. All of the steps S engaged in generated or preserved safety, yet her conclusion is not knowledge.

Tracking handles this type of example as if it was designed for it, as Vogel acknowledges (Vogel 2000: 615). The steps of S's procedure that are deductive— conjunction and the inference from 'F and the gauge says "F" ' to 'the gauge was accurate this time'—cannot be objectionable to recursive tracking, which allows that knowledge is preserved by deduction. However, neither deduction nor known implication is used in the other steps, so in order to be knowledge the beliefs S arrives at must meet the stricter standard of fulfilling the tracking conditions. S does this in her first steps: her perception is assumed normal so if the gauge did not read 'F' then she would not believe it did, and the gauge is assumed reliable so, presumably, if the tank were not full then it would not read 'F', and S would not believe that F. The adherence condition is fulfilled in both cases as well, and the conditional probability formulation gives the same answers. That she tracks these facts is consonant with our willingness to attribute to her knowledge of them.[3]

---

[2] The process reliabilist might protest that circular reasoning is not a reliable process. However, that is only the form of an answer. He would still need to supply an account of what a circular argument is, and do so in a purely externalist way. Remarkably, the tracking conditions tend to disqualify circular reasoning from yielding knowing belief without making special provisions, as we will see below.

[3] One might feel unhappy with the consequence of recursive tracking that says that this S knows the gauge was accurate this time, on the basis of her beliefs that F and that the gauge reads 'F', because

However, S's conclusion that the gauge is reliable manifestly fails to be knowledge on the recursive tracking view because that belief fails to track the truth. If the gauge were not reliable, then she might well believe it was, because she is not sufficiently disposed to check any other source of information about the state of the gas tank than the gauge whose reliability is in question and there is nothing to prompt her to. The same is true on the conditional probability formulation. Vogel's first argument played backup in his exposition, ensuring that though tracking escapes the second argument it is nevertheless not a viable form of externalism as regards questions about higher-level knowledge. Since the first argument causes no trouble for recursive tracking, this view remains unscathed by Vogel's important objections to externalism. Thus, recursive tracking is still standing in the face of problems that appear to me to make these other popular forms of externalism unrevivable.

In my opinion it is not a small matter that recursive tracking has a solution to its generality problem and escapes problems with higher-level knowledge, and that other externalisms fail on these scores. This is because these problems are not nit-picking or superficial but go to the heart of the challenges that pretty much inevitably follow on the move to externalism about knowledge. Externalism makes having knowledge a matter of a subject's factual relation to facts rather than a matter of a subject's awareness of facts and their relations. In so doing it becomes unmoored from any specification of the level of description of the relevant facts and must supply a substitute mooring. The internalist does not have this problem because her view is moored to a particular level of description by the fact that the belief whose knowledge status is in question has a particular level of description, the things which must be appropriately related to that belief are other (potential) beliefs, and rationality constraints decide whether the relation among the actual beliefs is appropriate. The fact that on an internalist view the supporting statements must be rationally related in certain ways to the knowing belief that they support fixes the appropriate level of generality of description that supporting beliefs must possess. Similarly, given that basically externalism says that knowledge need not be reflective we should not be surprised that such views have trouble accounting for those cases where it is. We should not be lenient when externalism fails to address the generality problem and problems about higher-level knowledge, because these are the challenges one chooses in the move to externalism, and they are problems the internalist never had. Such challenges keep alive the question whether the move to externalism was worth it at all. If we think it was, then we have to answer them.

Sensitivity and safety: direction of fit

My main intuitive objection to safety as what decides whether a true belief is knowledge is that it gets the direction of fit wrong for what knowledge is. Though

the former belief was based on the reading of the gauge itself. However, that can only be because one does not really believe that she knows F. (Otherwise, one thinks that we have here a counterexample to closure, which is doubtful.) The only ground on which one might think that she does not know F is the basic internalist intuition that one must always be aware of the reasons why one has a right to one's belief. This complaint would beg the question against externalism.

we want safe rather than unsafe beliefs, safety is surely not what makes a true belief knowledge, since knowledge is a matter of responsiveness to the way the world is and safety makes a demand in the opposite direction. I will begin to explain this somewhat uncharitably, since this helps to make the worry as clear as possible. Suppose the safety theorist is right that the appropriate extra criterion for knowledge of p is that $b(p) \rightarrow$ p, which ordinarily is read 'If S believed p then p would be true' (Sosa 1999*a*, 1999*b*).[4] Then imagine a case where S has a fairy godmother, whose special mode of operation is instantaneously to make true anything that S believes. If so, then for this S, for any p, if S believed p it would be true. This seems a happy scenario for S (although cf. King Midas), but it is surely not knowledge. This is so despite the fact that the fairy godmother guarantees that all of S's beliefs are safe.

It is illuminating to compare the analogous kind of case for sensitivity. The fairy godmother in this case looks at how the world is, and, directly or indirectly, affects S's belief-forming mechanisms. The fairy's activity is a node in the sequence that produces S's beliefs that makes sure for every p that if it weren't true then S wouldn't believe it and if it were true she would (except, possibly, when the belief is arrived at by known implication). If we formulate what the fairy does in terms of conditional probability, then my view is committed to accepting that this S has knowledge, and I do not regard this as objectionable, revealing, I suppose, my gut externalist instincts. This kind of case is analogous to cases of knowledge that we possess and encounter every day in the sense that many of the connections that run between the way the world is and our knowing beliefs about it are connections that we neither produced nor are aware of, and some are connections that we are merely lucky to obtain. That is a fact of life that we must accept, and sensitivity's fairy godmother is simply a vivid illustration of it.[5] What sensitivity gets right, even in this most extreme case, is that knowledge is a form of responsiveness to the world, and not a form of legislation.

I have drawn the challenge to safety as severely as possible, by choosing the formulation of the safety criterion that is most conducive to it. To my ear the formulations used by R. M. Sainsbury (1997) and Williamson (2000) support this challenge. They say that for my belief to be safe it must be that I 'couldn't easily have been wrong' and that I 'could not easily have falsely believed p,' respectively. Our subject with a fairy godmother instantaneously bringing about the truth of all of her beliefs surely satisfies these. It is similar in Vogel's 'neighborhood' formulation, where my belief should be something that would be true in all of the worlds in a neighborhood close by the actual world in which I believe it. Since I have a fairy godmother in the actual world, I would seem to have her in the close worlds too—not having her would be a big change. Or, in other words, my belief that is true in the actual world due to the fairy godmother is likely true in all very similar worlds.

---

[4] It is clear in Sosa (1999*a*) that he does not intend his '$b(p) \rightarrow$ p' to be read in the standard way, with '$\rightarrow$' the sign for a subjunctive conditional, $b(p)$ as antecedent, and p as consequent. I deal with the way he uses '$b(p) \rightarrow$ p' below.

[5] My response to the turned-on hologram projector (Nozick 1981; Shope 1984) is similar: this is knowledge. In this case a projector is set up just right for fulfilling the tracking conditions concerning a vase right behind the panel that you don't see in the normal way. This is another case of the blind luck discussed in Chapter 3.

However, Sosa has another formulation that he uses more frequently, and which seems to make a difference: S would not have held p without p's being true. This seems usefully false in the safety form of the fairy godmother case, since with the fairy godmother S might easily have believed something that *was* false, which then became true (thanks to the fairy godmother) as she decided to believe it. Sosa's subjunctive conditional seems to have a temporal dimension which makes the difference, though possibly because it has imported a bit of sensitivity. One natural reading of the sentence 'S would not have held p without p's being true' is the claim that if p weren't true then S wouldn't believe it. It is clear that Sosa does not intend his formulation to be equivalent to the sensitivity criterion $-p \rightarrow -b(p)$, but it is unclear how it should be written in the formalism of subjunctive conditionals if not as $b(p) \rightarrow p$, which led to the problem above.[6] In the language of conditional probability the obvious way to express safety would be as the requirement that $P(p/b(p))$ should be high, but this too brings with it the consequence that the subject with a safety fairy godmother has knowledge. At the very least, the safety position needs to be defined more rigorously, in order to show that it escapes this awkward consequence. Of course, on the basis of the other failures of safety discussed in this chapter, I personally do not think further refinement is worth the effort.

Sensitivity and safety: no trade-off

It is a familiar fact that neither sensitivity nor safety implies the other property. For a proposition that fulfills the sensitivity criterion but would not be a safe belief consider an obvious necessary falsehood. If it were false then one would not believe it because one would never believe it. Yet if one were to believe it, it could so easily be false that it is not possible for it to be otherwise. One may also have a safe belief that is not sensitive. Consider your belief, above, that your belief that Omar has new shoes is true. This is a safe belief because in all the nearby worlds in which you believe it, it is true that your belief that Omar has new shoes is true. However, this belief is not sensitive because if it were false that your belief that Omar has new shoes is true, you would still likely believe this statement. The same mutual lack of implication holds if sensitivity and safety are expressed not by subjunctive conditionals but instead via conditional probability, as I will express these properties below.

Let us admit, without making any commitment to either as a necessary condition for knowledge, that both sensitivity and safety are nice properties for a knowing belief to have. They strike us intuitively as good things, at first blush, even though each runs into trouble when taken alone as the sole extra necessary condition for knowledge. The ideal theory of knowledge, then, would have something of both of these properties rather than choosing one of them and excluding the other. The fact that there are cases of sensitivity without safety and safety without sensitivity tells us that

---

[6] Sosa (1999*b*) defends and clarifies the safety view further, but I do not see there clarification of this particular point. The clearest discussion of the intended counterfactuals seems to me Vogel's discussion of 'neighborhood' reliabilism (Vogel 2000). Sosa (1999*b*) also has to appeal to reliable processes to defend safety in the end, and such a move faces the unsolved generality problem as well as the problem of reflective knowledge above.

these two properties are not logically equivalent, but does not tell us anything about the kinds of cases in which we have one and not the other and whether those cases matter. When we look at this latter question we will find that there is an important asymmetry that is reason to prefer sensitivity to safety in an account of knowledge, because in the domain where it matters sensitivity brings safety along with it whereas the reverse is not true. Another way to say this is that the propositions which if S were to believe them would be sensitive but not safe are different in character from the propositions which if S were to believe them would be safe but not sensitive.

First consider the way in which sensitivity and safety are expressed in the terms of conditional probability. Returning to the shorthand expressions, a belief q is sensitive if and only if:

$$P(-b(q)/-q) > 0.95$$

while belief q is safe if and only if:

$$P(q/b(q)) > 0.95$$

I have set the thresholds somewhat severely. The point I am about to discuss remains if they are set somewhat lower or higher. It is not necessary that the two thresholds are the same to have the result I will describe, but having it so means that we are treating the two concepts fairly, rather than comparing a severe version of one property with a lenient version of the other. High $P(q/b(q))$ is a good way to probabilize the notion of safety because this strictly correlational statement says that the truth of q strongly tends to come along with the subject's belief in q; the truth of q tends to be present when S believes q. The probabilistic safety criterion does not say or require that S's belief *makes* q true, although as with the formulation of safety in terms of subjunctive conditionals such a case would make the safety probability high.

The sensitivity and safety probabilities have a definite relationship within probability theory, from which we can see in general the features of the cases where these two properties differ. (See Appendix 4.1.) This relationship can be written in either of the following two ways depending on convenience:

$$P(-b(q)/-q) = 1 - P(b(q))/P(-q)[1 - P(q/b(q))]$$
$$P(q/b(q)) = 1 - P(-q)/P(b(q))[1 - P(-b(q)/-q)]$$

The first equation gives us the sensitivity probability in terms of the safety probability and other factors. The second gives us the safety probability in terms of the sensitivity probability and other factors. Call the ratio

$$P(b(q))/P(-q)$$

'C', and call the ratio

$$P(-q)/P(b(q))$$

'D'. These ratios can be thought of as coupling constants between sensitivity and safety. Now, it follows from these equations that if our S and q are such that belief in q would be safe but not sensitive, then the coupling constant C is greater than 1. It also follows that if our S and q are such that belief in q would be sensitive but not safe, then the coupling constant D is greater than 1. This is all under the assumption that we evaluate these probabilities according to the rules of application for the tracking conditionals discussed in Chapter 3. For example, the actual fact, as it may be, that S believes p and that p is true are not assumed as background or fixed in the evaluation. Neither are their negations. Otherwise every true belief would be safe and every believed proposition would be insensitive, rendering the notions of safety and sensitivity useless.

The values of these coupling constants under the specified conditions tell us a lot about the examples where the sensitivity and safety properties are each present in the absence of the other. Consider first the kinds of examples where $D > 1$, that is, where belief in q would be sensitive but not safe. There are three possibilities:

$$P(-q) > 0.5 \text{ and } P(b(q)) > 0.5,$$
$$P(-q) < 0.5 \text{ and } P(b(q)) < 0.5, \text{ or}$$
$$P(-q) > 0.5 \text{ and } P(b(q)) < 0.5.$$

In the first and third possibilities, q is more likely than not to be false, and so, if believed, is more likely than not to be disqualified from being knowledge before we even get to the sensitivity and safety criteria. In the third possibility, in addition, q is not likely to be believed, and so is likely not to count as knowledge, again, before we even consider the sensitivity and safety criteria. In the second case, though q is more likely than not to be true, it is not likely to be believed, and so is not likely to be in the running for qualifying as a knowing belief.

Thus, with sensitivity all possibilities are covered, in the following sense. If we were to take sensitivity as a necessary condition for knowledge, then the true beliefs we would be counting as knowing beliefs would more likely than not also be safe. This follows from the fact that all of the beliefs that could be sensitive without being safe are more likely than not to be disqualified from being knowledge on other grounds, either of their falsehood or of their not being believed, or both. The same trend we see when asking what is more likely than not is continued when we ask what happens at the limit: because sensitivity without safety means $D > 1$, and the latter means $P(-q) > P(b(q))$, the more likely the subject is to believe p the more likely p is to be false, all the way to the limit. A sensitive but not safe belief is likely not to be knowledge on grounds of the belief's falsehood.

A look at the coupling constant for safety without sensitivity does not give the same assurances. If $C > 1$, then the following assignments are possible:

$$P(b(q)) > 0.5 \text{ and } P(-q) > 0.5,$$
$$P(b(q)) < 0.5 \text{ and } P(-q) < 0.5, \text{ or}$$
$$P(b(q)) > 0.5 \text{ and } P(-q) < 0.5.$$

In the first case, though one is more likely than not to believe q it is also more likely than not to be false, and hence one's belief in it is more likely than not to be disqualified from counting as knowledge before we get to the sensitivity and safety criteria. In the second case, although q is more likely than not to be true, one is less likely than not to believe it, and thus it is not likely to count as knowledge because the latter requires true belief.

The third possibility is not so reassuring. These are q which are more likely than not to be true, and more likely than not to be believed, so the only criteria that are likely to have a chance to disqualify them from being knowledge are the safety and sensitivity criteria. But by our assumptions these are cases in which belief in q would be safe but not sensitive. Thus, the safety criterion will have to count as knowledge many in a class of cases that are not sensitive. The limit phenomena are equally unsettling: for a safe but not sensitive belief $C > 1$, that is, $P(b(q))$ is greater than $P(-q)$. The more likely q is to be true the closer $P(-q)$ gets to zero, and under the $C > 1$ condition this allows for the probability that the subject believes p to take any value. There is not enough tendency against a true safe belief that is not sensitive, as there is against a true sensitive belief that is not safe. What sensitivity does for all classes of cases safety does only for some: in the domain of true beliefs, having the sensitivity property gives uniform (probabilistic) assurances that the belief also has the safety property whereas safety does not give the same assurances about sensitivity.

In fairness it is important to note that some of those cases of true beliefs that are safe but not sensitive have a right to count as knowledge. The case of your true belief above that your belief that Omar has new shoes is true, is a case of knowledge and a belief which is safe but not sensitive. As is now familiar, an unadulterated sensitivity criterion unjustly leaves out this kind of case. (Other such examples are discussed in Chapter 2.) The recursive tracking view puts these cases back in to the set of knowing beliefs by means of known implication. If all cases of safe but not sensitive beliefs were like this, then the safety view and a view with sensitivity plus deductive closure would pick out roughly the same set of cases as knowledge, and what we would have discovered is that there are two different ways of imagining (roughly) the same set.

However, this is clearly not so. These cases which strike us as knowledge are not the only kind of case in that set of safe but not sensitive true beliefs. Consider, for example, the belief above ('Higher-level knowledge') about the reliability of the gas gauge that our subject formed by an obviously question-begging bootstrapping procedure. That belief was safe but not sensitive, and also was obviously not knowledge. Unfortunately, a safety criterion cannot disqualify it. We might have hoped that the only examples of true beliefs that were safe but not sensitive were cases that intuitively count as knowledge, and that a sensitivity view needs to scramble to put back in to the set of knowing beliefs. The probabilistic relationships I have displayed do not rule out that possibility, but the gas gauge example does. Thus, choosing a safety criterion means having a view of knowledge that is patently too weak, whereas if we choose a sensitivity criterion with deductive closure we have uniform, though probabilistic, assurances of getting safety for free.

Why knowledge brings power

In the first chapter I conjectured that the reason knowledge brings us a capacity to make technological progress is that it brings us an ability to maintain a true belief about a matter over time and changing circumstances, and explained how taking knowledge to be due to the fulfillment of tracking conditions explains the latter ability directly. Not all knowledge has the power property on my view, since some knowledge comes by known implication from beliefs that track the truth and known implication does not preserve tracking. But when knowledge does have the power property it is due to the fact that the belief in question tracks the truth, and when it doesn't have the power property it is nevertheless implied by a belief that does. Externalist views of knowledge will naturally be superior to internalist views in explaining the power property because whereas for knowledge the internalist demands of the way the world is only a match between a truth and the content of the belief about it, the externalist demands in addition a relationship of some sort in the world between the truth and the fact that the correct content about it is believed. However, externalist views are not equally suited to explaining the power property.

As the safety fairy godmother makes plain, the safety view would be good at explaining why power of a certain sort brought knowledge if it did. But power of the fairy godmother's sort does not bring knowledge; one would not know p in virtue of the fact, if it was one, that if you were to believe p the fairy godmother would make it true. The direction of fit between the subject's belief and the world in the safety view is wrong for explaining why knowledge brings power, and we can see this more clearly by considering the asymmetry between the properties of sensitivity and safety in the domain of true belief discussed in the previous section. The sensitivity property of a knowing belief explains the subject's ability to maintain a true belief about that matter through time and changing circumstances, but if all we require for a true belief to be knowledge is that it has the safety property then according to the arguments of the previous section we have no uniform assurance at all that the belief will have the sensitivity property, because safety does not generally bring sensitivity with it. What the safety property does bring gives us no guidance as to what the subject would believe were the world to change because this property is concerned with the opposite direction of fit.

Process reliabilism is better at explaining the power property of knowledge because in demanding that a knowing belief be formed by a generally reliable process it demands that the belief be formed by a process that would give a true belief most of the time. A process couldn't do this if it didn't have some responsiveness to the way the world is. This gives some assurance that the subject has an ability to form the correct belief about the matter in a wider range of circumstances than just this occasion. However, it is worth noting the inferiority of this to the explanation that the new tracking view provides, even though the difference is subtle. The fact that a subject formed a belief by a generally reliable process on a given occasion does assure us that she has the ability on that occasion to form a knowing belief about the matter in a variety of circumstances, but gives us no assurance at all of her ability or disposition to form beliefs by that or another reliable process on other occasions in other circumstances. One can imagine a subject with normal sense organs who nevertheless has very little disposition to use them to form her beliefs; instead, say, she has a strong tendency to fabricate things to believe. At a certain minute of a certain day she uses her sense organs and comes to believe in the normal way that there is a table in front of her (which there is). Such occasions happen only once in a while, though, and are followed by periods of fabrication.

I do not see how the process reliabilist can deny that the belief the subject formed in the normal way when looking at the table was knowledge, since the process she used was reliable and there was no other reliable or conditionally reliable process available to her that would have resulted in her not believing that there was a table in front of her. There is some intuition supporting this judgment, but not one we can indulge in if we want an account of knowledge to explain why knowledge is power. Granted, the process reliabilist can deny that the subject has knowledge subsequently if, say, she later believes there is a table by fabrication. However, that this subject may not have knowledge at a later time is not the factor relevant to whether process reliabilism can explain the power property of knowledge. To explain the power property, it must be that having knowledge at a given time tends to give one power at later times due to an ability to maintain a true belief about the matter that is gained at the time, and due to the fact, that one does have knowledge. I don't see how we can explain this by process reliabilism, because having knowledge of p in the process reliabilist way imposes no requirement at all that one have a tendency to use the reliable process one actually used, or any other reliable process, in future wrestling with the matter of p, as the case of the habitual fabricator illustrates.

Fulfilling the new tracking conditions, by contrast, does mean fulfilling demands on one's future tendency to use good processes of belief formation because it puts demands on every tendency you have that is relevant to whether, for example, you can be expected to believe p in likely situations in which p is false. You must have a tendency to use a good process of belief formation, and not merely actually have used one, because the new tracking conditions are not relativized to the method the subject actually used, so the method the subject actually used is not per se fixed in the evaluation of what she has a tendency to believe about the matter in question. Thus, as an explanation of the power property of knowledge Nozick's tracking view has the same defect as process reliabilism. On the new tracking view, since the subject with the dispositions I described has a good chance of believing there is a table in front of her when there is not or—in case tables are too dull to be part of her fabrications—of not believing there is a table in front of her when there is, she does not know there is a table in front of her even on that rare occasion when she is looking at it with her eyes and believing what she sees. This, I think, is how it should be if we are to explain why knowledge brings power.

Relevant alternatives theories and 'lottery' propositions

There is a family of approaches to knowledge which have whether one knows p depend on whether one's evidence rules out alternatives to p (Goldman 1976, Stine 1976). However, lest the view be too strict not just every statement that entails −p needs to be ruled out. The subject must have evidence only against those alternatives that are relevant. In normal circumstances, the skeptical hypothesis in which there is no table in front of me because I am a brain in a vat is not considered relevant, and so need not be ruled out in order for me to know the mundane proposition that there is a table in front of me. If the question is whether one knows that one is not a brain in a vat then relevant alternative theories (RAT) can go in either of two directions. One might think that knowing the mundane proposition and that the falsity of the skeptical hypothesis follows from it does not mean that one knows the falsity of the skeptical hypothesis, since the skeptical hypothesis is in question and has not been ruled out, as in Dretske's form of RAT (Dretske 1981b). This will mean that knowledge is not closed under known implication. Or, one might think that knowing the mundane proposition does give one knowledge, via deduction, that the skeptical hypothesis is false, because or to the extent that the skeptical hypothesis remains irrelevant. The force of the irrelevance of an alternative on this view is that one need not have evidence against it in order to know that it does not obtain (Stine 1976). Such a view would retain closure for knowledge. Finally, recent RAT are often contextualist, allowing in particular that whether an alternative is relevant depends on context, and preserving closure within contexts (Cohen 1988; Lewis 1996).

RAT are particularly weak in their resources for dealing with 'lottery' propositions (Vogel 1999). These are propositions that are overwhelmingly likely, like the claim that my single ticket will not win the lottery, but which nevertheless there is some significant reluctance to admit that we know. For example, I have parked my car a few hours ago in a big city on a side street in a location I well remember. We are inclined to say that I know where my car is. However, hundreds of cars are stolen each day in big cities. There is some intuition that says I do not know that my car has not been stolen, even though it is very likely that it has not. It is as if in parking my car I have entered a lottery where having one's car stolen is the unhappy counterpart to winning the lottery. Some older RAT could deal with the car theft situation by denying closure: I know where my car is without knowing that it has not been stolen. More recent RAT will preserve closure, generally by citing a change in which alternatives count as relevant that occurs in asking the question about whether the car has been stolen. In discussion of the possibility that the car was stolen that alternative becomes relevant. Often this is identified as a shift in context. The result is that there is no one context in which I both know where my car is and do not know that it has not been stolen, so closure is preserved within every context.

However, the recent RAT or plain contextualist theories can make this answer work only by saying more about what makes an alternative relevant or makes for a shift in context that brings a new obligation to eliminate some particular alternative. Several ideas have been offered—salience, resemblance to actuality, salient resemblance to actuality, probability—but none do the job for all lottery-like propositions. It could be salience that tells us why once the question whether my car has been stolen is discussed I am obligated to rule out that possibility in order to be said to know where my car is. However, it is easy to describe other situations involving propositions with low probability where salience does not create the requirement to rule them out. Consider Vogel's Night Watchman case, in which if guessing the combination on the bank vault lock was the only possible way the night watchman could have stolen the money we take the jury to know that he did not do it. We think this even if the defense counsel for the real culprit makes the possibility that the night watchman guessed the combination salient by discussing it. Vividly entertaining an alternative to what one believes does not always make that an alternative one must rule out. So, salience is not a sufficient criterion for relevance of an alternative.

Resemblance to actuality is another popular way of attempting to spell out a criterion for when an alternative is relevant. This would explain the literal lottery case as follows. I do not know that my ticket will not win the lottery because the possibility in which my ticket wins closely resembles all of the possibilities where some other ticket wins. This means that I must eliminate the possibility in which my ticket wins in order to know that it will not win, and this I cannot do before the drawing. A similar move works for the car theft case because my car resembles all of the other cars that might have been stolen today. The resemblance criterion makes brains-in-a-vat type skeptical scenarios irrelevant, and hence not alternatives one needs to rule out in order to know mundane propositions, because a brains-in-a-vat world is not remotely like the normal world. The trouble with the resemblance criterion alone, though, is that it introduces significant skepticism of another sort. Presumably I can know that there is an amusement park in California called 'Disneyland', while not having ruled out the possibility that this park was destroyed by a terrible fire a few hours ago. But among alternatives to there being a Disneyland, a world in which it was destroyed resembles the actual world to a striking extent, and so, on this criterion, is an alternative that must be ruled out if I am to know the mundane proposition that there is a park called 'Disneyland'.

David Lewis combines resemblance to actuality with salience in a given context to determine which alternatives are relevant (Lewis 1996). However, this appears to classify too many alternatives as irrelevant. Imagine a case in which there has been a mishap at the aspirin manufacturer's as a consequence of which some of the bottles marked 'aspirin' on the store shelves actually contain acetaminophen, though no one has yet discovered this. In fact, one of the bottles on your store shelf contains the wrong medicine. It seems that you do not know that the bottle marked 'aspirin' that you bought has aspirin in it, even if it does, and it does not matter to this that no one has discussed the possibility of a manufacturing mishap. The possibility that the 'aspirin' bottle contains acetaminophen resembles actuality, but it is not salient, so according to the criterion you should not have to rule it out in order to know you got aspirin. However, without ruling it out you do not know that you have aspirin. So, salient resemblance is not necessary for an alternative to be relevant (Vogel 1999).[7]

Probability has been suggested as a criterion for which alternatives are relevant (Cohen 1988). The idea is that the relevant alternatives are the ones with sufficiently high probability, relative to our evidence, and the threshold changes with context. However, this will not do the job for the literal lottery proposition, for notice that the probability that my ticket will win can be made pretty much as low as we like, yet some intuition remains that I do not know that my ticket will not win. Taking sufficiently high probability as the criterion for relevance seems to undercut the motivation of the relevant alternatives view anyway. The point of this approach was to admit that there are some −p alternatives that we cannot rule out, but to submit that they need not be ruled out in order to know p, using the term 'irrelevant' to describe these possibilities. But if an alternative has low probability relative to our evidence then our evidence does go to rule it out. To adopt sufficiently high

---

[7] There is textual evidence that by 'salience' Lewis did not mean a speaker-sensitive trait, as Vogel and others have taken him. Even so, one would have to say what salience is in a way that did not yield a circular account of knowledge, and I don't know of anyone who has done that.

probability as the criterion of relevance would be to give up the relevant alternatives approach by making invocation of the relevance of alternatives unnecessary.

The relevant alternatives approach seems destined to fail in its account of lottery-type propositions. Process reliabilist and safety views fare no better. The belief that one will not win the lottery is formed by a reliable process, and though it might be wrong it could not easily be wrong; a scenario where a different ticket from the actual one is drawn is close by in the neighborhood around the actual world but there are at least a million tickets different from the actual winner's that aren't yours. Sensitivity-based accounts of knowledge, on the other hand, are famously resourceful in dealing with lottery propositions. Notice, for example, that on Nozick's account of knowledge you do not know that your ticket will not win the lottery, even if it will not, because you do not track the fact: you would believe your ticket was not the winner even if it was. DeRose has explained how the sensitivity criterion resolves a further puzzling fact. We do not think you know your lottery ticket is not the winner despite your knowledge of the vanishingly low probability that it is, but we will think you know that it is not the winner if you read a report that it is not in a newspaper with a higher probability of error than your ticket had to win (DeRose 1996: 570). It is clearly not the small probability of error that makes us think you do not know that your ticket is not the winner when you have not checked this. Tracking tells us what it is. You do not track the fact that the ticket will not win the lottery if you have not checked up on it, but notice that if you read a decent newspaper to check whether you won, then you will be tracking the fact that you did not: despite the newspaper's having a non-zero error rate, if you had won then you would believe it because the newspaper would have reported it.

All of this is very well, but of course these resources are not immediately available in the recursive tracking view, since in this view tracking is not a necessary condition for knowledge. You may know something without tracking it by knowing it follows from something you know. In one respect this represents an improvement on the Nozick view. For notice that though we do not think you know your ticket is not the winner if you have not checked, we do think you can know your ticket is not the winner by inferring from your knowledge that someone else's ticket is and that there is only one winner. Often getting to know your ticket did not win in this way will have you tracking the fact. For example, if your preferred way of learning who won was to watch for the winning number on television, then in the actual case you might learn that you did not win by seeing someone else's number drawn, and inferring—or simply knowing that that implies—that you did not win. If instead of someone else winning it was you who won, it would also be your number, not his, that came up and you would not believe you had not won. In this case you would count as knowing whether the new tracking view did or did not have the recursion clause, because the product of your inference from a tracking true belief also tracked the truth.

However, there are some cases in which knowing that one's ticket is not the winner by knowing that another is and knowing what that implies does not have one tracking the former fact, in either the subjunctive conditional or the new conditional probability sense. In this sort of case, if, contrary to fact, you did win, implying the other ticket did not, then you might well still believe you had not won. For example, suppose that you were someone who regularly bought lottery tickets but did not regularly watch for the numbers on television. (Perhaps you assumed, probably erroneously, that if you won then the lottery people would come and find you.) You learned that another ticket won because the winner was your friend, who came and told you about his windfall. If instead it was your ticket that had won, then you would believe that it was not because your friend, not having won, would not come to tell you that he had. The recursive tracking view can attribute to you knowledge that you did not win in case your friend (truthfully) told you he won, because you know that it follows from someone else's winning that you did not, you know (and track) from your friend's testimony that he won, and on this view one can know not only by tracking but also by known implication from a knowing belief.

From another side, the addition of closure to the tracking view looks like it might be an obstacle to giving the Nozickean account of lottery propositions, since known implication provides an extra route to knowledge of these propositions that tracking is supposed to tell us we do not have knowledge of. However, notice that we have not seen any cases where known implication gave us knowledge of lottery propositions that we did not think we had; if I know my friend won the lottery, then I do know that I did not win, for example. Also, known implication can give any subject knowledge that *probably* his ticket will not win. That is what follows from everything we know about how lotteries work and how many tickets are in the given lottery. But it is all that follows, and our intuitions don't balk at the idea that you know you *probably* won't win.

DeRose offers an example where we are supposed to think it follows deductively from something mundane that I know by tracking, that I will not win the lottery (DeRose 1996: 573–4). Yet the case is not convincing. So, suppose I know that I will not be able to pay off a large debt I have unless I win the lottery. Perhaps DeRose is right that we are willing to allow me to assert that I will not be able to pay off my debt this year, without even mentioning 'unless I win the lottery.' However, it does not follow from the fact that I will not be able to pay off my debt that I will not win the lottery. It is easy to imagine a counterexample: I am struck with a catastrophic illness whose medical bills swallow all of my lottery winnings and then some, and the situation may be set up legally in such a way that any assets I might acquire are turned over to the medical creditors without my having a say about it. If one naïvely thinks that medical bills could not possibly be so high, or medical creditors so insistent, imagine instead that on my winning the lottery the prize is promptly stolen from me and never recovered. It does follow from my not being able to pay off my debt by the end of the year that it is *probable* that I will not win the lottery, but this is not the proposition we are worried about, and the difference between the two is crucial at the moment, since intuitively I do know it is improbable I will win the lottery; what I do not know, intuitively, is the same statement with the probabilistic qualification removed.

One might think that though this example doesn't work an example could surely be constructed that did (Hawthorne 2004: 11). It is popular to suppose so but I seriously doubt it. The reason is that there is a trade-off involving the proposition one must know from which the claim that you will not win the lottery follows. In order that it imply that you will not win the lottery it must be very strong, but that makes it harder, and probably impossible, for you to know it. For example, we could get closer to having a proposition that implied I will not win the lottery if we considered 'I will not be able to pay off my debt and I will not be struck with a catastrophic illness and no money that I have will be stolen.' But it is evident that this is a much harder proposition to track and that I do not know it. This is so even though it is not yet strong enough to imply I will not win the lottery—what about the possibility that though I win the lottery the money will never be paid because the entity that sponsored the lottery will go bankrupt or out of existence at the appropriate time?

There are propositions that imply I will not win the lottery, but they do not help my opponent. One example is the claim that I will not be entitled to a very large sum of money any time in the future. I no more know this than I know that I will not win the lottery. (And if we put an end-date to specify the time when I will not be entitled to the money more closely, there is always the possibility that they postpone the drawing that decides the winner of the lottery, meaning that the proposition no longer implies I will not win the lottery. Implication cares about every possibility.) Another example is one that John Hawthorne has tried to use against the tracking view. It is obvious that if I know I don't own a lottery ticket then I do know I will not win the lottery. But this belief that I will not win the lottery does not fulfill Nozick's or my variation condition: if I will win the lottery then I will have to have had a ticket, in which case I am likely to believe I will not win, because my winning is so improbable. However, it is equally obvious that my closure clause handles this case, for I track the fact that I don't own a ticket, and I know that this implies I won't win. I do know that I won't win in this situation, but the recursive tracking view delivers that verdict.

The new tracking view also has a uniform approach to the lottery-like propositions considered by Vogel. The cases as described are all strictly like true lottery propositions in that the subject does not track the proposition in question. The subject tracks where he parked his car, but not where it is now or that it has not been stolen. The subject tracked the fact that there was a park called 'Disneyland' in California when he was last there and when he was watching CNN for a half hour two hours ago (they would have reported any fire that occurred today) but he does not track its existence now. And if the night watchman had guessed the combination of the bank vault a juror would still believe he had not. In none of these cases does the subject know, because he also does not know anything deductively stronger from which these propositions could be known to follow. On the other hand, in every case, the subject does know that the proposition he believes is probably the case. In cases of this sort that I have seen he tracks the probabilistic claim, and he also may know the probabilistic claim by known implication from other probabilistic claims.[8]

These cases are of the same type as the ice cubes and other such examples from Chapter 2 and, as I explained there, my own intuitions do not balk at these

---

[8] Note also that the jury we considered does know, by tracking, that the night watchman did not steal the money. If he had stolen the money then evidence to the effect would have appeared in court, and the jury would have believed it. This is because there is no reason to think that his (improbably) guessing the combination would have eliminated all evidence of his stealing the money. Thus, my view matches Vogel's observation.

implications about them. This is because knowledge of the probabilistic versions of such claims is secure, and the resemblance of these cases to true lottery propositions is impressive. The hesitation we have against claiming we know our lottery tickets will not win is a hesitation we ought to have in the other cases as well. It may even be a hesitation we do have that has gone unrecognized, for consider that denying that a person knows p does not require denying that the person believes p, even if the person is oneself. Sure, I would admit that I do not know that I will not win the lottery, but I also would assert that I will not win the lottery. Is it not similar with the parked car and ice cubes? Indeed, one would assert that those ice cubes have melted, or that one's car is parked on Main Street. If asked, though, whether one *knows* the ice cubes have melted, or one *knows* that one's car is parked on Main Street, the same hesitation creeps in as with the true lottery proposition. I don't think this is a sophisticated change of context, but a simple consequence of the fact that a different question has been asked. Though one believes the proposition in question, one does not believe that one knows it. That, I would say, is for good reason.

Lottery propositions and our attitudes toward them present a serious challenge to many theories of knowledge. The new tracking view performs as well as the old tracking view on these propositions, and in some cases even better, further confirming not just the viability but also the superiority of the new tracking view of knowledge.

Knowledge of logical and other necessary truths

Logical and mathematical truths and our knowledge of them are special in a number of ways. Taking our bearings from derivations in logic and proofs in mathematics we might even think that they are special in a way that favors the internalist about knowledge. For isn't the reason that the mathematician knows her theorem the fact that she is guided in her belief by a sequence of thoughts that bear the right rational relationships to one another to constitute a proof? And isn't her having of those thoughts a case of awareness of reasons, the stuff that uniquely internalist justification, and thereby uniquely internalist knowledge, is made of?[9]

There is no doubt that 'a sequence of thoughts' is one possible description of a mathematical proof, but more thought is required to decide what it is about that proof that makes it bring knowledge to its bearer. The idea that awareness may be in the service of something deeper here is suggested by the cases of mathematical and logical knowledge at the other end of the spectrum, cases like $2 + 2 = 4$ and if p and (if p then q) then q, which we have knowledge of without any ability to entertain a non-circular proof. Thinking about these kinds of cases makes externalist views more attractive, since these views do not require accessibility of reasons, proofs, justifications, or arguments for us to attribute knowledge.

However, there are peculiar problems with trying to understand knowledge of, say, logical truth through process reliabilism, a safety view, or a relevant alternatives view.

[9] Thanks to Nick White for pressing me (with his cloven hoof) as to how an externalist could appeal to knowledge of logical implication when this type of knowledge was so obviously a matter of thinking and awareness.

We might think that as long as the subject has (possibly unconscious) mechanisms that make sure she believes the logical truth p regardless of what else is true, the process reliabilist can count her as knowing p. After all, a process that outputs belief in p on any input is reliable if p is a logical truth, since in that case p is always true. However, on pain of counterexamples the process reliabilist has to demand that the process in question in any given case be described in a content-neutral way (Goldman 2000: 346). This means we cannot mention p in the description, and turns the process we are considering from one that is generally reliable to one that is patently not, since if the conclusion proposition is not a logical truth then one will not tend to get a true belief out of a process that makes one believe the proposition come what may. Thus, the process reliabilist is going to have to demand in the process that gives knowledge of a logical truth in this way a part in which the subject (possibly unconsciously) goes through operations that check and verify that the proposition in question is a logical truth. That is not a trivial thing, and seems to be more than what we do, even unconsciously, when we know that if p and (if p then q) then q.

A similar absence of an appropriate middle course in process reliabilism arises when we imagine the subject knowing a logical truth by reasoning, in particular by inferring it from something it is logically implied by. Logically valid inference is a conditionally reliable process. We get knowledge, on the process reliabilist view, when such a process takes a known truth as input. Suppose a subject knows that Jerry is at the movies, and that the subject infers from this that it is not the case that both grass is green and grass is not green. Then we must count her as knowing that it is not the case that both grass is green and grass is not green on the process reliabilist view. This is because this statement is logically implied by the known truth that Jerry is at the movies, making the subject's inference logically valid, since a logical truth is logically implied by every statement.

However, the assumptions we have made do not prevent this subject from being a person who thinks or behaves as if the truth of the logical truth mentioning grass actually depends on Jerry's being at the movies. This person would withdraw belief in the logical truth when Jerry got home from the movies, out of a sense that she had lost her grounds for inferring that it is not the case that both grass is green and grass is not green. There is something this subject does not appreciate about the logical truth, namely that it is true wherever Jerry may be and whatever else is true as well. One does not need to be an internalist to think that we should not count this subject as knowing that it is not the case that both grass is green and grass is not green. But process reliabilism cannot give us this verdict, as far as I can see. The process reliabilist could stipulate that the known truth from which the subject logically derives the logical truth must itself be a logical truth, but then he would still face the previous problem of telling us what it is to know the simplest logical truths that we know without reasoning.

A safety view fares no better. It is even simpler to see that a safety view is too weak to rule out the foregoing example as a case of knowledge of a logical truth. It has once again to do with the direction of fit that the property of safety imposes on knowledge. Because safety requires a fit of the world to the belief rather than of the belief to the world, this property can put no constraint at all on knowledge of logical truth, apart from the requirement that the belief be true. This is because a logical truth could not easily be false no matter which possible world a subject believed it in; it could not be false at all. This property of the logical truth itself means that as long as the subject actually believes it she has knowledge of it, regardless of why she believed it or what might make her stop believing it. Why? Because in any close possible world in which she believed it, it would be true.

A relevant alternatives view is equally impotent here to put any constraint beyond true belief on the subject who is counted as knowing a logical truth. This is because there are no alternatives to the truth of a logical truth; the type of alternative the view looks for must be a way the world might be such that the proposition is not true, but there is no way the world might be such that the proposition is not true. Knowing obvious logical truths ought to be fairly easy—not requiring access to a proof—but it should not be this easy.

Clearly there is a kind of responsiveness that we want a subject to have to a logical truth p, and to its necessity, before we count a subject as knowing p. In this we do well to take our bearings, I think, from the way I have defined knowledge of implication in Chapter 2. To know an implication, say that $q_1, \ldots, q_n$ imply p, I said, requires being responsive to that implication, having a strong disposition to believe the consequent when one believes the antecedent, and not believe the antecedent when one does not believe the consequent, properties captured by conditional probabilities as in conditions (*c*) and (*d*) of the official analysis of this knowledge concept:

(*c*) $P((-b(q_1) \vee \ldots \vee -b(q_n)) / -b(p)) > s,$
(*d*) $P(b(p)/b(q_1). \ldots .b(q_n)) > s,$ and

where I took $s = 0.95$ to fix ideas. This becomes an account of knowledge of logical implication through the additional stipulation that the implication in question is a *logical* truth. Now, one nice way of describing what it is about a logical truth that makes it right to believe it come what may, is to cite the fact that such a statement is logically implied by *every* proposition. This is a fact concerning a relation between every proposition and the logical truth, namely, that if the first is true then the second could not possibly be false.

To require in order for a subject to know p, a logical truth, that she *know* that every proposition implies p is obviously too much to ask. Knowledge that every proposition implies a particular logical truth typically only comes along with knowledge that this is a general property of logical truths because it requires a fine understanding of what implication is, and the latter pieces of higher-level knowledge usually only come from a course in logic. But people know lots of obvious logical truths without taking a course in logic.

However, we do not have to require knowledge of the special fact about the logical truth p that it is implied by every proposition in order to require responsiveness of the subject to this fact. A person need not even believe that every proposition implies p in order to satisfy the following condition: for every set of propositions $\{q_1, \ldots, q_n\}$,

(*c*) $P((-b(q_1) \vee \ldots \vee -b(q_n))/-b(p)) > s,$ and

for all $q_1, \ldots, q_n$ none of which is $-p,$

(*d*) $P(b(p)/(b(q_1). \ldots .b(q_n))) > s,$[10]

with $s = 0.95$. If clause (*d*) is true for every $q_1, \ldots, q_n$, none of which is $-p$, this informs us that no matter what the subject's beliefs (except $-p$), she believes the logical truth p. This is not exactly the property of believing come what may but tends strongly in that direction; it is believing come what may among the subject's beliefs (except $-p$). Given that we are quantifying over all possible beliefs of the subject (except $-p$), what we get from this is belief come what may for all eventualities that the subject's language could describe (except $-p$).[11] This will differ from all possible eventualities only if there are possible occurrences that the subject's language could not describe. Thus, we are very close to the property of belief come what may. I will call this slightly weaker property the belief-come-what-may property in what follows. It is anyway clear that we cannot go all the way to requiring what the phrase 'belief come what may' literally implies, since that would require immortality of the subject. We will avoid such absurd requirements in my view by care with the rules of application discussed below for conditions (*c*) and (*d*).

If clause (*c*) is true for every set of propositions $q_1, \ldots, q_n$, this says that for each set of propositions that doesn't contain $-p$, when the subject fails to believe the logical truth she tends to fail to believe some member of that set of propositions. This property makes her a person such that pretty much the only way we would find her not believing the logical truth would be if we found her not believing anything else either—every single proposition also forms a set of propositions—perhaps because her belief capabilities in general had failed. A subject who believes a logical truth p and has properties (*c*) and (*d*) with respect to it for all $q_1, \ldots, q_n$, and for all $q_1, \ldots, q_n$ none of which is $-p$, respectively, obviously has an appreciation of the necessity of the logical truth, and thereby of most of what is special about it. I say we should count such a person as knowing the logical truth p. Note that this does not mean that the subject knows that p is a logical truth; she may not have the belief that it is a logical truth or even know what 'logical truth' means. She need not have beliefs or ideas *about* the logical truth she believes in order to have the appreciation of its special character that I just defined purely in terms of dispositions to believe the logical truth itself in a variety of circumstances. So, for example, if p = 'It is not the case that grass is green and grass is not green,' then if we want to know whether she knows p we ask about her dispositions to believe this statement, not about whether she believes that this statement is a logical truth.

[10] One might wonder why I can't get away with single-premise implication here, simplifying the conditions to: (*c**) $P(-b(q)/-b(p)) > s$ and (*d**) $P(b(p)/b(q)) > s$, which are easier to scan. The reason is the same as the reason knowledge of implication had to be defined for multiple premises: the transition from conjuncts to a conjunction. Here, (*c**) and (*d**) would allow a subject to escape our net and count as knowing a logical truth when she shouldn't. This would happen if she believed q_1, believed q_2, did not believe $q_1.q_2$, and would not believe the logical truth if she did believe $q_1.q_2$.

[11] $-p$ is excepted here not because I think the subject should not believe p in case she believes $-p$, but for a technical reason. I think she should believe p in case she believes $-p$ because p is a logical truth and is implied by $-p$, a logical falsehood. However, the criterion of belief I adopted in Chapter 2 will not allow me to do this. That criterion can never count someone as believing both p and $-p$ when presented with the two—the subject can't bet more than the money we give her—which means that no one could ever fulfill condition (*d*) if the quantification ranged over $-p$.

While I will take the stand that the conditions I just described are sufficient for knowledge of a logical truth p (unless p itself takes the form of a logical implication)— a claim I will defend further below—it is evident that we cannot take satisfaction of clauses (*c*) and (*d*) for every $q_1, \ldots, q_n$ (not including $-p$ for (*d*)) as necessary. These clauses properly reward a subject who appreciates the necessity of a logical truth without having an ability to give a proof of it or to reflect on the fact that it is a logical truth. However, they unfairly penalize a subject who is able to give a proof of a logical truth, and is sensitive to whether or not the proof is valid. For notice that among the propositions q regardless of her belief in which the quantification of condition (*d*) expects a subject to hold on to belief in p, a logical truth, is a q that says 'That proof of p that I just did had an error in line n' for some n. A subject who believes a logical truth p because of having done a valid proof of p from another logical truth she knows should not be disqualified from thereby knowing p due to a disposition she has—and that a good reasoner should have—to withhold belief in the conclusion when she finds a mistake in the proof of that conclusion and has no other grounds for belief in it.

The solution to this problem of excessive stringency is by now a familiar trick: a recursion clause. To include among cases of knowledge of logical truth cases where the subject believes a logically true proposition of arbitrary complexity because of a logically valid proof of arbitrary complexity, while at the same time the subject is a person who has the praiseworthy disposition to be wary of the conclusion of a proof if she finds a mistake in the proof and has no other grounds for belief in that conclusion, all we need is to define knowledge of logical truth disjunctively and, more specifically, recursively. S will know a logical truth p (where p does not take the form of a logical implication) if and only if either S fulfills (*c*) and (*d*) for p and arbitrary $q_1, \ldots, q_n$ (excluding $-p$ in the case of (*d*)), or S knows that p is logically implied by a logical truth r not equivalent to p that S knows.

Analogously to the way in which deduction (or a fortiori the weaker known logical implication) does not preserve tracking, as we saw in Chapter 2, known logical implication also does not preserve the belief-come-what-may property that our knowledge of obvious logical truths has. This is clear intuitively on the basis of the example I cited of a person who knows a logical truth by an actually valid proof from a logically true premise that she knows but who would not believe that conclusion if she believed her proof was mistaken. To see that the recursive view I just sketched agrees that known logical implication does not preserve the belief-come-what-may property, we have to look more closely at the rules of application for conditions (*c*) and (*d*), which play several roles in that sketch and which I will finally specify.

The rules of application for (*c*) and (*d*) are relatively simple compared to those of conditions III and IV in the last chapter. We will fix the subject's existence, identity, dispositions, location in space and time when she has the belief, and her state of duress, and the laws of nature and other regularities, including logical truths, as before, since whether the subject knows logical truths has nothing to do with what she would do were these things to be altered. Everything else can vary insofar as the things that have been fixed allow them to vary, with an exception that is peculiar to knowledge of logical implication. Consider the fact we have already seen that when we ask whether someone who actually infers p from $q_1, \ldots, q_n$ and believes that $q_1, \ldots, q_n$ imply p knows that $q_1, \ldots, q_n$ imply p, it does not seem appropriate to disqualify her from this knowledge, assuming $q_1, \ldots, q_n$ do imply p, on the basis of the fact that she would withdraw belief in p though she believed $q_1, \ldots, q_n$ were she to believe that the inference she actually made from $q_1, \ldots, q_n$ to p was mistaken. That would be a good disposition to have, not one that we should allow to interfere with counting her as knowing that $q_1, \ldots, q_n$ imply p when she is actually confident in her inference. Likewise, it would be a good thing, and not a thing we should take to impugn her knowledge, if were she to believe that a proof of the proposition p was not possible she would not believe p on the basis of $q_1, \ldots, q_n$ as she actually does because, say, she actually does it by an inference, which is a proof, which in the scenario entertained she believes is impossible.

Thus we need to fix the probabilities of a few more propositions. One is the statement that the subject believes that the step she took from belief in $q_1, \ldots, q_n$ to belief in p was not mistaken. I refer not to her inference but instead to the more general 'step she took' since she may not have done any explicit reasoning, but still may have beliefs about whether what she did was legitimate, and varying those beliefs would often inappropriately disrupt our evaluation of her knowledge just the same. In addition, we need to fix the probability of the statement that the subject believes that a proof is possible. Whatever is the probability that she actually believes these statements is what all the probability functions will assign to her belief in these statements in the evaluation of conditions (c) and (d). Other reflective and modal statements may also need to be fixed. It will be obvious from the account below where to add them.

With these things in mind, the precise statements of conditions (c) and (d) respectively, where we imagine a subject who believes that $q_1, \ldots, q_n$ together imply p, are as follows:

(c):

For all P_i such that

(1) $P_i(s) = P_u(s)$ for s any statement regarding the subject's existence, identity, dispositions, location in space and time when she has the belief, the statement that the subject is under extreme duress, and any statement of a law of nature or other regularity, including a logical truth, and

(2) $P_i(b(s)) = P_u(b(s))$ for s the statements
   (a) the step I took from belief in $q_1, \ldots, q_n$ to belief in p was not mistaken and
   (b) a proof of p from $q_1, \ldots, q_n$ is possible,

$$P_i((-b(q_1) \vee \ldots \vee -b(q_n))/-b(p)) > 0.95, \text{ and}$$

(d):

for all P_i such that

(1) $P_i(s) = P_u(s)$ for s any statement regarding the subject's existence, identity, dispositions, location in space and time when she has the belief, the statement that the subject is under extreme duress, and any statement of a law of nature or other regularity, including a logical truth, and

(2) $P_i(b(s)) = P_u(b(s))$ for s the statements

(a) the step I took from belief in $q_1, \ldots, q_n$ to belief in p was not mistaken and

(b) a proof of p from $q_1, \ldots, q_n$ is possible,

$$P_i(b(p)/b(q_1). \ldots .b(q_n)) > 0.95.$$

The P_i in question are those that have the same domain as P_u, as explained in Chapter 3. The only difference between condition (*c*) and condition (*d*) is in their last lines, with (*c*) concerned about whether the subject refrains from believing at least one of $q_1, \ldots, q_n$ when she does not believe p, and (*d*) concerned with whether she does believe p when she believes each of $q_1, \ldots, q_n$.

I separate the case of knowledge of a logical truth that is a logical implication, that is, a logical truth of the form 'A ⊃ B' or '−(A.−B)' or 'B ∨ −A', from knowledge of other logical truths so that one cannot know a logical implication claim merely by possessing the belief-come-what-may property with respect to it.[12] My reasons for this will become clear below. Thus, a subject *knows that* $q_1, \ldots, q_n$ *imply* p if and only if $q_1, \ldots, q_n$ do imply p, she believes that $q_1, \ldots, q_n$ imply p, she fulfills conditions (*c*) and (*d*) as here stated, and condition (*e*) formulated in Chapter 2:

(*e*): if S believes that $q_1, \ldots, q_n$ imply p because of inferences S made from $q_1, \ldots, q_n$ to p, then every step of inference in this chain is one where S knows that the premises imply the conclusion.[13]

These conditions will be met by a subject who knows a simple or a complex claim of logical implication, and I think they are the only conditions we need to impose for knowledge of claims of logical implication apart from the stipulations that the implication is a logical truth and that the subject believes it.

For a logical truth p that does not take the form 'A ⊃ B' or '−(A.−B)' or 'B ∨ −A', a subject *knows* p, if p is logical truth, she believes p, and she fulfills condition (*c*) as here stated, for arbitrary $q_1, \ldots, q_n$, and condition (*d*) for arbitrary $q_1, \ldots, q_n$ none of which is −p, that is, if she fulfills (*c'*) and (*d'*), which are distinguished from (*c*) and (*d*) only by additional universal quantifications out front:

(*c'*): For all $q_1, \ldots, q_n$, and for all P_i such that

---

[12] One may worry that I cannot separate the cases of logical truths that do and do not take the form of implications, because p is equivalent to, and can be rewritten as, r ⊃ p for any r. However, we are concerned with beliefs and as beliefs 'p' and 'r ⊃ p' are not equivalent. The statement comes in one form or the other when we ask whether the subject believes it, and the claim that the other form is also believed is non-trivial. It is reassuring, though, that the two parts of this view of logical truth mesh to some extent in their evaluations of knowledge of p and knowledge that r implies p. If one knows p by the base clause for non-implicational logical truth, then one fulfills (*c*) for every q and (*d*) for every q not equal to −p, but these imply in particular that one fulfills (*c*) and (*d*) for r, and that together with belief that r implies p is sufficient for knowledge that r implies p.

[13] According to this formulation, a subject cannot know that −p implies p, even if it does—as when −p is a logical falsehood—and she believes it. This is an unhappy consequence of the formulation which is once again a result of the limitations of the belief criterion I have adopted, which doesn't count a person as believing unless she is point-consistent on the proposition in question. It may be possible to patch this here, but a more interesting approach would be to improve, by generalizing, the belief criterion. However, if one generalized away this feature of the belief criterion, one would lose the resolution of the paradox of entailment discussed below.

(1) $P_i(s) = P_u(s)$ for s any statement regarding the subject's existence, identity, dispositions, location in space and time when she has the belief, the statement that the subject is under extreme duress, and any statement of a law of nature or other regularity, including a logical truth, and

(2) $Pi(b(s)) = Pu(b(s))$ for s the statements

(a) the step I took, if any, from belief in $q_1, \ldots, q_n$ to belief in p was not mistaken and

(b) a proof of p from q is possible,

$$P_i((-b(q_1) \lor \ldots \lor -b(q_n))/-b(p)) > 0.95, \text{ and}$$

(*d'*): For all $q_1, \ldots, q_n$, none of which are $-p$, and for all P_i such that

(1) $P_i(s) = P_u(s)$ for s any statement regarding the subject's existence, identity, dispositions, location in space and time when she has the belief, the statement that the subject is under extreme duress, and any statement of a law of nature or other regularity, including a logical truth, and

(2) $P_i(b(s)) = P_u(b(s))$ for s the statements

(*a*) the step I took, if any, from belief in $q_1, \ldots, q_n$ to belief in p was not mistaken and

(*b*) a proof of p from $q_1, \ldots, q_n$ is possible,

$$Pi(b(p)/b(q_1). \ldots .b(q_n)) > 0.95.$$

This setup defines the base-case of knowledge of a (non-implicational) logical truth p by first defining knowledge of a logical implication, and then requiring for knowledge of p, roughly, that the subject behave as if she knows that p is implied by every proposition. In this way we do not require that the subject know that p is implied by every proposition in order to know p; we count her as knowing p if she is appropriately responsive to the fact that it is implied by every proposition. Being so responsive involves her having the belief-come-what-may property with regard to p, which is (*d'*). It also involves her having an appropriate deference to a sense in which all of her beliefs depend on this one, embodied in condition (*c'*); if this belief were withheld then the subject would not be believing anything.

This responsiveness to the special place logical truths have a right to in our belief structures is not the only way to know a (non-implicational) logical truth, though it is the reason we can be counted as knowing the most basic logical truths. Obviously, we can know more complicated logical truths by logically valid inference from, or, more generally, known implication from, other known logical truths. Thus, the account of knowing that q logically implies p has another role to play. It helped us to define the base clause for knowledge of (non-implicational) logical truth, and now it will provide a recursion clause. As a result, we get the following as the official account of knowledge of (non-implicational) logical truth: S *knows* p, for p a (non-implicational) logical truth, if and only if

(*a*) p is true
(*b*) S believes p, and

either (*c'*) and (*d'*)

or there are logical truths $q_1, \ldots, q_n$ none of which is equivalent to p such that S knows that $q_1, \ldots, q_n$ logically imply p and S knows $q_1, \ldots, q_n$.[14]

(c') and (d'), recall, are just the statements that (c) holds for all $q_1, \ldots, q_n$, and (d) holds for all $q_1, \ldots, q_n$, none of which is $-p$, respectively.

One surely cannot deny that valid logical inference from a known logical truth is a way of establishing knowledge of the inferred truth, but one might wonder why the recursion clause is necessary here. As mentioned above, the reason for this is that the result of valid logical inference from a known logical truth does not necessarily have the properties the base clause for knowledge of (non-implicational) logical truth requires; deduction does not preserve the (c') and (d') properties. In particular, the scenarios in which the subject has different beliefs from the actual ones about whether her inference from $q_1, \ldots, q_n$ to p was mistaken are not considered when we ask whether she knows that implication, because we deliberately fixed her actual belief about whether what she did was mistaken. But that possibility that is left out of account in scrutinizing knowledge of logical implication is in the domain of the quantification 'for all $q_1, \ldots, q_n$' that appears in condition (d'); fulfilling (d') means that the subject must be such that she is inclined to believe the logical truth even when she believes the inference she just made to it is mistaken, for she must believe the logical truth no matter what she believes (except $-p$).

This gives us an appreciation of just how strong the base clause for knowledge of (non-implicational) logical truth is. One consequence of this strength is that one cannot typically know a logical truth by authority, although nothing prevents one from learning it by authority. In a case of believing a proposition on the basis of authority one's belief is vulnerable to a change in one's belief about what the authority wants one to believe. This is so whether the authority is a bad one, e.g. Elmer Fraud or the *Weekly World News*, or a good one, e.g. one's elementary school teacher. Typically, if one bases one's belief in p on the fact that the authority says 'p', then in a case where one believes the authority says 'not-p' one will tend to withdraw belief in p. This disposition disqualifies one from knowing the logical truth by failure of condition (d'); one doesn't have the belief-come-what-may property with respect to p because a change in what one believes the authority says is liable to change one's belief in p. Similarly, one cannot know that q implies p by authority, since in defining conditions (c) and (d) we did not fix one's beliefs about what the authority says, so these may vary when conditions (c) and (d) are evaluated.[15] Since the belief of one who believes on the basis of authority is typically susceptible to change in case her belief about what the authority says changes, she does not fulfill condition (d). Nothing here says that one cannot learn logical truths by authority, as we do in early development. It is just that to know a logical truth requires leaving the authority behind at some point, and having a belief that is solid even if one should believe the

[14] If one was not moved by the example involving Jerry at the movies, then one will want to omit the requirement that the truths $q_1, \ldots, q_n$ be *logically* true.

[15] Change in one's belief about what the authority says can change the subject's sense that her step from the one belief to the other was legitimate. This change can happen despite our having fixed the probability that the subject believes the step was legitimate because the probability assigned was non-extreme. (See Chapter 3.)

authority has changed his mind, thus showing behaviorally one's appreciation of the fact that logical truths don't depend on what an authority says.

There are two possible types of exception I can think of to the consequence that one cannot know a logical truth by authority, one by an authority who is like Odysseus when tying himself to the mast, and the other the authority of one's linguistic community. However, I do not think these cases are actually successful. As Odysseus' ship was about to travel through the area of the seductive sirens whose song made captains steer their ships to destruction, he had himself tied to the mast of his ship with open ears and ordered his crew to plug their ears with wax and, crucially, not obey any order he should give to them while going through this area. The point is that he is an authority who gives an order accompanied by another order to the obeying subject *not* to listen to his subsequent orders. Could a subject not come to know a logical truth by trusting such an authority, one who abdicates his authority ever after? Would the subject not thereby acquire the belief-come-what-may property because he has been immunized, by the authority himself, against changing his belief in response to a change in what he believes the authority now says? He is indeed closer to having the belief-come-what-may property through such an experience, but this information alone does not insure that he has the property. This is because we know nothing about what the subject would do were he to misremember what the authority originally said. If he misremembered the authority as having said −p instead of p, he would believe the authority said −p, and wouldn't he also believe −p and not believe p? Well, maybe even if he did misremember what the authority said he would still believe p, because what the authority actually said had had such a strong effect on his belief-forming mechanisms. Maybe so, but in that case I would say he no longer believes on the *basis* of authority, and so does not know by authority, although it is certainly true that he learned by authority.

The authority of a linguistic community as a whole also seems close to being able to give a person knowledge of a logical truth by authority, according to my analysis of knowledge of logical truth. This is because if the subject comes to believe that the linguistic community does not affirm a logical truth that he believed, then chances are that he will not so much withdraw belief in that content as acquire a new belief that the community has changed the language. Here too, though, the person's having that disposition to believe the content even when he believes the linguistic community no longer affirms that statement suggests that his knowledge is not really *based* on the authority of the linguistic community. Of course, as in the other cases, one can still learn a logical truth by the authority of the linguistic community.

The account of knowledge of logical truth offered here counts valid inference of a logical truth from any known logical truth as giving one knowledge of the former, as we should expect. It also does not count mistaken proof or invalid inference as a way to get to know a logical truth from a known logical truth. Both of these consequences follow because of the way the recursion clause (involving knowledge of logical implication) is defined and because proof won't generally give one the means to satisfy the base clause. Ruling out mistaken calculations and proofs as giving knowledge represents an advantage of this account over Nozick's. For reasons discussed in Chapter 2, Nozick dealt with logical truths by giving the subject a pass on the variation condition, and taking the adherence condition as the only requirement for knowledge beyond true belief. This is not tragic but a better plan is desirable since, as Colin McGinn has pointed out, a subject who comes to a true logical or mathematical belief by means of a mistaken calculation will pass the adherence condition as long as the mistake was something the subject has a strong disposition to make (McGinn 1984: 534).

The new account deals with another type of case the adherence condition is not strong enough to rule out. This is the case of the premature logician, a subject who has a tendency to announce results confidently before checking the proof well or, indeed, before having a proof at all, and has, say, a 50–50 track record on the truth of these announcements.[16] We can imagine this person as behaving so concerning a p that actually is a logical truth, a sophisticated logical truth that is not easy to know. The problem here, and the reason we would not want to attribute knowledge to this person, does not seem to show up in evaluation of the adherence condition: if p were true this subject would believe it because he is so confident both in p and in his own powers, and nothing about the truth of p, or, we can suppose, anything else, will tip him off as to his prematurity. What we are inclined to object to is the track record of the person, saying something like 'he might have announced it even if it wasn't true', but the 'it' in this objection must refer generally to propositions he might announce and not specifically to p, since as a logical truth p could not fail to be true. It might be possible to define the variation condition more generally, to capture the intuition about this 'it', but I think it would be complicated.

The new account takes a different approach that has more power than the adherence condition did to catch out the premature logician if he should be caught. Either this subject did a sequence of inferences (perhaps unconsciously) from a known logical truth or he did not. (An analogous argument can be made if the logical truth is itself a claim of logical implication.) If he did a sequence of inferences and there is no mistake in any step, then he does have a right to be counted as knowing. He had good intuitions in this case; we have no right to condemn him. If he did a sequence of inferences and he does not have a right to count as knowing then at least one step of those inferences will have been invalid, and the analysis won't count him as knowing. If he did not do a sequence of inferences, even unconsciously, then the belief-come-what-may criterion applies. Someone with a tendency to announce results prematurely is likely to be fairly easy to shake from his belief under questioning because he has not worked out his grounds.

Of course, it is possible that despite his track record his confidence is unshakeable by any change in his other beliefs in a given case, and if this is true and he has not used inferences, then he counts as knowing on this account. This may be due to insight that does not involve inference. However, it is also possible that he has this property merely by good luck. But it is familiar that knowledge by luck is possible on a responsiveness-oriented view of knowledge. It is the case here, as with all other luck cases, that the account does not recommend luck as a forward-looking strategy for acquiring knowledge. (Believing every p come what may would be a disaster, and how would

[16] Thanks to Branden Fitelson for alerting me to this case and helping me think about it.

one choose?) The new account approaches the premature logician by scrutinizing what he actually does and picking up on any place where he made a mistake, even if unconsciously. It rightly makes room too for logical 'clairvoyants', who go through legitimate steps or flashes of insight unconsciously before or without ever having any ability to lay out the steps or insights explicitly.

One might wonder how this account handles the case I wielded against process reliabilism above, where a person infers a logical truth from a contingent truth, which implies it because a logical truth is implied by every proposition. I venture that the account handles this case just as we should want. The person cannot know the logical truth by the recursion clause, because that requires valid inference from a known logical truth and 'Jerry is at the movies' even if true is not a logical truth. Thus, she must know the logical truth by satisfying the belief-come-what-may property, or not be taken to know it at all. Could inference from a contingent truth, or a falsehood, give this to her? It need not, of course, which is what we saw above; she might mistakenly get the impression that the logical truth depends on whether Jerry is at the movies. However, it could give her this property, since for example she could have chosen the statement 'Jerry is at the movies' randomly, and on seeing that she could derive 'It is not the case that both grass is green and grass is not green', understood that the choice she made of 'Jerry is at the movies' didn't matter. This scenario would give her the belief-come-what-may property and in such a case we can count her as knowing the logical truth.

This account of knowledge of logical truth provides a natural resolution of the paradox of entailment. This paradox arises from the facts that (1) inconsistent statements together imply every proposition, (2) the belief set of any of us is probably inconsistent, and yet (3) we do not infer or believe every proposition. We think these facts are paradoxical because we suppose that we know (1). On the current account, (2) and (3) can be true despite (1) because, in the first place, we do not know (1), that inconsistent statements together imply every proposition. The reason we do not count as knowing this is the very fact that we do not behave in accordance with it and infer every proposition. For every set of inconsistent propositions one of us believes, knowing those propositions together imply every statement requires by clause (*d*) that one believe every statement, because one believes the inconsistent set. However, by observation (3), none of us do that. On the current account, our not believing every proposition when we believe an inconsistent set of propositions is not a distinct fact from our not knowing that the inconsistent set implies every proposition.

It is clear that this conclusion that we don't know that the inconsistent set implies every proposition matches what we think is true of the man on the street; I get puzzled looks even from students who have taken a logic course when I remind them of this fact. However, one will object, we who think about the paradox surely do know this fact about logical implication. We have derived it by valid deduction from known logical truths, and we even have the belief-come-what-may property with regard to the general fact that an inconsistent set implies every proposition, and to the instances of this generalization. Why shouldn't we be counted as knowing it?

This objection essentially asks me to justify my separation of knowledge of logical implication from knowledge of other (non-implicational) logical truths. It was that separation that gave us the consequence that belief-come-what-may or valid inference from a statement with this property would not alone make us count as knowing a logical implication. I would justify the separation by reference to all the other cases of knowledge of logical implication. I see no other case where we would attribute knowledge of a logical implication if the subject actually believes the antecedent and yet doesn't believe the consequent. There would be a kind of hypocrisy involved in supposing we know the implication when we don't display the deeds that that demands.

One might be concerned that my stand here is too strong, since the subject may know the implication and know the antecedent without having put the two together to make the inference. However, my account does not require that he has put the two together in order to know the implication. It only requires that he would put the two together if, when we verify that he actually believes the antecedent, we prompt him for his bet on the consequent vs. its negation. Because the stand my opponent expects me to take on the case of knowledge of the fact that an inconsistent set of propositions implies every proposition is different from the stand we would take on any other logical implication, I think it is better to go with the preponderance of cases and concede that despite the fact that we have a true belief that an inconsistent set of propositions implies every proposition, we do not know this. None of us knows it *because* we do not act in accord with it.

This seems to take the sting out of the paradox but one might protest: though my view implies we do not know that a contradiction implies every statement, I have admitted that we have a (true) belief that this is the case. Therefore the question remains why we do not infer every proposition. The answer, on the view expounded here, is that we do not have the premises for such an inference. That is, according to the belief criterion set out in Chapter 2 one cannot be counted as simultaneously believing two contradictory premises because that would require having a disposition to bet more money than the experimenter gives you, which is impossible. This resolves the paradox by declaring (2) above false. At least, (2) is false for the kind of inconsistent beliefs that could activate our belief in (1).

It remains to consider our knowledge of necessary truths that are not logical truths. Analytic truths that rest on the meanings of words, if one thinks there are any, are necessary truths, relative to a language, but though they are distinct from logical truths I think that the account of non-implicational logical truths will serve for this class as well, without modification except for the clauses indicating which type of truth is at issue. This is because though knowledge of meaning would require some extra premises in inferences, the analysis did not put any restriction on how many premises were allowed. One would of course have to change the requirements that the known p is a (non-implicational) logical truth and that premises from which one derives p are the same, to the requirements that the known p is an analytic truth depending on the meaning of a word or words, and that premises acknowledged by the recursion clause are known analytic truths depending on meaning. The conditions for knowledge of logical implication would remain unchanged. Of course, if one thinks that the set of analytic truths depending on meaning is empty, then one does not need an account of knowledge of such statements.

Mathematical truths are necessary. If one thinks that all mathematical truths are hypothetical, a view to which I am sympathetic, then the account of knowledge of logical implication will be sufficient to give conditions for knowledge of these truths. If one does not think that mathematical truths are all hypothetical, then the account of knowledge of non-implicational logical truth can be adapted for one's purposes, much as it can be for knowledge of analytic truths depending on meaning: one will know if either one fulfills the belief-come-what-may property and property (c') for the mathematical truth or one knows it is implied by a mathematical truth for which one does fulfill these properties.

My views provide two options for knowledge of laws of nature or physically necessary truths. My own inclination is not to count this as a special kind of necessity but rather to view what necessity pertains as logical and mathematical necessity relative to very general contingent facts. Because of this, and because the variation condition is not undefined for laws of nature—we can imagine worlds with different laws of nature—my inclination is to let the tracking conditions handle knowledge of so-called physical necessities. However, I think that special treatment for these propositions is available if one is so inclined. One can adapt the account of knowledge of non-implicational logical truth given above by restricting further the set of beliefs relative to which the subject must be inclined to believe the physical necessity statement. We expect a person who knows a logical truth to believe it even if she believes the laws of nature are different from what they actually are. We do not expect a person who knows a physical necessity statement to believe it even if she comes to believe the laws of nature are different from what they actually are. At the same time, we want to check that she is not likely to believe the laws of nature are different from what they actually are. Thus, one could adapt the account above to physical necessity statements by an additional fixing, in the rules of application for (c) and (d), of the probabilities of statements about the laws of nature at their actual values. If she is not likely to believe false things about the laws of nature, then roughly only true beliefs about the laws of nature and beliefs of any quality about other matters will figure in the variations we end up judging whether her belief in the physical necessity is good against.

I rely on the account of knowledge of implication in the account of knowledge of contingent truths given in previous chapters because I need this to define the recursion clause there. Otherwise, though, the account of logical and other necessary truths provided here is independent of the new tracking account of contingent knowledge. One could reject the new tracking account of knowledge and still accept the account of knowledge of logical and other necessary truths, and this might be an especially attractive option for the externalist views that have such trouble with necessary truth. However, this account of knowledge of necessary truth will remain best suited in spirit to a tracking account of contingent truth, because the two have in common what other externalist views on offer do not have: the idea that knowledge is a matter of responsiveness to the way the world is. A responsiveness-based theory splits into two parts simply because the type of responsiveness appropriate to knowledge is different for contingent truths and necessary truths.

Sensitivity and Safety

q, a belief held by S, is *sensitive* if and only if:

$$P(-b(q)/-q) > 0.95, \text{ and}$$

q, a belief held by S, is *safe* if and only if:

$$P(q/b(q)) > 0.95,$$

where 'b(q)' means that S believes q, and neither q nor $-q$, nor b(q), nor $-b(q)$, nor b($-q$) nor $-b(-q)$, is assigned probability 1 by P or fixed in the evaluation. Note that

$P(b(q)/-q) = 1 - P(-b(q)/-q)$	Total Probability,
$P(b(q)/-q) = P(-q/b(q)) \, P(b(q))/P(-q)$	Bayes's Theorem,
$P(-b(q)/-q) = 1 - P(-q/b(q)) \, P(b(q))/P(-q)$	algebra,
$P(-q/b(q)) = 1 - P(q/b(q))$	Total Probability,

yielding

$$\mathbf{P(-b(q)/-q) = 1 - P(b(q))/P(-q)[1 - P(q/b(q))]} \quad \text{algebra,}$$

which is sensitivity in terms of safety. This equation can be rearranged to yield safety in terms of sensitivity, thus:

$$\mathbf{P(q/b(q)) = 1 - P(-q)/P(b(q)) \, [1 - P(-b(q)/-q)]} \quad \text{algebra.[1]}$$

It is interesting to note that perfect safety and perfect sensitivity coincide. That is, if the safety level $P(q/b(q))$ is 1, then the sensitivity level $P(-b(q)/-q)$ is 1 also, and if the sensitivity level $P(-b(q)/-q)$ is 1 then the safety level $P(q/b(q))$ is 1 also. The two notions diverge only in the imperfect states that we typically find ourselves in.

---

[1] Thanks to John D. Norton for showing me that these relationships could be derived.

5

What is Evidence? Discrimination, Indication, and Leverage

Knowledge and evidence

It is a truism that the better one's evidence for a claim p the more likely one is to have knowledge that p. As with all truisms, we might find exceptions to it on closer inspection of the concepts. However, it ought to be true or mostly true, in particular, for the view of knowledge expounded in the previous chapters if that view is to be believed. Is there a view of what evidence is, compelling in its own right, that when combined with the recursive tracking view of knowledge makes the truism above come out true? This chapter argues that there is. This provides independent support for the view of knowledge on offer.

The recursive tracking view of what knowledge is puts constraints on what evidence must be like if it is to raise one's chances of knowledge. There are two ways to know p on that view. One might know p by tracking it, or one might know p by knowing that it follows from some $q_1, \ldots, q_n$ (none of which is equivalent to p) one knows. In the latter case there will be $r_1, \ldots, r_m$ (possibly including $q_1, \ldots, q_n$ themselves but not p) that one knows by tracking and from which p follows. Thus to know p one will have either to track p or track each of $r_1, \ldots, r_m$. Whether $q_1, \ldots, q_n$ that imply p should, when conjoined, count as evidence for p is a question I will postpone until my concrete proposal for how to understand evidence is on the table. In order for evidence to help one to know p by tracking p or tracking $r_1, \ldots, r_m$, though, obviously, the evidence will have to help one to track p or track each of $r_1, \ldots, r_m$. Without loss of generality we can use the letter 'h' to stand for statements like p or any of $r_1, \ldots, r_m$ since in both cases it will be right to say that we want the subject's belief in h to track h if we are to count her as having knowledge that h (and possibly thereby of one of h's deductive consequences, whether taken by itself or when combined with other known statements). In the most natural scenario, the evidence statement e will be an intermediary between the truth of h and one's belief in h, whether e is a statement believed or merely a content to which one responds with belief in h. Thus, the relationship of one's belief in h to the truth of e, the relationship between the truth of e and the truth of h, and the relationship of one's belief in e, if any, both to the truth of e and to one's belief in h, must be such as to support a relation between one's belief in h and the truth of h in which the former tracks the latter.

Suppressing some detail, it seems unlikely that such an intermediary will help one to have a belief in h that tracks the truth unless the intermediary tracks the truth, your belief tracks the intermediary, and tracking has a sufficiently robust transitivity property.[1] Only with a property something like transitivity, in which if A tracks B and B tracks C then A tracks C, will the intermediary be likely to do the job. To see how we can have the needed transitivity we must first take care to define tracking thoroughly generally. In Chapter 2 tracking was defined for the case where a belief tracks (or does not track) the truth of what the belief is about. This can easily be generalized for the case where one fact TRACKS another, a notion discussed in the first chapter and formulated there in terms of subjunctive conditionals. The official version of this notion will simply exchange the subjunctive conditionals for conditional probabilities, as we did in Chapter 2 for the restricted notion of beliefs that track truths. Thus A *TRACKS* B at level u if and only if:

(III) $P(-A/-B) > u$
(IV) $P(A/B) > u$ and if A=b (p) and B=p for some p then $P(b(-p)/p) < 1 - u$.[2]

As expected, these conditions say that for A to TRACK B is for it to be improbable that A given $-B$, and probable that A given B, with the added clause (carried over from the view of knowledge) for the special case where A is a belief. I will let the threshold u, which indicates how tight the correlation in question is, continue to be represented by the variable u instead of fixing it, for reasons that will become apparent.

With this account of TRACKING in mind we can prove that TRACKING possesses a transitivity property which is good enough for the purposes of allowing a tracking view of knowledge and of evidence to support the truism cited above. The bad news is that TRACKING is transitive in the usual, strict sense only in the case where the conditional probabilities in (III) and (IV) equal 1. That is, if A TRACKS B and B TRACKS C, then A does not necessarily TRACK C unless the tracking is perfect. This is because whatever error is allowed when we affirm that A TRACKS B (with $u < 1$) combines with the error allowed when we affirm that B TRACKS C (with $u < 1$) when we put the two claims together to try to infer that A TRACKS C. Though the first two claims have error levels below the threshold allowed for TRACKING when $u < 1$, the total error may exceed that threshold when the two claims are combined, because the errors also combine. We do not want to require that the conditional probabilities in

[1] It is possible for a belief to track the truth by an intermediary that perfectly anti-tracks the truth, as long as the belief perfectly anti-tracks the intermediary, as in a testimony example we saw in Chapter 1. However, it seems that this is unlikely enough that I can safely ignore it in this first foray into the topic of the relation between evidence and knowledge. Of course, this kind of case will represent a counterexample to the truism above on the tracking view of knowledge and evidence, since making the intermediary better evidence may make it track better which would make it do worse in bringing the subject knowledge because the subject is anti-tracking *it*.

[2] These conditions are labeled '(III)' and '(IV)' to indicate that they are generalizations of conditions III and IV from Chapter 2's analysis of *knowledge*. As earlier, one may of course want different thresholds for the two conditions.

(III) and (IV) be 1 in defining TRACKING since that would require, in particular, that there is no possible scenario in which we would believe the wrong thing when we have knowledge, and such an assumption flies in the face of a sensible fallibilism about knowledge. This is why in the earlier exposition of knowledge I set the thresholds at 0.95—high but not 1. On pain of infallibilism, we cannot get the transitivity we need by requiring perfect tracking.

Thus, everything depends on what happens when u < 1 and we try to put tracking claims end to end in order to infer a tracking claim about the beginning and the end of the chain. Do the errors multiply or grow exponentially? Do they grow out of control so that no tracking relation can be inferred between the beginning point and the endpoint? Fortunately, the answer is no. Errors no more than sum over links in a chain of TRACKING relations. This can be seen most easily in a diagram mapping the possibilities and their chances of happening under the constraints that A TRACKS B and B TRACKS C. Let $u + r = 1$, meaning that 'r' represents the error allowed when A TRACKS B at level u. Then Figure 5.1 indicates bounds on the chances of each possible scenario. The labeled chances in Figure 5.1 are those given by the assumptions that A TRACKS B and B TRACKS C, both at level u. From these we can calculate bounds on the possibilities of interest to the claim that A TRACKS C.

In particular, $P(A/C) > (1 - r)^2$, as can be seen by going to the C possibility and looking at the chances of all the paths that lead to an A. There is a path to A via −B but both of the nodes on that path give us upper bounds rather than lower bounds, so they are useless because they could be as low as 0. However, the path through B to A gives us a lower bound of $(1 - r)^2$ because the chances of A happening that way are the same as the chances of B and A happening given C, namely, the chances of the former

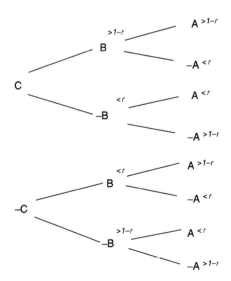

Figure 5.1

two multiplied. We can check our calculation by checking P(−A/C). There are two ways to get −A from C, one through the −B node and the other through the B node. The probability that the −B node gives us −A is less than r, which we get by supposing the worst case that −A always follows −B (that is, P(−A/−B) = 1), and noting that the probability of −B given C is less than r, and r multiplied by 1 equals r. The B node can give us −A only if B gives us −A, but the probability of that is less than r. Thus, P(−A/C) is less than r + r = 2r. This is consistent with P(A/C) > $(1 − r)^2 = 1 − 2r + r^2$. We can conclude, then, that P(A/C) > 1 − 2r. An analogous argument shows that P(−A/−C) > 1−2r. Thus, if A TRACKS B at level u and B TRACKS C at level u, then A TRACKS C at level 1−2r, i.e., at level u−r.

The error between the beginning and end of a series of tracking links 2 links long is less than 2 times the upper bound of error in each link. It is evident that this generalizes to n links: if A_1 TRACKS A_2, A_2 TRACKS A_3, ..., $A_{n−1}$ TRACKS A_n, where the TRACKING in each link is at level u, and u = 1 − r, then A_1 TRACKS A_n at level 1−nr. I call this property 'transitivity enough', since it is enough transitivity for better evidence to improve our chances of knowledge on a tracking view of both concepts. It is also enough to understand generally how it is possible for us to have knowledge, on the tracking view, by the intermediary of testimony. Error grows in a controlled and at most arithmetic manner when we put tracking claims end to end. In particular, if A TRACKS B at level 0.95, and B TRACKS C at level 0.95, then A TRACKS C at level 0.90, which is far from shabby. If my belief in p TRACKS a testifier's testimony that p at level 0.95, and that testimony TRACKS the truth of p at level 0.95, then my belief that p will TRACK p at level 0.90.

It is easy to see, though, that if one's TRACKING has no more than transitivity enough then there is a level of error beyond which putting TRACKING relations end to end will get you nothing at all. For notice that if r = 0.25 then 1− nr = 0.50 for n = 2. That is, putting two TRACKING claims end to end where each has an error rate possibly as high as 0.25 will mean only that the end TRACKS the beginning at a 0.50 rate, little better than random. If there are three links, then one gets to random with an even lower level of possible error in each link. And so on for greater numbers of links. Trusting to intermediaries to guide one's belief about a matter has a cost in error: the greater the number of (fallible) links the more error, and there is a point at which a greater number of (fallible) links makes the enterprise useless.

However, there are other costs that give us reasons to use intermediaries despite the danger. For example, it is not clear that we have any choice but to use the intermediary of inductive evidence in our efforts to track hypotheses. If we did not use such evidence we would avoid the cost of possibly tracking little better than random, but at the cost of not tracking hypotheses at all. Our trust in testimony also has a cost in error because there is at least one intermediary link, but the amount of error introduced would not always make the alternative to trusting testimony more attract-ive: tracking those truths directly would often require a lot more personal effort than does the determination of who to trust. This is especially true of trust in the testimony of scientific experts: not only are the links, we often suppose, more reliable than those in everyday life, but also the cost of tracking the matters in question directly oneself is very high, and for many prohibitive, because it involves difficult and expensive experiments and mathematical reasoning. Transitivity enough is not ideal, but it corresponds well to the trade-offs we actually make when we use intermediaries in the effort to know.

It is clear from these reflections that if one is to use intermediaries to know by tracking then, however this is accomplished, the tracking chain from belief in h to the truth of h must not be broken. If evidence is the intermediary, then at the far end it seems obvious that the evidence e must TRACK the hypothesis h—a claim that the remainder of this chapter will defend on independent grounds. However, at the near end, the relation between e and belief in h, it seems that there are two possibilities. Either the subject's belief in h TRACKS e, and e TRACKS h, or the subject's belief in h TRACKS her belief in e, her belief in e TRACKS e, and e TRACKS h. In the first case we might say that the subject's belief in h follows the evidence e, and that the subject uses the evidence e, but it would not necessarily be the case that the subject 'has' the evidence e, since belief in e is not required. Given my criterion for belief this means that such a subject would not even necessarily recognize the truth of e when the statement e was presented to her because she would not necessarily bet on it.

This may seem a strange way of coming to know things, but I am not willing to rule it out. There are plausible explanations for a subject's inability to recognize the truth of something that she in fact relies on in forming her beliefs. One possibility is that that truth is too complicated for her to understand when stated explicitly, though she has mechanisms for responding appropriately to whether it is true or false. Another possibility is simply that the subject does not recognize it when in a different form than the one she responds to, i.e. stated explicitly. The many cues that we respond to when deciding whether to trust someone, some of which dogs also respond to in evaluating the trustworthiness of a stranger, do not seem necessarily to be things we would recognize as true if they were put into explicit statements. If we think that it is possible that we are unable to become conscious of some things we rely on in our unconscious abilities, then we will think the way of using evidence currently under discussion is possible. Significantly, this would mean that a statement would not have to be part of our knowledge in order to be evidence that we make use of.

It would, I think, be inappropriate to say that a subject 'has' evidence e when she does not have a belief that e, even if she makes appropriate use of the truth of e in forming her belief about h. But we clearly do have evidence, at least in the sense of believing evidence statements, in many cases. In the other possible way I have described for a subject to come to know h through evidence e the subject is very likely to have e in the sense of believing e and even knowing e. This is because in this trajectory for knowing h not only is h true but also b(h) TRACKS b(e), b(e) TRACKS e, and e TRACKS h. Now, if h is true—as it must be for anyone to know it—and e TRACKS h then it is unlikely that e is false. And, if e is false, then because the subject's belief in e TRACKS e, the subject is unlikely to believe e. Since b(h) TRACKS b(e), the probability of b(h) given −b(e) is low too. All of this suggests that if the subject knows h through this trajectory, then because in order to do that she must believe h, e is likely to be true. Similar reasoning says that if the subject knows h through this trajectory then it is probable that the subject believes e. Does the subject also know e? Showing that the subject probably believes e and that e is probably true were the harder part in showing that she probably knows e, because knowing by an intermediary requires that the tracking chain not be broken and in the trajectory we are imagining one of the links is between b(e) and e. Therefore b(e) TRACKS e. Thus, if e is true and the subject believes e in this trajectory then the subject does know e. While it is not a necessary truth, it is probable that evidence that we have that helps us to know in the fashion under discussion now is itself part of our knowledge.[3]

In the foregoing discussion of the relation between knowledge and evidence on the recursive tracking view, I have inferred from the view of knowledge that evidence that helps us to have knowledge will normally stand in a tracking relation to the thing known. In the next sections of this chapter we will leave presumptions about what knowledge is behind, and see what reflections on the concept(s) of evidence lead us to believe about what makes evidence evidence. Through these independent reflections I will also conclude that inductive evidence stands in a tracking relation to what it is evidence for. At the end of this chapter I will come back to show that the concepts of evidence we arrive at do indeed combine with the recursive tracking view of knowledge to make the truism about knowledge and evidence with which this chapter began come out true.

Desiderata for a concept of evidence

Intuitively, good evidence for a hypothesis is a discriminating indicator of the truth of the hypothesis. It indicates, to whatever degree, the truth of the hypothesis in a way that discriminates between that hypothesis and its rivals. What is it to be an indicator, and what is it for an indicator to be discriminating? The 'check engine' lights in our cars are indicators to the extent that they go on when a problem is there, and if they are discriminating they go on *only* when a problem is there. This suggests that what it is for x to be a discriminating indicator of y is that x would be true if y were true, and false if y were false. Nozick wrote that e is *strong evidence* for h whenever if h were true then e would be true and if h were false then e would be false (Nozick 1981: 167–290). Substituting conditional probabilities for Nozick's subjunctive conditionals, we get that e is strong evidence for h whenever e TRACKS h at a high level. Tracking thus provides an analysis of what it is to be a discriminating indicator: x is a discriminating indicator of y when and only when x TRACKS y. Thereby it provides an analysis of what it is to be evidence.

It is not because Nozick had a tracking view of evidence or because I have endorsed a tracking view of knowledge that I will endorse a tracking view of evidence. Rather, the basis of a tracking view of evidence is in the first place the intuition that evidence is a matter of discrimination and indication. We will see in what follows that this intuition stands up to scrutiny that is based on the best that current confirmation theory has to offer. In conjunction with other arguments this intuition allows us to identify the most apt measure of degree of confirmation or evidential support.

By current confirmation theory I mean Bayesian confirmation theory, which is distinguished from non-Bayesian approaches to evidence in the first place by using

---

[3] This and the previous conclusion may be compared to Williamson's E = K thesis. See Williamson (2000: ch. 9).

probability models. That is, the Bayesian makes the idealizing assumption that all statements of the language in question possess probabilities. This is in contrast to the approach of classical statistics in which it is denied, for example, that hypotheses have probabilities.[4] The Bayesian use of probability to give an account of concepts of evidence contrasts with other approaches in another way: whereas, Peter Achinstein (2001), for example, insists that the concept of probability is insufficient to account for the concept *evidence*, and he supplements *probability* with the concept *explanation* in his own account of concepts of evidence, the Bayesian utilizes no concept other than *probability* to explicate concepts of evidence.

For my own part this is because I think one should explicate concepts in terms of concepts more fundamental because only then is the explication explanatory. While the concept of probability shows its fundamentality by its ability to be used in a myriad of contexts to define many other notions, the concept of explanation, for example, strikes me as no more fundamental than that of evidence. Indeed, there is an account of the concept of explanation, powerful and compelling to my mind, which uses only the concept of probability, namely, the statistical relevance account of *explanation* developed by Wesley Salmon (Salmon 1970). For related reasons of explanatory depth an analysis is better the fewer the primitive notions it assumes, so it is better to use only *probability* than to use *probability* and some other concept, whatever that other concept is. Achinstein might agree with this general principle but claims, through purported counterexamples, that *evidence* just cannot be analyzed through probability alone. In a later section of this chapter I argue that the examples he offers give us no reason to think this.[5]

This is not to say that the concept of probability as it is now understood will and must be the one we use forevermore. The standard Kolmogorov axiomatization of probability has limitations that affect its use in explicating concepts of evidence.[6] However, this suggests to me only that we should be open to generalizations and modifications of this axiomatization of *probability*, developments which are in any case a natural part of theoretical progress. It does not suggest that supplementation with concepts other than *probability* is necessary, or that illuminating universal claims about inductive evidence are impossible. It looks as if any future and better account of *evidence* will have to go through the concept of probability alone, however the latter is formulated. Thus, it is not merely because it is convenient for one who has committed herself to a view of knowledge in which subjunctive conditionals are jettisoned in favor of conditional probabilities that I will use *probability*, and no other concept, to explicate concepts of evidence. There is good independent reason to formulate what evidence is in terms of *probability* alone.

---

[4] For a defense of the avoidance of probabilities for hypotheses, see for example Mayo (1996). For a defense of the assignment of probabilities to hypotheses, see for example Fitelson (2005).

[5] For a more comprehensive defense of the claim that *probability* alone can explicate the notion of evidence as incremental support see for example Howson and Urbach (1993: 389–439) and Maher (2004). For dissent, see for example Glymour (1980: 63–93), Kelly and Glymour (2004), and Forster (1995).

[6] For a discussion of some of these, see Norton (2003: 659–62).

As will be evident from the discussion above, the notions of evidence that I am aiming for are objective in the following sense. That e is evidence for h is understood as holding in virtue of a factual relation between the statement e's being true and the statement h's being true, not in virtue of anyone's believing that this relation exists. Thus e does not become evidence, for example, only when some subject recognizes it as such. e is evidence for h or is not, in the sense I will be pursuing, regardless of whether anyone notices it. These latter issues give rise to the questions whether any subject *knows* or *believes* that e is evidence for h, not whether e is evidence for h. We can be wrong in claims that e is or is not evidence for h, for example by having false background beliefs that are relevant to the relation between e and h. To respect this fact we must regard the claim that e is evidence for h as a factual matter, not a matter dependent on anyone's beliefs.

One may worry that this is inconsistent with the Bayesian approach that I have endorsed, because of the personalist or subjective interpretation of probability associated with Bayesianism in which the probability of a proposition is some subject's degree of belief in that proposition. First, it is important to note that while the personalist interpretation of probability is useful for some purposes, e.g., exploration of rationality constraints, it is not the only interpretation of probability available to a Bayesian. Bayesianism can be defined, in the first place, by the commitment to assigning probabilities to all statements, including hypotheses, and is not necessarily restricted in the interpretation of probability. Second, I do favor an objective interpretation of probability for the purposes of this book, and such an interpretation is most natural in light of the externalist sentiment that whether one knows is not a matter of what one is aware of but of what is the case in the relation between one's beliefs and the truth.

Nonetheless, a personalist interpretation of probability could be used in conjunction with what I will say about evidence. It would involve a simple translation of statements like 'in order for e to be evidence for h, P(—) must be $\sim\sim$' to statements like 'in order for it to be rational for subject S to believe that e is evidence for h, her degree of belief in — must be $\sim\sim$'. The set of constraints that results from the translation is weaker than those I will present but the two are not inconsistent even though their verdicts may not match: it may be rational for a given subject to ascribe the concept of evidence to the relation between e and h given her set of beliefs, but that is not inconsistent with the possibility that her ascription is incorrect, that is, that e is not evidence for h. This could be so, for example, if her relevant background beliefs are false. Thus even if one adopts a subjective interpretation of probability one is not necessarily thereby saying that whether or not one statement *is* evidence for another depends on anyone's beliefs; one may simply admit the obvious fact that the conditions under which a certain relation holds may be different from the conditions under which it is rational for a particular subject to believe that it holds. If one chooses a personalist interpretation of probability, then the probabilistic conditions I will lay out will be not conditions under which e is evidence for h, but rather merely conditions under which a subject ought to regard e as evidence for h given her overall set of beliefs. That is not to deny that the relation __ is evidence for __ is objective.

Among Bayesians—or those we might call 'probabilists' given the weakness of my requirement for qualifying as a Bayesian—there is no disagreement I know of regarding the condition under which one statement supports another. That is, if we asked no question about quantity of support, but only whether e supports h to any (possibly minuscule) degree, probabilists would agree that the following is one way to formulate the answer:

e supports h if and only if $P(h/e) > P(h)$ †

This condition says that e is positively probabilistically relevant to h, that e raises h's probability above what it was without taking e into account. This is a notion of incremental support, which tells us nothing about how high the prior probability $P(h)$ or posterior probability $P(h/e)$ of the hypothesis is, but only whether e makes the posterior probability greater than the prior probability. It is what is usually referred to by the word 'confirmation' in the literature. In ordinary language the word 'confirmation' can also refer to a situation where evidence makes the posterior probability very high. That is a distinct notion that I will come to below, but I will reserve the term 'confirmation' and its cognates for the current incremental notion of support. Thus the term 'supports' is shorthand for 'incrementally supports' and is interchangeable with 'confirms'.

Significantly, there are other ways to formulate the condition for the existence of incremental support. Obviously, $P(h/e) > P(h)$ if and only if $P(e/h) > P(e)$, by a manipulation of Bayes's theorem. However, while $P(h/e)/P(h) = P(e/h)/P(e)$, there are even ways to formulate the accepted condition for support that do not yield ratios or differences equivalent to $P(h/e)/P(h)$. For example,

$P(e/h) > P(e/-h)$ if and only if $P(e/h) > P(e)$ if and only if e supports h,

but, except in special cases,

$P(e/h)/P(e/-h)$ does not equal $P(e/h)/P(e)$,

even if we ignore the cases in which either is undefined because of a zero denominator. What this means is that while those various formulations agree in all cases as to *whether* confirmation or support obtains, they disagree about *how much* obtains, because how much confirmation obtains is measured by the ratios or differences, and the ratios or differences are not generally equal. Branden Fitelson (1999, 2001*a*, 2001*b*) has pointed out and studied the significance and extent of this measure dependence of the confirmation relation for an ever-increasing set of claims of philosophical interest. (See also Christensen 1999) The various measures, of which there are many consistent with the condition of support given above, do not merely differ by degree but also ordinally. That is, they do not concur in general as to whether a piece of evidence confirms one hypothesis more or less than it does another hypothesis, or whether a piece of evidence confirms a hypothesis more or less than another piece of evidence confirms that same hypothesis. Thus, the differences between these measures are significant for any question that goes beyond the question whether e bears the relation of support to h at all.

I will be going beyond the question of when there is support or no support partly because the clear superiority of a tracking view shows up beyond this in questions about degree of support. I will also go beyond the question of support vs. no support because for purposes of the chapter that follows this one I am concerned to give an account of the type of evidence that gives us reason to believe a hypothesis is true, not merely more reason to believe the hypothesis than when we had not taken the evidence into account, that is, not merely incremental support. The reason for this interest of mine is that the scientific realist claims that our evidence for theories gives us reason to believe that some of those theories are true; he does not merely claim that our evidence gives us more such reason than we had before. To evaluate this claim of the realist critically we will ask whether our evidence does give such reasons, and for that we will need to know what properties evidence must have to achieve the said task.

What this means for the current chapter is that in addition to arguing for the superiority of a particular measure of degree of incremental support, I will also identify a second kind of condition that combined with sufficient incremental support puts a lower bound on the posterior probability of the hypothesis, that is, the probability that the hypothesis is true once the evidence is taken into account. If evidence not only supports a hypothesis but supports it sufficiently to make the probability of the hypothesis greater than 0.5, then I take it that the evidence in question gives one who has it some reason to believe the hypothesis is true. This kind of evidence I call *some evidence*. If evidence not only supports a hypothesis but supports it sufficiently to make the probability of the hypothesis high, then the evidence in question gives one who has it good reason to believe the hypothesis is true. This kind of evidence I call *good evidence*. This is a particular way of stating the idea that evidence and probability are guides to belief. Note that I have only stipulated what it is for evidence to give some reason or good reason to believe a hypothesis is true; I have taken no stand on whether evidence is the only way to acquire reason or good reason to believe a hypothesis is true.

An adequate notion of support or of the more absolute types of evidence just referred to should do justice to another assumption we tend to make about evidence. This is that evidence provides leverage on the truth of claims about the world. Specifically, knowing that the evidence statement is true is usually a lot easier than knowing that the hypothesis statement is true, and we use the former to help us make progress on the latter where we could not have made progress directly. This is analogous to the way in which we use a lever—a plank and a well-placed fulcrum— and our ability to lift a small weight in order to move a large weight we could not have lifted directly. The lever would not help us to move weights, of course, if for some reason the plank always had to be as heavy as the larger weight itself. For then we could not set up the connection between the smaller and the larger weight, for the same reason as we could not move the larger weight directly: the plank would be too heavy to put in place.

It is similar with evidence. Evidence would be useless to us if in order to judge its relation to the hypothesis it supports we had to know whether the hypothesis was true. If we already knew whether the hypothesis was true then the evidence, and its relation to the hypothesis, would not be needed, just as if we could put into place a plank as heavy as the object we wanted to move, a lever would not be necessary. The same point seen in reverse is that if we were not able to move the heavy weight in the first place then an equally heavy lever would not help us. Evidence is useful to us as a matter of fact, and we would not be able to explain the usefulness that evidence has if we were to depart dramatically from the leverage picture.

This leads to the idea that we ought not to define the criterion for a statement to be evidence for a hypothesis in a way that requires judgment of the truth of the hypothesis, if we want the criterion to be of any use in determining whether one statement is evidence for another, or in explaining the fact that we apparently often accomplish this determination. This idea explains, I think, the attraction of the qualitative syntactical views of confirmation that were popular among philosophers before they were discredited by Nelson Goodman's grue problem (Goodman 1983: 66–83). On these views, judging whether one statement was evidence for another was a matter of comparing the syntax of the two statements—was the first an instance of the second, did the first logically imply the second, etc.? No knowledge of whether the hypothesis was true, indeed no empirical knowledge whatsoever, was required to make such judgments.

Syntactic views of what the relation is in virtue of which one statement is evidence for another provide an easy way to conform to the leverage idea about evidence. But though Bayesian views of what evidence is are expressed formally they are not syntactical in the sense just described, because whether a formally expressed probabilistic condition for evidence, e.g. $P(e/h) > P(e)$, is fulfilled may depend on matters of fact, and usually does. However, we do not need to ban from the evidence relation all dependence on empirical fact in order to conform to the leverage idea. We go a long way by simply banning from the relation of evidence dependence on the truth or probability of the hypothesis itself, and maintaining the hope that the empirical facts on which the claim that one statement is evidence for another does depend are not themselves more difficult to assess than the hypothesis, though of course whether or not they are will depend on the case. I suspect that concerns about what I have called 'leverage' are part of the reason that the statistician I. J. Good took it as clear that the relation in virtue of which a statement is evidence for a hypothesis h should not be a function of $P(h)$ (Good 1985: 250–1, 266). Theorists can disagree about whether the confirmation relation should depend on $P(h)$, as James Joyce (2003) helpfully explains; thus, the leverage picture can be taken as my reason for going one way rather than the other on this issue.

The account of *evidence* that follows is thus guided by a number of expectations I have about the concepts I am aiming for. First are the intuitions that evidence is a matter of discrimination and of indication. Second is the requirement to explicate *evidence* purely in terms of *probability*. Third is the expectation that the relation in virtue of which one statement is evidence for another is objective. Fourth, I aim to identify not only the correct measure of incremental confirmation but also a kind of condition that together with sufficient incremental support will put a lower bound on the posterior probability of the hypothesis. Fifth, evidence and probability are taken to be guides to belief in the particular ways I stipulated. Finally, the idea that evidence works by leverage should be respected as far as possible. In addition to these guiding ideas, further particular considerations will weigh into my choices as those choices arise.

The discrimination condition on evidence

On my account there are two things we want to know when we want to know whether one statement is evidence for another. One thing we want to know, which may seem trivial but as I will argue is not, is that the truth of the purported evidence statement is an indicator of something. This will be connected, on my account, to its potential to be a reason to believe anything at all. Another thing we want to know is that the truth of the statement discriminates between the hypothesis and the negation of the hypothesis. For this, I will define a condition that incorporates the tracking ideas. If the indication condition is fulfilled, that will imply that the statement is evidence for *something*. If the discrimination condition is fulfilled, that will imply that the thing it is evidence for is the hypothesis rather than its negation.

It is natural to discuss the discrimination condition first since this discussion will motivate the particular form that the question about the indication condition takes on my view. To decide whether a potential evidence statement, e, discriminates between the hypothesis, h, and its negation, −h, we should compare two probabilities. It is natural, both intuitively and by some statistical traditions, to focus on the following:

P(e/h), the probability of e given h, and
P(e/−h), the probability of e given −h.

These probabilities, called 'likelihoods' of e on h and e on −h, have an obvious relation to Nozick's subjunctive conditional tracking conditions. If the first probability is high, then the probability of e is high when h is assumed, and if the second is low, then the probability of e is low when −h is assumed. These are close to Nozick's conditions on strong evidence that if h were true then e would be true, and that if h were false then e would not be true, respectively.

If the first probability, P(e/h), were high and the second, P(e/−h), low, then e would be significantly more probable assuming h was true than assuming h was false. In that case, the truth or falsity of h would make a difference to the truth of e, and in the right direction for imagining e as evidence for h. (The car's malfunctioning would make a difference, in the right direction, to the 'check engine' light's going on.) If so, then e's truth would in turn discriminate between h and −h. (Assuming the previous, the 'check engine' light's going on discriminates between the car's functioning and not functioning.) Thus, e discriminates somewhat between h and −h as long as P(e/h) is greater than P(e/−h), even if the first value is not absolutely high or the second absolutely low.[7]

We want P(e/h) to be greater than P(e/−h) if we are to count e as discriminating between h and −h. However, there is more than one way to measure how far e so

---

[7] A careful reader will have noticed that whereas I associated high P(e/h) with the intuitive idea of indication when I first discussed the check engine light example, I now associate it with discrimination. Indeed high P(e/h) will not show up later in the conditions I set for indication. Here is what has happened. The intuition of indication is more complicated than that of discrimination, and more

discriminates. We could measure, for example, by the difference between these likelihoods, P(e/h) − P (e/−h), as Nozick did when he discussed his tracking view of evidence in probabilistic terms.[8] This turns out to be a bad idea, not only because of individual counterexamples, such as those discussed by Richard Foley (1987), but because of this measure's violation of a general condition that is widely assumed, and on which many results in confirmation theory depend:

If P(h/e) > P(h/e′), then e confirms h to a greater degree than e′ confirms h.

(See Fitelson 1999, Joyce 2003.) The likelihood-difference measure violates the condition stated if we take degree of discrimination as explicating degree of confirmation, and we measure degree of discrimination by this difference between the likelihoods.

However, we would be poor probability theorists if we took this to mean the defeat of a tracking view of evidence, for there are other ways to use those likelihoods to measure degree of discrimination, that is, the degree to which P(e/h) exceeds P(e/−h). For example, we can measure the degree to which e discriminates between h and −h by the ratio of the two likelihoods in question:

$$P(e/h)/P(e/-h)$$

I will take this quantity, called the Likelihood Ratio (LR), to measure the degree to which e discriminates between h and −h and thereby the degree to which e supports or incrementally confirms h. Thus, e *confirms* h to some degree just in case this ratio is greater than 1 and e *disconfirms* h, and (as it happens) equivalently confirms −h, to some degree just in case this ratio is less than 1. e confirms h to a higher degree the higher this ratio is above 1, and e disconfirms h to a higher degree (and confirms −h to a higher degree) the lower this ratio is below 1. When the ratio is exactly 1 no confirmation or disconfirmation obtains. Since, as noted earlier, P(e/h) > P(e/−h) if and only if P(e/h) > P(e), the view advocated here is a specification of the general Bayesian picture of confirmation. In abiding by condition † it takes confirmation to exist if and only if e is positively probabilistically relevant to h, as on all probabilist accounts.

To see how the LR works, consider an example. Turning back the clock to late 2002, suppose we know that Saddam Hussein's Iraq succeeded in enriching uranium in past

complicated than it appears. When we think of the check engine light as indicating trouble, we make more than one assumption about that light's general behavior. One of those assumptions, that it is more likely to go on when there's trouble than when there is not, is naturally put in the discrimination part of my account. There is another assumption, that when the light goes on that should be taken seriously at all, that I will make the central idea in my condition(s) for indication. There is also a mathematical reason to divide the intuitions in this way: even if we put absolute requirements on the values of the likelihoods P(e/h) and P(e/−h), we would get no constraint on the posterior probability of the hypothesis, so we might as well just take the information that the ratio of those two quantities gives us and look somewhere other than the likelihoods for constraints that will determine absolute probabilities. This is what I do below.

[8] Nozick wrote most of his discussion of his tracking view of evidence in terms of probability rather than subjunctive conditionals, but seems to have regarded the probabilities as a kind of approximation. I am taking conditional probabilities as the real thing and subjunctive conditionals as an approximation, or picturesque thinking device.

efforts at a program for nuclear weapons. We discover that Iraq has recently purchased on the world market a particular kind of aluminum tube that—we are told—could be used for the enrichment of uranium. Do we have evidence that Iraq currently has a nuclear weapons program? What does that depend on?

The LR illuminates this nicely. Let,

e = Iraq has purchased high strength 81mm anodized aluminum tubes.
h = Iraq currently has a nuclear weapons program.

It appears that $P(e/h)$ is high, since apparently those tubes are suitable for enrichment of uranium, and if Iraq had a nuclear weapons program it would be trying to enrich uranium (as opposed to buying enriched uranium straight) because its scientists know how to do it, and that would be easier to hide than the buying of weapons-grade uranium straight. However, we sense that whether e is evidence for h depends on something else too, namely, whether those tubes are suitable for anything other than enriching uranium.[9] If the tubes could be used without modification for household plumbing, then there would be no case here against Iraq. Initial reports by the Bush administration of the discovery of aluminum tube purchases made it sound like those tubes Iraq bought were distinctive, and could not easily be used for anything else. If so, that would mean that $P(e/-h)$ was very low and, since $P(e/h)$ was high, that the LR was quite high, significantly greater than 1. This high value for the LR mirrors our sense that if all these assumptions were right, then we would have significant support for the claim that Iraq had a nuclear weapons program.

Subsequent reports about the US government's view of the matter divulged that there was significant dissension in the ranks about the aluminum tubes. The enrichment experts at the Department of Energy, officials at the State Department, and members of the CIA were of the opinion that the dimensions of those tubes made them suitable for things other than enriching uranium. They also protested that the dimensions of these tubes made them unsuitable for enrichment of uranium unless the tubes were made to undergo significant and costly modification. The IAEA and the report of the UN weapons inspectors in January 2003 concurred: those tubes were most suitable for use in conventional rockets of a sort Iraq was permitted to have under existing agreements, and was known to manufacture for itself. If the tubes were suitable for other things, things that Iraq was known to have done, then that would mean that $P(e/-h)$ was high: they would likely be buying those tubes even if they did not have a nuclear weapons program. If both $P(e/h)$ and $P(e/-h)$ are high, the LR is not going to be significantly greater than 1, mirroring our sense that this new information weakens our evidence for h significantly. Even worse for the prospects of evidence against Iraq from this direction, if the dissenting experts were right that the aluminum tubes were not as they stood suited to enriching uranium, that would make $P(e/h)$ much lower. With $P(e/-h)$ high due to the suitability of the tubes for the

---

[9] We might think we should also be asking whether things other than weapons could make the probability high that uranium enrichment is going on. Enriched uranium is very useful in peaceful nuclear reactors, after all. Weapons-grade enrichment is higher than reactor-grade enrichment, though, and, as I understand it, reactor-grade enrichment would not have required the process the aluminum tubes were imagined to take part in.

conventional rocket program, the LR would definitely not be greater than 1, in conformity with our intuition in that case that the aluminum tubes had turned out to be a misleading distraction.

Examples could be multiplied to convince the reader that the LR, or some measure ordinally equivalent to it, such as log(LR), sounds good as a measure of the degree to which evidence e supports hypothesis h. However, other measures of support have been considered and defended over the years, so it is important to say why this one should be preferred. Other people have already done a lot of work for me on this question. So, for example, I. J. Good's lifelong defense of his concept *weight of evidence* comes to my aid, since this concept is the same as the LR up to ordinal equivalence (Good 1983, 1985). Good wrote that he learned the tools involved in this concept from Harold Jeffreys and Alan Turing during their cryptanalysis work during the Second World War, and that they were instrumental in cracking codes. Good was convinced that his concept 'completely captures that of the degree to which evidence corroborates a hypothesis' and that 'it is almost as much an intelligence amplifier as the concept of probability itself' (Good 1983: p. xi).

More recently, Branden Fitelson has shown that the LR (or the ordinally equivalent log(LR)) is the only one of the familiar measures satisfying † above that satisfies several intuitive criteria for a confirmation relation to be able to give an account of independent evidence (Fitelson 2001*b*). He has also shown that the LR is the only measure that has been described, up to ordinal equivalence, that both respects the role of relevance in confirmation, that is, condition † above, and provides a quantitative generalization of deduction (Fitelson, private communication). This means that the LR can deliver the conclusion that if e deductively implies h (and e is not itself a logical falsehood) then e gives the strongest possible degree of support to h. This is because if e deductively implies h then $P(e/-h) = 0$, which means the LR is infinite provided that $P(e/h)$ does not equal 0, which it can do only if $P(e) = 0$, i.e. only if e is false.

To answer a question I left open at the beginning of this chapter, I view this treatment of deductive implication as the limiting case of inductive support as a good thing since it unifies our account of induction and deduction in the only way that makes sense. Deductive implication is seen in this treatment as the strongest possible kind of inductive support. It is of great significance that the LR can deliver this consequence and other relevance measures cannot. There are two additional quantitative problems that the LR measure does not have but at least one other popular measure does. One is the problem of old evidence, that when $P(e)$ is equal to or close to 1, e cannot count as evidence or much evidence for h even when it seems right to say that e supports h. The other problem is that when the probability of h is very high nothing can count as much evidence for h, even when it seems right to say that some e is strong evidence for h. I will discuss how the LR handles these issues as they arise below.

The reasons for preferring the LR measure of confirmation that I can add to these are best illustrated by comparing this measure to the popular ratio measure, according to which e confirms h to a greater degree the higher is the ratio $P(h/e)/P(h)$. An automatic prejudice has been created in favor of the ratio measure because Bayesian philosophers report the condition for the existence of confirmation at all in the form

$P(h/e) > P(h)$. But this favor is unwarranted since all of the relevance measures agree as to whether or not confirmation exists in a given case, so we could equivalently report the condition for confirmation as $P(e/h) > P(e/-h)$. To settle which is the better measure of the degree of confirmation we must compare the ratios $P(h/e)/P(h)$ and $P(e/h)/P(e/-h)$ as to how they are defined and how they behave.[10]

The intuition behind the ratio measure is that for e to be evidence for h, e should make the probability of h higher than it was before taking e into account. That is a sensible idea, but it is different from the discrimination dimension I have claimed is the intuitive key to evidential support. However, the ratio measure is similar to the LR, from a mathematical point of view. For $P(h/e)/P(h)$ is equivalent (via Bayes's theorem) to $P(e/h)/P(e)$, and the LR is $P(e/h)/P(e/-h)$. Since their numerators are the same, the two measures differ only by having $P(e)$ or $P(e/-h)$ in the denominator. What difference does this make?

Expanding $P(e)$, the answer becomes clear: the ratio measure contains a contribution from the prior probabilities of the hypothesis and its negation, that the LR does not have:

$P(e/h)/P(e/-h)$ Likelihood-Ratio Measure
$P(e/h)/[P(e/h)P(h) + P(e/-h)P(-h)]$ Ratio Measure

The prior probabilities of the hypothesis and its negation, on which the ratio measure depends, dilute the information there is in that ratio as to whether e discriminates between h and $-h$. The $P(e/-h)$ term, which tells us the probability of e on the assumption h is false, does occur in the denominator of the ratio measure, but it is tempered by the other three terms that also occur there.

The ratio measure dilutes information about how far e discriminates between h and $-h$ with information about prior probabilities of the hypothesis and its negation. This explains why the ratio measure does not strike us as measuring discrimination but as having a different guiding idea. But if discrimination is what a measure of confirmation should measure, as I think it is, then the ratio measure is not what we want and the LR measure is, because the latter gives us the information we want in a pure form, undiluted by other information. Dependence of the notion of how far e confirms h on the prior probabilities of h and $-h$ is objectionable for a second reason that I have discussed above. Namely, it will run us quickly afoul of the idea that evidence is something that gives us leverage. For in that case we would have to know how plausible the hypothesis is in order to know to what extent e is evidence for it. If we can avoid that kind of demand, we should, and going with the LR over the ratio measure avoids an obvious case of it. Of course, the term $P(e/-h)$ will have contributions from the priors relative to $-h$ of all of the possibilities that go to make up $-h$. However, though these are prior probabilities, they are not priors of the hypothesis in question or its negation, $P(h)$ or $P(-h)$. In any case, the $P(e/-h)$ term occurs in both measures so the dependence of this term on priors is immaterial to a comparative

---

[10] Some of the comparisons I make in what follows will also explain why the LR measure is superior to the difference measure: $P(h/e) - P(h)$, and the normalized difference measure: $P(h/e) - P(h/-e)$.

judgment of the two measures' leverage properties: both demand evaluation of this term $P(e/-h)$. I claim here only that the LR has a comparative advantage with respect to leverage, but this is enough to yield a preference if we care about leverage. In fact, the LR is the Bayesian relevance measure least dependent on priors, which makes it the measure of choice from the leverage point of view.

For clarity let me say explicitly that the '$-h$' term in the denominator of what I am calling the 'Likelihood Ratio' is the negation of h. It is not one particular hypothesis that contradicts h, or even the small group of hypotheses we have thought of so far that are inconsistent with h, but the full logical complement of h. That is, it is the disjunction of all logically possible alternatives to h. Thus, what I am calling the Likelihood Ratio is different from the likelihood ratio defended by Richard Royall (1997), who builds a view of evidence on a comparative measure, $P(e/T)/P(e/T')$, where T and T' are rival but not necessarily jointly exhaustive hypotheses. This comparative measure is not strong enough to constrain the posterior probability of the hypothesis, because $P(T) + P(T')$ is not necessarily equal to 1, or any particular value. (See Appendix 5.1.) This is so even if we add the kind of constraint I will adopt in the next section. Also, the so-called Law of Likelihood, roughly that e's support of h is shown only in what affects $P(e/h)$, is true on a comparative account of support such as Royall's but not on an account using the LR. This is because the LR takes into account $P(e/-h)$ in addition in determining how far e supports h.

Evaluation of the probability of e on this $-h$, the famous 'catch-all', is what I fully intend to require for determining whether e is evidence for h in the sense I am investigating. Objections to the effect that we are often unable to evaluate this probability for high-level theories will be forced to their natural, though unaccustomed, conclusion in the next chapter: so much the worse for our confidence that we have good reason to believe that those theories are true. We often can evaluate this probability term, and where we can is where our best evidence lies.

The indication condition on evidence

Something of the indication idea is already in the claim that $P(e/h)$ is high, but the first condition I have formulated, on the LR, is not enough to insure that $P(e/h)$ is high, since that is a ratio—the ratio could be high while both terms are low. Neither the condition that the LR be high nor a high ratio measure can be taken as sufficient conditions for e to be evidence for h, if we want the notion of evidence to include the notion of a reason to believe true, as I demanded above. This is because neither condition constrains the posterior probability of the hypothesis to be high, and we do not have good reason to believe, or even some reason to believe, a hypothesis is true, if we have no assurance that the posterior probability of the hypothesis is greater than 0.5. To see that high LR alone does not constrain the posterior probability, consider a hypothetical case with aluminum tubes.

e = Switzerland has purchased high-strength anodized 81mm aluminum tubes.
h = Switzerland has a nuclear weapons program.

To make the point, let us suppose that the dimensions and style of the tubes are indeed a good deal more suited to the enrichment of uranium than to anything else, which will give us that the LR is significantly greater than 1, and let us suppose that P(e/h) is 0.9, so the numerator of the LR is absolutely high not just much higher than the denominator. Nevertheless, the posterior probability of the hypothesis, h, will not be made high enough by this ratio to consider this a case in which we have a good reason to believe the hypothesis. This is because the prior probability of the hypothesis that Switzerland has a nuclear weapons program is so low that even multiplying it by four would not make it higher than 0.5. Doing the math, if the prior probability of the hypothesis is, as it seems to be, less than, say, 0.1, then the posterior probability of the hypothesis will still be less than 0.4, even on rosy values for the LR. High values for this ratio do not alone say that we have a good reason to believe a hypothesis; it seemed enough for the Iraq case only because there we were implicitly assuming that the prior probability of a nuclear weapons program was significant. The fact that neither high ratio measure nor high LR will insure high posterior probability for the hypothesis is a commonly cited limitation of both positive relevance and Likelihood Ratio conceptions of evidence.

An obvious solution to this problem is to adopt as a second condition for e to be evidence for h the demand that the posterior probability of h, P(h/e), be high. However, that is merely a restatement of our desideratum. Is there another condition that forces this desired outcome? There are at least two such conditions. The first is to require that the prior probability of the hypothesis, P(h), be high. A lower bound on the LR combined with a high P(h) will put a lower bound on the posterior probability of h, P(h/e), as can be seen using Bayes's theorem. However, this proposal conflicts with the leverage idea because in order to determine whether this condition holds you have to know the prior probability of the hypothesis explicitly. If there were no other options we might have to view this as a place where leverage is unattainable. However, it is possible to formulate a second condition and continue to uphold the leverage idea because there are other ways of getting at the same information.

It is an interesting algebraic fact that because P(e) is always between P(e/h) and P(e/−h), inclusive, at sufficiently high values of the LR a lower bound on P(e) constrains the posterior probability of the hypothesis to be greater than a certain value. This regularity can be visualized by taking the following equation, which is just a rearrangement of Bayes's theorem, as a starting point:

$$P(h/e) = [LR - P(e/h)/P(e)]/(LR - 1).[11]$$

We can see from this equation that values for P(e) and for P(e/h) and P(e/−h) are sufficient to determine the posterior probability of the hypothesis, because the two likelihoods determine the LR. Letting $y = LR$, $x = P(e/h)$, $P(e) = 0.4$, and the vertical axis z represent the dependent variable P(h/e), we can see how these terms affect the posterior probability of the hypothesis by looking at the surface that results from

---

[11] This equation can be derived by substituting (P(e) − P(e/−h))/(P(e/h) − P(e/−h)) in for P(h) in the standard Bayes equation. The equality of P(h) and the substitution can be derived by solving P(e) = P(e/h)P(h) + P(e/−h)P(−h) for P(h) and substituting 1 − P(h) for P(−h).

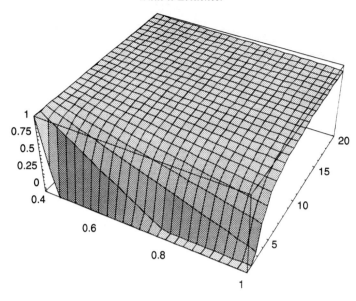

Figure 5.2a   P(e)=0.4

graphing the equation (Figure 5.2*a*). In general the LR may take any value, but I have graphed only the values between 1 and 20 because only values greater than 1 are cases of confirmation, and the effect I want to display shows up below LR = 20. The x-axis on which P(e/h) is graphed ranges between 0.4 and 1 because when P(e) = 0.4 and LR > 1, this restriction follows mathematically. The terms graphed on the x- and y-axes are independent, as they should be, because P(h) and P(−h) are understood here as dependent variables, taking whatever values x, y, and P(e) impose on them, not independent variables whose values fix relationships between the x and y terms.

Another way to think of how P(e), P(e/h), and P(e/−h) alone determine the posterior probability of h, and why P(h) and P(−h) are dependent variables in this scheme, can be seen in the following equations:

$$P(e) = P(e/h)P(h) + P(e/−h)P(−h)$$
$$1 = P(h) + P(−h)$$

Given values for P(e) and the likelihoods P(e/h) and P(e/−h), we have two equations in two variables, and can solve for P(h) and P(−h) if we wish. P(h) and P(−h) are best understood in this scheme not as priors but as weights, reflecting how well each of the likelihoods P(e/h) and P(e/−h) matches P(e), and thereby how good h and −h are at 'predicting' the actual probability of e.

If we imagine Figure 5.2*a* as sitting on a table, with the x- and y-axes resting flat on the table and the z-axis rising out of the table, and we rotate the graph clockwise while keeping it on the table, we get a graph with the y-axis, which was on the bottom right side, now going from left to right (on the bottom) in front of us, as in Figure 5.2*b*.

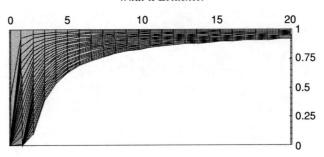

Figure 5.2*b*   P(e)=0.4

This is still a three-dimensional graph, but projected onto the two-dimensional page. The x-axis is now not visible because the reader is looking straight down it as the axis moves from higher to lower straight into the page. This particular graph illustrates how P(e) and the LR constrain P(h/e) because we can see that if P(e) = 0.4 and the LR is greater than about 4, P(h/e) will be greater than about 0.5.

This graph presents a convenient lower limit for the trends that we will see when we increase LR and P(e). The result is this: this surface bounds from below in the z dimension every graph with LR > 1 and P(e) > 0.4, and as these terms increase the z term increases. That is, as LR and P(e) increase above 1 and 0.4 respectively the value of P(h/e), for any given values of P(e/h) and the LR, monotonically rises to 1. We can see why this is by inspecting the equation

$$P(h/e) = [\text{LR} - P(e/h)/P(e)]/(\text{LR} - 1)$$

If we suppose that the LR is some fixed value greater than 1, then P(e/h) will be greater than or equal to P(e), since because P(e) is the weighted average of P(e/h) and P(e/−h), P(e) is always between P(e/h) and P(e/−h) inclusive, and LR > 1 tells us that P(e/h) is greater than P(e/−h). Since P(e/h) ≥ P(e), the term P(e/h)/P(e) subtracted in the numerator has a minimum value of 1, which it approaches on increase of P(e). In other words, increasing P(e) with fixed or rising LR will have the effect of increasing P(h/e).

For LR > 1, Figures 5.3–5.8 illustrate this trend. The fact that the x-axis is plotted into the page means that the empty space under the graphed surface shows that there are *no* values of P(e/h) for which P(h/e) is below the curve formed by the bottom of the visible graphed surface. Through graphing P(e/h), P(e), and the LR, we have found a result that is independent of P(e/h) and depends only on P(e) and the LR. For LR greater than about 3, fixed LR with increasing P(e) yields increased minimum values for P(h/e). Likewise, for LR greater than about 3, fixed P(e) with increasing LR yields increased minimum values for P(h/e). In general, putting a lower bound on the LR, and a lower bound on the value of P(e) will put a strict lower bound on the posterior probability of the hypothesis. (See Appendix 5.1 for an algebraic treatment.)

At sufficiently high values for P(e) and the LR, putting lower bounds on P(e) and the LR will put a lower bound on the posterior probability of the hypothesis. The next

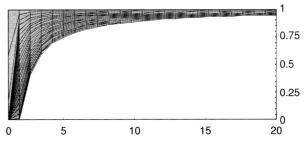

Figure 5.3 P(e)=0.5

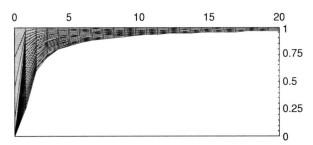

Figure 5.4 P(e)=0.6

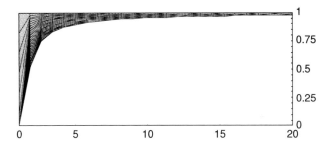

Figure 5.5 P(e)=0.7

question that arises is where we want to make cut-offs in conditions for evidence that exploit the cited trend. The general answer to this question is clear: we are interested in those values of the LR that are greater than the point from left to right where the graph lifts off the y-axis because that is where we start having a lower bound on P(h/e) that excludes values for P(h/e) not already excluded by the axiom that implies all probabilities are greater than or equal to zero.

The first point where a P(e) value of 0.5 gets you a meaningful constraint on the posterior, P(h/e), is roughly LR > 3, for there P(h/e) is greater than 0.5. That is, if it is more probable than not that e is true, and e is at least three times more likely if h is true than if −h is true, then it is more probable than not that h is true given e. This

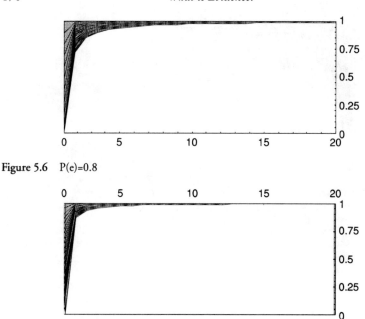

Figure 5.6   P(e)=0.8

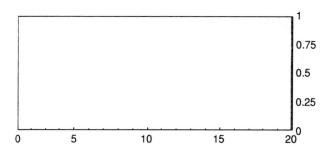

Figure 5.7   P(e)=0.9

Figure 5.8   P(e)=1

threshold is significant because it seems easier to determine whether a statement is roughly more probable than not, that is, has probability roughly greater than 0.5, than it is to assign an exact value to its probability. Also, if we know that the evidence makes the hypothesis more probable than not, that looks sufficient for counting us as having in e some reason to believe h. Thus, LR > 3 and P(e) > 0.5 will be jointly sufficient for our first notion of *some evidence*, evidence that gives some reason to believe the hypothesis. Many combinations of values for P(e) and LR (always greater than 1) will yield P(h/e) > 0.5. Thus, in general, one has *some evidence* for a hypothesis h when e is such that it has some combination of a lower bound greater than 0 on P(e) and a lower bound greater than 1 on the LR, that yields a lower bound of 0.5 on P(h/e).

Other points of interest occur as the LR and P(e) are pushed higher, since P(h/e) then approaches 1. There will be many and various combinations of values for the LR and P(e) that will make a high or very high probability for P(h/e), and which probabilities are easiest to judge in a given situation should play a role in deciding which combinations of LR and P(e) thresholds to use. One can also work backwards from the threshold on P(h/e) that is good enough to yield good reason to believe, which may vary with circumstances. For example, if P(h/e) > 0.82 seems sufficient for good reason to believe, then finding P(e) > 0.75 and LR > 3 will be enough to ensure it. If P(h/e) > 0.95 is desired, then LR > 3 and P(e) > 0.92 will ensure what you want. If it is hard to get a read on P(e), and you would like to show high P(h/e) by showing extremely high LR instead, you might choose to try to find that P(e) > 0.5 and LR > 21, because those together will insure that P(h/e) > 0.95. Another combination of interest is LR > 7 and P(e) > 0.75, for these conditions together force the posterior P(h/e) to be greater than 0.95. In general, e is *good evidence* for a hypothesis h if e is such that it has some combination of a lower bound greater than 0 on P(e) and a lower bound greater than 1 on the LR such that P(h/e) > x, where x, one's threshold for good reason to believe in the circumstances, is much greater than 0.5.

My proposal, then, is that the second condition on evidence, the indication condition, be a lower bound on the value of P(e). There are three broad questions to ask about this idea. One is whether, given that P(e) = P(e/h)P(h) + P(e/−h)P(−h), putting a condition on P(e) really does have an advantage with respect to leverage. A second is what the rationale could be for requiring a lower bound on P(e). A third is whether high P(e) is plausibly a necessary condition for evidence, since there seem to be counterexamples. I will address these questions in turn.

One might well wonder why it should be any better to require a lower bound on P(e) than to require that P(h) be high, when the objection to a condition on P(h) above was that requiring a determination of P(h) interfered with leverage, and when if P(e) is expanded so—P(e) = P(e/h)P(h) + P(e/−h)P(−h)—we see that it also contains information about the 'priors' of h and −h. Admittedly, information or misinformation about the 'priors' of h and −h is contained in any claim about the value of P(e). However, if we formulate the second condition on evidence as concerning P(e), it may not be necessary to ask for that information directly in order to have it. We can have that information, so far as we need it, without asking for it provided P(e) can be evaluated directly rather than calculated through its component parts. What I am concerned to argue, then, is that in some simple, paradigm cases of evidence P(e) can be evaluated directly, or at least without recourse to judgments of the priors on h and −h. I will not be able to show that the evaluation can be exact, but if I can show that it can be determined whether the value is roughly greater than 0.5 or roughly greater than 0.75 then that will suffice for a number of the thresholds of interest I mentioned above.

Consider a case where we are dealing with a blood test for a disease, where D is the disease and d is the blood marker this test is testing for. Let

e = Mary is a positive tester for d.
h = Mary has the disease D.

and suppose that the blood test for d is all we have to go on in Mary's case.[12] This means that we cannot estimate the prior probability that she has the disease, $P(h)$, or does not, $P(-h)$. Let us also suppose that we do not know the incidence of the disease in Mary's population, so we cannot use that to assign $P(h)$ and $P(-h)$ either. Suppose that the blood marker d is closely associated with the disease D: those with the disease have a 95 per cent probability of being positive testers for the marker d, and those without the disease have only a 15 per cent probability of being positive testers for the marker, meaning that $P(e/h) = 0.95$ and $P(e/-h) = 0.15$. We could figure out whether Mary has the disease by determining the probability that she is a positive tester for d, that is, by determining $P(e)$ directly.

As a start on this we could give her the test. If she comes up positive for d that's a start, but it isn't enough because one positive test does not a positive tester make: it could have been a fluke. However, if we tested Mary ten times and found her testing positive eight of those times, we'd be within our rights to assign a 0.8 probability to her being a positive tester. We'd have the intuition that we have good reason to believe she has the disease, and conformably the posterior probability of the hypothesis that she does, $P(h/e)$, would be 0.96 in that case. Suppose instead that in the ten trials of the blood test Mary had gotten a positive result in only two. Our intuition in that case is that our evidence that Mary has the disease is poor. This is in conformity with what happens to the posterior probability when we take the results of the blood tests to allow us to assign $P(e)$ the value 0.2: $P(h/e) = 0.3$. Notice too, that $P(e)$ is easy to evaluate in this case, whether one is a personalist or an objectivist about probability: all we need to do is give Mary the test repeatedly and keep track of the results.

Thus, clearly, real cases exist which exploit the mathematical fact I cited, that high $P(e)$ combined with high LR puts a lower bound on the posterior probability of the hypothesis. The task that remains is to articulate more fully what the rationale behind this is, to give an understanding of $P(e)$ that will allow us to exploit this mathematical fact more fully, and to understand other examples by redescribing them in this format. It is instructive in this regard to contrast the demand that $P(e)$ be high in order for e to be evidence for h, with what the personalist Bayesian typically says about the value of $P(e)$, and on what grounds.

The usual Bayesian story is that the value of $P(e)$ should be low. This comports on the one hand with the mathematical fact that since this term is in the denominator of Bayes's theorem, its being low should, other things being equal, make the posterior probability of the hypothesis high. (However, notice that other things are not always equal since the terms on the right-hand side are not independent.) It comports on the other hand with the idea that evidence that is surprising, or unexpected, is better confirmation for a hypothesis that predicts it than is evidence that is made highly probable by things we already know. As Howson and Urbach (1993: 123) put it, if a fortune-teller tells me that the first stranger I meet will have 10,467 hairs on his head, and that turns out to be right, I will be much more impressed with her powers than if

---

[12] e is thus a 'phenomenon' in the sense of Bogen and Woodward (1988). I use such an e, a general fact about Mary rather than a singular statement about her that we can verify at one go, because it is easier to see in such a case how the determination of $P(e)$ could be a process requiring several steps. The paradigm I am defending is not restricted to such cases, as I will discuss below.

she correctly predicts merely that I will meet a dark stranger sometime. Here h, the claim that the fortune-teller has powers of precognition, will be made more probable by e_1, the correct prediction of 10,467 hairs, than by e_2, the correct prediction that I will meet a dark stranger sometime. This is supposed to be because $P(e_1)$ is much lower than $P(e_2)$.

I think there is another way of modeling the idea that surprisingness of the evidence has significance for confirmation, if one is inclined to think it does (Roush forthcoming). For example, in the cases where Howson and Urbach think e is surprising, $P(e/h)$ is much greater than $P(e/-h)$, and $P(e/-h)$ is low. This can be so, and often is, without $P(e)$ being low. And notice that in the fortune-teller case $P(e_1/-h)$ is much lower than $P(e_2/-h)$, mirroring the fact that we find it more surprising that she is right about the number of hairs than about my meeting a dark stranger sometime. So, there is a place for surprisingness of the evidence, namely in $P(e/-h)$, but $P(e)$ need not be that place.

In fact, surely we would want it to be highly probable that the fortune-teller had been right in her prediction before using the statement of her correctness as evidence for anything. This corresponds to an important point about Bayesian strict conditionalization, the simplest Bayesian way of updating one's beliefs in response to coming to believe a piece of evidence. To see why it is good if $P(e)$ is high in real cases, we must be careful about what the term '$P(e)$' represents. $P(e)$ is often called the 'expectedness' of the evidence, but this phrase can lead to misunderstanding. We get a better understanding if we approach the matter in the most straightforward way. Assuming a personalist interpretation of probability for purposes of illustration, $P(s)$ is the degree of your belief in the statement s, and so, $P(e)$ is the degree of your belief in e, according to the function P. There is no sense of temporal priority or expectation built in to $P(e)$ that tells us under what circumstances to evaluate this term. Rather, evaluating it under different circumstances gives us different answers, and correspondingly different implications, because different probability functions are appropriate. For example, if we evaluate the probability of e after you have done a Bayesian strict conditionalization on e, then $P'(e) = 1$. If we evaluate the probability of e before such conditionalization on e then $P(e)$ will usually be less than 1. If we evaluate the probability of e after conditionalization on some statement that (you know) implies e, then $P''(e) = 1$, and if before then not necessarily.

The term 'expectedness' can be misleading because I may believe e to some high degree even though I did not previously expect e to be true. $P(e)$ reports actual degree of belief, not how much you expected at some prior stage that you would believe e at this stage. On the other hand, expectedness can affect my actual degree of belief in e. That e should have occurred may be so surprising that I am more willing to believe that my eyes are deceiving me than that e did actually occur. In such a case we might respond to witnessing that e occurs by saying 'I don't believe it,' and if that statement is true (as opposed to merely an expression of exasperation) then $P(e)$ is low. However, in a case where I have a very low degree of belief that e occurred, what reason could there be to think that e is evidence of anything for me?

It is similar in cases of surprising scientific evidence: no one takes a deeply surprising occurrence as evidence of anything until he satisfies himself that it did indeed occur, but then he has a high degree of belief that it occurred, and P(e) must be high. Back-scattering of alpha particles from thin gold foil was deeply surprising to Ernest Rutherford, but he wouldn't have taken the statement, e_s, that back-scattering occurred at a certain rate when atoms were bombarded, as evidence of the existence of a nucleus in the atom unless he had done some checking to reassure himself that e_s was true. On first report that the scattering had occurred, he might have been so surprised that he thought it more likely that his graduate student had blundered than that the report was true. In that case, and at that point, it hardly makes sense to think of the statement e_s as evidence for Rutherford of the existence of a nucleus. Once Rutherford had the experiment checked and repeated, e_s became evidence for him, but then his degree of belief in e_s was high, and thus so was P(e).

The claim that high P(e) is a good thing is (almost) implied by the principle of Bayesian strict conditionalization itself, which says:

> When your degree of belief in e goes to 1, but no stronger proposition also acquires probability 1, set $P'(a) = P(a/e)$ for all a in the domain of P, where P is your probability function immediately prior to the change. (Howson and Urbach 1993: 99)

This principle says that your degree of belief in e approaching 1 is a sufficient condition for strict conditionalization on e, that is, for you to update your beliefs on the assumption that e is true (provided that no claim logically stronger than e also had its degree of belief approach 1). Your degree of belief in e prior to the conditionalization is just P(e), so high P(e) is (almost) sufficient for you to take e as evidence for whatever e happens to be positively relevant to, that is, to conditionalize upon it. Roughly, if you are confident of e, then you ought to let your other beliefs feel the appropriate effects of e's truth.

Bayesians often think of P(e) as your degree of belief in e before you observe e, on the assumption that you can observe e and thereby come to be certain of it, at which point you conditionalize upon it. A lot of evidence is not like that, e.g. Rutherford's rate of back-scattering is not something one comes to be certain of in one observation, and Mary's being a positive tester is not shown by one positive test result. But even in cases where we do come to be confident of e through one observation, P(e) remains by definition your degree of belief in e before you conditionalize upon e. If, as is often assumed, P(e) is your degree of belief as far back as before you observe e, then you have no justification for strict conditionalization on e because you do not have confidence that e is true. It seems to me inescapable that in order for the value of P(e) that precedes Bayesian strict conditionalization to justify Bayesian strict conditionalization P(e) must be high.[13]

---

[13] Commentators are frequently misled by the fact that P(e) is in the denominator of Bayes's equation to conclude that P(e) is inversely proportional to P(h/e) (Howson and Urbach 1993: 124). This suggests that low P(e) will encourage high P(h/e). But there is no inverse proportionality here, because there is no constant of proportionality, since the other terms that stand between these two are variables that are not independent of P(e) or each other.

I am indebted to Brian Skyrms for helpful discussion of these issues. Of course, he should not be presumed to agree with my unorthodox view.

It is important to recognize that my conditions for some evidence and good evidence do not imply that such evidence always has a high value for P(e); high P(e) is sufficient but not necessary for (the indication condition for) some or good evidence. Though both sets of conditions include lower bounds for P(e), no particular lower bound is specified for all cases (except 0). P(e) may have a low value for either kind of evidence, as long as the value of the LR is high enough to offset it and make the two in combination yield a high value for P(h/e). I did not treat the LR similarly, but put a fixed lower bound of 1 on it, in order to insure some degree of discrimination in all cases. There are, however, practical reasons why higher P(e) is better than lower P(e). For one thing, if P(e) is very low, then the LR has to be proportionally higher to ensure a high posterior probability for the hypothesis. Very high values for the LR seem harder to verify than the claim that the LR is roughly greater than 3.

Secondly, as I have just argued, if you want to do Bayesian strict conditionalization, then low values for P(e) will not be sufficient. However, and this is one of the reasons I do not forbid low P(e), Jeffrey conditionalization, in which e gets assigned some probability less than 1 in the new probability function, does not require for its justification that P(e) approaches 1. Jeffrey conditionalization should be allowed since it is fully probabilistic and represents a needed generalization of strict conditionalization. Therefore low P(e) should not automatically make e evidentially powerless. Nevertheless, the facts remain that the graphs show that if used with the discrimination condition high P(e) is more powerful than low P(e), and also, justifying a strict conditionalization is a more powerful thing for e to do than justifying a Jeffrey conditionalization, because the former will allow e to have a greater effect on the probabilities of other statements. Thus, although high P(e) is not necessary for evidence, it is clearly superior to low P(e). Moreover, the point I have been developing in terms of conditionalization and a personalist interpretation of probability has an objective counterpart: if P(h/e) is high this cannot actually make the probability of the hypothesis high unless P(e) is also high, because P(h/e) is a conditional probability.

The idea that P(e) should be high may cause consternation from another direction. The problem of old evidence is the problem that when P(e) is 1, the highest value, then P(h/e) = P(h), so in such a case no relevance measure can count e as evidence for h. This includes the LR and any other measure we have considered minimally legitimate. How, then, can I say that high values of P(e) are good? A natural thought that many have had in response to the old evidence problem is to adopt a policy of avoiding assignments of extreme probabilities to any empirical propositions, thus avoiding the assignment of 1 to P(e). In this way we avoid having to deny that e is evidence at all for h. However, this approach leaves a quantitative problem if we use the familiar ratio measure. For when P(e) = 0.99, the ratio measure, which is equivalent to P(e/h)/P(e), has to be close to 1. That is, the degree of confirmation e bestows must be nearly negligible. It has been presumed on this as on other questions that what is true of the ratio measure is true of any other. However, importantly, it isn't so with this question and the LR measure. If P(e) = 0.99, or any higher non-unitary value, the LR may be arbitrarily high, according to a result due to Fitelson (forthcoming). This is an instance of the ordinal differences between the ratio and the LR measures of evidence, and of the superiority of the LR measure of support. The LR does not measure degree of support by the degree to which e has changed the posterior probability of the hypothesis or, equivalently, by the degree to which h changes e's probability. This allows those of us who rely on the LR to say that e is substantial evidence for h even when e is almost certain, and even when h is almost certain.

Let us consider some other challenging examples, cases where it may seem prima facie that it is the very improbability of e that makes it evidence for h. The following example was put to me by Achinstein:

e = There is one million dollars in my bank account.
h = I win the lottery.

On encountering the claim that there was a million dollars in my bank account, anyone who knew me would find that hard to believe. But which probability judgment does this incredulity correspond to? It is not patently clear, but the easiest category to force it into is a judgment about $P(e/-h)$: people who know me know that there is no way besides the lottery that I would have gotten a million dollars into my bank account. And, of course, it is partly because $P(e/-h)$ is so low, and then also because $P(e/h)$ is so very high, that we are inclined to take e seriously as evidence for h, even though, we assume, the prior probability of h is exceedingly low.

The question What is the value of $P(e)$? corresponds, on the personalist interpretation, to the question how far we believe that there is a million dollars in my account before we decide to conditionalize upon e. Anyone considering e will have heard this through some report or other, and even a bank statement can be in error. A person considering a report that e seems to me as likely to dismiss the report as to infer that I have won the lottery on its basis, unless there is good reason to think the report is accurate. And if good reason is forthcoming for thinking the report is accurate, the only circumstance in which we should take the statement e as evidence for h, then $P(e)$ is high. What makes e evidence for h is not that e has a low probability but that it has low probability on the assumption that h is not true.[14]

As we can see from the definitions and the examples, the way that my view of evidence as a whole works is that if the indication condition is fulfilled in the ideal way with $P(e)$ high, that will tell us that e is evidence for *something*. If the discrimination condition is fulfilled, that will tell us that the thing it is evidence for is more likely to be the hypothesis than its negation. I have argued elsewhere that this scheme corresponds to eliminative reasoning (Roush forthcoming). It is fair to wonder whether this scheme and interpretation of $P(e)$ could be used to understand every case of evidence. After all, cases immediately leap to mind where the phenomena most important in a

---

[14] Such an understanding of things makes sense of why the deviation of Mercury's perihelion from Newtonian prediction is better evidence for the Einsteinian theory that predicts it, t, than it is for the Newtonian theory, t′, even though that perihelion, e, was well known before Einstein's time, so e cannot be regarded as a novel prediction of Einstein's theory. What matters, it seems to me, is not per se whether a claim implied by a theory, t, is surprising or unknown before the theory's time but whether the probability of the evidence on the alternative (ideally −t) is low. The fact that $P(e/t′)$ was much lower than $P(e/t)$ meant that e gave more reason to believe General Relativity than it did to believe Newton's theory, assuming the theories have equal priors. Measurements of such things as perihelions always have error bars, so we need never grant that $P(e)$ becomes 1 on a personalist interpretation of probability.

scientific experiment are events that happen rarely. One solar neutrino will let itself be detected once a week, on average, in a gigantic facility that contains billions of opportunities for detection. If e is the claim that a neutrino is captured in the underground swimming pool, then surely the probability of e is very low.

There are several things to say about such examples. First, we should not suppose that a scientist takes the occurrence of one neutrino capture as evidence that tells between the two theoretical accounts competing in this case. What the theories disagree about in this case are the rates of neutrino detection, how many neutrinos will be captured over a given time period in a given facility containing a given number of opportunities. Although both going theories predict only a very small number of neutrino events, what matters in their predictions is that they be right about which small number that is, and thus that the experimentalists be right about the rate of detections and the conditions under which they occurred. It does not matter to this whether neutrino detection is a rare event. The probability that neutrinos were detected at a certain rate should ideally be very high before we take the claim that they were detected at that rate as evidence for anything. There will obviously be cases where it is not the rate of detection but a single occurrence that is taken as evidence— one thinks of the 'Golden Events' of the image tradition in experimental particle physics.[15] But these cases are like the case of my having a million dollars in my bank account. It had better be highly probable that I *do* have that much in my account before we take the statement that I do as evidence that I won the lottery.

I think that though many examples will not present themselves as cases where it looks like a good thing if P(e) is high, it will be possible to redescribe such cases in this form in which P(e) is high and the LR is high. That is, we should regard this as a normal form into which every case could be translated as the heuristics for doing so become clearer. As an indication of how this might go, consider another type of case. The condition paresis is familiar from discussions of explanation. This condition, a form of paralysis, is rare in the general population, almost never present unless a patient has latent, untreated syphilis, and even relatively rare in the class of latent, untreated syphilitics. This seems to present a problem for my view if one wants, as is reasonable, to treat the presence of paresis as evidence for latent, untreated syphilis, because it looks like the value of P(e) is going to have to be low.

However, that depends on how we understand P(e). If P(e) refers to the probability that a random member of the population has paresis, then it will be very low. But this is immaterial to the situations in which we would take the claim that a person has paresis as evidence that he has syphilis. If we chose a name randomly from the phone book, we would not take it that the statement that this person has paresis is evidence that he has syphilis, because the claim that he has paresis has a very low probability. Before taking that statement as evidence that he has syphilis we would want to know more about whether the statement is true. If P(e) refers instead to the probability that a particular patient in question, S, who complains of paralysis, has paresis, then it is clear that we would want the value of P(e) to be high if that paresis was to be a sign of

[15] See Galison's (1997) treatment of the 'Image' and 'Logic' traditions, two separate and epistemologically distinct approaches in experimental particle physics in the 20th century.

syphilis, or of anything. We would want to reassure ourselves that it was paresis, not some other form of paralysis not associated with syphilis. We would want it to be probable that it was paresis and not mere hypochondria. To check whether this probability was high, we might send the patient to ten different doctors to determine whether the condition the patient was suffering from really was paresis. If n of them said 'yes' then P(e) would be equal to .n.[16] A less costly option, of course, is to judge P(e) high on the basis of the expertise of one specialist of high reputation looking at the symptoms.

Only probability

Peter Achinstein (2001) has argued that no conception based only on probability can capture the concept of evidence, and in his own view of evidence appeals to the concept of *explanation* to supplement conditions on probabilities. One of his chief objections is that a view that takes positive probabilistic relevance (condition †) as its sole condition for evidence allows statements to count as evidence which do not make the probability of the hypothesis high. The same objection can be made to taking high LR as the sole condition for evidence. I have addressed this objection above in an unconventional manner, by setting the additional condition that P(e) be bounded from below, which together with high LR puts a minimum on the posterior probability of the hypothesis.

This first objection was to the effect that positive relevance (or high LR) is not sufficient for good evidence. The second objection is to the effect that positive relevance is not necessary for good evidence. If this objection stood then that would affect my view, since (ignoring cases where the ratio is undefined) LR > 1 implies positive relevance, and I have said that LR > 1 is necessary for e to be some or good evidence for h. However, the objection cannot be sustained, and I will treat here the two examples Achinstein presents, to show that probability, and especially the Likelihood Ratio, has more resources than he allows.[17] There are challenges involved in the project of using only the concept of probability to understand evidence, but they are not displayed in these examples.

Achinstein's first example involves a lottery:

e_1 = The *New York Times* (*NYT*) reports that Bill Clinton owns all but one of the 1,000 lottery tickets that exist in the lottery.

e_2 = The *Washington Post* (*WP*) reports that Bill Clinton owns all but one of the 1,000 lottery tickets that exist in the lottery.

b = This is a fair lottery in which one ticket drawn at random will win.

h = Bill Clinton will win the lottery.

[16] One may have noticed that a high value for P(e) in this case appears inconsistent with the low frequency of paresis in the general and untreated syphilitic populations, since P(e) is always between P(e/h) and P(e/−h), inclusive. However, P(e) is high only for the particular patient we considered, the one who complained of paralysis. Because it is background knowledge in this case that he complained of paralysis, it is clear that P(e/h) will be high, and still clear that P(e/−h) will be low. It is perfectly consistent for the likelihoods of a person randomly chosen from a population (low) to be different from those of an individual in that same population about whom one takes into account more information (high).

[17] Portions of this section are reprinted from Roush (2004).

e_1 and e_2 are both pieces of evidence, b is background knowledge, and h is the hypothesis. Achinstein submits that given e_1 and b, e_2 is strong evidence for h yet, he claims:

$$P(h/e_1.e_2.b) = P(h/e_1.b) = 999/1000. \text{ (Achinstein 2001: 70)}$$

In other words, he claims that once e_1 is incorporated as evidence, e_2 does not change the probability of the hypothesis, and therefore, on the positive relevance view, e_2 is not evidence for h in the circumstance described. Ergo, the positive relevance condition is too strong.

A little reflection shows that there is something amiss in the assignment of probabilities in this case. The probability that Clinton will win is 0.999 only if the probability that he owns 999 out of 1,000 tickets is 1. How are we supposed to get that? The only way to get from the claim that it was reported that Clinton owns 999 tickets to the claim that the probability he will win is 0.999 is to assume that a report in the *NYT* that c (where c = Clinton owns . . .) makes the probability of c equal to 1, that is, that the *NYT* is a perfect transmitter. This assumption makes the probability of a Clinton win as high as it could get (0.999) on the basis of any report that he owns 999 out of 1,000 tickets, and thereby prevents any other such report from raising the probability. The *NYT* is a respectable newspaper, but this assumption is inappropriate, not just because it is false—the existence of a 'corrections' section is sufficient to show this—but also because it automatically removes from consideration what goes on with probabilities when you have two imperfect sources of information, which is where all of the interest of this example lies.

It is obvious that if there exists evidence that we have and that makes the probability of a hypothesis equal to 1, then on the positive relevance view nothing else will count as evidence, because nothing can change a probability of 1. The question is whether there are any examples of that sort where the verdict strikes us as wrong. It is very hard to come up with examples where evidence makes the probability of a hypothesis equal to 1 where that probability was not already 1, that is, by raising it from a lower value, unless the hypothesis itself is taken as evidence. It is not enough simply to *assume* that a given case is one where evidence has made the probability of something, here c, equal to 1. That would have to be argued for, since it is the crucial, and difficult, premise of the argument against positive relevance. It is obvious that c in this example does not start out with probability 1, but it is also obvious that having the *NYT* report that c does not make $P(c) = 1$ either. What Achinstein would need to prove is implausible in this case, and that is enough to ruin this counterexample. Moreover, as we have seen above, there are reasons independent of this kind of case—e.g. the problem of old evidence—to adopt the practice of not assigning probability 1 to any but logical truths. If we make this move, as I have, then no examples of the sort Achinstein needs here can be constructed.

However, there is more to say. Even though the *NYT* report does not make the probability of c equal to 1, we may assume that it makes that probability high, and therefore the posterior probability of the hypothesis high. If one thinks being evidence is a matter of positive relevance, one may also think that the degree of this relevance is proportional to the strength of the evidence, although this is not implied. That is, one may think that the degree of evidential support is measured by the degree to which it positively changes the probability of the hypothesis, endorsing either what we have called the 'ratio measure' above, $P(h/e)/P(h)$, or the difference measure, $P(h/e)-P(h)$. If so, then the example looks strange, because it looks as if how good the *NYT* or *WP* report is as evidence depends on whether it was discovered first, since the one discovered second has little room to change the probability of h once the other evidence has been registered. If the two reports are not independent, if, say, both newspapers got their information from Reuters, then that seems far less strange. But the two reports could have been independent, and then there seems to be a problem. Nevertheless, this is not a reason to think positive relevance is not necessary for evidence. It is only a reason to think that neither the ratio of $P(h/e)$ to $P(h)$ nor the difference between $P(h/e)$ and $P(h)$ is the appropriate way to measure the *degree* to which one thing is evidence for another. However, as we have seen above, there are other measures of degree of confirmation.

It is instructive to compare the Likelihood Ratio measure as applied to this example, since this method not only gets the foregoing quantitative issue right, but also makes it harder to slip into presuming that a report of c makes $P(c) = 1$. On this view, recall, to determine whether e is evidence for h we compare $P(e/h)$ to $P(e/-h)$ and if the first is greater than the second, then e supports or incrementally confirms h. In our case, to decide whether e_2 is evidence for h when e_1 is already in the stock of evidence, we compare $P(e_2/h.e_1)$ to $P(e_2/-h.e_1)$. $P(e_2/h.e_1)$ is clearly greater than $P(e_2/-h.e_1)$, since in the second case the given fact that Clinton does not win the lottery casts doubt on the veracity of the *NYT* report that he owns 999 out of 1,000 of the tickets. If that report was false then, unless we can assume that the *WP* always copies the *NYT*, there is less reason to believe e_2 than there is if Clinton does win the lottery and the *NYT* report is the same. This means that the Likelihood Ratio is greater than 1 if we can assume that there is some chance the *WP* report is independent of the *NYT* report, which is anyway the only case where not counting e_2 as evidence is counterintuitive. Moreover, in general the Likelihood Ratio, and hence the *degree* of support, can be arbitrarily high regardless of how high(<1) e_1 makes the probability of the hypothesis.

Achinstein's second example involves an intervening cause:

e_1 = On Monday at 10 a.m. David, who has symptoms S, takes medicine M to relieve S.

e_2 = On Monday at 10.15 a.m. David takes medicine M' to relieve S.

b = Medicine M is 95 per cent effective in relieving S within two hours; medicine M' is 90 per cent effective in relieving S within two hours, but has fewer side effects. When taken within twenty minutes of having taken M medicine M' completely blocks the causal efficacy of M without affecting its own.[18]

h = David's symptoms S are relieved by noon on Monday.

In familiar form, Achinstein claims that given e_1 and b, information e_2 is strong evidence for h, because medicine M' is 90 per cent effective in relieving symptoms S. Yet the positive relevance account of evidence does not render this verdict, for:

---

[18] It is not stated but must also be assumed in the example that the symptoms S are such that if David did not take medicine then he would not recover.

$$P(h/e_1.b) = 0.95$$
$$P(h/e_2.e_1.b) = 0.90. \text{ (Achinstein 2001: 70–1)}$$

e_2 not only does not increase h's probability over what it was when e_2 was not taken into account, it decreases that probability.

In this case it is obvious that the probabilities are right. It is much less obvious that they yield counterintuitive judgments about evidence. When the example is first introduced Achinstein says we should believe that e_2 is strong evidence for h when e_1 and b are given 'since medicine M′ is 90% effective in relieving symptoms S' (Achinstein 2001: 71). However, the fact cited would justify the claim that e_2 is strong evidence for h given e_1 only if supported by one of two assumptions that are false, and that Achinstein has disavowed.

The first is that a sufficient condition for e to be evidence for h is that $P(h/e.b)$ is high. Achinstein rightly rejects this high probability condition as sufficient for evidence because it does not require that e be relevant to h, or, intuitively, that e 'made' the probability of h high (Achinstein 2001: 71). It would count the fact that a man consumed birth control pills as evidence that he will not get pregnant. The problem is that the probability that he would not get pregnant was already high, so his consumption of birth control pills has no work to do supporting it. The same is true of e_2 in the case of the medicines. The probability that David would recover was already high when the second medicine came along. e_2's role in making the probability that he would recover high is redundant with work that would have been done by e_1.[19] (I will have more to say in support of this claim below.) By Achinstein's own lights the mere fact that the probability of h is high after e_2 is taken into account does not make e_2 evidence for h when e_1 is given.

The other assumption that would make 'medicine M′ is 90 per cent effective in relieving symptoms S' a justification for the claim that e_2 is evidence for h once e_1 is taken into account is, as the quoted clause strongly suggests, that e_1 has not been taken into account! It is clear that if David had never taken medicine M, but had taken medicine M′, then the fact that he had taken M′ would be strong evidence that he would recover, because that medicine is 90 per cent effective. The probabilities also conform to that judgment, since $P(h/e_2.b) > P(h/b)$. However, these are not the probabilities we have to do with in Achinstein's claim that e_2 is evidence for h once e_1 has been taken into account, and do not obviously bear a helpful relation to $P(h/e_2.e_1.b)$ and $P(h/e_1.b)$.

We get a different justification when Achinstein later considers the same example (with minor changes):

Isn't the fact that I am taking [M]′ after having taken [M] evidence that my pain will be relieved, even though the probability that it will be relieved has decreased from 9[5]% to 90%? (Achinstein 2001: 84)

---

[19] This example is analogous to another Achinstein example dealt with by Patrick Maher (1996: 172), who drew the same conclusion I have as to whether evidence is present. My reply has the advantage of not relying on Maher's particular view of confirmation, some of whose assumptions Achinstein defended himself by attacking (Achinstein 1996).

The phrase 'the fact that I am taking M' after having taken M' is notably ambiguous. The reading that invites itself is 'the fact that I have taken M' and taken M.' It is obvious that this conjunction *is* evidence for h on intuitive grounds, but it is also clear that the corresponding positive relevance condition is fulfilled: $P(h/e_1.e_2.b) > P(h/b)$. That this conjunction is evidence is not the claim Achinstein needs to defend for his conclusion, but it is the claim the words suggest when he asks for our intuitions.

Achinstein's phrase could, and should, mean the fact that I am taking M' *given* that I have taken M. This would mean that the question is whether given the background and the fact that I have taken M, my having taken M' seems like further evidence, new information, that I will recover. Consider a concerned friend who knows that I have taken M. Would she be convinced if we told her we had new evidence that I was going to recover, namely that I had taken M'? She would undoubtedly be less confident that I would recover than she was before, if only by a little, and furthermore annoyed at the misleading advertisement. It is clear that when we have e_1, and we acquire e_2, we do *have* evidence that I will recover. It is not at all clear that given e_1, e_2 is evidence that I will recover.

Any lingering confusion in our intuitions about this case comes, I think, from the fact that if I do recover then it will have been due to the causal efficacy of M' alone, the medicine the taking of which is reported by e_2. In this the example differs from previous Achinstein examples of similar form, such as one in which there is a lottery and the first piece of evidence that Freddy will win is that he owns 999 of 1,000 tickets, and the second piece of evidence tallied says that by the next day 1,001 tickets have been sold of which Freddy still owns 999 (Achinstein 1983: 152). The probability of Freddy winning is still very high after the second report is in, but it has dropped from what it was with the first report, so e_2 does not count as evidence in this context on the probabilistic relevance view. Nor should it, on the basis of what I have argued above, since e_2 is redundant with part of e_1.

One might think that although e_2 has no right to count as evidence in this case, that is because there is no sense in which someone else's buying another ticket *causes* Freddy to win if he wins. The case of the medicines is different since if I recover then M', and not M, will be the cause of that. The latter claim is true but of no avail, I think, since other things are true as well. For example, I would have had an at least 90 per cent probability of recovery even if I had not taken M'. This is related to the peculiar fact that the only reason that M is not the actor in bringing about my recovery is a secondary action of M'. If I had not take M', then I also would not *need* M', for recovery. M' did not do anything relevant to whether I recover that M would not have done, supporting the claim that e_2, the report that I have taken M', is in the most important sense redundant with part of e_1. When we learn e_2, we learn something about the mechanism of recovery, but we learn nothing new about *whether* I will recover—the point at issue in the hypothesis—except the negative news that my chances have gone down, which does not change the fact that my chances are very good.

Each of M and M' raises the probability of recovery when acting alone, and when acting together they raise the probability over what it was with neither. This conforms to the fact that M and M' are jointly and each individually evidence for my recovery. However, once I know that M has been taken, learning that M' has been taken does not increase my confidence in recovery, and is not evidence for that recovery, since the information it gives about whether I will recover is redundant with information we already had.

Conclusion

I have defended a view of evidence according to which e is *some evidence* for h if and only if there is a lower bound greater than 1 on $P(e/h)/P(e/-h)$ and a lower bound greater than 0 on $P(e)$, such that $P(h/e)$ is greater than 0.5, and e is *good evidence* for h if and only if there is a lower bound greater than 1 on $P(e/h)/P(e/-h)$ and a lower bound greater than 0 on $P(e)$, such that $P(h/e)$ is greater than some high threshold appropriate to having good reason to believe. No concepts apart from probability are employed. While on this view LR > 1 is a necessary condition for either type of evidence, high $P(e)$ is not necessary but is ideal. This view preserves the leverage property of evidence better than its plausible rivals, and implies that some or good evidence gives some or good reason to believe. In addition, the analysis incorporates in formal probabilistic terms a satisfying picture according to which being evidence is being a discriminating indicator.

We have come to this view of evidence without depending on ideas about what knowledge is. But this view of evidence, compelling in its own right, combines with the recursive tracking view of knowledge to explain the truism that better evidence makes us more likely to know on its basis. When we use evidence e to form a belief about a hypothesis h we either believe the evidence e, and thereby believe h, or we respond to e in such a way that when our mechanisms say it is so we believe h.[20] If the subject's use of evidence e is such that she responds to belief in e or indication of e by believing h, then she cannot know h by tracking h via e unless e TRACKS h. Now, since it follows, lest the TRACKING chain from belief in h to h be broken, that the trajectory from the subject's belief in h to h must be by steps of TRACKING,[21] we can infer that not only does the subject who knows h by tracking h via e believe or otherwise respond to e and thereby believe h, it is also the case that her belief in h TRACKS either e or her belief in e.

If she believes e rather than merely responding appropriately in her h-belief behavior to e's truth, then if the TRACKING chain from belief in h to h is to be unbroken her belief in e had better also track e. This is not a matter of how good e is as evidence, but rather of how skilled the subject is at coming to know e. How good e is as

---

[20] Fixing ideas only this far implies that we are not imagining knowing h by anti-tracking e which anti-tracks h. Anti-tracking between e and h can be useful for knowing h only if the subject's belief in h anti-tracks e, which it does not in the cases just described. This is why the next sentence of the text follows. Of course, concerns about anti-tracking are somewhat semantic, since if anti-tracking exists tracking does too: if b(h) anti-tracks e which anti tracks h, then b(h) tracks −e which tracks h.

[21] It must be two steps of tracking rather than two steps of anti-tracking because due to our assumptions the second step, between e and h, is not anti-tracking so neither step can be or it would ruin the overall tracking chain.

evidence for h depends on something beyond this and contributes to knowledge of h in a way that we can now identify. The discussion of the last many pages has argued that when e is evidence for h at all, e is better evidence for h when either P(e) is higher or the LR is higher. This fits very nicely into the recursive tracking picture of knowledge via evidence. Begin with evidence that is better because of a higher LR. This can happen in one of two ways, either because the numerator of that ratio, P(e/h), is higher, or because the denominator of that ratio, P(e/−h), is lower. If the numerator is higher then that implies that e and h fulfill TRACKING condition (III) at a higher level, i.e. e TRACKS h better. If the denominator is lower, then that implies that e and h fulfill TRACKING condition (IV) at a higher level, i.e., e TRACKS h better. Since e TRACKING h was necessary for the subject to know h by tracking h via e, it is obvious that evidence for a hypothesis that is better by having a higher LR is more likely to bring the subject knowledge.

The other way that e can be better evidence, on the view of evidence on offer, is if P(e) is higher. To see why this enhances the prospects that a subject knows h on the basis of evidence e, consider the possibility that e TRACKS h at a high level. It follows from this that if e is false then h is probably false too. If h is false, then the subject cannot know h, by e or in any other way. Thus, in case e TRACKS h it is better for the prospects of knowledge of h if e is more likely to be true. If e does not TRACK h then the subject cannot know h via e, regardless of how other features may stand, and so, in particular, regardless of P(e).[22]

Of course, it may not be the case that all knowledge is via evidence on the recursive tracking view since there is the recursion clause that allows us to know by known implication from another known statement, which we have not yet considered. Does e count as evidence for h when e deductively implies h on my view? This area is slightly tricky because on the one hand I said that the LR measure makes inductive support a generalization of deductive implication, so the latter should count as a special, high-quality case of inductive support. Yet, on the other hand we know that the LR picture of inductive support incorporates tracking intuitions and that deduction does not preserve tracking. How could deductive implication be an instance of inductive support ('tracking') when we know that deduction does not preserve tracking and tracking has the transitivity-enough property?

The LR is a generalization of deductive implication, because if e implies h then P(e/−h) = 0, forcing the denominator of the LR to 0 and maximizing the LR. This means that e is maximally relevant to h, and thus e incrementally confirms h, on the measure of confirmation I have endorsed. However, e's deductively implying h does not alone make e good evidence or even some evidence for h under the analysis I have given of these concepts. This should not be surprising since I built in to the concepts of good evidence and some evidence the requirement that a statement that is either of these kinds of evidence puts a lower bound on the posterior probability of the statement it is evidence for. An e that makes for a high LR with respect to an h does not necessarily give such a bound, just as the fact alone that an e implies an h does not

---

[22] This is so in the scenario developed in the previous paragraphs because the anti-tracking possibilities were carefully eliminated.

give us any sense of whether h is true; we would need to know in addition, in the inductive case or the deductive case, something about the probability of e itself to have that.

If P(e) is high, we get what we expect in both the inductive and the deductive cases. If P(e) is high, and the LR is high, then it follows automatically that the posterior probability of the hypothesis is constrained from below. Since e's deductively implying h is one way to make the LR high, we also have the expected conclusion that a probable proposition that deductively implies another makes the probability of that other proposition high. Thus, if e is such that e implies h and P(e) is high, e does count as good evidence for h. But now it is also clear why despite the facts that a probable e that makes for a high LR with respect to h makes h probable, a deductive implication relation is one way to make the LR high, and the LR incorporates the tracking relations, nevertheless deduction does not preserve tracking. This is because of the way in which a deductive implication relation from e to h makes P(e/h)/P(e/−h) high. It does so by minimizing the denominator, but does not necessarily tell us anything about the numerator.[23] For there to be a tracking relation in which e TRACKS h it must be that there is assurance about both of these terms, that the denominator is low and that the numerator is high, meaning that e has the right behavior both when h is false and when h is true. If e implies h we have no assurance about what happens when h is true, unless we fallaciously affirm the antecedent. Thus it is clear why when a subject knows h by inferring it deductively from a known e, her belief in h will not in general track the truth: the tracking chain is broken because deductive implication is not itself a tracking relation. Non-extreme inductive support is weaker than deductive support, but there is a sense in which it gives us more information.

This fit between the concept of knowledge and the concept of evidence that I have proposed is more remarkable than it may at first appear. One would have expected that a tracking view of evidence would fit together with a tracking view of knowledge. However, for the connection to be more than homonymic, and the explanation of why better evidence makes knowledge more probable to be more than merely verbal, the details of the concepts of evidence and knowledge have to fit together properly. Anyone who has tried to analyze a concept knows that in the process many detailed choices arise that one makes with a view to getting the subject matter of that particular concept right. When one analyzes separately two concepts that have a connection at the intuitive level, one does not expect that the details of the two analyses will automatically mesh in a way that preserves the intuitive connection between the two concepts. But the two analyses here have fit together like pieces of a jigsaw puzzle.

The foregoing account of the relation between evidence and knowledge is more than merely verbal, since it explains why better evidence makes knowledge more probable at the deeper level of probabilistic relations. Yet, remarkably to me, I developed the view of knowledge and the view of evidence independently of each other and of the question of their relation, and made no adjustments to them in

---

[23] This can be seen in the following way: when P(e/−h) = 0, the equation P(e) = P(e/h)P(h) + P(e/−h)P(−h) goes to P(e) = P(e/h)P(h). This latter makes P(h/e) = 1, but we have no information about the values of P(e/h) and P(h) from this, and there are an infinite number of possible values for them that would make their product equal to P(e).

drawing out this explanation of why better evidence makes knowledge more probable. Thus, the views correctly predicted something they were not designed to predict, a feature that is generally taken to be a good sign about a theory. What it means in the present case, I think, is that tracking runs deep and wide in all of our epistemological intuitions, and a view that incorporates tracking is a good candidate for best possible systematization of our epistemological intuitions into well-defined and useful concepts.

The Likelihood Ratio, high P(e), and high P(h/e)

Why does high P(e) combined with high LR put a lower bound on P(h/e)? There are several ways to see why this happens of which I will explain one here. First, consider the following consequence of the axioms, which comes from substituting the right-hand side of this rearrangement of the Bayes equation,

$$P(e/h)P(h) = P(h/e)P(e),$$

in for the first term on the right-hand side of the equation of total probability for P(e):

$$P(e) = P(e/h)P(h) + P(e/-h)P(-h).$$

We get:

$$P(e) = P(h/e)P(e) + P(e/-h)P(-h),$$

which, solving for P(h/e), becomes:

$$P(h/e) = [P(e) - P(e/-h)P(-h)]/P(e).[1]$$

This equation is interesting, because the right-hand side takes the form:

$$(P(e) - X)/P(e).$$

This expression takes its highest value when X is 0, because X is dragging the expression away from taking its highest possible value, P(e)/P(e) = 1. Therefore, P(h/e) will be maximized when the term X is minimized.

This alone already suggests qualitatively why raising P(e) with high LR will raise P(h/e): the larger P(e) is, the less a fixed value of X will drag down (P(e) − X)/P(e). Of course, X is not necessarily fixed when P(e) goes up, because the terms P(e/-h)P(-h) and P(e) are not independent. However, in the conditions that I have discussed for evidence, in which we put lower bounds on both P(e) and LR, special things happen.

Consider what we can deduce if P(e) > 0.5 and LR > 3. From LR > 3 it follows that the maximum value for P(e/-h) is 0.33. This is because the maximum possible value for P(e/h) is 1, and LR > 3 says that P(e/-h) must be no more than one third of P(e/h). These conditions also impose an upper bound on P(-h), which we can see as follows. Note that because e is the weighted average of P(e/h) and P(e/-h), that is,

$$P(e) = P(e/h)P(h) + P(e/-h)P(-h),$$

P(e) will always be between P(e/h) and P(e/-h) inclusive. In particular, for any value for the LR that is >1, the ordering will be P(e/h) ≥ P(e) ≥ P(e/-h). Under our conditions, and with P(e/-h) at its maximum, 0.33, the highest value for P(-h) will occur when the LR is as low as possible, namely 3, because a higher LR would force a lower P(e/-h) than the maximum 0.33. The change that raising the LR produced would have to go to reducing P(e/-h) since P(e/h)

---

[1] I owe James Pearson thanks for discovering this equation.

cannot go higher than 1, the value it must have if $P(e/-h) = 0.33$ and LR is as much as 3. For maximizing $P(-h)$, $P(e)$ is best minimized to 0.5, because as $P(e)$ gets higher it moves away from the $P(e/-h)$ of 0.33, and thus lowers $P(-h)$, which is the weight on $P(e/-h)$ in the average that makes up $P(e)$. With these values that will yield the maximium value $P(-h)$ can have, we solve the following simultaneous equations:

$$0.5 = P(h) + 0.33P(-h)$$
$$0.33 = 0.33P(h) + 0.33P(-h)$$

to yield

$$P(h) = 0.25, P(-h) = 0.75.$$

The first of the simultaneous equations is an instance of

$$P(e) = P(e/h)P(h) + P(e/-h)P(-h),$$

and the second is a form of the axiom that says that the probabilities of a set of statements that exhaust the logical space must sum to 1:

$$1 = P(h) + P(-h)$$

This shows that the maximum value for $P(-h)$ under the conditions assumed is 0.75, and we showed above that the maximum value for $P(e/-h)$ is 0.33. The term X in the equation above is the product of these two, and so has maximum value 0.25. Thus, by the equation above,

$$P(h/e) = [P(e) - P(e/-h)P(-h)]/P(e),$$

when $P(e)$ is greater than 0.5 (and LR is greater than 3), $P(e/-h)P(-h)$ is less than or equal to 0.25, so $P(h/e)$ is greater than or equal to $(0.5 - 0.25)/0.5 = 0.5$.

   The fact that $P(e)$ is the weighted average of the two likelihoods we use, $P(e/h)$ and $P(e/-h)$, that is, that $P(e)$ is between these two likelihoods, and the fact that the hypotheses we consider exhaust the logical space, yielding the equation,

$$P(h) + P(-h) = 1,$$

played crucial roles in this derivation. This explains why a comparative likelihood ratio,

$$P(e/T)/P(e/T'),$$

where T and T' are rival hypotheses that do not exhaust the logical space, does not give us purchase on the posterior probability of the hypothesis, even if we combine a condition that this ratio be high with, say, a lower bound on $P(e)$. Since T and T' do not exhaust the logical space, their probabilities do not sum to 1. Also, $P(e)$ is not the weighted average of $P(e/T)$ and $P(e/T')$. Thus, neither of the equations we solved simultaneously above is available. This explains why if we want a notion of evidence in which it gives us a good reason to believe, comparative likelihoods are not enough, and we are forced to deal with the catch-all hypothesis. We may say that a high comparative likelihood ratio $P(e/T)/P(e/T')$ shows that e gives more reason to believe T than to believe T', but since both $P(T/e)$ and $P(T'/e)$ could be less than 0.5 (or less than 0.000000001!) for all the value of this ratio tells us, the amount of reason that e gives for believing either T or T' could be negligible.

6

Real Anti-realism: The Evidential Approach

Introduction

Philosophers have argued about whether we have reason to believe our scientific theories are true—roughly, the thesis of realism—at quite a high level of generality considering the variety of things that go on in science. The aim of generality is a fine one, especially for philosophers. However, some ways of getting to talk about generalities are based on classifications that are useless, and some are even misleading. Take, for example, the positions of epistemological realists and anti-realists, antagonists who agree that theories have truth values and that the world determines what those truth values are independently of what we believe, but disagree about how well we do at figuring out those truth values. Both types of adversaries in this debate typically ask us to adopt the same attitude toward all of a given group of scientific claims depending on whether they are or are not *well-tested* theories, or *successful* theories, or claims *involving unobservables*. But it is reasonable to take quite different views of different well-tested scientific claims involving unobservables depending on how ambitious the claims are.

The claim that there are atoms, meaning simply sub-microscopic entities moving at random or independently of each other,[1] and the claim that Quantum Mechanics is the true theory of the universe are both well-tested claims involving unobservables. (Atoms are unobservable by the philosopher's typical standard because detection does not count: an entity is observable only if the unaided human senses would take it in were it to be present.) Accordingly, the realist will say we have good reason to believe the two claims mentioned are true due to their well-testedness, and the anti-realist will deny that we have good reason to believe them due to their involvement with unobservables. Because of the classifications used in their debate neither has the resources to notice or explain the obvious fact that the claim that Quantum Mechanics is the true theory of the universe is wildly more difficult to confirm than the claim that there are atoms.

The unaided human senses cannot observe the interior of the sun—our sense organs, and much besides, would be destroyed by heat before even reaching the surface—yet we know things about the composition of the interior of this august body through analysis of the spectra of light that comes from it and comparison of those spectra with spectra from pure elements on earth. We cannot observe what caused the

---

[1] On this gross description of atoms, molecules also count as atoms.

white tracks of bubbles in the photograph on the cover of this book. Kaons and their decay products are too small to be observed by the naked eye. What we *see* is bubbles, not a kaon and its decay products. However, it seems absurd, given what we know about how the picture was produced, to deny that we know from the picture the paths of one particle becoming others. It is easy to cast aspersion on the idea that our knowledge is limited to claims about observables. However, the fact that we have good reason to believe claims about the internal composition of the sun or the existence of particles is very far from implying that we have good reason to believe that Quantum Mechanics is the true theory of the universe. One wants to say to the realist: do you have any idea how much content is in the claim that such a theory is true?

If the position of an anti-realist forces him to deny that we now have good reason to believe in the existence of atoms and molecules, and kaon decays, or to believe that the sun contains hydrogen and helium, then I think he must have a bullet hidden between his teeth. Prima facie, we have good reason to believe these things despite the fact that the entities involved are unobservable. But confidence that the observable versus unobservable distinction is not the place where our good reasons to believe true give out does not show that there is no such place. Prima facie, it is quite reasonable to doubt that we have good reason to believe that Quantum Mechanics is the true theory of the universe, despite the fact that it is probably the best-tested physics theory of all time. An adequate basis for realist and anti-realist views about scientific claims ought to be able to explain the difference between these two types of cases, but the distinctions that typical realist and anti-realist views offer do not.[2]

The view I will develop here does explain that difference by focusing more closely and explicitly than authors on this topic typically do on what it *takes* to have good (or some) reason to believe a claim is true, that is, on what confirmation or evidence requires, and by combining a discussion of standards for evidence on the one hand with descriptive claims about the evidence we actually have for theories and for weaker claims on the other.[3] In the section below called 'Empty strutting?' I consider various probabilistic measures of evidential support and some general consequences each has for the viability of familiar realist and especially anti-realist positions. In later sections I also do piecemeal evaluations of crucial types of cases, using one of the measures under discussion, to argue that we are actually neither so ignorant as the typical anti-realist position implies, nor nearly so blessed as the typical realist position implies. This approach, which takes a stand on cases by means of (facts about the cases and) an explicit and general evidential standard, differs from many typical anti-realist approaches in that it has no implications limiting a priori how far and in what cases scientists will be able to meet this standard in the future.

Claims about evidence have figured explicitly in the work of some authors on scientific realism. Thus, Richard Boyd wrote:

---

[2] For a different argument that our attitude toward mature theories should not be uniform in the way that classic scientific realists have supposed, see Achinstein (2002).

[3] Thus, I assume semantic realism, that is, that scientific theories can be construed literally and as such have truth values. The question at issue here is whether we have grounds for believing they are true rather than false.

By scientific realism I mean the doctrine that the sort of evidence which ordinarily counts in favor of the acceptance of a scientific law or theory is, ordinarily, evidence for the (at least approximate) truth of the law or theory as an account of the causal relations obtaining between the entities quantified over in the law or theory in question. (Boyd 1973: 1)

He went on to say that this means the evidence in question is not merely evidence that the theory has correct observational consequences, and to sketch what he took as necessary conditions for evidence. Whether we have evidence for claims that theories are true, good reason to believe our best theories true, was seen to be the issue. But my approach is relevant even to the projects of those who did not take this question about evidence as central. If I could show that our actual evidence for scientific theories, in the best cases, is good evidence that they are true according to a notion of evidence regarded as sound by independent standards, then the realist would have no need to concoct meta-abductions about the general relation of the success of a theory to its truth. On the other hand, if I can show that our actual evidence does not give us good reason, or even reason, to believe our theories true, according to an independently established standard for evidence, then that would cast serious doubt on any meta-abduction, a type of argument that is fishy to begin with (Laudan 1981).[4]

The realist might object that my formulation puts him at an immediate disadvantage. I say that the realist wants it to be the case that we have good reason, or at least reason, to believe our best theories true, ignoring the more qualified phrase 'approximately true' that allows him to hedge his bets and make a more plausible claim. In the first place, my reason for this is simply technical. The notions of good reason to believe true that I discuss are probabilistic and determinate, so any notion that I combine with them has to be as well, and I do not know of a notion of approximate truth that has both of these features.[5] Even if there is such a notion, incorporating it would add considerable complication to this analysis and, given my sympathies, I would just as soon leave it to a responding realist to do that further work. I do not know whether such work would make a difference to the results here; it may make none or may change them completely. Partly because I do not know how it would turn out, I think such work could be interesting and worthy of the realist's time.

However, in defense of the present analysis, I must point out that even without incorporating approximate truth my formulation of the realist position is hedged considerably, for notice that our having good reason to believe a theory true does not

---

[4] Philip Kitcher's Galilean strategy (Kitcher 2001) is a way of motivating a claim of relation between success and truth, but I would not call it a meta-abduction because the form of it is not to say there is no other way to explain success than truth; the inference looks more like a meta-induction. In any case, even if Kitcher's argument is successful this shows at most that it is gratuitous to assume that the success of the Galilean strategy is limited to observables. Since on the view I will develop here it turns out we have acquired reason to believe claims that go beyond observables, my view agrees with Kitcher's that far. However, general reflections on the Galilean strategy do not settle the question how far we actually get. One of the conclusions of the work of this chapter is that on this question the anti-realist was remarkably close to being right.

[5] Note that Niiniluoto's (1980) measure of estimated truthlikeness is not a standard of genuine approximate truth, but of how closely a theory corresponds to what we take to be the best conceptual systems we have so far found. Estimated truthlikeness does not obviously bear any necessary relation to genuine approximate truth.

imply that the theory *is* true. It does not even imply that the theory is probable in a sense independent of a particular evidence set. What it implies is that our actual evidence set makes the probability of the theory exceed a certain threshold. Granted, this is a lot for the realist to show, as we will see below in loving detail. But without those details it does sound exactly like a claim the realist is always making or depending on. Moreover, though I do not know it is impossible I have trouble imagining a notion of approximate truth that will allow that we have reason to believe a theory to have this property when the theory has a low probability on the evidence. High, or decent, probability on the evidence, not truth, is the criterion by which I end up judging the realist's position below.

If to be an anti-realist is simply to abstain from the realist conclusion—some would call this 'non-realism'—then all an anti-realist needs to do is to show that realists have not given a sound argument for that conclusion, and so some efforts have been (e.g., Laudan 1981). More ambitious anti-realists of a certain period involved themselves explicitly with the notion of evidence by arguing that no evidence we could get could possibly yield the realist conclusion. These arguments were based on the claim that empirically equivalent theories are evidentially indistinguishable, which was in turn based on the claim that only observations could be evidence. This mattered because of a conviction that there are a great number of possible theories empirically equivalent to the ones the realist wants to believe are true. If this anti-realist were right, and those alternative theories were not trivial variants, then our evidence could not possibly tell us our actual theories were more likely to be true than other theories that are empirically equivalent to them yet make significantly different claims about unobservable matters.

That anti-realist approach may seem odd since it tries to prove much more than is necessary. The anti-realist wins what may be the only battle worth fighting if our *actual* evidence does not warrant the realist conclusion, because this means that we do not now have and probably never yet have had good reason to believe scientific theories true. This would leave the realist with the task of showing that belief that we will be able to do in the future what we have never done in the past is more than a pious hope. Why, then, should the anti-realist attempt to prove something about the limited power of all possible evidence? I think the answer is that it looked like an easy mark for any empiricist who knew how logically to generate empirically equivalent alternatives to a theory. Remarkably, considering the extent of discussion on this topic and the explicit relevance of the notion of evidence to it, little more care was taken to define what it takes for one statement to support another than had been taken on the realist side. This may have been because of a presumption on both sides that this would not make much difference to the debate. Perhaps one assumed that confirmation theorists spend their time arguing about how best to capture obvious intuitions using probability, and in these arguments over realism one is appealing only to obvious intuitions, claims all confirmation theorists would have to agree on.[6]

---

[6] Laudan (1981: 23) offers a rather different explanation for the typical neglect of confirmation theory, at least on the realist side, namely, that it would be too strict a standard of success for the realist's purposes since it would make science largely 'unsuccessful' because unconfirmed. I think it

Whatever the reasons for the assumption, though, it is simply false that confirmation theory is irrelevant to realism about scientific theories. It turns out that we do not even need to make commitments that define evidence uniquely to get some interesting results about what are and are not possible and plausible views in the debate between realists and anti-realists.

In particular, as I will argue, no commonly discussed probabilistic measure of confirmation behaves in a way compatible with Constructive Empiricism, a more sophisticated anti-realist position I will discuss below that says we ought to take observations to confirm only claims about observables, and not any claims beyond these. This is because what characterizes Constructive Empiricism, a claim about evidence that I call 'Equal Punishment', though technically true on the ratio measure of confirmation (and not on other measures) is true only in a way that leaves the Constructive Empiricist position untenable, because of what is required to evaluate the terms of the measure. One is left with the choice to admit that we can sometimes evaluate a certain term, in which case one is no longer a Constructive Empiricist because one has admitted that we have knowledge of unobservables, or to maintain that we can never evaluate that term, in which case one must be doubtful even of inferences from observed to observable, and is not a Constructive Empiricist but a skeptic. This argument about Constructive Empiricism has similar implications for the approach that says empirically equivalent theories are evidentially indistinguishable, which is a more general version of the Equal Punishment claim.

The typical realist position fares little better, though. The realist is best served by the Likelihood Ratio (LR) measure of confirmation for reasons I will discuss, but evaluating this measure requires evaluating the probability of the evidence on the catch-all, the negation of the hypothesis. Although, as I argue below, we have evaluated this term for hypotheses that go beyond observables, it has been only slightly beyond, and any claim that we have evaluated this term for high-level theories like Quantum Mechanics would be preposterous. There are clear reasons why the term becomes harder and harder to evaluate as our hypotheses become more general. And one must evaluate this term or other terms just as difficult, I argue, to support the realist contention that we have reason to believe actual theories are true. I conclude by arguing that we don't know whether we will ever be able to evaluate this term for high-level theories, though the hope that we will is more than a fantasy. Along the way I give an account of theory testing that explains how it can be that theories are well tested while we have not thereby assembled good reason to believe that they are true.

On my own view, then, realist claims about science are best evaluated piecemeal from a principled view, or family of views, of what counts as confirmational support; for each scientific claim, do we have good (or some) reason to believe this claim is true by that or those standards, considering our actual evidence? Scientists actually do succeed in assembling good reason to believe true by my preferred standards for claims that go a little beyond observables, implying that observable versus unobservable is

would be a mark against a confirmation theory if it could find no sense in which science has been successful, since prima facie there is some sense in which it is successful and that sense is in part epistemic. However, the success may not be full-blown confirmation—reason to believe a theory true—as we will see below with my own view.

not the distinction most salient to realism and anti-realism. However, the criteria that show this also show, when brought to real examples, that the anti-realists were always right to doubt that we have actually got much further than that; further than that is very hard to get. The Constructive Empiricist type anti-realist was justified in his spirit of epistemic modesty, but wrong, and even immodest, in thinking that we could pronounce ahead of time through a priori arguments the limits of our ability to confirm high-level theories. If, as it sometimes seems, realism is the extremely modest claim that we do not know we will not be able to assemble good reason to believe high-level theories in the future, then I am a realist.

Lambs and sheep

As crimes that disproportionately target women came to be taken more seriously, well-intentioned people in the USA proposed to strengthen the laws against stalking by increasing the punishment for this crime. However, the folly of overzealousness in this direction was soon pointed out: if, as sometimes fantasized, the punishment for stalking in violation of a court protection order were to be equal to the punishment for murder, this might encourage stalkers to kill more often than they otherwise would. The punishment for murder would be no greater than that for stalking, the risk of detection might seem the same, and to a criminal in a stalking mood the murder would look more satisfying. Bas van Fraassen may be right when he says in defense of his Constructive Empiricist position about scientific theories that 'it is not an epistemological principle that one might as well hang for a sheep as for a lamb,' but, as Alan Musgrave pointed out, as a practical principle this is pretty sensible advice (van Fraassen 1980: 72; Musgrave 1985: 199). If the risk is the same, one should opt for the higher payoff.[7]

Van Fraassen's quip has often been construed as a denial that it is better to have more than to have fewer true or potentially true beliefs, or as saying that the realist's claim that certain theories are true should be shunned because it has a greater chance of being wrong than the Constructive Empiricist's belief merely that those theories are empirically adequate, true to the observables. If these were the meanings, though, then why rest at the belief that certain theories make true predictions about observables? Why not take risk-aversion to its limit and believe nothing at all? Van Fraassen's quip, I think, was not so much about the risk of being wrong, as about the risk of punishment for being wrong, and was not a complaint that the realist took too great a risk of being wrong but rather that he took too little risk of punishment for it. What van Fraassen meant, it seems to me, was that the principle that one does well to take the same risk for more rather than for less does not apply to the case where we imagine the realist belief about theories as the sheep and the Constructive Empiricist's belief about theories as the lamb. This is because whereas it is obvious that a sheep is a greater payoff than a lamb, it simply is not true, according to van Fraassen, that the realist

---

[7] The sheep–lamb quip depends on taking the sheep to be more valuable because larger, giving more meat and wool. For present purposes, banish all thoughts that lamb might be more valuable because tastier or more tender.

belief about a theory—that it is true—constitutes a greater payoff than that of the Constructive Empiricist—that it is empirically adequate.

The realist belief does not represent a greater payoff, according to van Fraassen, because in this special case that the risk of punishment would be the same actually destroys the extra value that the realist option initially appeared to have. It is van Fraassen's position that the realist claim that a scientific theory is true is no more liable to be punished by any possible experience than the Constructive Empiricist claim that the theory is empirically adequate. The point of his comment about sheep and lambs was then to say that the lack of need to have more fear of punishment for the realist claim than for the Constructive Empiricist claim is not a reason to believe the realist claim. As he later elaborated his point, since 'the extra opinion is not additionally vulnerable, the risk is ... illusory, and *therefore so is the wealth*. It is but empty strutting and posturing, this display of courage not under fire' (van Fraassen 1985: 255). To the extent that the realist claim about a theory goes beyond the claim that the theory is empirically adequate the claim cannot be impugned by empirical tests, van Fraassen implies. If the further claims cannot be punished by experience then far from adding value they are merely a certain kind of hot air. If the assumptions of van Fraassen's position are right, then the choice we have in our attitude toward scientific theories is between a weaker belief that we can investigate—the theories are empirically adequate—and a stronger belief that we cannot—the theories are true.[8]

While illusions have their attractions, van Fraassen seems to me right that the second option does not have a more valuable payoff if we assume that the risk of punishment is the same. I cannot see how anyone could defend the view that the business of science is to aim for the second option, a stronger belief that we cannot investigate, since whatever else is true it seems that the business of science is investigation and not hot air. Thus, the controversial core of van Fraassen's view lies elsewhere, in the intermediate conclusions that yield the consequence that these are our choices. Much critical attention has focused on his distinction between observable and unobservable entities, and it is true that if there is no such distinction then there also is no distinction between the empirical adequacy and the truth of a theory, implying that the hanging gambit is ill posed. However, van Fraassen's distinction between observables and unobservables needs only the assumption that there is a vague distinction between things the unaided human senses can observe and things that they cannot, and this I am inclined to grant. And though the existence of a

---

[8] There are several reasons why it may not be obvious to a casual reader of *The Scientific Image* that this comment about lambs and sheep has the significance I am attributing to it. One is that despite van Fraassen's commendable reformulation of the positivist position as an epistemological claim rather than a linguistic claim, he tends to postpone serious discussion of the epistemological issue I am interested in when it arises. (See van Fraassen 1980: 19, 72.) This, in turn, I think, is because the burden of the book is to argue that one is not rationally compelled to be a realist rather than that the realist is wrong. Thus, the main work of the book is to describe a possible non-realist position that can make sense of scientific practice rather than to show that this position is epistemologically superior or even feasible. The lonely and show-stopping role of the lamb–sheep remark when the question of the epistemological viability of the Constructive Empiricist position arises, and the fact that my interpretation of it fits with the positivist spirit of concern about idle metaphysics and with his later comments about the remark, have convinced me that this is the core of van Fraassen's epistemological defense of Constructive Empiricism.

distinction between empirical adequacy and truth of a claim goes beyond this, and faces the problem of saying how to identify the part of a theory that is about observables, this distinction has been compelling and useful even to philosophers with no sympathy for Constructive Empiricism.[9]

However, that this observable versus unobservable distinction exists, and that the empirical adequacy versus truth distinction should exist, are not enough to defend Constructive Empiricism. What that view depends on, and the important question for any discussion of van Fraassen's style of anti-realism, is why this or any similar distinction should have an epistemological significance. Why should the confirming (or disconfirming) action that successful (or unsuccessful) empirical predictions by a theory yield for that theory stop short at the level of the empirical generalizations the theory implies, rather than flow up in a smooth, if attenuated, path through its deductively stronger claims?[10] If confirmation and disconfirmation ever flow up beyond observables then the realist option of believing that a theory is true is not always empty strutting.

There is an immediacy to unaided observation that our justifications for beliefs about other matters do not have. It is thus tempting to privilege beliefs based on observation in one's epistemology because of a sense that we know things we observe with our unaided senses better than we know other things. Empiricism tends along these lines. Further, though one might doubt, as I do, that claims about observables deserve a privileged status without exception, one must admit that from an epistemic point of view the distinction between observables and unobservables is not simply arbitrary. The privileging of claims about observables is built on the sound idea that we can acquire stronger reasons to believe claims about matters we have better access to.

One might think that assuming that observations are more trustworthy than other sources of justification would yield van Fraassen's options, since privileging observables in a hierarchy of justification provides an epistemological distinction between observables and unobservables. However, what those options depend on is not merely that observations are privileged as *sources* of evidence but also the further claim that what our evidence *yields* in further justified beliefs or knowledge does not extend beyond the domain of observables. I do not doubt that a strong enough empiricist position would imply that what we can have good evidence for or against is limited to the realm of observables, or that such a view could be internally consistent. An assumption that might yield this claim is that nothing except beliefs about observables can either be evidence or make a difference to claims that one statement is evidence for

---

[9] For discussion of the aboutness problem, see Musgrave (1985: 208) and Sober (1985).

[10] Kitcher (2001) provides several arguments against the epistemological significance of the distinction between observables and unobservables, not all of which I agree with. For example, he charges the idea with hubris for implying that the general reliability of the inference from the practical success of beliefs to their truth fails for inferences involving unobservables, for why should the world stop behaving in a certain way just at the arbitrary place where our ability to observe gives out? However, the Constructive Empiricist need not claim that the reliability of the success–truth inference fails for unobservables, but only that he does not know or have good reason to believe that it succeeds. And, for that claim the distinction between observables and unobservables does not look arbitrary, since it is a claim that depends on what we have 'access' to.

another.[11] However, this is a rather strong claim to take as an assumption and one that many scientists would not agree with, so I am not going to assume either it or its negation at the outset. Instead, I am going to start by treating the claim that undergirds van Fraassen's position directly as a claim about evidence.

That van Fraassen's options are our choices depends on a claim about evidence or confirmation. The realist option of believing that a theory is true is empty strutting if, and only if, it takes no further chances of punishment in the tribunal of experience than the claim of the Constructive Empiricist does, that is, if and only if no evidence could disconfirm the claim that a theory is true more than it disconfirmed the claim that the theory is empirically adequate. It seems that this claim is so central to van Fraassen's view that if we believe the claim then we ought to be Constructive Empiricists (lest we indulge in hot air) and if not then not (because it's not hot air). I am going to address the question whether this claim is true in terms of probabilistic conceptions of evidence. In discussions of realism and anti-realism, assumptions about confirmation and how it works often get made on the basis of arguments about other things, without explicit arguments about confirmation as such. Here I will turn this around: asking questions about confirmation explicitly, I will build a view of realist and anti-realist issues on the basis of what confirmation theory teaches us about evidence. It will turn out that van Fraassen's charge that the realist claim about theories is empty strutting is false on all but one of the currently discussed measures of confirmation, but that this provides less comfort to the realist than the realist generally assumes it would.

Empty strutting?

Call the claim that no observational evidence could disconfirm the realist belief that a given theory is true more than it did the Constructive Empiricist claim that that theory is empirically adequate 'EP', for equal punishment. By 'disconfirm more' we mean, of course, that the evidence lowers the probability of one hypothesis more than it lowers the probability of the other hypothesis; evidence that disconfirms to some degree need not knock a hypothesis out of all consideration. There are conceptions of confirmation on which the claim EP is true, as I will show. However, most of the conceptions I am aware of on which it is true are primitive, and patently inadequate. Among sophisticated conceptions of confirmation, the claim EP is measure-dependent. That is, the claim is true for the ratio measure of confirmation, but false for all other measures that are in common use, including the LR which was argued in the previous chapter to be superior to other known measures of confirmation on a number of grounds. Though I think the ratio measure is inapt, reasonable people have defended it, but even embracing this measure on which the claim EP is true will not make the Constructive Empiricist coherent. This is because, as I will show, use of this measure (and all the others) requires commitments to claims about unobservables even to evaluate evidence claims about observables.

---

[11] Van Fraassen has embraced this claim at (1985: 254) and probably elsewhere.

We can represent the realist's belief that a hypothesis, h, is true by 'h', and the claim that h is empirically adequate by 'CE(h)', for Constructive Empiricism.[12] It is plausible that on the enumerative induction view of confirmation the claim EP is true. On this view, the form that every case of confirmation takes is that an instance lends support to its generalization. Disconfirmation of a generalization occurs when one of the generalization's instances is found to be false. h and CE(h) have the same observational consequences, and it is plausible that any statement about observations which is an instance of some claim included in the hypothesis is also an instance of some claim that is part of CE(h).[13] Hence both h and CE(h) will be disconfirmed whenever any of that common set of consequences that is an instance of something in the first is found to be false. Thus, it follows from the assumptions that no observational instance that disconfirms h could fail to disconfirm CE(h), on the enumerative induction view of ampliative reasoning. This view has no quantitative measure, so allows no sense in which a given instance disconfirms one statement more than it disconfirms another except by disconfirming one without disconfirming the other.

Thus, it is plausible that EP is true on the enumerative induction conception of confirmation. However, the limitations of this view of confirmation are extreme and well known. Not only does it lack a quantitative or even comparative measure, but a great deal of scientific reasoning just does not take the form of inferring from an instance to a generalization. (We will see an example of this below.) In the search for a form for ampliative reasoning that is more general than this, it is natural to consider the possibility that what makes the instance-generalization inference compelling is not the relation of instance to generalization but the more general relation of a statement to another statement that implies it. The idea in other words is that it is a mark of the truth of a hypothesis if it implies the evidence one has. A hypothesis is disconfirmed if it implies a claim that is false, and disconfirmed by a true statement about observables if it implies that that statement about observables is false. As with enumerative induction, this conception does not have a way of talking about degrees of confirmation or disconfirmation, so the only way that h could be more disconfirmed than CE(h) would be for h to be disconfirmed while CE(h) was not.

It is easy to show that on this conception of induction, known as the hypothetico-deductive account, EP is true. Since CE(h) is simply the claim that h makes all the right claims about observables, h and CE(h) have the same observational consequences, that is, they imply all of the same things about observables. Any finding that a statement about observables that was implied by h was not true would also be a finding that a statement about observables implied by CE(h) was not true. Any disconfirmation of h by true statements about observables would be a disconfirmation of CE(h) by true

---

[12] Van Fraassen could object that in representing the issues as I will I am assuming a syntactic view of theories that he rejects. I do this, to the extent that I do, in the first place because I do not know how to formulate confirmation theory with a semantic view of theories. However, I am also suspicious of the claimed advantages of the semantic view of theories over the syntactic view, in general and in light of the arguments of William Demopoulos (2003: esp. section 5).

[13] It is not plausible the other way around, namely, that any statement about observations which is an instance of some claim included in CE(h) is also an instance of some claim included in h. We will see a counterexample to that below.

statements about observables, and since there are no degrees of comparison on this conception that is all we have to know in order to know that EP is true. We could soften the hypothetico-deductive account to say that a hypothesis is disconfirmed by observations when, and only when, it makes those observations improbable. If we did, it would not change the result that EP is true, because it is natural to expect from the assumption that CE(h) has all the same observational consequences as h that CE(h) predicts the same probability as h does for every statement about observables that h has a prediction for.

EP is true on the hypothetico-deductive account and on its probabilistic version, but both views of confirmation are known to be inadequate. The best-known reason is that they make confirmation indiscriminate in ways that we do not think it is: on these views all hypotheses that imply a set of true claims about observables are equally supported by those claims, and there are an infinite number of such hypotheses, not all of which we think are so supported. Logical conjunction provides an obvious way of constructing examples of this problem. We do think that the result of observation during an eclipse of the precise amount by which light bends around the sun supports Einstein's general theory of relativity over Newton's theory of gravity. However, we do not think of that observation as supporting the conjunction of Einstein's theory with the statement that all herrings are red, though the latter conjunction implies the observation as surely as Einstein's theory (with auxiliaries) does.[14]

I have just described two broad conceptions of induction on which the claim EP is true. However, the Constructive Empiricist has nothing to be proud of in these results, since the conceptions or assumptions on which these views are based are known to be inadequate or false. The inadequacies of these views are not common-sense knowledge, though, and the views of evidential support as coming through enumerative induction or hypothetico-deduction are familiar, which raises the suspicion that a primitive conception of induction is what leads some (though not necessarily van Fraassen himself) to think that EP is true. On more sophisticated probabilistic accounts, confirmation admits of degrees, and the currently popular measures of this sort give different answers as to whether EP is true. That is, the claim EP is measure-dependent, which is sufficient to show the relevance of disagreements within confirmation theory to the debate over realism and anti-realism. According to the LR measure, the difference measure, and the normalized difference measure, the claim EP is false, while according to the popular ratio measure EP is true. I will show that EP is false for the LR measure with counterexamples, and I will show algebraically that EP is false for the difference measure and normalized difference measure and true for the ratio measure.[15]

---

[14] The ratio measure, $P(e/h)/P(e)$, apparently cannot register this distinction, but the LR, $P(e/h)/P(e/-h)$, with its attention to the probability of the evidence on the negation of the hypothesis can. Taking T as Einstein's theory and r as the red herring claim, it is obvious that $P(e/-T)$ does not equal $P(e/-(T.r))$, for the conjunction of T and r could be false while T is true, for example if r is false.

[15] In discussing these probabilistic measures I ignore the fact that one can use the log of the measure instead of the measure itself in the case of the ratio measure and the Likelihood Ratio measure. This is innocuous because the logged versions of these measures are ordinally equivalent to the measures themselves.

EP is not true on a LR conception of confirmation. This can be illustrated easily with a simple counterexample. Suppose h ≡ O.U, where 'O' is a conjunct that contains all and only h's claims about observables, and 'U' is a conjunct that contains all and only h's claims about unobservables. For EP to be true on this measure it must be the case for every example that P(e/h)/P(e/−h) = P(e/CE(h))/P(e/−CE(h)), but this equality need not hold on the LR measure for the type of example described. The numerators P(e/h) and P(e/CE(h)) are equal, since e is observable and h and CE(h) imply the same things about observables. However, the denominators P(e/−h) and P(e/−CE(h)) are not in general equal. Notice that,

$$P(e/-h) = P(e/-(O.U)),$$

and

$$P(e/-CE(h)) = P(e/-O).$$

Suppose that O entails e, and that O is true but U is false. O true and U false is a possible way to fulfill the condition that −(O.U), and in this case P(e/−(O.U)) will be 1 due to O's entailment of e. However, in this case P(e/−O) can be less than 1, since −O need not entail e just because O does.[16]

EP is false on the LR measure of confirmation, but the counterexample just described assumed that the theory was resolvable into two conjuncts which neatly separate the observable 'parts' and the unobservable 'parts' of the theory's claims. Real examples could be more complicated, and this example does not give us any conclusion about them. Real examples are indeed more complicated, but relaxing the separability assumption does not favor EP, as the following example shows. Suppose that F and G are observable types of phenomena. Perhaps F is a red flash and G is a blue flash. Suppose J and K are unobservable types of events. The hypothesis, h, is a conjunction of five claims:

h$_1$: After a J occurs, a K occurs exactly 5 seconds later > 90 per cent of the time.
h$_2$: After a J occurs, invariably an F occurs within 5 seconds.
h$_3$: After a K occurs invariably a G occurs within 5 seconds.
h$_4$: There is no occurrence of an F without a J preceding it within 5 seconds.
h$_5$: There is no occurrence of a G without a K preceding it.

h is equivalent to (h$_1$.h$_2$.h$_3$.h$_4$.h$_5$), and contains claims about unobservables as well as claims about observables. Figure 6.1 provides a schematic picture of the situation, where time passes from left to right. The claim, CE(h), that h is empirically adequate is the following:

After an F occurs a G occurs within 10 seconds > 90% of the time.

CE(h) and h have the same observational consequences, namely CE(h).

---

[16] I owe the last bit of this example to Eric Barnes who used it to argue against a claim I made in an earlier version of this chapter that EP was true on the LR measure if one made the simplistic (and not generally true) assumption that the observable and unobservable 'parts' of a theory can be separated into conjuncts.

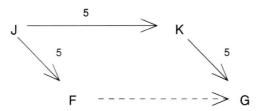

Figure 6.1

Note first that, confirming the reflections above, this example does not undermine EP on an instance-generalization account of induction. The only observable instances there could be of either h or CE(h) are instances in which F occurs and then G occurs. However, these are not instances of h, since there is no statement in h that is the generalization of any of these instances. Thus, if Fs occurred without Gs, that would provide some disconfirmation of CE(h) but no disconfirmation at all of h. 'After an F came a G' is not an instance of h, although it is an instance of a statement implied by h, namely CE(h). In fact, h does not have any instances concerning observables and so could never be disconfirmed by any finding about observables on the instance-generalization view of induction. What we see here is the severe limitations of the instance-generalization form. This example also bears out the reflection above that EP is true on the hypothetico-deductive account of confirmation, since h and CE(h) have the same set of implications about observables, and that is the only thing the hypothetico-deductive account uses as a criterion.

However, EP is false on the LR conception of how to measure degree of confirmation, and this example shows it for cases where observable and unobservable parts of a theory are not separable as conjuncts. To say that EP is false on this measure is to say that on this measure one set of truths about observables can disconfirm h more than it disconfirms CE(h). Consider the following possible evidence gathered about observables:

e = There was an F not followed within 10 seconds by a G in eight out of ten runs.

The statement e, if true, intuitively disconfirms both CE(h) and h to some degree since in the first case e reports a frequency of F-without-G instances that the hypothesis says is unlikely, and in the second case what e says is something the hypothesis implies is unlikely. e disconfirms both hypotheses to some degree judging by the LR too, since the ratios:

$$P(e/h)/P(e/-h) \text{ and}$$
$$P(e/CE(h))/P(e/-CE(h))$$

are both less than 1. e is made more probable by the negations of these hypotheses than by the hypotheses themselves. h will be *more* disconfirmed by e than CE(h) is, according to the LR conception, if the ratio:

$$P(e/h)/P(e/-h)$$

is less than the ratio:

$$P(e/\text{CE}(h))/P(e/-\text{CE}(h)),$$

because in that case the negation of h is more favored over h by e than is the negation of CE (h) favored over CE(h) by e. It is easy to see that the numerators of these ratios are equal, that is,

$$P(e/h) = P(e/\text{CE}(h)),$$

because e is a statement about observables, and h and CE(h) yield the same predictions about observables. In fact, for our case $P(e/h) = P(e/\text{CE}(h)) < 0.28$.

Since the numerators of these ratios are the same, any difference there may be between the ratios will be found in the denominators. The denominators do not disappoint; since the negation of h is very different from the negation of CE(h), there is no reason to expect the denominators to be the same. In fact, it would be a miracle if they were. For a counterexample to EP, we need only that

$$P(e/-h) > P(e/-\text{CE}(h)).$$

Since $-h$ is a disjunction of the negations of h_1 through h_5, $-h$ is true if and only if either

  $-h_1$: After a J, a K occurs exactly 5 seconds later $\leq$ 90 per cent of the time, or
  $-h_2$: Js sometimes occur without an F occurring within 5 seconds after, or
  $-h_3$: Ks sometimes occur without a G occurring within 5 seconds after, or
  $-h_4$: An F sometimes occurs without a J preceding it within 5 seconds, or
  $-h_5$: A G sometimes occurs without a K preceding it.

The negation of CE(h) is the claim simply that:

After an F occurs a G occurs within 10 seconds $\leq$ 90 per cent of the time.

It can be calculated that $P(e/-\text{CE}(h))$ is greater than or equal to 0.72. It is not necessary but is fully allowable and plausible to assign a higher value to $P(e/-h)$ than to $P(e/-\text{CE}(h))$ since $-h_1$ by itself gives a probability greater than 0.28 to the failure of G to follow F on eight out of ten runs, and other possibilities $-h_3$ and $-h_4$ provide other ways in which G could fail to occur after F. Of course, it is possible that $P(-h_1/-h)$ is extremely low, that is, that if the hypothesis h is false the problem is not with h_1. However, I only need one example to show that EP is false on the LR view, and therefore I only need for it to be possible that $P(-h_1/-h)$ is high enough, or the probability that all of h_1 through h_5 are false is high enough, that $P(e/-h)$ is higher than $P(e/-\text{CE}(h))$, and that is certainly allowable and realistically possible. For an example that will guarantee this, assign $P(h_6/-h) = 1$, where h_6 is a strengthening of $-h_1$ which says that exactly five seconds after a J there is a K exactly 20 per cent of the time. Therefore, on the LR view of confirmational support EP is false, and the realist option is not always empty strutting.

Note that the inequality of punishment of h and CE(h) by e could also go in the other direction. That is, the logically weaker claim CE(h) can be more disconfirmed by the given evidence than h is disconfirmed by it. To get this in our example, suppose that exactly five seconds after a J occurs, a K occurs exactly 80 per cent of the time.

This makes h_1 false, and thus makes h false. Suppose the remaining conjuncts of h are true. That is, $P(-h_2/-h) = P(-h_3/-h) = P(-h_4/-h) = P(-h_5/-h) = 0$. If so, then $-h$ implies that G follows F exactly 80 per cent of the time. From this we can calculate that $P(e/-h) = 0.32$. Because 0.28/0.32 is greater than 0.28/0.72, CE(h) is more disconfirmed than h is by e in the circumstances just imagined. This blocks an out that the Constructive Empiricist might be considering, namely, to give up the claim EP and rest one's epistemic modesty instead on the claim that the realist hypothesis that a theory is true always takes more chances both of being wrong and of being exposed as wrong by evidence. On the LR measure, at least, the logically stronger hypothesis is not always more disconfirmed by a given set of evidence. We have just seen that it may be disconfirmed less.

Note that the result that EP is false has a significance more general than that for our attitude toward Constructive Empiricism, for the claim EP is an instance of the more general claim, much discussed in the realism-anti-realism debate of an earlier period, that empirically equivalent theories are evidentially indistinguishable (EEEI). If theories that imply all the same things about observables are not evidentially distinguishable, then the anti-realist can make hay since our evidence cannot tell us which potentially wildly different such theory to believe true in a given domain. According to the LR measure, though, EEEI is false; this is obvious from the fact that one of its instances, EP, is false, but its falsity is more widespread than that implies. For notice that the argument that showed EP is false is general: empirically equivalent theories are not generally evidentially indistinguishable because two theories may have the same implications about a restricted domain while the negations of those two theories have very different implications for that domain. The LR measure of confirmation registers the implications of the negation of a hypothesis as well as the implications of the hypothesis in judging how far the evidence we see confirms a hypothesis, and it serves the realist to do so.[17]

As I have said, though, the claim EP is measure-dependent. If we assume the ratio measure of confirmation, $P(e/h)/P(e)$, then the claim EP is true, as can be seen immediately. On the standard way of measuring disconfirmation on this view, a hypothesis h is more disconfirmed the lower is the ratio $P(e/h)/P(e)$. $P(e)$ must be the same for our hypotheses h and CE(h) since the e in question is the same. Therefore, e can disconfirm h more than it disconfirms CE(h) only if $P(e/h) < P(e/CE(h))$. However, $P(e/h)$ must be equal to $P(e/CE(h))$ because h and CE(h) have the same implications about observables and e is observable. A similar argument would show that the claim EEEI is true on the ratio measure. I will have more to say below about whether this support for EP and EEEI can be taken as a victory for Constructive Empiricism or anti-realism in general.

The difference measure and the normalized difference measure occupy a ground in between the LR measure and the ratio measure in that they agree with the LR that the claim EP is false, but the way in which this happens is not very useful to the realist argument against the anti-realist. The difference measure, $P(h/e) - P(h)$, is equivalent

---

[17] This way of showing EEEI to be false can be seen as a further, more general, step in a discussion begun by Larry Laudan and Jarrett Leplin (1991: 465–6).

to $P(h)[P(e/h)/P(e) - 1]$, and a hypothesis is disconfirmed by e if this difference is less than 0. A hypothesis is more disconfirmed the lower is the value of $P(h/e) - P(h)$, or the lower is the value of $P(h)[P(e/h)/P(e) - 1]$. Since $P(e/h)/P(e)$ is just the ratio measure, and we have just shown that the ratio measure gives the same results for h and $CE(h)$, the only way that the expressions

$$P(h)[P(e/h)/P(e) - 1]$$

and

$$P(CE(h))[P(e/CE(h)/P(e) - 1]$$

could be different would be if $P(h)$ and $P(CE(h))$ were different. Indeed, these two terms, the prior probability of the hypothesis and the prior probability of the Constructive Empiricist version of the hypothesis, will not in general be the same; since the hypothesis is usually a stronger and never a weaker claim than its Constructive Empiricist counterpart, it will often have a lower prior probability. Thereby, h's difference measure will be lower than that for $CE(h)$, and h will be more disconfirmed than $CE(h)$ if both are disconfirmed to some degree by the observational evidence e. According to the difference measure, e can disconfirm h to a greater degree than it does $CE(h)$, so EP is false. The normalized difference measure gives exactly the same result since the normalization factor, $1/P(-e)$, can be different only if $P(e)$ is different, but as noted $P(e)$ must be the same for h and $CE(h)$. A similar argument would show that both measures make the claim EEEI false.

Thus the consistent advocate of the difference measure or the normalized difference measure of confirmation should reject Constructive Empiricism (and EEEI-based anti-realism in general). However, there is an important difference in the grounds that the advocate of the difference measure and the advocate of the LR have for this preference. The difference measure made EP false because that measure contains a weighting by the prior probability of the hypothesis. The LR made EP false because the LR incorporates a term concerning the relation of e and the negation of the hypothesis. A realism based on the difference measure will be vulnerable to the Constructive Empiricist digging in his heels with a charge of adhockery. The only reason the advocate of the difference measure got excused from assenting to EP, he will say, was that he *defined* confirmation as containing a weighting by the prior of the hypothesis, not because of a difference that the *evidence* was shown to make to the degree of confirmation. Without that weighting by the prior, the difference measure has no sensitivity to the relation of the evidence and the hypothesis beyond what the ratio measure has, and according to the ratio measure EP is true. The advocate of the LR is not vulnerable to this rather reasonable objection.

So far, then, it looks as if the debate between realism and Constructive Empiricism (or EEEI-based anti-realism in general) comes down to a disagreement over whether to adopt the ratio measure or the LR measure of confirmation. It would be natural for the Constructive Empiricist to reply to these results with an empiricist-style argument against the LR measure. It is all very well, he might say, that the LR makes EP false, but it is not really punishment if one never feels the pain. That is, maybe it is true that on the basis of a given set of statements about observables the realist's belief about a given hypothesis can *be* more disconfirmed than the Constructive Empiricist's belief about that hypothesis, on a certain view of what confirmation is. Still, that does not show that we can *know* that the realist's belief is more disconfirmed. From the derivation above it is clear that, in the example given, knowing the realist's belief is more disconfirmed on the LR measure would require some knowledge of unobservable entities, since the likelihood of e on −h depends on the probabilities of claims about unobservable entities, e.g., on $P(-h_1 / -h)$. Therefore, the realist can claim that we can *find out* his belief about a hypothesis is more disconfirmed than the belief of the Constructive Empiricist only if he assumes that we can have knowledge of unobservable entities, and the latter is just what the Constructive Empiricist has doubted from the beginning.

The Constructive Empiricist can point out that it is not quite enough for the realist if there are significant cases where EP is in fact false on her chosen measure; it must also be true that she can evaluate the terms that tell us this is so. But what's good for the goose is good for the gander, and it is not quite enough for Constructive Empiricism that EP be true on one's chosen measure either. The Constructive Empiricist also needs to be able to commit himself to the claim that CE(h) is confirmed by observations without making any assumptions about unobservables, for he professes not to be able to confirm assumptions about unobservables and yet to be able to acquire reason to believe on the basis of actual observations the claims a theory makes about *all* observables. To make this commitment in the case of incremental confirmation of CE(h), the Constructive Empiricist needs to evaluate the terms of the ratio measure for this hypothesis, $P(e/CE(h))$ and $P(e)$. I claim that he cannot do this without making commitments to claims about unobservables. (I will consider in the next two sections how far the realist is able to evaluate the measure on which EP is false.)

Consider the likelihood, $P(e/CE(h))$, where e is not a disconfirming run of instances, as above, but, intuitively, a confirming run of instances. For example, let

e = An F was followed by a G within 5 seconds in ten out of these ten runs.

We must not be misled by the fact that the term $P(e/CE(h))$ only mentions observables: evaluation of this term requires commitments about many claims involving unobservables. This is because the truth values of many claims about unobservables are probabilistically relevant to this conditional probability, a point analogous to a point concerning auxiliary hypotheses made long ago by Pierre Duhem. To see this, we will have to be more precise about what the claim CE(h) is. We never test claims about correlations between observables that do not have implicit circumstances qualifying the claims, because such unqualified claims are typically false and not what we mean. For example, we do not test the claim that blue lights follow red lights more than 90 per cent of the time, since that claim is patently false, as shown by the widespread existence of stoplights. We were not thinking of stoplights when we formulated the claim that blue lights follow red lights. We were thinking of a particular experimental or observational situation. The stoplight, in which a red light is followed by a green light and not by a blue light, would be a counterexample to the unqualified claim about lights, but it is not a counterexample to the claim that was actually meant. That claim was, say, that any red light will be followed within

5 seconds by a blue light more than 90 per cent of the time in this location on this square machine if its switch has been turned on for a run. Notice that I have described the circumstances that qualify the claim CE(h) purely in terms of matters that are observable.

We can see that P(e/CE(h)) is underdetermined by claims about observables by noticing that there are an infinite number of statements like the following, whose probabilities make a difference to P(e/CE(h)). Call this statement 'EXOTIC':

> During the runs referred to in e there was a transient and highly local force field in the vicinity whose only possible effect on observables was to prevent G after an F had occurred, and it had a 90 per cent probability of doing so when an F had occurred.

Suppose EXOTIC (and all statements like it) were false. Then P(e/CE(h)) would be very high, just as we assumed it was above, because CE(h) says that red lights are followed quickly by blue lights more than 90 per cent of the time (in the circumstances described in the previous paragraph) and the falsity of EXOTIC and its friends tells us that nothing is interfering with that. However, if EXOTIC had a high probability, then P(e/CE(h)) would *not* be high because even if CE(h) was true, there was also likely a disturbing factor on these runs with a good chance of preventing G after F occurred. EXOTIC affects the probability of e given CE(h), and EXOTIC is consistent with the truth of CE(h), because it refers only to the time during the ten runs referred to in e, whereas CE(h) refers to all times that could be observed and makes a statistical claim. One has to assign a probability to EXOTIC in order to evaluate the likelihood term that is needed to decide whether the ratio measure is greater than 1, indicating confirmation.

On the ratio measure of confirmation, probabilities must be assigned to claims about unobservables in order to know how far e confirms (or disconfirms) the Constructivist Empiricist belief about h, because those probabilities are needed to evaluate the term P(e/CE(h)). Since the term P(e/CE(h)) occurs explicitly in all the common measures it must be evaluated for confirmation (or disconfirmation) of CE(h) no matter which of those measures one chooses. Thus, the Constructive Empiricist cannot escape commitments to claims about unobservables if he is going to claim that he can confirm a theory's empirical adequacy. If he is going to deny any knowledge or confirmation of claims about unobservables, he is going to have to be a full-blown skeptic who does not think we know anything beyond our current observations, a consequence which, of course, van Fraassen never intended. The ratio measure is encouraging to the Constructive Empiricist because it makes EP true, but this measure cannot be used to defend Constructive Empiricism. A more general version of this argument can be used against any anti-realism based on EEEI via the ratio measure: you can refrain from judging between theories that have the same implications for all possible evidence, but only if you also refrain from all commitments that go beyond our actual observed evidence. Perhaps there are anti-realists who would wish to go that far, but I think that among anti-realisms van Fraassen's style had an advantage in that it appeared not to require one to be quite that skeptical.

One might protest to this argument against the coherence of Constructive Empiricism that there is no reason that a Constructive Empiricist must assign probabilities to statements like EXOTIC; he can just leave those spaces in the probability function blank. However, the Constructive Empiricist's semantic realism says otherwise. When we ventured into the epistemological realism and anti-realism debate we left social constructivism and instrumentalisms of all sorts at the door; theories and indicative statements of the language (and their negations) that are potentially parts of a theory have truth values independently of us, and the issue is about whether we find reasons for belief about what those truth values are. EXOTIC is an indicative statement of our language that according to semantic realism has a truth value. Thus any probability function assigns EXOTIC a probability, or at least has a name for EXOTIC and a place for assigning it a probability. Given that, what the Constructive Empiricist could have hoped for was that no statement about unobservables would be *relevant* to the question how far statements about observations were evidence for statements about observables, because then we could get away with assigning it no value since it would make no difference to the quantity we are interested in. However, EXOTIC is probabilistically relevant to e given CE(h) in our example above, and what this means is that the idea of assigning no probabilities to EXOTIC and its negation is a non-starter: because the truth of EXOTIC would make a difference to $P(e/CE(h))$, assigning EXOTIC no probability is *effectively* assigning it a low probability because one thereby defuses the ability of the truth of the claim to make any difference to that likelihood. One might want to complain that EXOTIC is just too exotic to concern us, but this idea cannot stand: the Constructive Empiricist (or anyone else) has to assume a high probability for the negation of EXOTIC to get the probabilities that he normally gets, and the negation of EXOTIC is far from exotic.

At this point two replies are available to the Constructive Empiricist, but neither is convincing. The first, put to me by Kyle Stanford, concedes the point that assumptions are made about unobservables in assigning the likelihood that one needs to evaluate in order to judge the claim that empirical adequacy of a theory has been confirmed by observed events. Still, this reply continues, those commitments about unobservables are a restricted set, and conceding that we make assumptions there is still a far cry from full-blown realism. First, I do not see that the set of things about which there could be statements like EXOTIC is terribly restricted. For any time period or place during which an observation could take place, and any idea one might concoct of what is going on in the unobservable realm there and then, we can concoct a statement like EXOTIC which is either true or false. The truth value of each of these statements is going to matter to the evidential import of some possible observation. If in the full course of future scientific evaluation of evidence the Constructive Empiricist has to have us make a commitment about each of these statements about unobservables, I do not see that he is left with any meaningful restriction.

However, there is also a serious motivational problem with this attempt at damage control on behalf of Constructive Empiricism. The idea that we have access to observables in a way that we don't have to unobservables was the motivation behind the divisions that got made between those claims we can find good reason to believe and those we can't. If we now admit that we have access to reasons to believe claims about unobservables that, note well, may have any degree of difficulty whatever, what is the reason to think we are unable or unallowed to do the same for other claims about unobservables, the ones that occur in actual theories? I can see none. The claims like EXOTIC and its negation which this reply is going to allow also may themselves occur in actual theories. Are we going to say that we are allowed to evaluate those because they could have occurred as auxiliaries in claims about evidence and we would have supposed we were allowed to evaluate them then, or are we going to say that we cannot evaluate them here as they occur in actual theories, whereas we could evaluate them there as auxiliaries, because here they occur in theories? The first option is a quite realist approach in so far as it puts little a priori limit on what we may in the future be able to find good reason to believe, while the second option lacks any obvious defense.

Another kind of reply on behalf of Constructive Empiricism, which Eric Barnes alerted me to, would be to suggest that I have overlooked an important option. Instead of making commitments about EXOTIC and its relatives in order to get to judgments about confirmation of CE(h) and the like, why can the Constructive Empiricist not merely make commitments to the claims that such statements as EXOTIC are or are not empirically adequate, true in what they say about observables? The answer, I think, is that the empirical import of statements like EXOTIC—in particular, the difference that the truth or falsity of EXOTIC makes to $P(e/CE(h))$— cannot always be captured in statements that are only about observables. To see this, consider EXOTICA, a slight variation on our earlier statement:

> During the runs referred to in e there was a transient and highly local force field in the vicinity whose only possible effect on observables was to prevent G after an F had occurred, and it had a 5 per cent probability of doing so when an F had occurred.

It might seem as if we could capture the empirical import of such a statement simply through a condition on the frequency of Gs after Fs. For example, we might think that what EXOTICA says about observables is captured in an assignment of probability less than or equal to 0.95 to the occurrence of G given F, i.e., $P(G/F) \leq 0.95$. (The transient force acted with 5 per cent success on somewhere between 0 per cent and 100 per cent of cases of F depending on what fraction of cases of F had been actually about to bring forth G when this was prevented.) When we combine this assignment with the assignment that comes from affirming CE(h) we get the result that $0.90 \leq P(e/CE(h)) \leq 0.95$, which is intuitively the result we would expect from the existence of the force described by EXOTICA.

However, the denial of this paraphrase of EXOTICA has a different empirical effect than the denial of EXOTICA itself, which means that we have not properly captured EXOTICA's empirical import. If we deny EXOTICA itself, we deny that there is a disturbing force, and $P(e/CE(h))$ goes back to being merely greater than 0.90. If we deny, on the other hand, that $P(G/F) \leq 0.95$, we affirm that $P(G/F) > 0.95$, which means that we are expecting a higher frequency of Gs after Fs than we did when affirming CE(h) alone. Whatever statement captures the empirical import of EXOTICA should make $P(e/CE(h)) > 0.90$ when it is false, but this candidate makes $P(e/CE(h)) > 0.95$ in that circumstance. This divergence can be made much larger by manipulating the numbers in the example. The natural way to try to capture the empirical import of EXOTICA with assignments of probabilities to frequencies of Gs after Fs does not succeed. Denying statements about the frequencies of Gs after Fs does not have the same empirical consequences as denying EXOTICA.

Better luck may be had with the Ramsey sentence of EXOTICA. This is EXOTICA with its claims about unobservables, here a disturbing force, replaced with an existential quantifier and a variable over predicates about unobservables, while what it says about observables is left intact. However, I am unable to see how to formulate what EXOTICA says in such a way that the truth and falsity of its Ramsey sentence has the same effect on $P(e/CE(h))$ as the truth and falsity of EXOTICA does. What happens when the substituted sentence is false is once again the problem. But even if the Ramsey sentence of some form of EXOTICA behaved as EXOTICA does with $P(e/CE(h))$, the problem for the Constructive Empiricist would be that there is a clear sense in which the Ramsey sentence is not about only observables. It does not specify details about unobservables, but it quantifies over them. Thus I see no way that the option of assigning probabilities only to claims that statements like the denials of EXOTIC and EXOTICA are empirically adequate is going to succeed in rescuing Constructive Empiricism.

To sum up, the realist belief about a hypothesis can be more disconfirmed by a set of statements about observables than the Constructive Empiricist's belief is, that is, EP is false, on most of the measures of confirmation commonly defended. In addition, though we do need to know or assume something about unobservables in order to know how far the realist belief is disconfirmed (or confirmed), we also need to know something about unobservables to know how far the Constructive Empiricist's claim is disconfirmed (or confirmed), no matter which measure of confirmation we choose among those currently popular. To get some knowledge of unobservables, we must start with some knowledge of unobservables. However, the same is true of observables: to get some knowledge of observables out of our knowledge of what is actually observed, we have to have some knowledge of unobservables. Unless there is a compelling conception of confirmation that we have not canvassed, to be a Constructive Empiricist one has to be more of a skeptic, or else more of a realist, than van Fraassen ever intended to be. There is something of a victory for realism in these results. Moreover, the results are stronger than many of the arguments realists typically make, for notice that although I have shown that empirically equivalent theories can be evidentially distinguishable, this has not been by means of dubious assumptions that considerations like simplicity, parsimony, or abduction have any intrinsic evidential significance.

Natural defenses

Epistemic modesty suggests, to me at least, that there is something right in the anti-realist position that we do not know we have good reason to believe our successful scientific theories are true.[18] The scope and depth of our theories ought to make the

---

[18] I use the locution 'we do not know we have good reason to believe . . .' because according to my notion of what it is to have good reason to believe, discussed in Chapter 5, having this means believing a statement that is good evidence for a hypothesis. It is possible to believe, and even to know,

realist queasy about such a claim. At least, one ought to acknowledge the vast difference in difficulty between finding good reason to believe that there are atoms and finding good reason to believe that Quantum Mechanics is the true theory of the universe. The distinction between observables and unobservables has been attractive to some anti-realists because it presents an intuitively accessible bright line between things we know well and things we know less well if at all. However, I have shown in the previous section that this distinction cannot be used in combination with any common probabilistic measure of confirmation we know of to sustain a Constructive Empiricist type anti-realist position. Realists typically celebrate at the point in an argument when the power of the observable–unobservable distinction is defused. In this section and the one that follows I will argue that such celebrations are premature.

Sympathy for anti-realism can make one cling longer than one ought to the distinction between observables and unobservables. Like the river in a battlefield this distinction leaps out as a natural barrier, and it is easy to presume that if it is breached then all is lost or, for the opponent, that all is won. However, even if, as it seems, there are no other visible barriers to realism in the landscape here, it does not follow that there are no serious barriers. In fact, as I see it, after the river it is uphill all the way for the realist, and so far we have not actually climbed very high at all. This is because the measure of confirmation that is most favorable to realism among those I have discussed, the Likelihood Ratio, contains the term $P(e/-h)$, the probability of the evidence on the catch-all, and though we know how to evaluate this term for some modest hypotheses, it is extremely difficult to evaluate for a high-level theory. Indeed, I think we have so far not done so for any high-level theory. The problem of the catch-all is, it seems to me, one of the best ways of thinking about what is wrong with the realist assertion that we have reason or good reason to believe our successful theories are true. This problem also provides a nice explanation of why it is so much harder to confirm that Quantum Mechanics is the true theory of the universe than it is to confirm that there are atoms.

The LR is the best measure of confirmation for the realist, as we have seen, because it implies that the Equal Punishment claim is false, and so provides for the possibility that observational evidence distinguishes between the truth and the empirical adequacy of a theory. It implies more generally, by a similar argument, that empirically equivalent theories are not necessarily evidentially indistinguishable. Moreover, unlike the difference measure and the normalized difference measure, the LR does this through a contribution of the *evidence* to the degree of its support of a hypothesis rather than through an extra assumption that the prior probability of a hypothesis contributes to the degree to which evidence supports that hypothesis, an assumption which could fairly be considered cheating in the realist-anti-realist game.

---

statements that are good evidence for our theories without knowing *that they are* good evidence because of inability to evaluate how well they indicate a hypothesis and discriminate it from alternatives. Evaluating whether we know we have good evidence is the relevant matter here, since we are evidently not evolved to have automatic and unconscious knowledge of the matters scientific theories concern themselves with, as we are to have knowledge of, say, the location of middle-sized dry goods. In the case of science we have to approach the question whether we have good evidence consciously.

These are advantages of the LR for the realist regardless of whether he believed a word of the previous chapter, where I argued for the superiority of the LR measure on other grounds.

It will be necessary for the realist to evaluate the LR in order to get a handle on whether the posterior probability of a hypothesis is high, that is, whether the hypothesis is probably true given the evidence, but of course this will not be sufficient. The LR, like the other measures I discussed, is an incremental measure of support that tells us the degree to which e supports the hypothesis but does not alone constrain the posterior probability of the hypothesis; that is, it does not alone tell us how probable the hypothesis is once the evidence is taken into account. For this, a further ingredient is needed regardless of which incremental measure one favors, but if the scheme discussed in the previous chapter is sound then the extra ingredient one needs with the LR is pretty easy to get. If I am right that $P(e)$ can often be evaluated directly and found to be high, in repeatable experiments for example, then one only needs to verify an appropriately high lower bound on the LR in order to have purchase on the posterior probability of the hypothesis. Thus, on my scheme the LR may be the *only* difficult step that stands in the way of finding good reason to believe our theories are true.

Whether or not it is the only challenging step, evaluation of the LR is a necessary step to establishing the posterior probability of the hypothesis, especially for the realist. The LR has two terms to evaluate, $P(e/h)$, just like the ratio measure, in the numerator, and $P(e/-h)$ in the denominator. Evaluating $P(e/h)$ has its challenges, as we saw earlier, since there are an infinite number of relevant auxiliary statements, many about unobservables, that we must make commitments about to get the value of $P(e/h)$. However, let us set this challenge to one side for now since I am interested in the limiting step of the process of getting good reason to believe a theory is true, and evaluating $P(e/-h)$ has the challenges of $P(e/h)$ and more besides.

It is intuitively obvious that $P(e/-h)$ is easier to evaluate when h is the hypothesis that Mary is pregnant than when h is the hypothesis that Quantum Mechanics is the true theory of the world, for suitable e. There are at least four levels of reasons for this. First, though negation of a proposition that refers always yields a proposition with a definite reference, it does not always yield a proposition that conjures up a definite or unified understanding in a human mind. Whether it does so or not is largely dependent on the complexity of the original proposition. 'Mary is pregnant' attributes one predicate to an individual. The negation of this proposition has a definite sense because of its simplicity, which is a consequence of the simplicity of the original proposition; the negation denies the simple thing that the original proposition affirms, namely, that Mary is set to give birth to a baby in the near future. Sometimes we do, and sometimes we do not, treat '__ is pregnant' as a simple predicate, one that cannot be broken down into a conjunction of simpler predicates. When we do, 'Mary is pregnant' counts as an atomic sentence.

When h is more complex than an atomic sentence, its negation is also more complex. Suppose that any hypothesis can be expressed in the first-order predicate calculus. (This assumption errs in the direction of simplifying, and so will underestimate the complexity of real scientific cases, which helps my argument by putting me at a disadvantage.) Then every hypothesis has a conjunctive normal form; that is, it is equivalent to a statement that is a conjunction of disjunctions of atomic sentences and negations of atomic sentences. It is plausible that the complex predicate '__ is a black and white checkered floor' could be expressed in the first-order predicate calculus as a conjunction of disjunctions of atomic sentences. Its negation would then be a disjunction of conjunctions of negations of atomic sentences. But while the original predicate conjures up a mental picture, its negation does not. Some of the negations in the negation of the predicate could be simplified away, but we would still be left with the fact that there are many ways of failing to be a black and white checkered floor. A thing could fail to have black tiles, fail to have white tiles, fail to be a floor, fail to be checkered in any of a number of spots, fail to have black tiles, *and* fail to have white tiles while yet being a floor, fail to be a floor yet have black tiles, etc. The possibilities may not be endless, but they are many. If we unpack it, we see the definite meaning of the negation of the predicate, but still it fails to conjure up a single image.

If a complex predicate is associated with a single intuitive image, its negation nevertheless usually does not have a single intuitive image. If we do unpack the negation and find its definite meaning, then in complex cases we will run into a further, computational problem. Do we have the resources to compute the combination of the consequences of each of those circumstances? For it is not merely that we have to check whether the lengthy disjunction, $-h$, is true, where verifying one disjunct would suffice. Determining $P(e/-h)$ requires evaluating the expression,

$$P(e/-h_1)P(-h_1/-h) + P(e/-h_2)P(-h_2/-h) + P(e/-h_3)$$
$$(-h_3/-h) + \ldots + P(e/-h_n)P(-h_n/-h),$$

for h_1 through h_n the conjuncts of the conjunction h. We have in addition to the computational problem of listing and combining all of these values, also the problem of assembling knowledge of what they are: how probable is e given that h_2 is false, and how probable is it that h_2 is false given that h is false?

When we ask how probable it is that Mary tests positive for HCG hormone given that she is not pregnant, we have a question we can address by means of empirical data. This is so despite the fact that the predicate '__ is not pregnant,' which is simple as far as its application allows us to exclude the birth of a baby in the near future, is also complex in that there are many ways for a woman to be when she is not pregnant. For those many ways of being a non-pregnant woman are well represented in a random sample of women. Thus, to find out the false positive rate of the HCG test we can assemble hundreds of non-pregnant women of a variety of types, give them an HCG test, and see how many test positive. Then we wait nine months, and check for abortions, to be sure the false positives were really false. When we ask how probable it is that the deflection of light around the sun during an eclipse is just what it is measured to be given that the general theory of relativity is not true, there is not an obvious experiment we can do to answer this question. We would have to calculate the probability of that deflection on every possible theory (consistent with background knowledge, including auxiliaries) that is incompatible with the general theory of relativity, and weight those theories as to their probability if general relativity is false.

Not only would that be a lot of computation if we had the terms in our hands, but how should we determine how probable it is that a particular theory of the world should be true if general relativity is false? There is a problem of lack of knowledge.

Physicists do make non-arbitrary judgments about such things, when they distinguish between those aspects of established theories that they think will have to be part of any future theory and those parts that seem less secure. The latter are more probably what is wrong if the theory in question is wrong. For example, it looks like any successor to Quantum Mechanics will have to be non-local, but surely it might have a different and better formalism. Physicists trying to build the next better theory have to make some judgments and guesses about these matters, because they face the question of which aspects of successful theories to keep and generalize, and which to throw away. However, we should not pretend that these judgments have the same kind of security as the results of experimentally determining the false positive rate of the HCG test for pregnancy.

In addition to the fact that our knowledge of which part of an established theory is most likely to be wrong if the theory is wrong is quite limited, there is a fourth problem that we do not know what all of the possible alternative theories are. It looks like $P(e/-h)$ cannot be calculated without having the likelihood of e on each of those alternatives, and a weighting of all of those alternatives. However, our track record as inquirers strongly suggests that at any given time there are possible and even conceivable theories consistent with all of our actual evidence, even possible theories expressible in our language, of which we have not yet actually conceived. Maxwellian physicists did not conceive of special relativistic physics, though the language existed to express the central ideas. Every predecessor of a great new theoretical discovery seems to have been in the same situation of not having actually conceived a possibility that was conceivable and that was consistent with all of the actual evidence at hand. Why should we think we are any different?

Kyle Stanford has called this inference the 'new induction' over the history of science, and he argues that it is the one kind of underdetermination of theory by data that we must take seriously (Stanford 2001). The LR provides further understanding of why the unconceived conceivables Stanford discusses matter epistemically: in order to know that you have good reason to believe h, you have to evaluate $P(e/-h)$ well enough to know that it is significantly less than $P(e/h)$, and in order to evaluate $P(e/-h)$ it looks like you have to conceive—in some sense of 'conceive'—all of the relevantly distinct possibilities that make up $-h$.[19] Notice that, in harmony with Stanford's point that what matters to what we actually have a right to believe is not all possible evidence but our actual (accumulated) evidence, the hypotheses the probability calculus is looking for in the term $P(e/-h)$ are those consistent with our background knowledge. However, following the LR measure of confirmation I cannot quite agree with Stanford's conclusion that unconceived conceivables are the set of

---

[19] I say 'it looks like' because though it is clear that you have to know $P(e/-h)$, and that the brute force way of doing that would be to determine all the terms that occur in its full expansion, perhaps a clever statistician could figure out a way of estimating $P(e/-h)$ without as much information (and perhaps one already has). That would be a step forward for knowledge, though, as with anything else, we should not expect such an advance to give us something for nothing.

alternative possibilities that we must take seriously, for the image this conjures up is both too strong and too weak. It is too strong because, as I will illustrate below, we do not need to conceive of possibilities *explicitly* in order to rule them out. It is too weak because the term '−h' refers not just to possibilities that we *can* conceive but to the logical complement of h, all possibilities not consistent with h (but consistent with background knowledge).

This is a set that is very humbling indeed, but background knowledge takes us a long way in case the hypothesis we are trying to confirm is modest. We know that there are very few if any possible but unconsidered types of non-pregnant woman that are relevant to our hypothesis that Mary is pregnant and relevantly distinct from the types we will find in a large enough and varied enough sample of the current human population. There probably are possible unconsidered types of personality, hair color, and physique, for example, but we know that personality, hair color, and physique are highly unlikely to be relevant to the chances of a false positive in an HCG test. In many thousands of years there could come to be significant proportions of non-pregnant women relevantly distinct from the types we find in the population today, but we are not looking to know whether to trust the HCG test on distant future products of evolution when we ask about Mary. General theories are much more ambitious than the hypothesis that Mary is pregnant, and problems of definiteness, computation, knowledge, and unconsidered possibilities present challenges that the simpler case does not and that the background knowledge we have does not help much with, in our efforts to determine whether we have good reason to believe our theories are true.

From EP to e·p·t: dream on

Some will say that while I am obviously right that it is difficult to estimate $P(e/-h)$ for h a complex and general theory, where I am wrong is in thinking that this is what we have to do in order to know we have good reason to believe a theory is true. Besides, they will say, we do test theories, and find evidence for theories, and these things seem to be nearly impossible on the view of evidence described here. There must be something wrong with that view of evidence.

Thinking about comparative Likelihood Ratios addresses both of these objections. First, we do test theories, but what we are typically able to estimate after the testing of a general, complex theory, t, is a comparative Likelihood Ratio, the probability of the evidence e on t, $P(e/t)$, divided by that on a rival theory t′, $P(e/t′)$, where t and t′ do not exhaust the logical space of theories compatible with our background knowledge. Second, comparative Likelihood Ratios do not constrain the posterior probability of the hypothesis, even when an extra constraint, like high $P(e)$, is added. No notion of good reason to believe true that will do the job that the realist intends would take us to have this when we have no purchase whatsoever on the posterior probability of the hypothesis. It was the realist, not me, who set the goalpost at the truth, or probable truth (or approximate truth), of the hypothesis.

Consider one of the most impressive connections ever established between experimental results and high theory, the Bell inequalities. These are inequalities that Quantum Mechanics predicts will be violated and that classical and commonsense assumptions imply will not be violated. Experimentally, Quantum Mechanics makes the correct prediction, since the inequalities are violated by subatomic particles. Most would agree that these experimental results provide an important test that Quantum Mechanics passed. But what exactly do we get from such tests? One of the reasons the experiments, and the theorem that provoked them, are so impressive is that we do get more than usual in this case. We are not simply comparing the likelihood of fulfillment of the Bell inequalities on Quantum Mechanics and on one rival theory, say, a particular version of Newton's theory. We are comparing what Quantum Mechanics predicts with the predictions of an entire class of possible theories: all of the theories that share a few extremely general assumptions, including locality, single-valuedness of reality, fair distribution of microstates, and hidden variables. Any theory with all of those assumptions is shown to be highly unlikely in light of the experimental falsification of the inequalities that follow from them.[20] And we did not have to describe those possibilities in detail, that is, we did not have to conceive of all the theories in that class explicitly and individually, in order to rule them out. Quantum Mechanics is not just better than one particular theory according to a certain set of evidence, but better than an entire class of possible theories. Learning this was a stupendous epistemic achievement.

However, though the likelihoods evaluated in this case are not restricted to comparison of just two theories, they are still comparative. We learned the surprising fact that a whole class of possible theories is very probably false, and that our leading theory does not have the particular problem that those theories do. We did not, however, learn that Quantum Mechanics is the only possible theory of the world on which the Bell inequalities are violated, or that it is the most likely of the possible theories of the world on which those inequalities are violated, information that would be needed to evaluate the posterior probability of this theory. The developments did not give us reason to think that we have considered all of the possible theories compatible with our evidence that violate the Bell inequalities, and though as with Mary's pregnancy we do have background knowledge that knowledge here does not give us reason to think we have considered all the relevant possible theories compatible with what we know. Consequently, we did not evaluate $P(e/t)/P(e/-t)$, where t is Quantum Mechanics, but rather $P(e/t)/P(e/t')$, where t' is some fraction (of unknown magnitude) of the $-t$ space. It is both mathematically possible and in this case highly realistic that $P(e/t)/P(e/t')$ be very high while $P(e/t)/P(e/-t)$ equals 1. That is, Quantum Mechanics may show its superiority to a particular set of theories in the Bell inequality experiments while there exists a theory incompatible with Quantum Mechanics that makes the same successful prediction. The experiment would thereby have given us reason to prefer Quantum Mechanics to any of a huge set of theories without having given us reason to believe that Quantum Mechanics is true or even probably true on our evidence.

[20] However high its prior probability, the posterior probability of any of these theories will be extremely low if, as we are assuming, the probability of violation of the inequalities given such a theory is very, very low, and the probability that the inequalities *are* violated is high.

What, one might then wonder, is the 'stupendous achievement' I referred to? The achievement, in this case, is the falsification of a large class of otherwise plausible theories and the survival of only one known theory. The point, echoing in probabilistic terms once again an old argument of Duhem's, is that falsifying one or many theories in a domain does not tell you how the unfalsified theory ranks relative to the remaining possible theories. You do not have an estimate of the probable truth (posterior probability) of the unfalsified theory until you do have an estimate of its rank relative to those others, and you do not have an estimate of that rank if you have not adequately characterized the entire remaining possibility space. With high-level theories our background knowledge does not typically give us enough information about that remaining possibility space to say that we know what the remaining possible theories would predict.

The case of the Bell inequalities is somewhat special in that since $P(e/t')$ is essentially zero the t'-theories are effectively eliminated by the evidence; in this case we can say that the surviving theory ranks *higher* in posterior probability than those that were falsified. When that special situation does not obtain comparative likelihoods, which is what we typically do have available in theory-testing, are even less potent. If we evaluate $P(e/h)$ and $P(e/h')$, for h and h' rival theories, as we often can due to models that fill in the auxiliary hypotheses that determine these probabilities, and we find that the first probability is greater than the second, that gives us a moderately reliable ranking of h and h' relative to e. However, the moderately reliable ranking given by these likelihoods bears no necessary relation to the ranking of the posterior probabilities of the hypotheses, the ranking that the realist needs to support his claims. For it is just a mathematical fact that $P(e/h)/P(e/h')$ may be high while $P(h/e)/P(h'/e)$ is low. That is, h' may be more probable than h once the evidence is taken into account while the likelihood of e on h is much higher than the likelihood of e on h'. We are quite good at evaluating and comparing likelihoods for high-level theories, and this is sufficient to explain our sense that we test theories very successfully, but this alone implies nothing about our ability to evaluate the posterior probabilities of theories, which the realist needs for his claim of probable truth.[21] (See Appendix 5.1.)

One may still be worried that evaluation of $P(e/-h)$ is too high a standard for evidence that gives us good reason to believe a claim true or probably true. Essentially

---

[21] In this sense, it is clear, contra Peter Lipton, that our best may not be good enough for the realist's claim. Lipton (1993) argues that there can be no reliable comparative evaluation of theories without a reliable absolute evaluation, and thus no middle ground between realism and skepticism. However, that conclusion must be false in light of my discussion here of ranking by comparative likelihoods. Lipton also claims that scientists evaluate contradictories (h and −h) and that there is no coherent way to ban the ranking of contradictories while allowing the ranking of rivals. But we do not need to ban the evaluation of contradictories in order to avoid both skepticism and realism: all we need to do is point out that the evaluation of contradictories gets exponentially more difficult as we move from questions about low-level hypotheses, such as whether Mary is pregnant or she is not, to questions about high-level theories, such as whether Quantum Mechanics or its negation is true. The issue is whether we can understand the worth of what we have actually done in theory evaluation without finding any grounds for beliefs about the probable truth of our theories, and the answer is yes. Note that since I do think we successfully evaluate contradictories in many situations, I do think we thereby gain reason to believe some hypotheses are true. For this and other reasons, my view is thus not a Popperian falsificationism.

the same question might be raised from the anti-realist side, with a different import: though the LR measure of confirmation makes the claim EP false, what is the reason to think that when we look at the cases where we actually have and actually haven't evaluated this term we will not come up with effectively the same line between claims about observables and claims about unobservables that van Fraassen pointed to? Maybe he had the right conclusion but the wrong argument for it. How exactly do the cases where I do think we have good reason to believe claims about unobservable entities escape the problems I just discussed for tests of high theory?

We have already seen one example of how we secure a claim about unobservables by having the capacity to evaluate the probability of the evidence on the catch-all, $P(e/-h)$, namely, the case of the claim that Mary is pregnant. Suppose Mary is only between four and five weeks pregnant. If so, then the pregnancy is unobservable because the embryo is less than one seventeenth of an inch; the naked eye would not be able to tell that it was an embryo. And, although HCG hormone is spiking in Mary's blood by this time, the hormone is also unobservable because microscopic. Nevertheless, as is familiar, because the presence of HCG hormone is detectable— there are discriminating indicators for its presence—an HCG test at five weeks can give us good reason to believe that Mary is pregnant.

On the present account of evidence this is because, among other things, we do so well evaluating the probability that HCG tests yield false positives. That gives us an estimate of the probability of e, that Mary is a positive tester, given that −h, Mary is not pregnant. We can do this, as I discussed above, because of the simplicity of the hypothesis, and the fact that we have good reason to believe that there are no relevant unconsidered possible types of human women that will not be represented in a large and varied sample of the current human population. It takes a mad skepticism to suppose that we do not know that relevant unconsidered possible types of current and near future women who exist in any appreciable numbers will show up in large and varied samples of the current human population. It does not require mad skepticism to suppose that we do not know of all the possible generalizations of Quantum Mechanics that are consistent with our evidence and background knowledge. This is what physicists believe when they try to imagine better theories.

The difference between the two cases is in part a matter of how far our background knowledge is able to take us. We have background knowledge about pregnancy, human physiology, degree of variation in the human population, the time scale of human evolution, and statistics which are together sufficient to tell us that the variations we need to see in order to estimate false positives for the HCG test will show up in a large, varied sample. We do not have enough background knowledge to be confident that we know what all possible generalizations of Quantum Mechanics look like. This is terra incognita, as we should expect from the fact that a theory like Quantum Mechanics is far more ambitious in the complexity and scope of its claims than is the hypothesis that Mary is pregnant. Its being more ambitious means in part that it attempts to go further beyond the knowledge we already confidently possess. In the case of Quantum Mechanics we have the added trouble that its generalizations will differ from it in areas beyond the place where our commonsense assumptions have already been shown to be false; therefore, we know we cannot trust common sense as a guide.

218 *Real Anti-realism*

Our ability to detect early pregnancy already gets us past the line between observables and unobservables, and the Likelihood Ratio tells us why. But perhaps this is a special borderline case where we are able to get knowledge about an unobservable state because that state is a temporary way station between an observable event (sex) and an observable state ('showing' pregnancy). Early pregnancy cannot occur without a particular observable event preceding it, the unobservable state of early pregnancy reliably progresses to an observable phenomenon if left to itself, and our species has long experience of these stable facts.

All this is true, but it does not change the fact that this is a counterexample to the claim that our knowledge does not extend beyond observables. Also, importantly, our knowledge of early pregnancy fits precisely the form of the counterexample to EP described above with J early, unobservable pregnancy, K the unobservable aspects of late pregnancy, and G the birth of a baby. F is the observable marker—a line in a little window, for example—that an early pregnancy test shows when J is the case. This shows that it is not only that the claim EP is false in principle, but that it is false in actual cases that are useful to the realist cause. Moreover, if one thinks that we have too much species familiarity with pregnancy for this case to count, consider all of the blood tests we have for early detection of disease, at a stage before observable symptoms are exhibited. We do not have longstanding familiarity as a species with the course of cancer, but we do have tests that are extremely good at detecting some of them before they show observable symptoms. These tests follow the same form as early pregnancy and the counterexample to EP above, and if a number of markers of this sort that were known to be reliable showed up positive I suspect few of us would deny that we have good reason to believe we have cancer.

What about harder cases? Does a LR-based view allow that we have good reason to believe claims such as that there are atoms and molecules, as I advertised above? As I have said, the typically most difficult part of acquiring good reason to believe a claim on the view of evidence I advocate, and that the realist needs, is evaluating P(e/−h), the probability of the evidence on the catch-all. It is congenial to my view of evidence that exemplary experimentalists also attach great significance to determining that what they count as evidence could not have been produced by something other than what they would like to take it as evidence for. We saw this already in the cases of Michelson and Morely, Rutherford, and Meselson and Stahl, discussed in Chapter 1. Jean Perrin was no exception to this rule.

In discussing the reasons Perrin gave us for belief in atoms and molecules, commentators frequently focus on his determination of Avogadro's number, which is interesting because it looks like an argument from coincidence (Harman 1965; Cartwright 1983: 84; Salmon 1984: 213–27). However, Perrin confirmed the existence of atoms and molecules to a substantial degree before the step in which he determined Avogadro's number from the motion of Brownian particles.[22] Measurement of Avogadro's number is needed to confirm the particular, quantitative, molecular-kinetic theory of Albert Einstein and M. von Smoluchowski, but not to

[22] See Deborah Mayo's detailed discussion of this argument in ch. 7 of Mayo (1996), which I make use of here.

confirm the more modest hypothesis that there are atoms and molecules, understood merely as spatially discrete sub-microscopic entities moving independently of each other, i.e., at random. The sense in which these entities are spatially discrete must be understood as vague, to accommodate the possibility, later discovered, that atoms exhibit the quantum mechanical property of not being fully localized, which did not make us cease to believe there are atoms and molecules, and was not intended to be excluded by the modest atomic hypothesis.

Brownian particles, the tools of many an investigation into atoms, are not observable to the naked eye, so we will have to violate van Fraassen's strictures even to believe the evidence whose significance we want to evaluate. However, the arguments so far should have got one over any resistance to knowledge via microscope. Brownian particles are special because they have a useful size, since they are big enough to be visible under a microscope, yet small enough to be moved as a consequence of a collision with a sub-microscopic atom or molecule, as macroscopic objects are not. Brownian particles were long an object of fascination because they have a perpetual agitated motion whose cause was unclear, and sub-microscopic atoms provided a possible explanation: heat kept the atoms in motion, and they buffeted each other and the Brownian particles in a random walk.

What is interesting and advantageous about the content of the modest atomic hypothesis is that it is a hypothesis of no effect. If there are atoms, in the sense specified above, then the motion of the Brownian particles will be a random walk, that is, that motion will exhibit no systematic effects, no dependencies or correlations between the motions of one particle and another or tendencies in the motion of a single particle. Since the modest atomic hypothesis is so devoid of detail, for example, as to the structure and precise size of atoms, there do not seem to be any hypotheses that could explain a random walk in the Brownian particles that are not included within this atomic hypothesis. The hypothesis of atoms and molecules is not equivalent to the hypothesis that Brownian motion is fully random, but it is close to being so. Thus, what Perrin had to verify in order to confirm that there are atoms and molecules was that the motion of Brownian particles has no systematic effects.

The possibilities that Brownian motion is a random walk and that it exhibits a systematic effect exhaust the logical space, since the motion is either random or it is not. If there were any factor external to the liquid housing the Brownian particles that caused their characteristic motion, that would yield a systematic effect, a lack of independence between the motion of one Brownian particle and another, or lack of randomness in the motion of a single particle over time. One such factor after another—vibrations, light, temperature gradients, magnetism, electricity, shaking, evaporation, air currents, capillarity, motions of the observer's hands, etc.—had been investigated in the nineteenth century, and ruled out as causes of the motion. But this, after all, had been a process of ruling out alternatives by listing them. One could always wonder: is there an external cause we have not considered? With the formulation of the problem as a choice between a random walk and a systematic effect, and the tools to distinguish the two, Perrin was able to investigate this question with a dramatically new level of completeness.

Perrin did not judge whether the motion of Brownian particles was random or systematic merely by the naked eye. Familiarity with the outputs of standard chance mechanisms and the statistical theory of the random walk were quite sophisticated by the time of his experiments. Perrin could display the frequency distributions that could be expected from a chance apparatus which had been programmed to incorporate a slight dependency, without any regard for what might have been the cause of the dependency. Thus he could investigate large chunks of the possibility space of causes of the Brownian motion without describing, listing, or explicitly imagining the possibilities in that space. He could generate the frequency distributions for many different chance apparatuses with slight dependencies in order to show what could be expected in the motion of a Brownian particle if anything were introducing a systematic effect. It could be calculated that if any of these dependencies were present they would be very likely to show up in Perrin's various experiments on gamboge particles, the particular Brownian particles he found to be most uniform in size. Since none of them showed up, Perrin concluded that 'the irregular nature of the movement is quantitatively rigorous.' 'Incidentally,' he added, 'we have in this one of the most striking applications of the laws of chance' (Perrin 1990: 119).

It remains logically possible that there are chance mechanisms we have not conceived of which, when a dependency is introduced into them, would generate a distribution that the Brownian motion matches better than it does the normal distribution. That is, it remains logically possible that there are hidden dependencies in the Brownian motion. It also remains logically possible that something other than atoms, in the largely indeterminate sense described above, could explain a random distribution of the motion of Brownian particles. However, these possibilities would require the existence not just of a correlation but of a *type* of correlation, and a type of entity, that we have not encountered before.[23]

Lest we conclude that these unknown types of things are more probable than they are, notice that the unknown type of correlation and type of entity referred to must occur at the scale of atoms and molecules and not merely below that scale. Perrin did not know how the entities smaller than quarks behave, and we may not either, but effects that occur only at a level of resolution below that of atoms are of no relevance here because the question here is whether there is a systematic effect of any sort at the scale of atoms. On this issue we are in a better position than Perrin was because of the passage of a century of time during which a vast amount of experimental work has been done at the scale of atoms and molecules. Even though these experimenters were not looking for a systematic effect in the Brownian motion, since they were taking Perrin's work for granted, it is hard to believe that nothing they did would have tipped them off to an unknown type of effect in the Brownian motion if there were one.

Suppose, quite modestly, that the most we know is that such unknown types of correlations and entities underlying the Brownian motion are no more probable than

---

[23] New types of correlations found subatomically, in particular of a quantum mechanical sort, will not impugn the modest atomic hypothesis we have considered, which has nothing to say about their presence or absence. It is possible for atoms to exhibit quantum mechanical types of correlations, but though Perrin probably did not do enough to rule these out explicitly, there is also no reason to expect such correlations to exist in a fluid.

known types; their probability is no more than 0.5. Then through all of Perrin's experiments in the step prior to determination of Avogadro's number we will have brought the likelihood of e, the actual motion of the Brownian particles, on −h, the hypothesis that there are not atoms, only as low as 0.5. Still, since the likelihood of e on h, P(e/h), is 1, the LR would be 2. Figure 5.4 shows that LR $\geq$ 2 combined with a very modest P(e) $\geq$ 0.6 yields a posterior probability for the hypothesis, h, of $\geq$ 0.6, better than more likely than not. Thus, even on extremely generous assumptions about unknown rivals to the atomic hypothesis, and very stingy assumptions about our right to be confident of the evidence, we have through Perrin's first experiments and collective experience since then reason to believe in the existence of atoms, even without counting determination of Avogadro's number from the Brownian motion. And, Perrin's determination of Avogadro's number from the Brownian motion is one of several phenomena that the atomic hypothesis explains and that I have not discussed, e.g., the constant ratios of chemical combination, the independently suspected inexactness of the Carnot Principle, and the perpetuity of the Brownian motion. The effect of these pieces of evidence would be to increase the probability that there are atoms above the minimum probability I have argued for here.

One might wonder, as Eric Barnes has done out loud, why we cannot make a 'modest' assumption in the case of high-level theories as I have just said we can for Perrin's hypothesis. Why can we not suppose that unknown types of alternative explanatory theories are no more likely than not when we evaluate the probability of the evidence on the catch-all of a theory, when I say we are allowed to do such a thing here in the case of the hypothesis about atoms? The answer to this question is that in the case of the atomic hypothesis we do, and in the case of a high-level theory we do not, have the relevant information. This in turn is because there is less that is relevant to the atomic hypothesis than to, say, Quantum Mechanics.

The modest atomic hypothesis is about a restricted scale that we have by now a lot of experience with. The claim and hope of a universal theory on the other hand is that it gives the right story at every scale. There are possible rivals to Quantum Mechanics that make the same predictions as that theory does at the atomic scale—say, that there are atoms, in the modest sense—while making different predictions at finer scales. We need not evaluate explicitly what these theories say in order to evaluate P(e/−h) for h the atomic hypothesis because since these do not disagree with the atomic hypothesis they are not part of −h. Instead, in effect, they are part of the atomic hypothesis. By contrast, when we attempt to evaluate P(e/−h) for h Quantum Mechanics and e evidence at a scale finer than atoms we do need to take those theories that disagree with Quantum Mechanics into account, whatever they are. Thus, there is a clear sense in which we need to know more to evaluate P(e/−h) for a high-level theory than we do for the modest atomic hypothesis.

Possible rivals to Quantum Mechanics that make *different* predictions than it does at the atomic level are relevant to P(e/−h), but then they also are being considered— not under that name—in investigations of whether the Brownian motion has a systematic effect. We do not need to know what those alternatives to Quantum Mechanics are in order to study the relevant part of the difference they might make at the atomic scale; we are studying those alternatives to the extent that they need to be studied by investigating the existence of a systematic effect in the Brownian motion. No restriction of this sort can be made in the case of a high-level theory due to its generality, and that is why we have no right to a 'modest' assumption in such a case.

I have focused on the first step of Perrin's argument for the existence of atoms and molecules partly because it (together with our experience since then) establishes a minimum probability for the atomic hypothesis, and partly because it is one of many examples that I think could be employed in a positive induction on the history of science that we would do well to put alongside Stanford's new negative induction. The instances of this positive induction would be all of the cases we have of dramatic improvements in our ability to estimate the probability of the evidence on the catch-all, $P(e/-h)$. There was a time when we did not know how to develop a blood test that would give evidence for or against a bodily state or disease, but we now know how to determine a false positive rate for such a test because we know how to do experimental control. There was a time when scientists knew how to eliminate alternatives to the atomic hypothesis only by listing and ruling out specific causes, and this did not amount to a determination of $P(e/-h)$ because it did not involve a general grasp of the space of possibilities. Theoretical advances and the experiments of Perrin changed that; the first step of his experiments with gamboge particles, together with our experience since then, put a maximum on the probability of the evidence on the catch-all to the atomic hypothesis and thereby a minimum on the probability of the atomic hypothesis, without his having to conceive of the possibilities he was ruling out in any explicit detail.

There are, in general, tough challenges in the estimation of $P(e/-h)$, and we have in fact not succeeded at this estimation very often for claims that go significantly beyond observables. Thus, where the anti-realists are right is in thinking that we do not actually have reason to believe our current high-level theories are true or probably true. However, nothing I have pointed to constitutes an a priori argument that we can never acquire good reason to believe high-level theories true. An epistemology that takes a high LR as a requirement for good evidence, as mine does, is even more general and ambitious than van Fraassen's stricture that no evidence can disconfirm the claim that a theory is true more than it disconfirms the claim that it is empirically adequate. Yet this more general requirement does not alone imply limits in principle to our knowledge, as van Fraassen's assumption does. The LR tells us only what we have to know in order to evaluate a given claim about evidence, and though for a given claim or type of claim at a given time we may not be able to acquire the knowledge that will tell us that we have good evidence, and we may not have good evidence, nothing in the LR says that we will never have good evidence for a particular claim or be able to know that we do. Thus, the view that results from my reflections incorporates van Fraassen's admirable spirit of epistemic modesty, without committing us to immodest conclusions about what science can and cannot achieve.

I do not see grounds for declaring ahead of time any limit in principle to our capacity to find ways to estimate $P(e/-h)$. How would we know what the future of science can and cannot bring? In times of doubt about our ability to estimate $P(e/-h)$ one should remember that Perrin's predecessors would not have expected that he could do what he did either, and their lack of conception of something that was conceivable thus has a positive significance as well as the negative significance that Stanford draws out. Honesty in the evaluation of our actual evidence for actual theories entitles us to say to the typical scientific realist, *Dream on*, with a tone of sarcasm. But our knowledge that we do not know what we can and cannot do, and our record for surprising ourselves positively as well as negatively, allow us also to say *Dream on* without any sarcasm at all.

Conclusion

One might wonder how I can be an externalist about knowledge and evidence and an anti-realist about (many) scientific theories. Externalism has great deference to the way the world is, and many anti-realist positions one has heard of do not even acknowledge the existence of a world independent of our beliefs. Of course, the anti-realist position defended here is nothing like those anti-realisms. As I have indicated, I am a semantic realist, like van Fraassen and others before me. Theories have truth values—when determinately formulated, they are either true or false, and which they are does not depend on our imagination or beliefs. The question that has occupied me in this chapter—epistemological realism versus anti-realism—is how good we are at figuring out what those truth values are.

Externalism about knowledge and evidence in no way implies epistemological realism about scientific theories. To think so would, I think, be to confuse a criterion with the verdict one gets by applying it. Externalism is a framework for saying what is required to have knowledge or evidence; knowledge is a relation between belief that p and the fact that p, and a statement is evidence in virtue of a relation in the world between one fact (the evidence) and another (the hypothesis). It is an independent question, once a set of requirements is set forth, whether we meet them in actual cases. My anti-realist position rests on arguments to the effect that in the case of high-level theoretical claims we do not yet actually meet a reasonable (externalist) standard that the realist should approve of. There is no reason to think that an externalist standard is unable to yield negative verdicts in particular cases. One may be concerned that an epistemic anti-realist position implies that it is not possible for us to evaluate whether our evidence meets an externalist standard—as I purport to have done—since whether that standard is fulfilled may depend on matters unobservable to us. However, my anti-realism does not depend on or imply a priori empiricist principles saying that what we can know is restricted to observables.

Another nagging suspicion may come from the fact that in discussing science I seem to be describing people, scientists, who have and are aware of their reasons, make arguments, and have justifications available for (some of) their claims. If I am right that the best way of formulating what makes knowledge knowledge and evidence evidence is through tracking relations in the world that the bearer of the belief in question need not be aware of, why then is there so much awareness and deliberate seeking of reasons on the part of scientists? Externalism does not, of course, imply that none of our knowledge has justification or that we never have conscious access to our reasons. It only denies that conscious accessibility of reasons is necessary for knowledge or for the possession of evidence. However, I take the point, in that if justification and accessibility of reasons are not what make our results knowledge, why are these things so prominent in our biggest knowledge-producing institution?

In Chapter 1 I conjectured that the function of justification and more generally of higher-level cogitations about the processes through which our beliefs are formed and our evidence comes to us is simply the tracking of truth, and that justification is a means to the end of knowledge but is not part of the thing itself. There I pointed out many advantages of our conscious deliberative faculties for improved tracking of the truth—more truths, more accurately, and more efficiently. It is no mystery why it is good for us to seek justifications—in cases where this is cost-efficient—if we seek knowledge and knowledge is the tracking of truth. There is an additional reason why it should be no surprise on my externalist view that scientists in particular deliberately, consciously, and constantly seek justifications, arguments, and evidence. The kinds of matters about which we acquire knowledge without higher-level reasoning about our sources, and about which to seek justification consciously would be highly inefficient, are matters with respect to which our unconscious mechanisms, like perception, are naturally endowed with the ability to track the truth. The questions scientists ask— beyond questions like 'where was the pointer?' which used to be called 'observation statements'—go so far beyond what we are naturally endowed to track the answers to unconsciously that the *only* way they can expect to come to knowledge is to create mechanisms for tracking the truth, such as experiments, instruments, and tested hypotheses that connect one phenomenon with another. There is no way that one can expect created mechanisms to work as one wishes unless one consciously plans them to work so (and even then it is a gamble). Scientists consciously and deliberately produce and evaluate justifications because they have no choice but to do so if they want to know, that is, to track the truth.

References

ACHINSTEIN, PETER (1983). 'Concepts of Evidence,' in P. Achinstein (ed.), *The Concept of Evidence*. Oxford: Oxford University Press, 145–74.

—— (1996). 'Swimming in Evidence: A Reply to Maher,' *Philosophy of Science*, 63: 175–82.

—— (2001). *The Book of Evidence*. New York: Oxford University Press.

—— (2002). 'Is there a Valid Experimental Argument for Scientific Realism?' *Journal of Philosophy*, 99/9: 470–95.

ADAMS, ERNEST (1965). 'The Logic of Conditionals,' *Inquiry*, 8: 166–97.

—— (1966). 'Probability and the Logic of Conditionals,' in J. Hintikka and P. Suppes (eds.), *Aspects of Inductive Logic*. Amsterdam: North Holland, 265–316.

ADLER, JONATHAN (1994). 'Testimony, Trust, Knowing,' *Journal of Philosophy*, 91/5: 264–75.

ARMSTRONG, D. M. (1973). *Belief, Truth and Knowledge*. New York: Cambridge University Press.

AUDI, ROBERT (1997). 'The Place of Testimony in the Fabric of Knowledge and Justification,' *American Philosophical Quarterly*, 34/4: 405–32.

BOGEN, JAMES, and JAMES WOODWARD (1988). 'Saving the Phenomena,' *Philosophical Review*, 97: 303–52.

BONJOUR, LAURENCE (1980). 'Externalist Theories of Empirical Knowledge,' *Midwest Studies in Philosophy*, 5: 53–73.

—— (1985). *The Structure of Empirical Knowledge*. Cambridge, Mass.: Harvard University Press.

BOYD, RICHARD (1973). 'Realism, Underdetermination, and a Causal Theory of Evidence,' *Nous*, 7: 1–12.

CARROLL, LEWIS (1895). 'What the Tortoise Said to Achilles,' *Mind*, 4: 278–80.

CARTWRIGHT, NANCY (1983). *How the Laws of Physics Lie*. New York: Oxford University Press.

CHALMERS, ALAN (2002). 'Experiment and the Growth of Experimental Knowledge,' in P. Gärdenfors et al. (eds.), *In the Scope of Logic, Methodology and Philosophy of Science*. Dordrecht: Kluwer Academic Publishers, 157–69.

CHRISTENSEN, DAVID (1999). 'Measuring Confirmation,' *Journal of Philosophy*, 96/9: 437–61

CHURCHLAND, PAUL M., and CLIFFORD A. HOOKER, eds. (1985). *Images of Science: Essays on Realism and Empiricism, with a Reply from Bas. C. van Fraassen*. Chicago: University of Chicago Press.

CLARK, MICHAEL (1963). 'Knowledge and Grounds: A Comment on Mr. Gettier's Paper,' *Analysis*, 24/2: 46–8.

CLUTTON-BROCK, TIM (2002). 'Meerkats Stand Tall,' *National Geographic*, 202/3: 52–73.

COADY, C. A. J. (1992). *Testimony: A Philosophical Study*. New York: Clarendon Press.

COHEN, STEWART (1988). 'How to Be a Fallibilist,' *Philosophical Perspectives*, 2: 91–123.

CONAN DOYLE, Sir ARTHUR (1986). 'Silver Blaze,' in *Sherlock Holmes: The Complete Novels and Stories*. New York: Bantam Books, 455–77.

CONEE, EARL, and RICHARD FELDMAN (1998). 'The Generality Problem for Reliabilism,' *Philosophical Studies*, 89: 1–29.

DEMOPOULOS, WILLIAM (2003). 'On the Rational Reconstruction of our Theoretical Knowledge,' *British Journal for the Philosophy of Science*, 54/3: 371–403.

DEROSE, KEITH (1995). 'Solving the Skeptical Problem,' *Philosophical Review*, 104: 1–52.

DeRose, Keith (1996). 'Knowledge, Assertion and Lotteries,' *Australasian Journal of Philosophy*, 74: 568–80.

Dretske, Fred (1970). 'Epistemic Operators,' *Journal of Philosophy*, 67/24: 1007–23.

—— (1971). 'Conclusive Reasons,' *Australasian Journal of Philosophy* 49/1: 1–22

—— (1981a). *Knowledge and the Flow of Information*. Cambridge, Mass.: MIT Press.

—— (1981b). 'The Pragmatic Dimension of Knowledge,' *Philosophical Studies* 40: 363–78.

Elgin, Catherine Z. (1996). *Considered Judgment*. Princeton: Princeton University Press.

Faulkner, P. (2002). 'On the Rationality of our Response to Testimony,' *Synthese*, 131: 353–70.

Feldman, Richard (1995). 'In Defence of Closure,' *Philosophical Quarterly*, 45: 487–94.

Fitelson, Branden (1999). 'The Plurality of Bayesian Measures of Confirmation and the Problem of Measure Sensitivity,' *Philosophy of Science*, 66: S362–78.

—— (2001a). 'Studies in Bayesian Confirmation Theory.' Ph.D. dissertation, University of Wisconsin, Madison.

—— (2001b). 'A Bayesian Account of Independent Evidence with Applications,' *Philosophy of Science*, 68: S123–40.

—— (2005). 'Likelihoodism, Bayesianism, and Relational Confirmation,' *Synthese*.

—— (forthcoming). 'Earman on Old Evidence and Measures of Confirmation.' Manuscript.

—— and Neil Thomason (forthcoming). 'Bayesians Sometimes cannot Ignore even Very Implausible Theories.' Manuscript.

Fogelin, Robert J. (1994). *Pyrrhonian Reflections on Knowledge and Justification*. New York: Oxford University Press.

Foley, Richard (1987). 'Evidence as a Tracking Relation,' in Luper-Foy (1987: 119–36).

Forbes, Graeme (1984). 'Nozick on Skepticism,' *Philosophical Quarterly*, 34/134: 43–52.

Forster, Malcolm (1995). 'Bayes and Bust: Simplicity as a Problem for a Probabilist's Approach to Confirmation,' *British Journal for the Philosophy of Science*, 46/3: 399–424.

Franklin, Allan (1986). *The Neglect of Experiment*. New York: Cambridge University Press.

Fricker, Elizabeth (1987). 'The Epistemology of Testimony,' *Proceedings of the Aristotelian Society*, 61, supplement (1987): 57–83.

—— (1995). 'Telling and Trusting: Reductionism and Anti-Reductionism in the Epistemology of Testimony,' *Mind*, 104/414: 393–411.

Galison, Peter (1987). *How Experiments End*. Chicago: University of Chicago Press.

—— (1997). *Image and Logic: A Material Culture of Microphysics*. Chicago: University of Chicago Press.

Gettier, Edmund, Jr. (1963). 'Is Justified True Belief Knowledge?' *Analysis*, 23: 121–3.

Glymour, Clark (1980). *Theory and Evidence*. Princeton: Princeton University Press.

Goldman, Alvin (1967). 'A Causal Theory of Knowing,' *Journal of Philosophy*, 64/12: 357–72.

—— (1976). 'Discrimination and Perceptual Knowledge,' *Journal of Philosophy*, 73/20: 771–91.

—— (1979). 'What is Justified Belief?' in G. S. Pappas (ed.), *Justification and Knowledge*. Dordrecht: D. Reidel, 1–23.

—— (1983). 'Philosophical Explanations,' *Philosophical Review*, 92: 81–8.

—— (1986). *Epistemology and Cognition*. Cambridge, Mass.: Harvard University Press.

—— (1999). 'Internalism Exposed,' *Journal of Philosophy*, 96/6: 271–93.

—— (2000). 'What is Justified Belief?' in E. Sosa and J. Kim (eds.), *Epistemology: An Anthology*. Oxford: Blackwell, 340–53.

Good, I. J. (1983). *Good Thinking: The Foundations of Probability and its Applications*. Minneapolis: University of Minnesota Press.

—— (1985). 'Weight of Evidence: A Brief Survey,' in J. M. Bernardo et al. (eds.), *Bayesian Statistics 2.* Amsterdam: Elsevier Science, 249–70.

GOODMAN, NELSON (1983). *Fact, Fiction, and Forecast* (4th edn.). Cambridge, Mass.: Harvard University Press.

HACKING, IAN (1983). *Representing and Intervening: Introductory Topics in the Philosophy of Natural Science.* New York: Cambridge University Press.

HARDWIG, JOHN (1985). 'Epistemic Dependence,' *Journal of Philosophy*, 82/7: 335–49.

—— (1991). 'The Role of Trust in Knowledge,' *Journal of Philosophy*, 88/12: 693–708.

HARMAN, GILBERT (1965). 'Inference to the Best Explanation,' *Philosophical Review*, 74: 88–95.

—— (1973). *Thought.* Princeton: Princeton University Press.

—— (1980). 'Reasoning and Evidence One Does Not Possess,' *Midwest Studies in Philosophy*, 5: 163–82.

HAWTHORNE, JOHN (2004). *Knowledge and Lotteries.* Oxford: Oxford University Press.

HITCHCOCK, CHRISTOPHER, ed. (2004). *Contemporary Debates in Philosophy of Science.* Oxford: Blackwell Publishers.

HOWSON, COLIN, ed. (1976). *Method and Appraisal in the Physical Sciences: The Critical Background to Modern Science, 1800–1905.* New York: Cambridge University Press.

—— and PETER URBACH (1993). *Scientific Reasoning: The Bayesian Approach* (2nd edn.). La Salle, Ill.: Open Court Publishing.

JOYCE, JAMES (2003). 'Bayes' Theorem', in Edward N. Zalta (ed.), *The Stanford Encyclopedia of Philosophy* (winter edn.). **http://plato.stanford.edu/archives/win2003/entries/bayes-theorem/**.

KANT, IMMANUEL (1965). *Critique of Pure Reason*, trans. N. K. Smith. New York: St Martin's Press.

KELLY, KEVIN T., and CLARK GLYMOUR (2004). 'Why Probability does not Capture the Logic of Scientific Justification,' in Hitchcock (2004: 94–114).

KITCHER, PHILIP (1993). *The Advancement of Science: Science without Legend, Objectivity without Illusions.* New York: Oxford University Press.

—— (2001). 'Real Realism: The Galilean Strategy,' *Philosophical Review*, 110: 151–97.

KLEIN, PETER (1987). 'On Behalf of the Skeptic,' in Luper-Foy (1987: 267–81).

KORNBLITH, HILARY (2002). *Knowledge and its Place in Nature.* New York: Oxford University Press.

KUSCH, MARTIN, and PETER LIPTON (2002). 'Testimony: A Primer,' *Studies in the History and Philosophy of Science*, 33: 209–17.

KVANVIG, JONATHAN L. (2003). *The Value of Knowledge and the Pursuit of Understanding.* Cambridge: Cambridge University Press.

LACKEY, JENNIFER (1999). 'Testimonial Knowledge and Transmission,' *Philosophical Quarterly*, 49/197: 471–90.

LAUDAN, LARRY (1981). 'A Confutation of Convergent Realism,' *Philosophy of Science*, 48: 19–49.

—— and JARRETT LEPLIN (1991). 'Empirical Equivalence and Underdetermination,' *Journal of Philosophy*, 88/9: 449–72.

LEHRER, KEITH (2000). *Theory of Knowledge* (2nd edn.). Boulder, Colo.: Westview Press.

LEWIS, DAVID (1976). 'Probabilities of Conditionals and Conditional Probabilities,' *Philosophical Review*, 85: 297–315.

—— (1979). 'Counterfactual Dependence and Time's Arrow,' *Nous*, 13: 455–75.

—— (1996). 'Elusive Knowledge,' *Australasian Journal of Philosophy*, 74: 549–67.

LIPTON, PETER (1993). 'Is the Best Good Enough?' *Proceedings of the Aristotelian Society*, 93/2: 89–104.

—— (1998). 'The Epistemology of Testimony,' *Studies in the History and Philosophy of Science*, 29: 1–31.

LOFTUS, ELIZABETH F. (1996). *Eyewitness Testimony*. Cambridge, Mass.: Harvard University Press.

LUPER-FOY, STEVEN, ed. (1987). *The Possibility of Knowledge: Nozick and his Critics*. Totowa, NJ: Rowman & Littlefield.

McGINN, COLIN (1984). 'The Concept of Knowledge,' *Midwest Studies in Philosophy*, 9: 529–54.

MAHER, PATRICK (1996). 'Subjective and Objective Confirmation,' *Philosophy of Science*, 63: 149–74.

—— (2004). 'Probability Captures the Logic of Scientific Confirmation,' in Hitchcock (2004: 69–93).

MARTIN, RAYMOND (1983). 'Tracking Nozick's Skeptic: A Better Method,' *Analysis*, 43: 28–33.

MAYO, DEBORAH (1996). *Error and the Growth of Experimental Knowledge*. Chicago: Chicago University Press.

MESELSON, MATTHEW, and FRANKLIN STAHL (1958). 'The Replication of DNA in Escherichia coli,' *Proceedings of the National Academy of Science*, 44: 671–82.

MOORE, G. E. (1962). *Philosophical Papers*. New York: Collier Books, 144–8.

MUSGRAVE, ALAN (1985). 'Realism vs. Constructive Empiricism,' in Churchland and Hooker (1985: 197–221).

NICHOLS, SHAUN, STEVEN STICH, and JONATHAN M. WEINBERG (2003). 'Meta-Skepticism: Meditations in Ethno-Epistemology,' in S. Luper (ed.), *The Skeptics: Contemporary Essays*. Aldershot: Ashgate Publishing, 227–47.

NIINILUOTO, I. (1980). 'Scientific Progress,' *Synthese*, 45: 427–62.

NORTON, JOHN D. (2003). 'A Material Theory of Induction,' *Philosophy of Science*, 70: 647–70.

NOZICK, ROBERT (1981). *Philosophical Explanations*. Cambridge, Mass.: Harvard University Press.

PAIS, ABRAHAM (1986). *Inward Bound: Of Matter and Forces in the Physical World*. New York: Oxford University Press.

PERRIN, JEAN (1990). *Atoms*, trans. D. Ll. Hammick. Woodbridge, Conn.: Ox Bow Press. Reprint of *Les Atomes*, Librairie Félix Alcan, 1913.

PLANTINGA, ALVIN (1993). *Warrant and Proper Function*. New York: Oxford University Press.

RAMSEY, FRANK, P. (1960). 'Knowledge,' in R. B. Braithwaite (ed.), *The Foundations of Mathematics and other Logical Essays*, Paterson, N.J.: Littlefield, Adams, and Co., 258–9.

REICHENBACH, HANS (1949). *The Theory of Probability* (2nd edn.). Berkeley and Los Angeles: University of California Press.

ROUSH, SHERRILYN (2004). 'Discussion: Positive Relevance Defended,' *Philosophy of Science*, 71: 110–16.

—— (forthcoming). 'The Probability of the Evidence.' Manuscript.

ROYALL, RICHARD (1997). *Statistical Evidence*. London: Chapman & Hall.

RUTHERFORD, ERNEST (1911). 'The Scattering of α and β Particles by Matter and the Structure of the Atom,' *Philosophical Magazine*, 21, 669–88. Reprinted in R. T. Beyer (ed.), *Foundations of Nuclear Physics*. New York: Dover, 1949.

SAINSBURY, R. M. (1997). 'Easy Possibilities,' *Philosophy and Phenomenological Research*, 57/4: 907–19.

SALMON, WESLEY (1970). 'Statistical Explanation,' in R. Colodny (ed.), *The Nature and Function of Scientific Theories*. Pittsburgh: University of Pittsburgh Press, 173–231.

—— (1984). *Scientific Explanation and the Causal Structure of the World*. Princeton: Princeton University Press.

SHAPIN, S. (1994). *A Social History of Truth*. Chicago: University of Chicago Press.

SHOPE, ROBERT K. (1984). 'Cognitive Abilities, Conditionals, and Knowledge: A Response to Nozick,' *Journal of Philosophy*, 81/1: 29–48.

SOBER, ELLIOTT (1985). 'Constructive Empiricism and the Problem of Aboutness,' *British Journal for the Philosophy of Science*, 36/3: 11–18.

SOSA, ERNEST (1999a). 'How to Defeat Opposition to Moore,' *Philosophical Perspectives*, 13: 141–53.

—— (1999b). 'How Must Knowledge Be Modally Related to What Is Known?' *Philosophical Topics*, 26: 373–84.

STANFORD, P. KYLE (2001). 'Refusing the Devil's Bargain: What Kind of Underdetermination Should We Take Seriously?' *Philosophy of Science*, 68: S1–S12.

STERELNY, KIM (2003). *Thought in a Hostile World: The Evolution of Human Cognition*. Oxford: Blackwell Publishing.

STINE, GAIL (1976). 'Skepticism, Relevant Alternatives, and Deductive Closure,' *Philosophical Studies*, 29: 249–61.

VAN FRAASSEN, BAS (1980). *The Scientific Image*. New York: Oxford University Press.

—— (1985). 'Empiricism in the Philosophy of Science,' in Churchland and Hooker (1985: 245–308).

—— (1989). *Laws and Symmetry*. Oxford: Clarendon Press.

VOGEL, JONATHAN (1987). 'Tracking, Closure, and Inductive Knowledge,' in Luper-Foy (1987: 197–215).

—— (1990). 'Are there Counterexamples to the Closure Principle?' in M. D. Roth and G. Ross (eds.), *Doubting*. Dordrecht: Kluwer Academic Publishers, 13–27.

—— (1999). 'The New Relevant Alternatives Theory,' *Philosophical Perspectives*, 13: 155–80.

—— (2000). 'Reliabilism Leveled,' *Journal of Philosophy*, 97/11: 602–23.

WATSON, J. D., and F. H. C. CRICK (1953). 'Genetical Implications of the Structure of Deoxyribonucleic Acid,' *Nature*, 171: 964–7.

WEBB, MARK OWEN (1993). 'Why I Know About as Much as You: A Reply to Hardwig,' *Journal of Philosophy*, 90/5: 260–70.

WILLIAMS, MICHAEL (1991). *Unnatural Doubts: Epistemological Realism and the Basis of Scepticism*. Oxford: Blackwell.

WILLIAMSON, TIMOTHY (2000). *Knowledge and its Limits*. Oxford: Oxford University Press.

WRIGHT, CRISPIN (1983). 'Keeping Track of Nozick,' *Analysis*, 43: 134–40.

Index

abduction 191, 209
accidentality 2–5, 39, 49, 68–9, 73
Achinstein, P. 155, 176, 178–83, 190
Adams, E. 51
adherence condition 42–3, 45–6, 50–1,
    59, 68, 75–81, 83–5, 87–91, 94–6,
    109, 111, 113, 120, 144
Adler, J. 17, 22
anti-luck 5, 40
anti-realism 32–4, 189–94, 196–7,
    199, 203–4, 206–7, 209–10,
    217, 222–3
    anti-tracking 19–20, 150 n, 183 n, 184 n
approximate truth 191–2, 194
Armstrong, D. M. 8 n, 112
atoms, 3, 189–90, 210, 218–22
Audi, R. 17

backtracking counterfactuals 65, 113–16
Bacon, F. 4
Barnes, E. 200, 208, 221
barns, Kripke 100–6
Bayesian 154–7, 159, 161, 163, 165, 172–5
belief 9, 48, 50, 51, 72, 87, 108, 140 n, 146
    animal 8–9
    basis of 41, 44, 70–1, 112–13, 143
    -come-what-may property 137–8, 140–3,
    145, 147
    justified 3–5, 7–8, 17, 19–20, 22–6, 29,
    35–6, 49, 54, 56, 43, 91, 103–4, 106–7
    true 2–3, 5, 22–7
Bogen, J. 172 n
BonJour, L. 23
Boyd, R. 190–1
brain in a vat 38, 53–6, 88–91, 128, 130
Brandt, S. 19 n
Bristow, B. 23 n
Brownian motion 218–22

Carnap, R. 32
Carroll, L. 43
Cartwright, n 218
catch-all 33–4, 165, 188, 193, 210,
    217–18, 221–2

Christensen, D. 157
circularity 30, 43, 47, 86, 119–20,
    130 n, 134
clairvoyant 23–4, 145
Clark, M. 49 n
closure, deductive 27–8, 31, 41–2, 49,
    51, 53–4, 56–7, 63, 66, 74, 102, 113,
    118–19, 121, 126, 129, 132–3, 184
Clutton-Brock, T. 7
Coady, C. A. J. 17, 20
Cohen, S. 129–30
Conan Doyle, A. 53
conditionalization:
    Jeffrey 175
    strict 173–5
Conee, E. 29, 69
confirmation 10, 32–4, 154, 157–9, 161,
    163–5, 167, 172, 175, 180–1, 184,
    189–90, 192–211, 213–14, 217–19, 222
    degree of 154, 157–61, 163–6, 175–6,
    180, 184, 190, 193, 197–201, 203–6,
    209–13, 217
        incremental vs. absolute 155, 157–9,
        161, 180, 184
    measure-dependence 33, 157–61,
    163–5, 175–6, 180, 190, 193,
    197–201, 203–6, 209–10, 216–17
    measures 32 n, 154, 157–61, 163–6,
    175–6, 180, 184, 190, 193, 197–201,
    203–6, 209–13, 217
Constructive Empiricism 33, 193–9,
    203–10
contextualism 38, 41–2, 46 n, 54–7, 59,
    129–30, 134
correlation 33, 40, 45, 76, 124, 150, 205,
    219–20
counterfactual 28, 30, 41–2, 45, 72, 92–3,
    112–14, 117–18, 123 n
Crick, F. H. C. 14–15

deduction 24–6, 29, 41, 43–4, 49, 51–4, 56,
    63, 66, 91, 113, 119–20, 126, 129,
    132–3, 138, 142, 145, 149, 163, 184–5
Demopoulos, W. 198 n

DeRose, K. 38, 42, 56–7, 59, 131–2
detection systems 10, 18–19
dictator assassination 93–6
difference measure 164, 199, 203, 204
  normalized 164, 199, 204
direction of fit 117, 121–2, 127, 135
disconfirmation 161, 196–9, 201–6,
  209, 222
discrimination 149, 154, 159–61, 164,
  175–6, 183, 199, 210, 217
DNA replication 14–16
dreaming 54 n
Dretske, F. 1, 8 n, 40–1, 54, 81, 129
Duhem, P. 205, 216

E = K thesis 153, 154 n
EEEI 203–4, 206
effort 52, 56, 60
Einstein, A. 11, 176, 199, 218
Elgin, C. 2
empirical adequacy 194–8, 200,
  206–10, 222
empirical equivalence 192–3, 203, 209–10
empiricism 192, 196, 204
entailment, paradox of 140 n, 145–6
EP 197–207, 209, 214, 217–18
equal punishment 33, 193, 197–207,
  209–10, 214, 217–18
equivalence schema 61–3
ether 11–13, 52, 60–1
evidence Ch. 5 *passim*, 190–9, 201–4,
  206–11, 213–19, 221–4
  analysis of 149, 170, 175, 183–4
  deductive 149, 163, 184–5
  desiderata 154–60
  good 154, 158, 171, 178, 183–5
  and knowledge 149–54, 183–6
  old, problem of 163, 175–6
  probability of 166–78, 211
  some 158, 170, 175–6, 178, 183–4
  strong 11, 154
  surprising 172–4
example:
  clairvoyant 23–4, 145
  dictator assassination 93–6
  fairy godmother 122–3, 127
  Gumshoe and Tagalong 96–8, 100,
    103–5, 114
  hit rock 63–4

  hologram projector, turned-on 122 n
  ice cubes 63–7
  Jesse James 68–70, 113
  Judy and Trudy 98–100
  Kripke barns 100–6
  missed rock 63–4
  Mr Nogot 107–10
  not falsely believing 38, 59–63,
    118–19, 122
  newspaper 93–6, 131
  Oscar and Dack 57–9, 63, 71
  rookie 63–7
  thermometer 81–3
  trash chute 65 n
  veteran 64–7
EXOTIC 206–8
EXOTICA 208–9
experiment 9 n, 11–17, 153, 174, 177, 205,
  211–15, 218, 220–2, 224
externalism 8, 21–3, 29–30, 43, 50, 121 &
  n, 127, 223
externalist 8, 20, 21–3, 30–1, 36–7, 50,
  50 n, 57, 60, 117–20, 122, 127, 134,
  147, 156, 223–4

fairy godmother 122–3, 127
fallibilism 26, 41, 46, 60, 151
Faulkner, P. 22
Feldman, R. 29, 42, 69
Field, H. 61 n
Fitelson, B. 155 n, 157,
  161, 163, 175
Fogelin, R. 40, 45 n, 92
Foley, R. 161
Forbes, G. 68
Forster, M. 155
Fricker, E. 17, 21–2 & n

Galison, P. 11, 177 n
generality problem 29, 30, 69, 76, 78–9,
  91–3, 117, 121, 123 n
Gettier, E. 4–5, 39, 48–50, 108 n
Glymour, C. 155 n
Golden Events 177
Goldman, A. 1, 3 n, 8 n, 23, 29, 35–6, 57,
  59, 81, 98–9, 104, 128, 135
Good, I. J. 159, 163
Goodman, n 159
grandmother 70–1

grue 86, 159
Gumshoe and Tagalong 96–8, 100, 103–5, 114

Hardwig, J. 17
Harman, G. 36, 49, 93–4, 104, 108 n
Hawthorne, J. 132–3
HCG 212–14, 217
hit rock 63–4
hologram projector, turned-on 122 n
Howson, C. 155 n, 172–4
Humean 45

ice cubes 63–7
indication 154, 159–61, 165–78, 183
induction 23, 26, 32, 52, 67, 119–20, 163
  enumerative 198–9, 201
  hypothetico-deductive 198–9, 201
  instance-generalization 198–9, 201
  instance-to-instance 67, 113–16
  meta- 191 n
  'new' 213, 222
  pessimistic 33
  positive 222, 33–4
inference 24–6, 43–4, 47, 49–50, 65 n, 67, 108 n, 119–20, 134–5, 139–43, 145–6, 198, 223–4
instrumentalism 207
internalism 8, 10, 21–2, 29–30, 36, 91
internalist 7–9, 20, 22–3, 29, 35–6, 121, 121 n, 127, 134–5

James, A. 79 n
Jeffrey, R. 175
Jeffreys, H. 163
Jesse James 68–70, 113
Joyce, J. 159, 161
Judy and Trudy 98–100
justification 3–5, 7–8, 20 n, 22–6, 29, 35–7, 40, 43, 49, 54, 56, 86, 91, 103–4, 196, 223–4

Kant, I. 9
kaon decay 2, 190
Kelly, K. 155 n
Kitcher, P. 191 n
Klein, P. 64, 67
knowledge:
  analysis of 42–3, 45–7

of analytic truths 146
animal 7–10
anti-luck views 5, 40
and authority 3, 17–22, 25 n, 142–3
basic 51–2
causal view of 40, 93, 112
counterfactual views 1, 41, 117–26
of conjunctions 110–12
of disjunctions 62–3
empirical Chs. 1–4
and evidence 149–154, 183–6
of future 113–16
higher-level 30, 61–2, 117–19, 121, 123 n, 139
of implication 42–5, 47–8, 52, 117, 134, 136–8, 140–7
of laws of nature 147
of logical truths 134–46
of mathematical truths 147
of necessary truths 134–47
reflective 26, 30, 60–2, 66, 105–6, 117–19, 121, 123 n, 139, 223–4
structure of 51–3
value of 2–3, 5–6, 26–7
value of account of 2–4
Kolmogorov probability 46, 76 n, 84, 92, 155
Kornblith, H. 8 n
Kripke barns 100–6
Kusch, M. 17
Kvanvig, J. 2

Lackey, J. 17, 19
Laudan, L. 191–2, 203
Law of Likelihood 165
Lehrer, K. 100
Leplin, J. 203
Lewis, D. 31, 36, 51, 65, 129–30
leverage 158–9, 164–6, 171, 183
Likelihood Ratio (LR) 161–71, 175–8, 183–5, 187–8, 193, 197, 199, 210, 214, 218
likelihood ratio, comparative 164–5, 188, 214–16
Likelihood Ratio (LR) measure 161, 163–5, 175–6, 184, 193, 197, 199
Lipton, P. 17, 216 n
Loftus, E. 69
Logical Empiricism 195 n
lottery 176–8, 180, 182

lottery propositions 31, 67,
    117, 128–34
luck, epistemic 5, 26, 39–40, 49–50, 81,
    102–7, 122, 144

Maher, P. 155 n, 181 n
McGinn, C. 40, 73, 92–3, 144
Martin, R. 96
Maxwell, James Clerk 12, 213
Mayo, D. 155 n, 218 n
Meselson, M. 218
method 2, 28, 34, 41, 61, 63–4, 68–71, 79,
    82, 94, 97 n 103, 112–13, 128
Michelson, A. 11, 13
Michelson–Morely experiment 11–13
missed rock 63–4
model, probability 29–30
Moore, G. E. 46 n, 54, 56–7
Morely, E. 12
Mr Nogot 107–10
Musgrave, A. 194, 196 n

necessary truth 31, 134–47
neighborhood reliabilism 117–18, 120,
    122–3, 131
newspaper 93–6, 131
neutrino 177
Newton, I. 176 n, 199, 215
Nichols, S. 2
Niiniluoto, I. 191 n
non-realism 192
Norton, J. 148 n, 155 n
not falsely believing 38, 59–63, 118–19, 122
Nozick, R. 1–2, 7–8, 11, 17–18, 22, 27–9,
    31–2, 38–43, 45, 51, 53–4, 57, 64–5,
    67–70, 73, 75, 82, 94, 96–103, 108,
    110, 112–13, 122, 128, 131–3, 143,
    154, 160–1
Nozick-knowing 42–3, 46, 57, 59, 63–4,
    68, 119

observables 32–3, 189–211,
    217–19, 222–3
old evidence problem 163, 175–6
Oscar and Dack 57–9, 63, 71
overdetermination, causal 112–13

Pais, A. 13
paradox of entailment 140 n, 145–6

Pearson, J. 187 n
Perrin, J. 218–22
Plantinga, A. 8 n
Popper functions 76 n
positive relevance 157, 166, 178–80, 182
positivism 195 n
power 1–2, 4, 6–7, 23, 25, 26, 31,
    117, 126–8
pregnancy 211–18
Principle P 49, 109
probabilistic relevance 46, 80, 83, 91–2, 98,
    101, 114, 155, 157, 161, 163–6, 174,
    178–82, 184, 205, 207
probability:
    conditional 2, 28, 30–1, 41, 43, 45–7, 51,
        62, 64 n, 75–8, 83–4, 87–94, 96,
        98–101, 107, 110, 112–15, 120–4,
        131, 136, 150, 154–5, 161, 175, 205
    interpretation of 45, 50, 76–7, 92,
        156, 173
    Kolmogorov 46, 76 n, 84, 92, 155
    objective 45, 156
    personalist 45, 76–7, 156, 173
    subjective 45, 50, 76–7, 156, 173
probability function, 30, 46 n, 75–9, 83–6,
    92, 102, 109, 113, 139, 207
    ur- 83–6, 92, 98, 101
probability model 29–30
process reliabilism 19, 29–31, 36, 40,
    69, 78–9, 117–20, 123, 127–8, 131,
    134–5, 145

quantum mechanics 189–90, 193, 210–11,
    213–17, 219–21

Ramsey, F. 8 n
Ramsey sentence 209
ratio measure 33, 163–6, 175, 180, 193,
    197, 199, 203–6, 209, 211
realism, 33–4, 158, Ch. 6 *passim*
    epistemological 189, 223
    scientific, 33–4, Ch. 6 *passim*
    semantic 189–90, 207, 223
reasoning 24–6, 43–4, 47, 49–50, 65 n, 67,
    108 n, 119–20, 134–5, 139–43, 145–6,
    198, 223–4
Reichenbach, H. 32
reflection 3–4, 21, 26, 105–7, 111, 119, 121
relation 93

relativity 11, 176 n, 199, 213
relativization to method 28, 41, 63–4, 68–71, 79, 82, 94, 97, 112–13, 128
relevance measure 163–6, 175, 180
relevant alternatives theories (RAT) 31, 38, 117, 128–31, 134, 136
reliabilism, neighborhood 117–18, 120, 122–3, 131
reliabilism, process 19, 29–31, 36, 38, 40, 69, 78, 79 n, 117–20, 123, 127–8, 131, 134–5, 145
representation, decoupled 9 n
responsiveness 8, 9 n, 18, 25, 31, 40, 44, 52, 68, 80, 94, 104, 106, 112, 122, 127, 136, 141, 143–4, 147
rookie 63–7
Royall, R. 165
Rutherford, E. 13, 14, 174, 218

safety 30–1, 40–1, 44, 117–28, 148
Sainsbury, R. M. 122
Salmon, W. 155, 218
semantic view of theories 198 n
sensitivity 12, 40–1, 56, 58 n, 71–2, 112, 117–27, 131, 138, 148
Shapin, S. 17
Sherlock Holmes 53, 63
Shope, R. 68, 94, 108, 122
skepticism 38, 41–2, 51, 53–7, 60, 73, 89–91, 118, 128–30
Skyrms, B. 61 n, 174 n
Sober, E. 196 n
social constructivism 207
Sosa, E. 40, 59, 65 n, 118, 122–3
Stahl, F. 218
Stanford, P. K. 207, 213, 222–3
Sterelny, K. 9 n, 10 n
Stich, S. 2
Stine, G. 128–9
subjunctive conditionals 1, 2, 5 n, 7, 27–32, 35, 40–1, 45–7, 63–4, 73, 75, 77, 92, 98–100, 107, 110, 122–4, 131, 150, 154–5, 160–1
success 189, 191–3, 196, 209–10, 213, 215–16
support, incremental 32, 35, 154–5, 157–9, 161–5, 175–6, 180–2, 184–5
syntactic view of theories 198 n

testimony 17–22, 55
theories:
   semantic view 198 n
   syntactic view 198 n
   testing 189–90, 193, 195, 205, 212–18, 222, 224
thermometer 81–3
Thomson, J. J. 13
tracking:
   recursive 28, 41–9, 51–3, 55–7, 59–63, 65, 67–8, 70–1, 100, 102–3, 105, 110, 117–21, 126, 131–3, 138
   second-order 20, 37, 60, 105–7, 119
   transitivity of 11 n, 19 n, 20 n, 32, 35 n, 150–2
   transitivity enough of 152–3, 184
TRACKING 8, 11 n, 150–4
tracking conditions 1–2, 5–7, 9, 12–17, 20–3, 27–9, 31, 35–6, 41–52, 55 n, 56–7, 75–6
   rules of application 76–93
transitivity 11 n, 19 n, 20 n, 32, 35 n, 150–2
transitivity enough 152–3, 184
trash chute 65 n
truth, approximate 191–2, 214
T-sentence 61–3
Turing, A. 163

underdetermination 192, 213
unobservable 189–90, 192–3, 195–7, 200–1, 205–11, 217–18, 223
Urbach, P. 155 n, 172–4

van Fraassen, B. 33, 194–9, 206, 209, 217, 219, 222–3
variation condition 42–6, 50–1, 56–9, 62, 64, 68 n, 69 n, 71, 73
veteran 64–7
Vogel, J. 42, 59, 62–5, 67, 117–23, 129–30, 133

Watson, J. D. 14–15
White, N. 134 n
Williams, M. 92
Williamson, T. 40, 56, 58 n, 71–2
Wright, C. 42
Woodward, J. 172 n